।। षष्ट्यब्दसंस्कृतम् ।।

Sixty Years of Sanskrit Studies

Vol. 1

Published on the occasion of

15th World Sanskrit Conference

being jointly organised by the

International Association of Sanskrit Studies (IASS)

and the

Rashtriya Sanskrit Sansthan

(under the Ministry of Human Resource Development,
Government of India)

।। षष्ट्यब्दसंस्कृतम् ।।

Sixty Years of Sanskrit Studies

(1950–2010)

Vol. 1: India

Edited by

Radhavallabh Tripathi

Rashtriya Sanskrit Sansthan

D.K. PRINTWORLD

Publishers of Indian Traditions

Cataloging in Publication Data — DK
[Courtesy: D.K. Agencies (P) Ltd. <docinfo@dkagencies.com>]

Ṣaṣṭyabdasaṁskṛtam = Sixty years of Sanskrit studies (1950–2010) / edited by Radhavallabh Tripathi.

2 v. cm.
Contributed articles.
Includes bibliographical references.
Contents: v. 1. India — v. 2. Countries other than India
ISBN 13: 9788124606285 (set) 9788124606292 (Vol. 1)

1. Sanskrit language — Study and teaching — India. 2. Sanskrit language — Study and teaching. 3. Sanskrit literature — India — History and criticism. 4. Sanskrit literature — History and criticism. I. Tripathi, Radhavallabh, 1949- II. Rashtriya Sanskrit Sansthan.

DDC 491.20710954 23

ISBN 13: 978-81-246-0628-5 (set) ISBN 13: 978-81-246-0629-2 (vol. 1)
First published in 2012

Published by:
RASHTRIYA SANSKRIT SANSTHAN
56-57, Institutional Area, Janakpuri, New Delhi - 110 058
Phones: (011) 2852 4993, 2852 1994, 2852 4995
e-mail: rsks@nda.vsnl.net.in
Website: www.sanskrit.nic.in

and

D.K. PRINTWORLD (P) LTD.
Regd. Office: *'Vedasri'*, F-395, Sudarshan Park
(Metro Station: Ramesh Nagar), New Delhi - 110 015-11
Phones: (011) 2545 3975; 2546 6019; Fax: (011) 2546 5926
e-mail: indology@dkprintworld.com
Website: www.dkprintworld.com

Printed by: D.K. Printworld (P) Ltd, New Delhi

Preface

The world Sanskrit Conferences organised under the authority of the International Association of Sanskrit Studies (IASS) have been providing periodical opportunities to take stock of Sanskrit studies and their future prospects. Volumes devoted to the progress of Sanskrit studies have been published earlier on the occasion of some of the World Sanskrit Conferences. The exercise of bringing out these volumes not only involves the assessment of accomplishments, but envisaging the future prospects also. Considering the details that have been covered in earlier such volumes, we thought it proper to make a modest attempt to present documentations and analyses of the latest developments in Sanskrit studies in various states of India specially between 1950 and 2010, and present important issues related to Sanskrit studies in the national perspective in this volume being issued on the ceremonial occasion of the 15th WSC.

We are grateful to all the learned scholars who have contributed their papers for this volume at our request. The volumes edited by Prof. K.K. Mishra (1997) and (late) Prof. Vachaspati Upadhyaya (2001) under the same title *Sanskrit Studies in India* have been helpful in chalking out the plan for the present volume and in avoiding repetitions. This volume would not have taken the present shape but for the meticulous and assiduous efforts of Shri Susheel Mittal of D.K. Printworld. Thanks are also due to Dr. Prakash Pande, Officer on Special Duty for Publications at the Rashtriya Sanskrit Sansthan, for collecting and formatting the articles and corresponding with their authors.

Radhavallabh Tripathi

Contents

Introduction*

Radhavallabh Tripathi

IT is almost an impossible task for a single person to present a comprehensive view on the status and trends of Sanskrit studies in a vast country like India. What is being done here would just appear to be a sketchy account, containing snippets of information, that is to be further corroborated, properly analysed and explored.

India is divided into 28 states, 7 union territories and 644 districts. There is hardly any district or region where Sanskrit is not studied in some form or the other. Sanskrit is mentioned in the list of 22 major languages, officially accepted in the Constitution of India, and it is also one of the three languages there, that have an all India character.

Teaching, Education and Research

In India there are 282 universities as per the records with the AIU, at least 112 of which have postgraduate and research departments of Sanskrit. The number of colleges teaching Sanskrit is around 10,000. "Modern methods" are adopted in these institutions for teaching programmes in Sanskrit. Apart from these universities and colleges, there are 16 Sanskrit universities and a number of Sanskrit *pāṭhaśālā*s or Sanskrit

---

* This is an enlarged and revised version of my paper "Sanskrit Studies in India" published in the Bulletin of IASS, 2012.

colleges where traditional method also known as *pāṭhaśālā paddhati* is practised.

As per a recent state-wise survey conducted by the Rashtriya Sanskrit Sansthan (RSkS) the number of Sanskrit *pāṭhaśālā*s in Madhya Pradesh is 644, in Chhattisgarh 32, in Uttar Pradesh 1347, Uttarakhand 115, in Karnataka it is 290, in Orissa 433, Punjab 8, Rajasthan 1698, Sikkim 36, Tamil Nadu 55, and in Himachal Pradesh 129, Andhra Pradesh 509, Assam 83, Bihar 717, Goa 4, Gujarat 63, Haryana 74, Jammu & Kashmir 43, Jharkhand 3, Kerala 31, Maharashtra 63, Manipur 8. There are also 21 model Sanskrit colleges under the RSkS. In the state of H.P. there are 27 Sanskrit colleges apart from the two model Sanskrit colleges under the RSkS. There are 84 Sanskrit colleges in the state of Uttarakhand. More than 1000 Sanskrit *vidyālaya*s function under the supervision of Bihar Sanskrit Shiksha Board (estd. 1982).

All in all, there are approximately 8000 Sanskrit *pāṭhaśālā*s in the country, with around 1.8 million students pursuing their studies in them. Apart from these, a number of the *vedapāṭhaśālā*s are being run across India for cultivating the tradition of chanting and studying some particular *śākhā* of Veda. The MSRVVP has supported 54 *vedapāṭhaśālā*s during 2009-10. In addition to this, the MSRVVP has also been funding 187 units of traditional Vedic learning. In each of such units, one *guru* of a particular *vedaśākhā* imparts training to the disciples (all male). These units are spread over in remote areas even in such far off provinces as Sikkim. Besides the *vedapāṭhaśālā*s aided by the MSRVVP, several independent organisations and also the four *maṭha*s founded by Ādi Śaṅkarācārya, are running their own *vedapāṭhaśālā*s or *gurukula*s. In Maharastra itself there are more than 25 *vedapāṭhaśālā*s, preserving the tradition of the oral transmission of the Vedic texts. In addition to those *pāṭhaśālā*s there are *vaidika*s that are not running the *vedapāṭhaśālā*s formally but teaching the students privately in a temple or in their house. *Vedapāṭhaśālās* or *veda-vidyālayas* are also functioning in the states of Assam and Tripura.

The provisions of the RTE Act are not applicable to the Sanskrit *pāṭhaśālās* and the *vedapāṭhaśālās*, so that the uniqueness of the *pāṭhaśālā paddhati* is maintained.

The divide between the *pāṭhaśālā paddhati* and the "modern method" was a colonial legacy. The Sanskrit universities established in post-Independent India have worked to demolish the compartmentalisation between the two systems. Students of *pāṭhaśālās* are now being trained in modern technological devices — computer software and programming, with a view to create a corpus of Sanskrit literature for e-learning. Even though all such efforts appear to be extremely insufficient, the efflorescence breathes with immense potential. A more promising area for cultivation of Sanskrit education is opening through distance learning mode, IGNOU, RSkS, RSV and some other institutions are running various programmes for distance learning in Sanskrit. Cultivation of spoken Sanskrit has received sustained support from various organisations. Nearly 1 million persons have been so far benefited from the non-formal Sanskrit Education programme of the RSkS; a few thousands teachers for this programme have been trained.

General Studies

There are Sanskrit Academies established by the respective state governments in some states like Madhya Pradesh, Uttar Pradesh, Uttarakhand, Gujarat, Haryana and Delhi. They conduct several extracurricular programmes for promotion of Sanskrit studies at regional and national levels. Amongst some of the NGOs that have taken initiative for promotion of Sanskrit studies, SSP is one of the oldest and the most renowned institutions with a long-standing reputation of publications and research. Academy of Sanskrit Research,

Melkote has made a mark in the fields of Āgama and computational Sanskrit. Veda Vani Vitanam (Satna, M.P.) — specially promotes studies and researches on Veda, scientific literature in Sanskrit and epigraphy; Vrindavan Shodh Sansthan at Vrindavan in U.P. has a rich collection of manuscripts and has taken up projects on medieval culture; Brahmaswam Vedic Research Centre at Thrissur (Kerala) conducts teaching and seminars, etc. for promotion of Vedic learning.

Amongst the research journals, *PJDIS*, was termed by Suniti Kumar Chatterji as "a most useful production of Indological studies" that "has got an immense bibliographical value", has been a creditable attempt at indexing of indological researches, the only discredit lies in its irregularity in publication. The volume XXXIX-XL of 2003-04 was issued in 2008, after that the next number XLI-XLII of the year 2005-06 has been issued in 2011. There are a number of research journals being published; the journals brought out by the Special Centre for Sanskrit Studies at JNU; RSkS, MSRVVP, Sanskrit Department, Pondichery University; School of Vedic Studies, Rabindra Bharati; *JICPR* by ICPR are a few to mention.

There is a mushrooming growth of the so-called Indological research journals, while the old journals like *ABORI* (*Annals of Bhandarkar Oriental Research Institute*), *IA* (*Indian Antiquiry*), *IHQ* (*Indian Historical Quarterly*), *JGJKSV* (*Journal of the Ganganatha Jha Kendriya Sanskrit Vidyapeetha*), *JORI* (*Journal of Oriental Research Institute*), JOIB (*Journal of Oriental Institute, Baroda*), and *JASB* (*Journal of the Asiatic Society, Bombay*) are somehow carrying on. There are research journals exclusively in the Sanskrit medium, like *Sāgarikā* and *Sārasvatīsuṣamā* which sometimes publish articles of very high standard. Some newly-established institutions have launched research journals, and these attempts are reassuring. *Vāgīśvarī* is an annual bi-lingual research journal of Sanskrit department of Assam University,

Silchur and its issue number V was issued in 2010. The first issue of the *Karṇāṭaka Saṁskṛtādhyayanam* started by the Karnataka Sanskrit University, has come out in January 2011 and this bilingual half-yearly journal re-establishes the Śāstric traditions with modern techniques of research.

With the inception of Sanskrit universities in the states of Madhya Pradesh, Karnataka and Assam there are now 16 Sanskrit universities, including the Vedic university at Tirupati. Sampurnand Sanskrit University is the oldest amongst these, Rashtriya Sanskrit Sansthan with its eleven campuses located in different parts of the country is the biggest and the only multi-campus Sanskrit University in India. These Sanskrit universities together with their affiliated colleges and *pāṭhaśālā*s promote traditional Sanskrit learning.

CIF, VSM, PPSM and Sanskrit Academy Hyderabad are recognized as model research institutes under the scheme of the Government of India operated by the RSkS. CIF has been cultivating studies in Advaita-Vedānta and manuscripts; VSM is very well known for its editions of Vedic texts; the faculty at PPSM has rare scholarship in Mādhvavedānta and Mīmāṁsā. The BORI, Pune; KSSRI, Chennai; ORI, Vadodara; ORI, Mysore and ORI Chennai have enormously contributed to the Sanskrit studies by publishing critical editions of important Sanskrit texts. In Bihar, K.P. Jaiswal Research Institute has been one of the premier centres of researches on ancient Indian history and archaeology, Buddhism and Tibetology. The list of publications of this institute contains 28 volumes in the Tibetan Sanskrit series, 5 volumes in the classical Sanskrit series, 15 volumes in the historical research text series. The contribution of the Institute is unique as the works published in the Tibetan series, like *Pramāṇavārttika-bhāṣya* of Prabhākaragupta (ed. Rahul Sankrityayana), Nalinaksa Dutta's *Bodhisattvabhūmiḥ* and *Abhidharmakośa-bhāṣyam* (ed. P. Pradhan and A. Halden) would not have seen the light of the day but for the initiatives taken by this Institute. ORI at Madras was established in 1926. Kunjuni Raja was the first professor of Sanskrit appointed in this institute in 1927. The early enthusiasm and motivation of late nineteenth and early twentieth century has now dwindled, and a feeling of helplessness has taken place in all these institutes.

Very few serious attempts at investigating the interrelationships of Sanskrit with medieval literatures in other languages or regional/folk literatures have been made. Some important works surveying Sanskrit literature in different regions, of course, provide valuable references. Kunjuni Raja had produced a big volume on the history of Kerala Sanskrit literature, and a similar attempt was made by P. Shri Ram Murti for Andhra Pradesh in his unpublished thesis at the Andhra University. The RSkS has brought out a volume on contribution of north-east states to Sanskrit.

That Sanskrit remains a force to reckon with in this country was substantially established by some recent events. One of them has been the International Sanskrit Book Festival organised by some voluntary institutions at Bangalore from 7 to 10 January, 2011. Eight thousand delegates participated in various events organised on this occasion, and more than half a million visitors frequented the book stalls. There were 154 stalls put up by 128 publishers. Books worth more than Rs. 4 crore were purchased.

Tradition of *śāstrārtha* (intellectual debates amongst the *paṇḍits*) has re-surfaced through modern technological device — the internet. Bharatiya Vidvat Parishad (a group) has been serving as a vibrant platform for the *śāstrārtha* and also for exchange of ideas, dissemination of knowledge and sharing of information on the latest studies and researches.

Vedic Studies

The present century began with the discovery of a new

manuscript of *Ṛgveda* with additional *mantras* (total about 11000). MSRVVP is going to publish this manuscript. During the last two decades of the twentieth century, sustained efforts were made for the revival of the Vedic school of Madhusudan Ojha. Study centres for studies on his *prasthāna* started functioning. Madhusudan Ojha Research cell at the university at Jodhpur (Rajasthan) especially took up to publish the works of Ojha (more than hundred in number, all in Sanskrit and all original Śāstric writings). Due to these efforts now more than 60 works of Ojha are in circulation and researches on them are being carried on in different universities. Even though the discussions on Ojha's school of Vedic interpretation remained limited to places like Jaipur and Jodhpur, their echoes can be heard in distant southern parts, and have accelerated the studies on the scientific perspectives of the Veda. Dayanand Bhargava, Anant Shastri and G.L. Suthar have enormously contributed to the study of Ojha's school during the past 20 years. Institute of Scientific Research on Vedas (ISERVE) has collaborated with eminent scientists to explore scientific perspectives in Veda.

Pune in Maharashtra has been a great centre of the Vedic studies. Bhagyalata Pataskar in her write up here has given an account of some recent activities carried out there. Critical editions of some of the Vedic texts that have come out during the past few decades are worth mentioning. Dr. P.D. Nawathe is still working on the Kāṭhaka school and has so far published very rare works about this almost extinct branch of *Kṛṣṇa-Yajurveda*. After publishing the critical edition of *Ṛgveda-Saṁhitā* with *Sāyaṇa Bhaṣya* with *padapāṭha*, VSM launched the project on *Taittirīya-Saṁhitā* with *Sāyaṇa* and *Bhaṭṭabhāskara Bhāṣya*, and *padapāṭha*. The last (5th) volume comprising indices completes the VSM edn. of this Saṁhitā. The *Kāṇva-Saṁhitā* of the *Śukla-Yajurveda* with *Sāyaṇa Bhāṣya* (on first 20 *adhyāyas*) and *Anantācārya Bhaṣya* (on last 20 *adhyāyas*) and *Ānandabodha Bhāṣya* (on the entire Saṁhitā) is also critically edited and published by VSM. While some other *bhāṣyas* on *Ṛgveda* have been brought out, Kapali Shastri wrote his one *Siddhāñjana Bhāṣya* on some of the hymns of *Ṛgveda* often interpreting them in the light of Aurobindo's philosophy. On the other hand, S.A. Dange promoted studies of mythology, rituals and symbolism with an anthro-pomorphological approach.

Out of Śrautasūtras, recent publications are — *Baudhāyana Śrautasūtra* (critically edited and translated by C.G. Kashikar, IGNCA, 2003), *Āpastamba Śrautasūtra* (text with English translation and notes by G.U. Thite, NBBC, 2004), *Bhāradvāja Śrautasūtra* (C.G. Kashikar, VSM, 1961), *Laṭyāyana Śrautasūtra* (H.G. Ranade, IGNCA, 1998), *Kātyāyana Śulbasūtra* (S.D. Khadilkar, VSM 1974), the *Kātyāyana Śrautasūtra* (G.U. Thite, NBBC, Delhi, 2006). VSM has also published the *Kaṭhāraṇyakam* (text with English translation and notes by Mrs. Bhagyalata Pataskar, 2010), *Śatapatha Brāhmaṇa*, Sanskrit text with English translation by Eggeling and Notes (ed. Maitreyee Deshpande NBBC, 2008) — all being inevitable sources for the Vedic studies.

The *Śrauta Kośa* of the VSM (both Sanskrit and English versions) is the encyclopaedic work on the Śrauta ritual. The *Dictionary of Vedic Rituals* (IGNCA) is a more valuable reference work. It gives the texts right from the Brāhmaṇas up to the Sūtra texts, regarding one particular ritual.

FISH organised a three-day international conference on decoding the Veda Vidyā at Putige in collaboration with the Rastriya Sanskrit Sansthan. The attempts to rediscover the corpus of lost *śākhās* and as well as the later Vedic texts have also borne some welcome results. The MSRVVP is going to publish the newly discovered *śākhā* of *Ṛgveda* — the Śāṅkhāyana *śākhā* with 11,000 *mantras*. The manuscript of this lost *śākhā* was discovered at Ajmer. The Paippalādaśākhā of *Atharvaveda* could also be restored.

Some other important publications in this area during the past decade are — *Atharvavedīyavrātyasūktam* and *Bāṣkalamantropaniṣad* both edited by Shrikishor Mishra; *Vaidikakhilasūktamīmāṁsā* – O.P. Pandey; *Holistic Approach of Vedas* — Dayanand Bhargava (both by MSRVVP).

On the other hand, Dayakrishna raised certain questions about the structure of the text of *R̥gveda*, and he proposed to present a new version of the text based on the way of rearranging all hymns on the basis of the seers and their families. (A Sanskrit translation of the preface of this proposed new edition, that could not be published, has been presented by V.R. Pandurangi and published in *Sanskrit Vimarśa*, no. V, 2011. Bhagyalata Pataskar (VSM, Pune, 2010) presents multidimensional studies on the Āraṇyakas.

The publication of the two volumes of G.C Pande's *R̥gveda* (text with new Hindi translation in verse form) covering books III to VI is an important event in respect of making available an authentic literary translation of *R̥gveda* (with comments and interpretive notes) to a larger section of readers. SAKSI has brought out translation of some Vedic texts.

The problem of the date of *R̥gveda* is being re-examined on the basis of new historical and archaeological findings. In his *New Light on the Date of R̥gveda* (1994) N.R. Waradpande is in favour of taking the period of *R̥gveda* back to 8000 BCE, considering Abhyankar's findings on the motion of winter-solstice in Aśvinī constellation in *R̥gveda*. He also refers to Magasthenes corroborating the Kaliyuga date, washing away of Hastināpur and 50,000 year old relics unearthed in Kurukṣetra and Ayodhyā regions.

The MSRVVP was established by the Government of India for preservation of Vedic practices and cultivation of Vedic studies. WAVES (Worldwide Association of Vedic Studies) has done significant work by the way of organising conferences on Vedic studies on selected themes in India and other countries. Proceedings of conferences on Revisiting Indus-Sarasvatī Age and Ancient India (1998), Contemporary Views on Indian Civilization (2003), New Perspectives on Vedic and Ancient Civilisation (2000, 2008), Contemporary World Order: A Vedic Perspective (2009) as well as Haṛappan Civilization and Vedic Civilization (2010) have been brought out. WAVE's conference on Creation and Existence: Indian Perspective (2009) provided a platform to scientists and Vedic scholars for exchange of their views. ISERVE was established in 2004 for scientific study of Vedic and post-Vedic literature. It has taken up a project on extraction, translation and sequential dating of astronomical references in Sanskrit literature in correlation to archaeo-logical, geological, ecological, anthropological, geographic and oceanographic findings.

The research journals of MSRSVVP and SVS have continued.

Vyākaraṇa and Linguistics

In the last decades of the twentieth century, publications on Bhartṛhari (English translation) and also some portion with commentaries edited by K.A. Subramania Iyer, generated interest in the study of *Vākyapadīya*. Iyer also discussed interrelations between Bhoja and Bhartṛhari in Venkatachalam V. (1999). While *Ambākartṛvyākhyā* still remains one of the most indispensable studies on *Vākyapadīya*, studies by Saroja Bhate, and publications of the proceedings of several seminars, Bhartṛhari has occupied a central position in the study of philosophy of grammar. *The Central Problems of Bhartṛhari's Philosophy* (Devendra Nath Tiwari), and *Bhartṛhari* (ed. Mithilesh Chaturvedi) offer some brilliant expositions into this area. A pioneer work on the philosophy of grammar in Sanskrit was earlier produced by Pt. Ram Prasad Tripathi, one of the most renowned *vaiyākaraṇa*s from Kāśī (SSU, 1997). Pragya

Devi who worked for promotion of teaching of Vyākaraṇa on the basis of *Aṣṭādhyāyī*-system had produced a critical study of *Kāśikā* in Sanskrit. *Sanskrit-bhāṣādarśanam of Yajña Vīr Dahiyā* (BVP, 2001) takes into account the linguistic theories as envisaged in Śāstric traditions.

P. Ramachandudu establishes interconnections between Bhoja, Pāṇini and Candragomin in Venkatachalam V. (1999).

Impetus to studies on Patañjali was provided by the volumes of *Mahābhāṣya* edited by S.D. Joshi and J.A.F. Roodbergen. Equally remarkable work of the same editors is the *Aṣṭādhyāyī* of Pāṇini, with the translation and explanatory notes. The *Dictionary of Pāṇinian Grammatical Terminology* (ed. Roodbergen J.A.F. and published by the BORI in 2008) serves very important tool for the study of these works. One of the noteworthy attempts is the complete Marathi translation of the *Vyvākaraṇa Mahābhāṣya* of Patañjali with short notes by Abhyankar Vasudevashastri. *Tantrapradīpa* a commentary on *Kāśikā* and *Nyāsa* has been edited with fresh manuscript material by D.K. Kanjilal (2007). Seminar on Pāṇini and Chomsky (Bangalore) marked a new initiative. G.B. Palsule's *Yubhātaḥ Saṁskṛtam Prati* provides insights in the study of the Indo-European linguistics in Sanskrit. Some other important publications in the field of Vyākaraṇa and Linguistics have been — *Sarasvatīkaṇṭhābharaṇa of Bhoja* (Vedic Vyākaraṇa portion) ed. N.M. Kansara, *Vyākaraṇasiddhānta-sudhānidhiḥ* of Viśveśvara Pāṇḍe edited by Bhargava and Dube, *Siddhāntaratnākara of Rāmakṛṣṇa on Siddhāntakaumudī* edited by Ajad Mishra.

Some of the major projects that have been carried out in this field are: *Grammatical Traditions of Sanskrit and Tamil* (by Siniruddha Das, Madras) and preparation of a new *Kaumudī* by Pushpa Dikshit.

The *Indo-Āryan Languages* (2003) edited by George Cardona and Dhanesh Jain is a very important work on the study of

Indian languages and Indo-European linguistics. It comprises minute studies of various MILs giving accounts of their scripts, history of development and morphological as well as semantic distinctions.

Philosophy

Ashok Aklujakar (2011) re-examines the question of unity of Pūrva and Uttara Mīmāṁsās refuting the arguments of H. Bronkhorst against the initial unity of the two systems. Studies in Mādhva Vedānta and Mīmāṁsā have been seriously pursued in Karnataka, some of the institutions like DVSRF and PPSM have developed as centres for study and research on these two systems. Shree Vallabh Vidyapeeth, Pune and Shri Sharada Peetham, Śṛṅgerī have remained devoted to studies in texts related to particular Vedāntas. The ICPR has produced some very important text studies thereon, such as Studies on Gadādhara's and Gaṅgeśa's philosophy by Sibajivan Bhattacharya (1990, 1993, 1996), on Patañjali by Surendranath Dasgupta (1991, 2001), on Cārvāka by Debi Prasad Chattopadhyaya (2006) on Gautama's Nyāya system by Ananta Lal Thakkut (1996, 1997) are worth mentioning. Excerpts on Upādhi from Gaṅgeśa has been translated by Stephen H. Phillips and N.S. Ramanuj Tatacharya. Kaliprasad Sinha has made enormous contributions through his writings on Nyāya philosophy — his *Nyāyadarśanavimarśaḥ* in Sanskrit is a *magnum opus* providing an easy access to the methodology of Navya-Nyāya, that has assumed added significance in the recent studies under computational linguistics. Jivan Krishna's *Nyāyaprakāśikā* (1946) and *Tarkāmṛtavivṛttiḥ* (1956) are also important treatises in Sanskrit.

Nagsampige and K.B. Subbarayudu have produced dissertations on the synthesis of various Vedānta philosophies and 18 systems of Indian philosophy respectively.

In the area of philosophy of grammar, a new edition of

Śābdabodhataraṅgiṇī of Vepatturu Subrahmanya Shastri edited by K.T. Pandurangi was issued in 2006. *Śābdabodhamīmāṁsā* in four volumes by Ramanuj Tatacharya published by RSkS, is definitely the biggest original Sanskrit work of the past decade.

The first Asian Philosophy Congress was organised by ICPR in March, 2010. As many as 763 scholars participated. This Congress can be termed as a significant event in the sense that it initiated a massive organisational move for studying "Asian Philosophies" and their contribution to world thought. The session of *paṇḍita pariṣad* in this Congress presented the continuity of Śāstric traditions of Nyāya, Vedānta, Vyākaraṇa and Mīmāṁsā. A forum for Asian Philosophy and Philosophers was actualised in this congress. Volume XII of *Encyclopaedia of Indian Philosophies* edited by G.J. Larson and Ram Shankar Bhattacharya is focused on the history and literature of Yoga philosophy. Dayakrishna and Oscar Püjol have initiated dialogues between the Eastern and Western philosophical traditions. The theory of "Dehātmavāda" postulated by Badarinath Shukla was subjected to interesting debates amongst the traditional pundits of Nyāya and scholars of modern philosophy.

Focus to a large extent has remained on exposition of the texts on Vedānta during last few decades. R. Balasubramanian (2011) in *Śārīrakacatuḥsūtrīvicāra* has edited the commentary of Bellaṅkoṇḍa Rāmarāyakavi (1875-1914) on first four *sūtras* of *Brahmasūtra*. A detailed introduction to Rāmarāyakavi unearths facets of studies on Advaita Vedānta and Hindu way of life. Mithila Prasad Tripathi has edited fragments of an unknown *Bhāṣya* by Viśvanāthasiṁha on the *Brahmasūtra*. *Śaṅkarabhāratī* (vol. 36, nos. 1-2 of *The Voice of Śaṅkara*) edited by N. Veezhinathan have been issued in 2011.

Epics and Purāṇas

By and large the attention of the scholarly world and the

academicians outside the traditional Sanskrit scholarship remained focused on the *Mahābhārata* (*Mbh*) in the last decade. A number of interesting seminars were organised on *Mbh*. Proceedings of the seminar organised by the NMM in 2007 have been published under the title *Text and Variations of the Mahābhārata*. MSP has been publishing a journal *The Mahābhārata Studies* and has also taken up projects on the *Mbh*. Mohan Gupta (2003) has made a fresh attempt to calculate the date of the Mahābhārata war. Basing his thesis on astronomical, historical and Purāṇic sources, he adjusts the birth of Kṛṣṇa in 2045 BCE, and the year of Mahābhārata war in 1952 BCE.

An important contribution to Bhāgavata studies is made by V.P. Mishra with the fresh edition of *Mantrabhāgavatam* of Nīlakaṇṭha, the well-known commentator of the *Mbh*. Nīlakaṇṭha has established how the life and deeds of Śrī Kṛṣṇa have been visualised in the *mantra*s of *Ṛgveda*. In a number of seminars and conferences, there have been discussions on science, ecology and environment in Purāṇas. A seminar on Environment in Purāṇas organised by DVSRF in 2000 had streamlined these discussions.

Alaṁkāraśāstra

The discovery of the manuscripts of *Śṛṅgāraprakāśa* of Bhoja around 1918 was as much an important event as the discovery of the Bhāsa plays in 1910. Raghavan's studies on *Śṛṅgāraprakāśa* created a new era of understanding the whole tradition of the history and growth of literary theories in Sanskrit. After Josyer's edition of this most voluminous work on Alaṁkāraśāstra between 1955 to 1974, and Raghavan's first volume of his edition from Harvard in 1996, the publication of its complete critical edition by Rewa Prasad Dwivedi in the first decade of the twenty-first century has brought Bhoja and his school of Alaṁkāra at the forefront of Indian Aesthetics. Mukunda Madhava Sharma (1934-2009), Rama Ranjan

Mukerjee and C. Rajendran have made studies in comparative aesthetics. *Vyañjanāprapañcasamīkṣā* (1979) by Mukunda Madhava Sharma initiated studies in comparative symbolism.

Some very important papers on Bhoja's aesthetics have been collected in V. Venkatachalam's *Bhoja and Indian Learning*. K. Krishmamurti's edition of *Vakroktijīvita* initiated fresh discussions on Alaṁkāraśāstra in the context of post-structuralism and postmodernism. Gopichand Narang's voluminous study as well as *Coleridge and Abhinavagupta* by R. Mishra are important contributions in the area of comparative aesthetics. Works by Ramaranjana Mukherji and T.S. Nandi may also be mentioned. The latter has published studies in "thought currents" of Indian literary theories in three volumes under the title *Sahṛdayāloka*.

After the edition and translation by K. Krishnamurti, the publication of *Dhvanyālokalocana* with three commentaries from Kerala by C.M. Neelkanthan has resuscitated interest in *dhvani* theory. L.D. Institute of Indology, Ahmedabad, has re-issued Hemacandra's *Kāvyānuśāsana* with *Cūḍāmaṇi* and *Viveka* edited by T.S. Nandi.

New categories and theories are still being evolved by traditional *paṇḍits* and scholars and there is a series of original works in Sanskrit on Alaṁkāraśāstra. *Sāhityavinduḥ* by Chajjurama Shastri, works of Brahmananda Sharma, *Kāvyālaṁkārakārikā* by Rewa Prasad Dwivedi, *Abhirājayaśobhūṣaṇam* by Abhiraj Rajendra Mishra and *Abhinavakāvya-alaṁkārasūtram* by the present author have been much discussed works during the past decades. The latest work offering hermeneutics in this Śāstra is *Sāhityavallarī* by N. Lakshminarayana Bhatta (2011). *Anvīkṣā* (Journal of Department of Sanskrit, vol. XXXII, March, 2011) is a tribute to the late Prof Rama Rajan Mukherji with a focus on interdisciplinary studies in Indian Aesthetics. New concepts like surrealism have been evaluated in the light of Indian aesthetics (pp. 191-98). Ratna Basu discusses the Indo-German interaction in aesthetics (pp. 199-209).

History and Epigraphy

The Cultural Heritage of India published by the Ramkrishna Mission Institute of Culture remains a singularly largest and the most exhaustive reference work on all the aspects of Indian history and culture. After its first edition in 1937, the work went on assuming larger proportions to accommodate comprehensive treatment in a wider perspective. Veteran scholars like Sarvepalli Radhakrishnan, Haridas Bhattacharya, R.C. Majumdar and Suniti Kumar Chatterji were associated with its editing. Volume VII pt I issued in 2006 under the editorship of Kapila Vatsyayana is devoted to epigraphy, arts and architecture. The eight volumes of *Indian Culture: Encyclopedic Survey* were launched in 2008 by the Bharatiya Vidya Mandir. This Encyclopaedia covers all the aspects of culture and civilization comprising articles by veteran scholars like T.M.P Mahadevan, S.S. Barlinge, Goswami Shyama Manohar, Satyavrata Shastri, Sitakanta Mahapatra and a host of others. The Devanāgarī edition of 89 inscriptions from Nepal, earlier edited by Reneiro Knolii has been published by RSkS with Hindi translation (2010). The publication of corpus of inscriptions dating from the earliest period to CE 1600 in chronological sequence in 10 volumes was taken up by Uṭṭaṅkita-vidyāraṇya Trust established at the instance of H.H. Chandrashekharendra Saraswati in 1984. Volume I was brought out in 1985. The sixth volume (2010) comprises 106 inscriptions belonging to a period between CE 800 to 900. Volume VII comprising inscriptions from CE 900 to 1000 was released on 23 January 2011 at Mumbai by H.H. Shankaracharya of Kanchi and volume VIII is in the planning. A reprint of copperplate inscriptions belonging to Śaṅkarācārya of Kāmakoṭi Kanchi Peeth edited by T.A. Gopinath Rao and published in 1916 has been issued (2011). It contains 10 inscriptions beginning from the period of Vijaya Gaṇḍagopāladeva (CE 1291) to Śaka Saṁvat 1608 (CE 1688).

Āgama and Tantra

After Swami Lakshman Joo (1907-91), Pandit Baljinath was one of the last stalwarts in the line of traditional *paṇḍits* devoted to the pursuits on Tantra and Āgama under Śaivism. His *Kāśmīraśaivadarśanabṛhatkośa* (2001) is a monumental work in two volumes. K.C. Pande had done pioneering work on Abhinavagupta. Many important texts of Śaivism were brought out under the prestigious Kashmir Sanskrit Series. L.N. Sharma presented his critical and comparative studies on absolutism in Kashmir Śaivism and Advaita Vedānta in his *Kashmir Śaivism*, BVP, 1972. K.A. Subrahmaniya Ayer, K.C. Pandey and R.C. Dwivedi have presented a better edition of *Īśvarapratyabhjñāvimarśinī* of Abhinavagupta. Navjivan Rastogi and Bettina Baümer have continued philosophical investigations on Śaivism. The new edition of *Parātriṁśikā* by Bettina Bäumer is an important contribution. Publication of *Sahṛdaya* — studies in India and South-East-Asian Art in the honour of R. Nagaswami present some newly unearthed facets of Kashmir Śaivism.

The proceedings of a seminar on interrelationships between Śaiva, Śākta and Vaiṣṇava Āgamas have been edited by the present author (NBBC, 2010). Saṁvidālaya — the Abhinavagupta Research Library being run by Bettina Baümer is devoted to activities for promotion of Āgama studies.

Asoke Chatterjee Shastri has made an extensive survey of religious sects in ancient Kāmarūpa — various tantric cults, Buddhism and Vaiṣṇavism. Prof. Chatterji also presents the process of synchronisation between these sects. In fact, the land of Assam described as Kāmarūpa and Prāgjyotiṣapura, is known for the practice of Śāktism and has been a seat of tantric cults. A vast mass of literature in Sanskrit on the cult related to the Goddess Kāmākhyā was created here in the past. The scriptures like the *Yoginītantra*, the *Kālikā Purāṇa*, the *Dharma Purāṇa* and the *Haragaurīsaṁvāda* were composed here. Vishvanatha Narayan Shastri, one of the doyens of Sanskrit studies of this state has produced a number of volumes making in-depth study of the tantric cults that have developed here.

Buddhism

Buddhist Society of India has continued holding annual conventions and other programmes and volumes on Ocean of Buddhist Wisdom published through its initiatives have marked the continuity of Buddhist studies.

Kāvya

The critical edition of *Abhijñānaśākuntala* by D.K. Kanjilal still remains a landmark, *Kālidāsagranthāvalī* edition by Rewa Prasad Dwivedi has appeared in the third revised and enlarged edition. *Kirātārjunīyam* of Bhāravi has assumed an added significance with the publication of four rare commentaries. Ambalal Prajapati has edited the Sanskrit Communication *Pradīpikā* of Dharmavijayagaṇi (2010). Composed around CE 1742, this commentary is one of the most brilliant and comprehensive expositions of Bhāravi's *magnum opus*. Virupaksha Jaddipal has prepared a critical edition of first three cantos of the *mahākāvya* with commentaries of Nṛsimha, Prakāśavarṣa and Jonarāja. The publication of *Cakrapāṇivijayamahākāvyam* by Bhaṭṭalakṣmī-dhara in 1956 has changed the whole scenario of the study of Sanskrit *kāvya* literature. Bhaṭṭalakṣmīdhara was a contemporary of King Bhoja and his epic has to be treated at par with the trio of Bhāravi, Māgha and Śrīharṣa. A new edition of *Cakrapāṇivijayamahākāvyam* with a Sanskrit commentary by Purnachandra Upadhyaya has been published in 2007. In the Platinum Jubilee publication (2008) of Jayadeva's *Gītagovinda* with commentary of Dhanañjaya's *Sarvāṅgasundarī*, the whole illustrated manuscript has also been reproduced. The unique value of this manuscript lies in the fact that the commentator Dhnañjaya himself drew the illustrations on each stanza of all the songs in the manuscript. After her earlier publications of Jayadeva, Kapila Vatsyayana has brought out 'The Darbhanga Gītagovinda'. Sanskrit Academy of Hyderabad had published complete *laghukāvyas* of Kṣemendra and Paṇḍitarāja Jagannātha. A revised edition of *laghukāvyas* of Kṣemendra by Shrinivas Verkhedy (2009) is definitely an invaluable reference.

Studies on Kālidāsa and Sanskrit literature are being promoted by Kalidasa Akademi at Ujjain by organising national and international seminars, and workshops on Sanskrit theatre. Recent publications of this academy include the edition of all the works of Kālidāsa edited by Rewa Prasad Dwivedi with Hindi translation and edition of *Meghadūta* with commentaries. Meanwhile, N.P. Unni's translation of complete works of Kālidāsa (NBBC, 2009) has come out to meet a popular demand.

The corpus of Sanskrit literature is being viewed and reviewed from new angles and modern notions with a view to create hermeneutics. C. Rajendran initiated studies of Sanskrit *kathā* literature on the basis of theories of narratology and has published the volume edited by him (NBBC, 2010).

Naṭyaśāstra and Śilpa

English translation by M.M. Ghosh has become obsolete. New translations of *Naṭyaśāstra* in the last quarter of the twentieth century and the first decade of the present one have appeared; those translated by Adya Rangacharya, N.P. Unni and Pushpendra Kumar are worth mentioning. T.S. Nandi has produced voluminous works on *NŚ* and Alaṁkāra — offering fresh insights in textual criticism. A project to prepare a new critical edition of *Naṭyaśāstra* based on the hitherto unutilised

Newārī manuscript, was taken up by Kamlesh Datta Tripathi in 1986 at Kalidasa Akademi, Ujjain. The project is still being carried on by him at Varanasi. Meanwhile, T.S. Nandi and Rajendra Nanavati separately brought out fresh editions and Vadodara edition was revised by K. Krishnamurthy and T.S. Nandi. Anvita Sharma in her thesis (2011) has re-edited chapters VI and VII of the *NŚ* on the basis of fresh manuscripts material obtained from Nepal.

V. Raghavan, Kapila Vatsyayan, Govardhan Panchal, K.D. Tripathi, Tarala Mehta, the present author and Gajanan Hegde have made studies on *Naṭyaśāstra* with reference to the performance traditions. Theatres of Kūṭiyāṭṭam and Yakṣagāna were studied in the light of edicts of *Naṭyaśāstra*. K. Raja, C. Rajendran and K.G. Paulose have considerably contributed to the study of Kūṭiyaṭṭam. A life long work in this area was done by G. Panchal in his *Kūṭṭampalam and Kūṭiyāṭṭam* (1984) where he reproduces the plan of some of the *Kūṭṭampalam*s from Kerala temples — Vadakkunathan, Guruvayoor, Kādālamaṇikom and Subrahmaṇya establishing them as descendants of Bharata's classical theatre. Panchal also considers Kūṭiyāṭṭam as a landmark in the history of Asian theatre. International Conference on Naṭyaśāstra organised under the auspices of IGNCA, Varanasi in collaboration with Lincoln University, UK (8-20 March 2011), explored the possibilities of what the text and tradition of *Naṭyaśāstra* has in its store for the world of art and aesthetics today. Some of the noted dancers have made studies in co-relationships between *Naṭyaśāstra* and the classical dance forms. Padma Subrahmanyam's studies focusing Bharatanāṭyam evince the acumen of a scholar-cum-artist. Maya Das has made studies on interrelation between *Abhinayachandrika and Oddissi Dance* (Eastern Book Linkers Delhi, 2001).

The Kalāmūla Series of IGNCA published critical editions of a number of valuable texts on *śilpa*, *nāṭya* and *saṅgīta*.

Śilparatna of Śrīkumāra has been reprinted with an elaborate introduction by Manabendu Banerjee. Manabendu Banerjee has presented an authentic account and ancient Indian Architecture through Sanskrit sources in his *Aspects of Architectural Texts*.

Computational Sanskrit

That this area is attracting a sizeable number of young scholars was evident from the deliberations of section on Computer and Sanskrit in the 10th World Sanskrit Congress organised at Bangalore. While there is no major breakthrough in the projects to devise Sanskrit as a language suitable for the machine, neither the tools created under the projects on Machine translations have proved to be very effective, there has been all the same an enormous growth of presentations of Sanskrit texts in electronic format and the tendency to utilise these has also been finding footage. A CD and software developed by RSkS on *Śabdakapadruma*, one of the most voluminous encyclopaedic dictionaries of Sanskrit is an example of how technology can help in preservation and cultivation of Sanskrit-based knowledge systems. The major centres of studies that have emerged from presentations of Sanskrit texts in electronic format during the past decade are IIIT, Sanskrit Department of Central University, Hyderabad and Sanskrit Parishad at Osmania University; Special Centre for Sanskrit Studies, JNU, New Delhi. Proceedings of the IV International Symposium held in New Delhi in 2010 have been published. RVSS Avadhunulu has made attempts at hermeneutics of Sanskrit based knowledge systems from the viewpoint of Computer Science in Vedas and Computers.

Studies on Manuscripts

With a view to cultivate scholarship on manuscripts, and further the cause of preservation of manuscripts the Government of India announced the formation of the National

Manuscript Mission (NMM) on 5 February 2003. The NMM has established a network of Resource Centres in the country and has conducted extensive surveys throughout its length and breadth. More than 4,000 personnel have been trained in the area of preserving manuscripts; cataloguing and conservation work has also been done. In 2006-07, the first phase of this Pilot Project was completed and digitisation of manuscripts in various repositories is now in progress. Publication of the periodical *Kṛtti Rakṣaṇa* by NMM and other works have gone a long way towards creating awareness about the manuscripts Heritage. Tattavabodha — the lecture series of NMM running monthly at their headquarters and annually at many of the centres created by it — has been of substantial value for the furtherance of manuscript studies and creating awareness about the manuscripts. Selected lectures are being published in a series of volumes. Volume III of *Tattavabodha* — edited by Dipti Tripathi has been published (2010).

It was V. Raghavan who started one of the most voluminous works in the field of manuscripts studies by NCC. He also brought out five volumes of the NCC, a project now being funded by the NMM; 25 volumes have been prepared and published, to complete the work up to the alphabet *ra*. The digitisation of these volumes will supplement the whole project of digitisation of manuscripts. The mission has digitised the existing volumes of the New Catalogus Catalogorum for preserving the valuable data in these books. Presently they have completed 200 books and work is still in progress. RSkS has published a catalogue of 13,000 manuscripts in their G.H. Jha campus; a complete catalogue of 56,000 manuscripts in this library is being published now. *Sanskrit and Allied Manuscripts in Europe* (2005) by D.K. Kanjilal and Kripamayee Kanjilal presents a survey of manuscripts in 21 libraries of Europe. Besides producing the lists of manuscripts in these libraries it also gives descriptions of some rare and important manuscripts.

Other important contributions to manuscript. studies are *Prākṛt-pāṇḍulipi-cayanikā* and *Apabraṁśa-pāṇḍulipi-cayanikā* edited by K.C. Sogani. One of the important surveys with reference to manuscripts on science was made by K.V. Sarma and his account of manuscripts related to astronomy, astrology, medicine, veterinary science chemistry, physics, botany, architecture draws one's attention towards some very valuable literature that lies in the repositories in south India. Pustaka Prakasha — a research institute at Jodhpur (Rajasthan) — has launched an annual journal on manuscripts studies titled *Mānaprakāśa*. The first number released in 2011 gives a detailed account of 77 manuscripts preserved in the library of this institute; some of these manuscripts dealing with lives of the local rulers are very important from the point of view of history of the Jodhpur state.

Manuscriptology and manuscript studies have become most significant emerging areas and some of the budding scholars have devoted themselves to these. Works by Virupaksha Jaddipal have been referred to above. He has also translated S.M. Katre's book on textual criticism in Sanskrit. Basant Kumar Bhatta has done an authentic work on the manuscripts of *Abhijñānaśākuntala* and *Uttararāmacaritam* and has also produced critical editions of these. Malhar Kulkarni has worked on manuscripts of *Kāśikā*. Rajesh Chunilal Vyas has worked on the commentary of Puñjarāja on *Sārasvatavyākaraṇa*. Ajad Mishra has prepared critical edition of *Siddhāntaratnākara* — a commentary on *Siddhāntakaumudī*.

Kośas and Laxicography

The Kalātattvakośa sponsored by the IGNCA is an ambitious attempt to present exhaustive and authentic account of key concepts of art, aesthetics and culture. So far, six volumes have been published another 8 volumes are in the planning. An encyclopaedic dictionary of Sanskrit is a monumental project taken up at the Deccan College Pune. Volume IX was brought out during 2010-11 with words beginning with *apa* and the work still continuous. This dictionary covers as many as 62 branches of Sanskrit-based knowledge systems and references have been collected from 1,500 Sanskrit texts. Virupaksha Jaddipal has presented a critical edition of *Nānārthaśabdaratna* (2008) — a unique lexicon of homonyms called from diverse sources, and attributed to Kālidāsa, said to be the court-poet of King Bhoja of Dhārā, and accompanied with the commentary of Niculakavi.

Scientific Literature

P.C. Ray did a pioneering work on Indian Chemistry citing various Sanskrit sources. Satya Prakash covered a vast spectrum of scientific traditions in his work on Ancient Indian Science. There has been an upsurge of studies on Kauṭilya's text after the critical edition and its English translation by R.P. Kangle. Environmental studies, mathematics, astrology, architecture and Āyurveda with reference to Sanskrit literature were especially discussed in a seminar organised in 2001 at Sri Sankaracharya University, Kaladi. Proceedings under the title *Sanskrit in Technological Age* have been published (2006). In the volume of proceedings of a similar seminar edited by Manabendu Banerjee *Ancient Indian Science and Technology* (SSP, Kolkata, 2003) Mira Roy makes an interesting study of *Garbhopaniṣad* — a text on embryology and a Mokṣaśāstra as well. Volume VI of *The Cultural Heritage of India* published by Ramkrishna Mission Institute of Culture edited by eminent scientists like Priyadaranjan Ray and S.N. Sen covers articles on the Vedic and post-Vedic mathematics, agriculture, Āyurveda, etc. During the last two decades a number of seminars were organised on scientific literature and scientific traditions as envisaged in the Sanskrit literature. The proceedings of the seminars held at Tripunithura (1991), Jabalpur (2000) and Allahabad (2005) have already been published. The deliberations in such seminars have been marred with repetitions, over simplifications and spirit of glorification of the past. However, the Tripunithura event could bring out the Kerala traditions in mathematics. A series of seminars on environmental studies and Sanskrit have been held in recent years, the earliest one being organised by V.N. Jha (1990). R.K. Sharma edited *Jñānabhaiṣajyamañjarī* of Gumānīkavi, an interesting work on Āyurveda presenting a blending philosophical thoughts with Āyurvedic prescriptions. Sanskrit scholars like R.S. Sarma (who now has settled in Germany) and Rama Subrahmaniam have devoted themselves to the study of scientific literature in Sanskrit. The translation of *Caraka-Saṁhitā* by a one of the most reputed medical practitioners, after taking pains to study Sanskrit and the original text, is a landmark. The writings of Sudyumnacharya specially on mathematics and scientific perspectives in Vedic and philosophical literature have helped to create an awareness amongst the common people. *Triśatikā of Śrīdharācārya on Pāṭigaṇita* edited by Sudyumnacharya is worth mentioning. The Vedavani Vitana established by him organised a seminar on Āryabhaṭa. Several other institutions have come up during the last decade for studies on scientific literature in Sanskrit.

The emphasis now has shifted on the search for a logical view of life and the scientific elements in Sanskrit traditions. Amartya Sen in *The Argumentative Indian* has already presented a viewpoint in this regard. Works like *Vedic Mathematics for all Ages* (2007), *Vedic Physics* (2008) have resulted out of an enthusiasm to unravel perspectives of science and technology of the Vedic lore. A more serious work has been done by Somraj Gupta in *Word Speaks to the Faustian Man* by presenting interpretative studies of Prasthānatrayī.

Ancient India Insights and Modern Science (1996) carries the findings of a UGC project done by Kalpana M. Paranjape. She explains modern theories of Einstein, quantum theory, theory of dynamic law, refers to David Bohm and then proceeds to draw parallels with Paramāṇuvāda, Kaṇāda's view, etc. She follows the same method in the treatment of cosmographical and cosmological theories, the theories of evolution, etc. In her *Biographical Dictionary of Indian Scientists* (2002) Anjana Chattopadhyaya covers the vast area, but a larger part of it treats the modern Indian scientists. There are 2,063 entries in 1,573 pages. It has entries on Āryabhaṭṭa I and Āryabhaṭṭa II, Varāhamihira, Brahmagupta, Nīlakaṇṭha Padmanābha (sixteenth century) but the author of *Dhruvabhramaṇayantra* has not been listed.

Abbreviations:

AIU : Association of Indian Universities, New Delhi

DVSRF : Dvaita Vedanta Studies & Reseach Foundation, Bangalore

FISH: The Foundation of Indian Scientific Heritage

ISERVE: Institute of Scientific Research on Vedas, Hyderabad

MSP: Mahabharata Samshodhana Pratishthana of Bangalore

MSRVVP: Maharshi Sandipani Rashtriya Veda Vidya Pratishthana, Ujjain

NBBC: New Bharatiya Book Corpotation, New Delhi

NGOs: Non-Government Organisations

NIVS: National Institute of Vedic Sciences, Bangalore

PJDIS: *Prācījyoti* – Digest of Indological Studies, Institute of Sanskrit and Indological Studies, Kurukshetra University

PPSM: Purna Prajna Samshodhana Mandir, Bangalore

RSkS: Rashtriya Sanskrit Sansthan, New Delhi

RTE: Right to Education Act of the Govt. of India

SAKSI: Sri Aurobindo Kapali Sastri Institute of Vedic

	Culture
SSP:	Sanskrit Sahitya Parishad of Kolkata
SVS:	School of Vedic Studies, Rabindra Bharati University, Kolkata
VSM :	Vedic Samshodhana Mandala, Pune
WAVES:	Worldwide Association of Vedic Studies

References

Aggrawal, Krishan Dev, *Importance of Nepalese Sanskrit Inscriptions*, RSkS, 2010.

Aklujakar, Ashok, "Unity of the Mīmāṁsās", in *Vācaspativaibhavam* (Delhi, 2011).

Avadhunulu R.V.S.S., *Vedas and Computers*, Veda Bharati, Hyderabad, 2007.

Balasubramanian, R., *Śārīrakacatuḥsūtrīvicāra*, Adi Shankar Research Centre, Chennai, 2011.

Banerjee, Manabendu, *Ancient Indian Science and Technology*, SSP, Kolkata, 2003.

Banerjee, Manabendu, *Aspects of Architectural Texts*, Kolkata, 2010.

Cakrapāṇivijayamahākāvyam by Bhaṭṭalakṣmīdhara with a Sanskrit commentary by Purnachandra Updhyaya, New Delhi, 2003.

Cakrapāṇivijayamahākāvyam by Bhaṭṭalakṣmīdhara, ed. Kesav Ram Kashi Ram Shastri, RII, Jodhpur, 1956.

Cardona, George and Dhanesh Jain, *The Indo-Āryan Languages*, Routledge, London & New York, 2003.

Chakravaty, Kalyan Kumar (ed.), *Text and Variations of the Mahābhārata*, NMM, IGNCA & MRML, Delhi, 2009.

Chattopadhyaya, Anjana, *Biographical Dictionery of Indian Scientists*, Rupa & co. Delhi 2002.

Chaube, B.B. (ed.), *Śrauta Prayogakḷpti of Ācārya Śivaśroṇa*, NMM, 2011.

Gopinath Rao, T.A. (ed., 1916, 2011), *Copperplate Inscriptions Belonging to Shankaracharya of Kāmakoṭi Kanchi Peeth.*

Gupta, Mohan, *Mahābhārata kā Kālanirṇaya*, Varanasi, 2003.

Gupta, Somraj, *Word Speaks to the Faustian Man*, MLBD, 2008.

Jaddipal, Virupaksha (ed.), *Kirātārjunīyam of Bhāravi with Commentary of Nṛsiṁha, Prakāśavarśa and Jonarāja*, Delhi, 2008.

Jaddipal, Virupaksha (ed.), *Nānārthaśabdaratna Kālidāsa, with the Commentary of Niculakavi*, Amar Granth Publications, Delhi, 2008.

Jha, V.N., *Proceedings of National Seminar on Environmental Awareness Reflected in Sanskrit Lierature*, CASS, Pune, 1991.

Kanjilal, D.K. and Kanjilal Kripamayee, *Sanskrit and Allied Manuscripts in Europe*, Sanskrit Pustak Bhandar, Kolkata, 2005.

Malla, Bhagyalipi (ed.), *Jayadeva's Gītagovinda*, Orissa State Museum, Platinum Jubilee publication 2008.

Muraleemadhavan, P.C. (ed.), *Sanskrit in Technological Age*, New Delhi, 2006.

Nandi, T.S., *Sahṛdayāloka*, L.D. Institute of Indology, Ahmedabad.

Neelakanthan, C.M. & K.A. Ravindran (eds.), *Veda, Society and Modernity*, Kunamkulam, 2007.

Neelkanthan, C.M & K.A. Ravindran (eds.), *Vedic Texts and the Knowledge Systems of India*, SSUK, 2010.

Neelkanthan, C.M & K.A. Ravindran, *Preservation of Techniques of Ṛgveda Chanting of Kerala*, SSUK, 2010.

Neelkanthan, C.M. (ed.), *Dhvanyālokalocana with three commentaries from Kerala*, vols. I and II, Centre for Heritage Studies, Tripunithura, 2011.

Palsule, G. B., *Yubhātaḥ Saṁskṛtaṁ Prati*, RSkS, 1978.

Pandita, Baljin Nath, *Kāśmīraśaivadarśanabṛhatkośa*, Ranbir Sanskrit Vidyapeeth, Jammu, 2001.

Pandurangi, K.T., *Purāṇeṣu Nisarga Parisaravarṇam*, DVSRF, Bangalore, 2000.

Paranjape, Kalpana M., *Ancient India Insights and Modern Science*, BORI, Pune, 1996.

Prajapati Amba Lal (ed.), *Kirātārjunīyam of Bhāravi with Commentary Pradīpikā*, Surat, 2010.

Prajapati, Ambalal, *Kirātārjunīyam with Sanskrit Commentary of Dharmavijayagani*, Veershasana, Surat, 2010.

Sanskrit Computational Linguistics, ed. Girish Nath Jha, Springer, 2010.

Sarma, K.V., *Science Texts in Sanskrit in Manuscripts Repositories in Kerala and Tamil Nadu*, RSkS, 2002.

Sen, Amartya, *The Argumentative Indian.*

Sharma, Hari Dutta (ed.), *Sanskrit meṅ Vijñana aur Vaijñānika Tattva,* Allahabad, 2006.

Sharma, R.K. (ed.), *Jñānabhaiṣajyamañjarī of Gumānīkavi,* RSkS, 2005.

Śilparatna of Śrīkumāra, intro. by Manabendu Banerjee, SPB, Kolkata, 2009.

Singhal, Vandana, *Vedic Mathematics for all Ages,* MLBD, 2007.

Sogani K.C. (ed.), *Prākṛt-pāṇdulipi-cayanikā,* Apabraṁśa Sahitya Academy, Shri Mahavirji, 2006.

Sogani, K.C. (ed.), *Apabraṁśa-pāṇdulipi-cayanikā,* Apabraṁśa Sahitya Academy, Shri Mahavirji, 2007.

Śṛṅgāraprakāśa of Bhoja, ed. Rewa Prasad Dwivedi, IGNCA, New Delhi & Kalidasa Samsthan Verabasi, 2007.

Sudyumnacharya (ed.), *Triśatikā of Śrīsharācārya,* RSkS, 2004.

Sudyumnacharya, *Bhāratīya Darśana tathā Ādhunika Vijñāna,* Satna, 2nd edn., 2002.

Sudyumnacharya, *Gaṇitaśāstra kī Bhāratīya Paramparā,* MLBD, 2006.

Vatsyayan, Kapila, *The Darbhanga Gītagovinda.*

Veezhinathan, N. (2011), "*The Voice of Śaṅkara*", *Śaṅkarabhāratī,* vol. 36, nos. 1-2.

Venkatachalam, V. (1999), *Bhoja and Indian Learning,* Vikram University, Ujjian.

Verkhedy, Shrinivas, Srinivsas Sharma and Surya Prakash (eds.), *Kṣemendra-laghukāvyasaṁgraha,* Hyderabad (2009).

Verma, Keshav Dev (ed.), *Vedic Physics,* MLBD, 2008.

1

Sanskrit Studies in Andhra Pradesh (I)

K.E. Devanathan

ANDHRA Pradesh has a rich tradition of having contributed towards enrichment in the Sanskrit studies. This land produced hundreds of eminent scholars through *gurukula* system. The contribution of the scholars from this part of our country by way of authoring texts on subjects of the Sanskrit literature, philosophy and grammar, etc. and sustaining the traditional system of learning is well known and acknowledged by one and all. The present state of Sanskrit studies in Andhra Pradesh is also very encouraging. This is being reported in this paper.

Institutions

Institutions which are preserving and propagating Sanskrit can be classified as 1. Veda Pāṭhaśālās, 2. Oriental Colleges, 3. Institutions with Sanskrit Departments, and 4. Sanskrit Institutions.

VEDA PĀṬHAŚĀLĀS

There are several *veda pāṭhaśālā*s in Andhra Pradesh Most of them are being run as in-house *gurukula*s. These *gurukula*s are probably having three or four students only, and these children belong to the family of the only teacher who figure as students. These *vedapāṭhaśālā*s, though not the organised ones, the teaching standard is considered of high value.

The second kind of *vedapāṭhaśālā*s are well organised and well maintained, like professional schools. There are 22 such institutions available in Andhra Pradesh. Most of these institutions are being financed by the T.T. Devasthanams, a famous temple authority of India. These are:

1. Sri Kanchi Kamakoti Sri Maruthi Devalayam, Guntur.
2. Jagadguru Sankaracharya Vedapathasala Pendurthi, Visakhapatnam.
3. Srimad Bhagavath Bharathi Trust, Narasarao Pet.
4. Sri Bharadwaja Maharshi Veda Vidyamandir, Ongole.
5. Sri Sanatana Dharma Seva Ashrama, Guntur.
6. Bashyakara Educational & Service Trust, Bheemavaram.
7. Sri Dattatreya Veda Vidya Gurukulam, Rajahamundry.
8. Srimad Upanishad Siddantha Acharya Peetham, Kakinada (Saranya Vedapathasala).
9. Veda Parishat, Guntur.
10. Sri Sachidananda Gurukula Mahavidyalaya, Tuni.
11. Veda Vedantha Gurukula Mahavidyalaya, Madipadu.
12. Jeeyar Educational Trust, Sitanagaram.
13. Sri Sankara Vidyalayam, Bapatla.
14. Sridevi Veda Vidyalayam, Srisailam.
15. Sri Sankara Gurukula Vedapathasala, Vedabhavanam, Hyderabad.
16. Sri Bramari Suryaprakasika Vijyasankara Veda Smartha Patasala, Secunderabad.
17. Sri Gurumadananda Saraswathi Peetham, Medak.
18. Sri Seethrama Veda Samskrutha Vidyapeetham, Medak.
19. Sri Sadananda Vaidika Patasala, Siddipeta.

20. Sri Mahadeva Vedapathasala, Achalapur.
21. Sri Pushpagiri Bharatha Samskrutha Vedapathasala, Secunderabad.
22. Sri Srirangam Srimad Andvan Vedapathasala, Tiruchanur.

Besides the *vedapāṭhaśāla*s mentioned above, the T.T. Devasthanams authority is running *vedapāṭhaśāla*s in Tirumala, Hyderabad and Secunderabad.

T.T. Devasthanams are feeding almost all *veda gurukula*s in the state. The Devasthanams are also doing priceless service in preserving the Veda traditions by providing bright employment to the successful Vedic students.

ORIENTAL COLLEGES

Oriental Colleges were the backbone for the development of the Sanskrit during the last century in the state. They moulded hundreds of scholars during the last century. But they have slowly lost the attraction due to lack of financial support from the private donors, who had been helping these colleges. Most of those colleges are no more existing and the remaining colleges also cannot attract students for Śāstras in good number. These colleges are mostly concentrating on Telugu language. The Oriental colleges have courses called B.A. (OL). The list of Oriental colleges is given here.

1. AKLR Government Oriental College, Hyderabad
2. Andhra Sanskrit Kalasala for Women, East Godavari
3. Government MR Sanskrit College, Vizianagaram
4. Matrusri Oriental College, Guntur
5. MR Sanskrit College, Vizianagaram
6. Oriental Sanskrit College, West Godavari
7. PSM Sanskrit College, East Godavari

8. SB College of Sanskrit & Indian Languages, Nellore
9. SBS Oriental College for Women, West Godavari
10. SGVPKJ Oriental College, East Godavari
11. SKRS Oriental College, West Godavari
12. SPSSR Oriental College, East Godavari
13. Sri Gogineni Kanakaiah Oriental Degree College, Guntur
14. Sri Gorantla Venkanna Oriental College, Prakasam
15. Sri Nagasimha Sanskrit College, Krishna Chitigudur
16. SV Oriental College, Tirupati
17. SVJV Sanskrit College, West Godavari
18. Veda & Sanskrit College, Nellore

INSTITUTIONS WITH SANSKRIT DEPARTMENTS

Most of the universities in Andhra Pradesh have Sanskrit departments. Some of them like S.V. University, Tirupati; Osmania University, Hyderabad; University of Hyderabad, Hyderabad; Sri P.S. Telugu University, Hyderabad and SPW Vishvavidyalayam, Tirupati have been actively engaging their Sanskrit departments towards the promotion of Sanskrit language.

There are several colleges in A.P., having Sanskrit departments. In junior colleges and high schools too Sanskrit is being taught as a subject. In Andhra Pradesh thousands of school boys and girls have a basic knowledge of Sanskrit since it is an optional subject. Government degree colleges situated at Vijayawada, Rajahmundry, Nagarjunasagar, Tirupati and other places are offering Sanskrit at Graduation level.

The government-aided teaching institutions and schools like Kendriya Vidyalayas, Bharatiya Vidya Bhavans and some other private schools give priority to Sanskrit education by way of including Sanskrit in their curriculum, arranging competitions on *Bhagavad-Gītā*, etc.

It is noteworthy to mention that the Oriental High Schools run by the T.T. Devasthanams, Sri Malayalaswamy Ashramam, Erpedu and other prominent institutions, are encouraging Sanskrit-learning at the school level.

SANSKRIT INSTITUTIONS

Andhra Pradesh has many institutions exclusively for the Sanskrit-learning and preservation and promotion of the traditional Śāstras. These are classified as (a) Government Sanskrit institutions, (b) Private institutions, (c) Religious institutions and (d) *gurukulas*.

Government Sanskrit Institutions

The Rashtriya Sanskrit Vidyapeeth (deemed university), Tirupati, S.V. Vedic University, Tirupati, Sanskrit Academy in Hyderabad and S.V. Oriental College, Tirupati are the prominent government-run Sanskrit institutions:

Rashtriya Sanskrit Vidyapeeth, Tirupati: This university has produced many eminent scholars and proficient Sanskrit orators. The university celebrated its Golden Jubilee in the year of 2010-11. In this central university Sāhitya, Vyākaraṇa, Nyāya, Mīmāṁsā, Vedabhāṣya, Āgama, Advaita Vedānta, Viśiṣṭādvaita Vedānta, Dvaita Vedānta, Jyotiṣa, Purāṇetihasa, Dharmaśāstra, Śikṣā Śāstra and Sāṁkhya Yoga are offered at B.A., M.A., M.Phil. and Ph.D. levels. The medium of instruction in Sanskrit.

This university has been recognised by the UGC as a Centre of Excellence in the subject of traditional Śāstras.

S.V. Vedic University, Tirupati: The Vedic University has been established recently with the financial help by T.T. Devasthanams. It offers courses on different Vedic branches like Vedabhāṣya, Vedāṅgas, Mīmāṁsā, Āgamas, etc.

Sanskrit Academy, Hyderabad: This institution is being financially assisted by the Rashtriya Sanskrit Sansthan, New Delhi, under

Adarsha Samskrit Shoda Samsthas scheme. This Institution is engaged in research & publications.

Private Sanskrit Institutions

There are a good number of private Sanskrit institutions located in A.P.:

1. Gururaja Seva Samiti's Gurusarvabhouma Mahavidyalaya at Mantralayam.
2. Sastra Patashala at Sringeri Sankar Math, Hyderabad.
3. Sri Sri Chinna Jeeyar Swami Veda Sastra Vidyalaya, Sitanagaram, Vijayawada.
4. Sri Jeer Integrated Vedic Academy, Samshabad.
5. Surabharathi Samithi, Hyderabad.
6. Samskrit Bhasha Pracharini Sabha, Chittoor.
7. Svadharma Svarajya Sangha, Secunderabad

Religious Institutions

1. The T.T. Devasthanams, Tirupati.
2. The Satyanarayana Swamy Devasthanams, Annavaram.
3. Sri Narasimha Devasthanams, Yadagirigutta.
4. Sri Venkateswara Swami Devasthanams, Dvaraka Tirumala.

The above-said are some non-private religious institutions serving the Sanskrit language and the Vedas.

Gurukulas

In Andhra Pradesh Sri Kanchi Veda Vedanta Sastra Sabha, Tenali, is doing praiseworthy service to the preservation of Vedabhāṣya and the Śāstras. This Sabha is conducting regular examinations and awarding the successful students with citations. The students are studying at different places in *gurukula* method under the supervision of this Sabha. The students also get enough stipend to pursue their studies from this Sabha. This sabha has produced great scholars in different streams of Śāstras.

Research and Publications

There are several institutions engaged in the research and publications in Sanskrit. These are:

1. **Sanskrit Academy, Hyderabad**: This is a part of the Osmania University but financially supported by the Rashtriya Sanskrit Sansthan, New Delhi. This institution has done yeoman's service in the field of research and publications. This academy has already published 63 books besides, publishing regular research journals.
2. **Oriental Research Institute, Tirupati:** This institute is part of the S.V. University. This is known for a big collection of rare manuscripts and books. This institution has published many books and regular research journals.
3. **Rashtriya Sanskrit Vidyapeetha, Tirupati:** This prestigious institution has already published 260 reputed books in the last one year itself of which 50 books were under the banner of Golden Jubilee publications. This Vidyapeetha has a rich collection of manuscripts.

   This university has also produced CDs containing lectures on different Śāstras delivered by eminent scholars. To popularise Sanskrit, this Vidyapeetha has also produced CDs for Sanskrit-loving beginners.
4. **S.V. Vedic University, Tirupati:** More than 50 publications have been done during the span of last 3 years. The ancient texts were preferred for preservation.

5. **Tirumala Tirupati Devasthanams:** T.T. Devasthanam has been publishing works pertaining to various disciplines like Vedas, Vedānta, Purāṇas and Āgamas. This institution is also supporting translation of *bhakti* literature into different languages. The *Śrīmad Bhāgavata* has been taken up for translation into the Telugu language. The T.T.D. is also encouraging writers through aid-to-author scheme.

Some other institutes are:

6. Arsha Bharati Trust, Hyderabad.
7. Sadhana Grantha Mandali, Tenali.
8. Sanskrit Bhasha Prachara Samithi, Hyderabad.
9. Surabharati Samithi, Hyderabad.
10. Sanskrit Bhasa Pracharini Sabha, Chittoor. This Sabhā is publishing a Sanskrit monthly journal called *Gairvani*. This Sabha also conducts many meaningful examinations, namely Parichaya, Abhijna, etc. for the benefit of Sanskrit knowledge seekers.

Teachers

VEDIC TEACHERS

There are hundreds of Vedic teachers in Andhra Pradesh. They teach in Gurukula Vedapathashalas, etc, and S.V. Vedic University. Some of the noteworthy Ganapathis are:

1. Vishnubatla Subrahmanya Sastri Ghanapathi, Hyderabad.
2. Venkatarama Ganapathi, Hyderabad.
3. Chandrasekhara Ganapathi, Tirupati.
4. Maddulapalli Suryanarayana Ganapathi, Tirupati
5. U. Kasipati Ganapathi, Tirupati.

VEDABHĀṢYA TEACHERS

Andhra Pradesh has a unique privilege in having a more number of Vedabhāṣya teachers. Some of them are:

1. Ch. Srirama Sarma, Rajahmundry
2. P. Ramakrishna Somayaji, Tirupati.
3. Dandukuri Narayana Sarma, Tirupati.
4. Gullapalli Sitaramachandra Ganapathi, West Godavari.
5. C. Srinivasa Ganapathi, Tirupati.
6. Satyavageeshwara Ganapathi, Tirupati.

And many more experts are available in Andhra Pradesh.

ŚĀSTRA TEACHERS

A.P. has a rich resource of Śāstra teachers. There are also a number of budding scholars ready to join the galaxy of eminent scholars.

Traditional teachers include:

1. V. Gopalakrishna Sastry, Rajahmundry (Nyāya and Vyākaraṇa).
2. K. Satyanarayana Sastry, Rajahmundry teaches Vyākaraṇa Śāstra to traditional students and has produced many scholars in that subject. He has been awarded with Vyākaraṇa Vibhūṣaṇam for producing a number scholars in Śāstra.
3. K.E. Devanathan, Tirupati has taught Nyāya, Mīmāṁsā and Vedānta to several students successfully. He has been awarded as Nyāyavibhūṣaṇam for this contribution.
4. O.S. Ramalala Sarma has been teaching Nyāya Śāstra in the traditional method.
5. Ch. Srirama Sarma, Rajahmundry has been teaching Mīmāṁsā in Gurukula Method.

6. S.T.G.K. Rangacharya, Rajahmundry — Vyākaraṇa.
7. S.V. Rangaramanujacharya, Samshbad — Alaṁkāra, Viśiṣṭādvaita Vedānta.
8. S. Sudarsana Sarma, Tirupati — Sāhitya, Veda.
9. Kompella Ramasuryanarayana, Tirupati — Sāhitya, Nyāya.
10. K.E. Govindan, Tirupati — Nyāya, Viśiṣṭādvaita Vedānta.
11. R.L.N. Sastry, Tirupati — Vyākaraṇa.
12. J. Ramakrishna, Tirupati — Vyākaraṇa.
13. G.S.R. Krishna Murthy, Tirupati — Sāhitya.
14. Sripada Bhat, Tirupati — Jyotiṣa.
15. Sripada Subrahmanyam, Hyderabad — Vyākaraṇa, Nyāya.
16. Sripada Satyanarayana Murthy, Tirupati — Vyākaraṇa
17. K.V. Ramakrishnamacharyulu, Tirupati — Vyākaraṇa, Viśiṣṭādvaita
18. D. Prabhakara Sarma, Rajahmundry — Nyāya
19. K. Viswanatha Sarma, Tirupati. — Nyāya, Advaita Vedānta
20. M.L.N. Murthy, Tirupati — Advaita Vedānta.
21. Narsimhachar Purohit. Tirupati
22. K. Ganapathi Bhat, Tirupati — Nyāya, Advaita Vedānta.

Individual Publications

The contribution of Andhra Pradesh in the Sansksrit publications field at individual level is highly commendable.

1. Padmashri Pullela Srirama Chandrudu has authored and edited many books in Advaita, Alaṁkāra, etc. He

has edited and brought out Sri Appayya Dixita's highly reputed works.

2. N.S.R. Tatacharya has authored many books for the benefit of Śāstra students. He has written commentaries on almost all Nyāya texts which are in the curriculum of Sanskrit universities. In this way his service to Śāstra is unparalleled and ever memorable.
3. Hare Krishna Satapathy has written a work entitled *Bharatayanam* for which he has been awarded with Dalmia Srivani Puraskar.
4. S.S. Murthy has written a commentary on Nageshas Lagusabdendu Sekhara.
5. K.V. Ramakrishnamacharyulu has authored a treatise on Bhūṣaṇasāra, i.e. *Bhūṣaṇasāra Tattvaprakāśikā*.
6. K.E. Devanathan has edited two volumes of Śrībhāṣya with commentaries. He also authored *Śrībhāṣya Bhāvaprakāśa* and *Saktivadasthavicarasangraha* on Vedānta and Nyāya. He has edited *Nyāyakusumāñjali* with Vistara commentary of Sri T. Veeraraghavacharya.
7. S.V. Rangaramanujacharyulu has authored *Kāvyaprakāśa-Hr̥dayaprakāśa*.

Only a few of the recent Sanskrit publications in Andhra Pradesh have been mentioned here. There are hundreds of other publications which need a mention.

Conclusion

The Andhra Pradesh has been preserving and promoting Sanskrit studies without any interruption. It needs to be mentioned here that the Navya-Nyāya Śāstra which had roots in Mithila and flourished in Navadveepa of Bengal and north India, is being preserved in Andhra Pradesh by the mode of *gurukula* system. Many authors of philosophical works and other literary works were from Andhra Pradesh. Pandita Raja

Jagannatha lived in this holy land. It is heartening to say that still the people of Andhra Pradesh have got a great affection towards Sanskrit and traditional Śāstras. The T.T. Devasthanams of Tirupati and the Government of India are making significant contribution in the preservation of Sanskrit in the state, since erstwhile royals and landlords are no more in a position to contribute in this direction.

2

Sanskrit Studies in Andhra Pradesh (II)

Shrinivasa Varakhedi

THE Andhra Pradesh State, though formally announced as a province as part of the republic of India in 1970s very late after the Independence a had been a linguistically identified territory for long. It is one of the biggest states spreading from the banks of river Godāvarī in the north, till the end of Rayalseema region in the south in the southern part of India. It has been a great seat of Śāstric learning particularly in villages along the banks of the Godāvarī just like the traditional learning continued for ages in Varanasi on the banks of Gaṅgā. During the colonial rule in pre-Independent India, traditional Vedic and Sanskrit studies enjoyed the patronage of the local royal families, with the exception of the northern part of current Telangana region, which was then under the Nawab's rule. Following India's Independence the whole tradition of learning got affected and lost its royal patronage. This has led to some severe damage to the traditional learning in the state. Many Sanskrit study centres, like the government Sanskrit colleges that were supported by the British government continued to enjoy the same status. But, the later developments in the education system have greatly impacted the Sanskrit education. The oriental *pāṭhaśālā*s (schools and colleges) started diminishing due to the shortfall of student strength. Government grant was decreased. Endowment from trusts and *maṭhs* was very meagre. Notwithstanding the university departments, institutions supported by some local trusts, later on religious institutions like TTD stepped in and took the responsibility of keeping the Sanskrit studies alive. It is noteworthy to record the post-Independence developments of Sanskrit studies in Andhra Pradesh as there is a good prospect of promoting Sanskrit studies in the state.

This write-up records some important contributions of institutions as well as individuals in this direction. For the purpose of clarity the article is divided into various sections.

The institutions endeavouring for preservation and propagation of Sanskrit in Andhra Pradesh can be classified into, viz. governmental, government-aided, and private. These can be further catagorised as educational, research and publication wings. Again, the teaching institutions are of various levels like schools, colleges and universities.

Educational Institutions

The Government of Andhra Pradesh has a sound system of general educational set-up which offers Sanskrit as a language for study. The schools and colleges under this system form the backbone for Sanskrit studies in the state.

SCHOOL LEVEL

In select schools of the state government, the students have to study Sanskrit at the level of class X and below. Almost all the residential schools are equipped with a Sanskrit teacher. In some other schools the subject of Sanskrit is optional. In Andhra Pradesh, thousands of school boys and girls thus study Sanskrit for the basic knowledge of the language.

ORIENTAL SCHOOLS

Apart from the general educational set-up, there is a marginal but unique system of education that was categorised under the title "oriental schools" in Andhra Pradesh These oriental schools offer classical language courses in the Telugu and Sanskrit. Students used to get a certificate named as OSSLC after completion of 10 years study in these schools. There was substantial scope for Sanskrit studies in this set-up. As per the records there were hundreds of these oriental schools in the whole state. Unfortunately, most of these schools either closed down or changed to modern schools as the times changed. Now we hardly find 20 oriental schools in the whole state. In the sector of government-aided educational institutions, the Oriental High Schools deserve to be specially mentioned. These schools are offering Sanskrit as a compulsory subject from class 7 to class 10. These Oriental High Schools are also serving as feeders to the Oriental Colleges.

JUNIOR COLLEGE LEVEL

The Government of Andhra Pradesh is running hundreds of junior colleges, at the undergraduate level. Students are admitted for a two-year course of Intermediate. In these colleges too, along with other subjects Sanskrit is offered as a language. In Andhra Pradesh more than 80 per cent of Intermediate level students opt for Sanskrit. In this regard, the encouragement given by the parents is praiseworthy. Hundreds of private colleges too encourage the Sanskrit studies. The reason for this choice could be the possibility of getting high scores in the exams. Whatever be the reason, due to this phenomenon a good amount of job opportunities are created for Sanskrit students. This has resulted in a boom for students' entry in university departments of Sanskrit. According to the Intermediate Board of Education of Andhra Pradesh sources, 18,99,689 students have appeared in the Intermediate examinations in the academic year 2010-11. More than 10 lakh students out of them, might have opted Sanskrit as optional for second language. Same number of students will opt Sanskrit in degree colleges. Reason behind this phenomenon is the most of the EAMCET oriental colleges in Andhra pradesh offer Sanskrit as the second language.

DEGREE COLLEGES

Government degree colleges situated at Nagarjunasagar, Rajahmundry, Vijayawada and other places are offering Sanskrit subject at the graduate level. The syllabus is prepared with a balanced blend of various dimensions of Sanksrit language by the respective university departments.

At the degree and intermediate levels, Sanskrit, Telugu, English and Hindi languages are the medium of instruction while teaching Sanskrit. Annual examinations in Sanskrit are also conducted in these languages. Based on merit, scholarships and stipend are also provided to Sanskrit students. Traditional and modern teaching methodologies are adapted while teaching Sanskrit. Educational institutions at these levels are well equipped with all infrastructural facilities. Employment for the Sanskrit students is also provided. Sanskrit syllabus is generally very scientific, interesting, simple and well framed. With the passage of time the number of students opting for Sanskrit is decreasing at these levels in the educational institutions as unemployment is discouraging students to opt for Sanskrit. Less usage of Sanskrit language is also another factor for the diminishing popularity of Sanskrit studies. Sanskrit is opted with the view that it is an ancient and classical language of India. In universities, degree colleges and *vidyāpīṭhas*, literary debates, essay writing, elocution, poetry reading and playing Sanskrit dramas, etc. are included in literary activities.

In the oriental Sanskrit degree colleges, Sanskrit is studied as a compulsory subject.

Universities concerned themselves frame the guidelines for the academics of Sanskrit *mahāvidyālayas*. Directorate of College Education, Hyderabad, has the administrative control over these *mahāvidyālaya*s. Various courses in the *mahāvidyālaya*s are: Intermediate (PDC), B.A. — Oriental Languages, Vidya Praveena, and Bhasha Praveena.

No postgraduation course is offered by Sanskrit *mahāvidyālayas*. Postgraduation course has to be pursued only in the universities. Duration of various courses is as follows:

Entrance Examination	3 years
Intermediate or PDC	2 years
BA	3 years
Vidya Praveena	5 years
Bhasha Praveena	5 years

Sanskrit *mahāvidyālaya*s impart Sanskrit studies in a traditional way in Alaṁkāraśāstram, Vyākaraṇaśāstram, Navīnanyāyaśāstram, Prācīnanyāyaśāstram, Mīmāṁsā, Dharmaśāstram, Jyotiṣaśāstram, Advaitavedāntaśāstram, Viśiṣṭādvaitaśāstram and Dvaitavedāntaśāstram. These *mahāvidyālaya*s are designated as Oriental Colleges.

ORIENTAL COLLEGES

More than 50 per cent of the contribution of Andhra Pradesh to Sanskrit is owing to the oriental colleges. These colleges are exclusively for oriental languages among which Sanskrit is the predominant one. Some of the colleges are offering full-fledged degree course in Sanskrit with various sub-stream options like Sāhitya Vyākaraṇa and Nyāya. Higher texts of these Śāstras are taught in traditional methods in these colleges which are intended for the preservation of Sanskrit in its traditional form. In this category, S.V.V.V.S College, Hyderabad; S.V. Oriental College, Tirupati; M.O. College, Jillellamudi; Sanskrit College, Nellore; Malayalaswamy Oriental College, Proddatur; K.V.K.S. College and Saradaniketan College, Guntur; Andhra Geervana Vidyapeetham, Rajahmundry, are known for their priceless contribution to Śāstras and Sanskrit language in general. Also there are some orienal colleges at Agiripalli, Repalle, Narasaraopet, Tenali, Kakinada, Eluru, Bhimavaram and other places. In these colleges, Telugu is offered at the degree level as the main subject and Sanskrit as a compulsory second language. These oriental colleges have produced several hundreds of Sanskrit *paṇḍit*s. To record the service rendered by these institutions, a detailed report is given hereunder:

Maharaja's Sanskrit college is a monumental contribution of the Raja's of historical Vizianagaram. Vijayarama Gajapati of Vizianagaram established this college here 150 years ago, i.e. in the year 1860, with the noble intention of spreading the Vedic knowledge through all its branches. This historic institution was transferred to the Government of Andhra Pradesh in 1956. Courses like Bhasha Praveena, Vidya Praveena in Vyākaraṇam and Sāhityam with five years' duration are offered here. The college was awarded the U.G.C. status in-between 1960 and 1980. In 1980 the college was converted into an oriental degree college, offering B.A.(O.L.) 5 years integrated course as Sanskrit (main) and Telugu (main) by introducing English and History as compulsory subjects. Postgraduate courses were started here in Telugu and Sanskrit. It produced many academic stalwarts in Sanskrit language.

SRI VENKATESWARA ORIENTAL COLLEGE, TIRUPATI

This prestigious college, during its establishment, began as a *vedapāṭhaśālā* under the auspices of Sri Govindarajaswami temple. It flourished receiving the patronage of Tirumala Tirupati Devasthanam. In 1920 this school became an affiliated institution of Madras University and courses like Siromani in Sanskrit and Āyurveda were offered. After the establishment of Andhra University in 1926, the school was affiliated to Andhra University. In 1933, again the school was brought under the managing committee of TTD. Vidvan courses in

Telugu and Tamil, in 1939 and Vidvan course in Hindi, in 1947 were introduced. With this development the school was elevated to the status of Sri Venkateswara Oriental College. Departments pertaining to Veda, Āgama and the holy scriptures were separated from this college and were brought under Sri Veda Sanskrit Pathasala. It underwent hardships for a period of 8 years. In 1964 the college was revived by reintroducing the previous courses and also introducing B.A. degree course in Sanskrit with the intention to provide employment to Sanskrit scholars. Students of this college are encouraged by the government with the provision of stipend. Degree courses are offered even in the Vedas and the Śāstras. In 1956 pre-university course in Sanskrit Śāstras and in 1966 B.A. course in Sanskrit Śāstras was introduced. Introduction of Veda-Śāstra at the matriculation level was another milestone in the college's history. In 1972 a two-year intermediate course was started. In 1986, the traditional courses like Siromani and Vidvan were replaced by degree courses and English and Hindi were added to the curriculum. An FM radio station was established in 2007 for the educational development of this college. In the academic year 2009-10, M.A. Telugu course was introduced. B.A. with the combination of epigraphy, musicology and tourism in the medium of English was also introduced. The college library comprises more than 60,000 valuable books. Thus, this Sanskrit educational institution contrinued bringing educational reforms according to the changes and needs of the society and keeping in step with the Indian educational system. Having a strength of 850 students and imparting Sanskrit knowledge to the people, this college can be stated as a fine feather in the cap of Sanskrit education.

With the noble aim of promoting women's education, in 1920, at Rajamahendravaranagar, on the banks of the holy river Godāvarī, the late Ramalingaiah Gupta established Vysasevasadanam. The institution, which functioned in a private residence for 12 years, was then shifted to its own separate building. Gradually, this institution was elevated from primary school level to college level. After its elevation as Andhra Mahila Sanskrit Kalasala, it produced numerous female Sanskrit scholars. Affiliated to the Andhra Pradesh Government and Andhra University, it offered primary level, secondary level, Pravesakaksha Vidyabhasha Praveena courses, etc. which are prescribed by the Andhra University. It was further empowered by the establishment of oriental high school in 1930. Girl students, after the completion of Sanskrit high school education from this school, could pursue PUC, BA, Vidya Praveena and Bhasha Praveena courses. Music, stitching, arts etc. are also a part of education here to promote self-employment. These two institutions, with the total strength of 389 students, are flourishing because of their own hostel building.

KLN SANSKRIT KALASHALA

Established as a Sanskrit *pāṭhaśālā* in Kolluru in the beginning, was shifted to Tenalinagaram in 1910 and elevated to Sanskrit Kalashala. Getting the affiliation of Madras University in 1912, it offered courses like Sahityavedantasiromani and got the recognition as Adarshamahavidyalaya. Generous financial aid extended by individuals gave the needgul financial stability to the institution. So far, 1,200 students could acquire Sanskrit education from this institution. Sanskrit education was imparted in the domains of Vyākaraṇa, Sāhitya, Nyāya, Advaita Vedānta, etc. Sanskrit Nataka Parishad, a part of this institution, is engaged in spreading the Sanskrit knowledge by staging plays of Bhāsa, Kālidāsa, etc. A monthly Sanskrit magazine, with highly research oriented articles, is also published by this institution. The additional attraction brought to this institution is its library with a vast collection of rare Sanskrit and Telugu books.

SRI MUNNALAL SANSKRIT KALASHALA

Established by Sri Munnalal, at Secunderabad, this college offered courses like BOL, etc. produced numerous scholars and writers in Sanskrit. It occupies second place among all Sanskrit colleges in the Telengana region. It offers courses prescribed by Osmania University for oriental colleges. The institution is empowered by the hostel facility with munificent funding. Another additional attraction of the Sanskrit Kalashala is its library with a vast collection of rare Sanskrit books which are source of the research and studies.

SRI YADAGIRI LAXMINARASIMHA SHASTRA-VIDVAT PARISHAT

Located at Nallagonda district and established in 1950, this institution is engaged in preserving and propagating the Vedic and Śāstric studies. Literary debates were rgularly organised and the meritorious were honoured. This renowned Vidvat Parishat attained fame by encouraging the Vedic and Śāstric studies and honouring Sanskrit scholars by conferring on them awards and titles. Established in 1953, at the pilgrim centre Yadagiri and spreading the fragrance of Sanskrit knowledge, this *vidyāpīṭham* is progressing with generous financial aid of the Yadagiri and Devasthanam. Osmania University's oriental colleges curriculum is adopted by this institution. Mathematics, English and Telugu are also included in the curriculum. With the strength of 32 students, the *vidyāpīṭham* is imparting quality education in Sanskrit studies. Evidence to this statement is, students of this *Vidyāpīṭham* come out with flying colours in the university examinations.

SRI RAJARAJESHVARA SANSKRIT PATHASHALA, VEMULAVADA

The Devasthanam established this Sanskrit Pathashala in 1947 and is extending financial support for the educational activity. Fifty students are seeking education in Sanskrit in this *pāṭhaśālā*.

A library, with rich collection of Sāhitya, Vedānta, Vyākaraṇa, etc. is of immense help to the *Ācaryas* and students of this *pāṭhaśālā*, to enhance their Sanskrit knowledge.

SRI RAGHUNATHA SANSKRIT PATHASHALA

This *pāṭhaśālā* is spreading Sanskrit knowledge for the past 25 years. Recognised by the Osmania University, the *pāṭhaśālā* is now educating 20 Sanskrit students. Mathematics and English are also a part of curriculum.

SRI RAMANUJA SANSKRIT PATHASHALA

This institution, established on 27 February, 1957, is imparting Sanskrit education, in Sāhitya and Vyākaraṇa domain, to many students. The *pāṭhaśālā*, while extending hostel facility, is encouraging students to seek Sanskrit studies.

SRI VISHVESHVARA SANSKRIT-ANDHRA KALASHALA

This Kalashala offers courses following the curriculum of DOL and BOL of the Osmania University. The *kalāśālā* imparts education in both Sanskrit and Telugu. Government financial assistance is also provided to this institution. Eminent Sanskrit scholars are involved in edifying students and thus serving the Sanskrit field.

SRI VEDIKA KALASHALA, WARANGAL

Recognised by the Osmania University, with sufficient funds, this *kalāśālā*, under the auspices of Sanskrit Vidyasamiti, Hyderabad, is putting in immense efforts to develop Sanskrit studies for the past 30 years.

MAHARAJA SANSKRIT KALASHALA

In CE 1848 the King Vijayaramagajapati of Vijayanagara Samrajyam, inspired by Sanskrit educational institutions and observing the progress of Sanskrit studies in Kāsī, established a Sanskrit *pāṭhaśalā* in his hometown and appointed Sanskrit scholars who had pursued their Sanskrit studies in Kāsī. The founder of this *kalāśālā* was the great grandfather of ex-minister of A.P. Vijayaramagajapati. He encouraged so many Sanskrit scholars to go to Varanasi and Navadweep in order to attain scholarship in various Śāstras. Coming back to Vijayanagaram, these scholars would impart their knowledge of Sanskrit to the disciples who were equivalent to their preceptors in knowledge. The *kalāśālā* received the patronage of the Maharaja for 32 years. After the demise of the Maharaja, his son Anandagajapati Maharaja reigned the *saṁsthāna* and rendered his patronage like his forefathers. He further encouraged the scholars to author so many Sanskrit works. Gradually the school was elevated to the status of a college. Over the years so many Sanskrit Vyākaraṇa scholars were produced by this *kalāśālā*.

VEDANTAVARDHINI SANSKRIT KALASHALA

GudimellaVenkatarangacharya, a renowned scholar, on the instruction of his preceptor Venkatanrisimhacharya, established Vedantavardhini Sanskrit Kalashala in Korutla village. Śāstric studies flourished in this kalāśālā. The founder Gudimella Venkatarangacharya for many years ran the institution with his hard earned money. He further collected Rs. 2 lakh as donation from the generous people and helped the institution to gain financial stability by depositing the said amount. Many renowned Sanskrit scholars rendered their services to the institution. It now functions under the Sanskrit Vidya Samiti receives government financial aid and has been recognised by the Osmania University.

SRI VENKATESHVARA SANSKRIT PATHASHALA

Located on the banks of the Godāvarī, under the auspices of Dharmapuri Nrisimhaksetram was established in 1848, by Sri Taduri Sitaramaiah Ganapati after receiving munificent funds from the philanthropists; this institution started imparting Śāstraic studies. Renowned Sanskrit scholars served both the Sanskrit literature and the institution without taking a single paisa from the institution. Since 1965 the institution underwent severe financial crisis. It was however revived by the intense efforts of Burgula Ramakrishnarao, by bringing it under the Sanskrit Vidya Samiti, Hyderabad. Two hundred students are receiving Sanskrit from this institution education following the DOL curriculum of the Osmania University.

SANSKRIT VISHVAPARISHAT, DHARMAPURI

This branch was established under the auspices of Dharmapuri Nrisimhaksetram, in 1964. Since it establishment, 300 students have sought Sanskrit studies and 40 students have sought Sanskrit Śāstraic studies. Vālmīki, Vyāsa, Kālidāsa Jayantīs are celebrated here and dramas in Sanskrit are staged every year to propagate Sanskrit language and literature.

SRI VEDANTAVARDHINI SANSKRIT MAHAPATHASHALA

H.H. Sri Satakoparamanujacharya established "Ubhayavedantavardhini" school in Sitarambagh, Hyderabad. The school functioned for many years with the generous help of philanthropists. Boarding and lodging facilities facilitated the students here to pursue Sanskrit studies. Not only the local but also the non local students were drawn towards this institution for its quality of studies in Nyāya, Vyākaraṇa, Sāhitya and Vedānta systems, renowned preceptors and facilities. As number of students kept increasing the functioning of the institution got effected. Mobilisation of funds brought some stability to the institution. More than 12 Sanskrit scholars, taking lesser salary only, are imparting Sanskrit studies, in order to preserve and propagate Sanskrit. The educational curriculum of this institution is based on Siromani examination of Madras University and Vidya Praveena examination of Andhra University. Numerous students have come out successfully in Siromani and Vidya Praveena examinations. Affiliated to the Osmania University, now it conducts entrance, DOL, BOL examinations. Currently the institution has been undertaken by the Tirumala Tirupati Devasthanam. Students are pursuing their studies in the various systems of Sāhitya, Vyākaraṇa, Nyāya and Vedānta.

SRI SANATANA DHARMA SANSKRIT PATHASHALA

Pt. Harinarayana Sarma, Secretary, Sanatana Dharma Sabha, Begum Bazaar, Hyderabad, played key role in establishing this Sanskrit *pāṭhaśālā*. It is engaged in imparting education in the Vedic studies to the knowledge seekers.

SANGA VEDA PATHASHALA

With the noble intention of imparting education in the Vedas along with six auxiliaries to the students to preserve and promote Vedic studies, R.V. Sitarama Sastri established this *pāṭhaśālā* in 1928. Vedic scholars of great reputation, rendered services and enlightened the students. The *pāṭhaśālā* could produce more than 30 profound Vedic scholars. H.H. Vidyasankara Bharati Swami is nurturing this old institution by providing financial aid collected from generous devotees.

SRI SUBRAHMANYA BHARATI PATHASHALA

To preserve the Vedic tradition, Sri Challa Subrahmanyam, an ardent follower of Vedic culture, established this *pāṭhaśālā*, at Narendrapura village, in 1919. After his demise, his wife took over the responsibility and developed the institution further. More than 100 students could acquire profound scholarship in Kṛṣṇa Yajurveda, Sāhitya and Vyākaraṇa from this *pāṭhaśālā*.

UNIVERSITY DEPARTMENTS OF SANSKRIT

The role of universities in Sanksrit studies in Andhra Pradesh is predominant. Andhra University, Vizag; Osmania University, Hyderabad and Sri Venkateswara University, Tirupati, had separate departments for Sanskrit studies from the very beginning, offering Diploma, Postgraduation, M.Phil and (Ph.D) Doctorate level courses. Recently, Nagarjuna

University in Guntur, Sri Krishna Devaraya University in Ananthapur and Kakatiya University in Warangal, have also opended postgraduate study centres for Sanskrit studies. Very recently, the prestigious central university in Andhra Pradesh, the Hyderabad University, has started a department for Sanskrit studies where Sanskrit is taught as an interdisciplinary subject. Hundreds of great Sanskrit scholars were produced by these old universities. At these universities, Vedic study is also undertaken. Though Nagarjuna, Kakatiya and Srikrishnadevaraya universities do not have departments exclusively for Sanskrit, they do provide Sanskrit teaching for the students of M.A. (Telugu) and other languages.

THE RASHTRIYA SANSKRIT VIDYAPEETH, TIRUPATI

As far as the Sanskrit studies are concerned, above all, the Rashtriya Sanskrit Vidyapeetha, Tirupati, a deemed university funded by the UGC exclusively for Sanskrit, has grown as a model university in the whole country. It is the first of its kind in the south India. The quantum of its contribution is larger than that of any other university in the state. This university has produced excellent Śāstric experts, proficient in Śāstric tradition. In this Central University, Sāhitya, Vyākaraṇa, Nyāya, Mīmāṁsā, Veda Bhāṣya, Advaita Vedānta, Viśiṣṭādvaita Vedānta, Jyotiṣa and Śikṣāśāstra (Pedagogy) are offered within the Sanskrit domain at Prak-Sastry Inter level, Sastry B.A., Acarya M.A., Vidyavaridhi Ph.D. levels. The unique nature of this university is that the medium of instruction is Sanskrit. Established in 1956, this Kendriya Sanskrit Vidyapeeth was elevated to the status of a deemed university in 1987. Thought it started with just two departments, today it has got 22 departments under five faculties with more than 70 teaching positions. The Vidyapeetha is the first Sanskrit institution that has started the Computer Science department and undertaken many computer related projects like Sanskrit, etc. Later in 2004, it also opened a new interdisciplinary department for studies in Sanskrit Computational Linguistics, which is a novel field of research. This department offers postgraduate course in Shabdabodha and Language technology. With all this, the Vidyapeetha has achieved a rare honour of being recognised as the centre for excellence in Traditional Sanskrit śāstras by the UGC. The NAAC has accredited the Vidyapeeth with the A+ level in 2003.

Other Educational Institutions

Right from the pre-Independence era, it is the private educational institutes which served the noble cause of preserving and propagating the Vedas, Śāstras and the general Sanskrit. The *saṁsthānams* of Wanaparthy, Gadwal, Pithapuram, Vizianagaram, etc. established and run these Veda Śāstra *pāṭhaśālā*s, with free boarding and lodging facilities for the students. The yearly cash honours arranged by these *saṁsthānams* enthused many to teach and study the Vedas and Śāstras. Thus, the private institutions have played a key role in preservation and propagation of Sanskrit in Andhra Pradesh. On the decline of the *saṁsthānams*, persons with philanthropic views formed into societies to shoulder the responsibility of preserving and propagating Sanskrit. At present the Veda *pāṭhaśālā*s are continuing at Agrigalli, Bapatla, Chautapapayapalem, Draksaramam, Eluru, Guntur, Kapilesarapuram, Keesara, Machilipatnam, Rajahmundry, Sitanagaram, Tirupati, Vijayawada, Visakhapatnam, Vemulavada, Yadagirigutta and other places. These are run exclusively by private organisations, without any financial help from the government.

At Agitipalli, Hyderabad, Nellore, Vizianagaram, Mantralayam and other places there are some Śāstra *pāṭhaśālā*s, where Vyākaraṇa, Nyāya, Mīmāṁsā and Vedānta Śāstras are taught in traditional methods.

Religious Institutions

Organisations of different religious faiths have established various institutions, which render invaluable service in promoting Sanskrit. It is not out of context to recall their contribution to Sanskrit. The TTD is seriously engaged in spreading Sanskrit studies through different schemes. Besides running the two oriental colleges one each at Hyderabad and Tirupati and Veda *pāṭhaśālā*s at Tirupati and Keesara, the TTD launched a scheme called "Kumaradhyapana". Under this scheme a father who imparts Veda education to his son is given some monthly financial grant. Later this scheme was broadened by removing the clause "son". Therefore any *paṇḍit* teaching Veda to any student is entitled for getting the financial grant. The "Śāstra Rakṣaṇa Scheme" provides the same kind of facility for Śāstric teaching. Apart from this, TTD through its Vedaparāyaṇa scheme, is tremendously influencing and attracting the public towards the Vedic studies.

SRI VENKATESHVARA VEDIC UNIVERSITY, TIRUPATI

In 2006, Tirumala Tirupati Devasthanam Board established a new university for the Vedic studies in Tirupati. This university offers postgraduate and undergraduate courses in all *śākhā*s of Vedas. A Veda *pāṭhaśālā* in Dharmagiri of Tirumala is a famous place for Vedic studies under this university.

The Viravenkata Satyanarayana Swamy Devasthanam is running a Veda *pāṭhaśālā* at Annavaram. Sri Venkateswaraswamy Devasthanam of Dwarka Tirumala, is running a Sanskrit high school. Narasimha Swamy Devasthanam at Yadagirigutta is also running a Sanskrit *pāṭhaśālā*. Sri Rajarajeswara Swamy Devasthanam, at Vemulavada, is running a Sanskrit College. Not just the above mentioned, but many other *devasthānam*s are also contributing, at their best possible level, to the teaching of the Vedas, Śāstras and general Sanskrit. The efforts of Srisaila Devasthanam in running the Veda *pāṭhaśālā* are praiseworthy.

Under the auspices of Sri Raghavendraswamy Mutt, a Śāstra *pāṭhaśālā* is being run at Mantralayam. Vyākaraṇa, Sāhitya, Nyāya, Māmāṁsā and Dvaita Vedānta Śāstras are taught here.

Similarly, the Jagadguru Peetham of Sringeri is running a Śāstra *pāṭhaśālā* at Hyderabad, where Nyāya and Advaita Vedānta Śāstras are imparted. The Kanchi Kamakoti Peetham is helping to run the Veda *pāṭhaśālā*s at Nellore, Vijayawada and other places. Sri Chinnajeeyar Swamy Veda Visvavidyalaya of Seetanagaram has promoted a Veda Śāstra *pāṭhaśālā*, near Jaggayyapet, Krishna district, where Yajurveda and Vaiṣṇavāgamas are taught. Higher texts of Viśiṣṭādvaita Vedānta are also taught here.

Some non-governmental organisations are also doing a tremendous job for Sanskrit language promotion and propagation in Andhra Pradesh

SANSKRIT BHASHA PRACHARA SAMITHI, HYDERABAD

This Samiti, established in 1978, is offering short-term Sanskrit courses for public with nearly 100 teachers and 20,000 students.

SURABHARATI SAMITHI, HYDERABAD

Apart from maintaining a Sanskrit library for the benefit of research scholars, this samiti conducts evening classes for Sanskrit lovers in the premises of Osmania University, Hyderabad.

SANSKRIT BHARATI, HYDERABAD

Sanskrit Bharati, a branch of All India Sanskrit Bharati, is doing yeoman's service in propagating Sanskrit among people. Short-term courses such as Sanskrit Shibiram, Geetha-Shikshana, etc. have great impact on the society in general.

SANSKRIT BHASHA PRACHARA SABHA, CHITTOR

The *sabhā* is conducting regular classes for Sanskrit learners, and preparing students for examinations like Praveshika, Vichakshana, Kovida, etc. that are recognised by several other educational institutions. Established 20 years back, this *sabhā* is dedicated in spreading Sanskrit knowledge in Andhra Pradesh as well as in Tamil Nadu. Another special feature of this institution is its examination branches are located in Sri Lanka also. Sanskrit Parichaya, Sanskritbhijna, Sanskrit Vichakshana, Sanskrit Śamartha and Sanskrit Kovida are examinations conducted by the *Sabhā*. These examinations help the seekers to acquire knowledge in Sāhitya, Dharmaśāstra, Mīmāṁsā, Vyākaraṇa, Vedānta, Jyotiṣa, etc. Its fame spread far and wide of the country as numerous knowledge seekers were benefited by it. Owing to this, it attained a prominent place among all the Sanskrit institutions which propagate Sanskrit. *Girvani*, a monthly journal with scholarly articles, is also published by the institution. Library of this institution, having a rich collection of rare Sanskrit works, draws many Sanskrit students and seekers.

Educational institutions established in Andhra Pradesh by the Arya Samaj are open to everyone. These traditional Arya Samaj *gurukula*s, established all over India, are imparting the Vedic studies without any discrimination of gender, caste, creed, religion and nationality. In Andhra Pradesh, five prominent *gurukula*s are playing key role in spreading Vedic studies. To name a few : Arsha Shodha Sansthan, Aliyabad, Shameerpet (M), Rangareddy district; Swami Brahmanand Saraswati Arsha Gurukul, Vadlur, Kamareddy-Indur; Nigama Needam, Pidiched, Gajwel, Medak district. The Panini Prabhat Kanya Mahavidyalaya, Vayu Shakti Nagar Lane, Krishnanagar Extension, Dommaiguda, Ranga Reddy district Keesar Mandal, started with just two students in 2004. This budding *gurukula* is imparting Vedic, Śāstric studies along with modern studies under the guidance of Smt. Savita Arya and Pandit Syamprasad. It is run with some munificent funds donated by philanthropists. Computer science, Indian classical as well as folk dance, music, Yoga, martial arts are also included in the educational curriculum for the all-round development of the students. The *gurukula*, having the strength of 33 students, is striving hard to bridge the gap between the ancient and modern educational systems.

ANDHRA GEERVANA VIDYAPEETHAM

Located at Kovvuru, West Godavari district and established in 1912, Andhra Geervana Vidyapeetha is imparting education in Sanksrit and Telugu for both, boys and girls. Vyākaraṇa, Sāhitya, Nyāya and other Śāstric studies are offered. There are about 15 oriental Sanskrit colleges functioning in the state, where Sanskrit along with Śāstric studies is taught. Apart from these about 10 oriental Telugu and Sanskrit colleges are also functional. Among these institutions, Maharaja Sanskrit College, Vijayanagaram; Matrusri Oriental College, Jillelamudi; SV oriental College, Tirupati and S.V. Vedantavardhini Sanskrit College, Hyderabad, are the ones where currently Sanskrit studies are actively pursued.

By conducing annual examinations and organising cash award oriented functions many institutions have contributed so much to the Veda and Sanskrit learning. Guntur Mandala Veda Vidvatpravardhakapariksamahasabha, the Krishnatiraveda Sabha, Rajahmundry Vedapariksa Sabha, Konasimaveda Sabha, Swadharma Swarajya Sangha, Kouta Purnanbam Trust, Kouta Lalita Manohar Trust, etc. conduct Vedic examinations for the students and award then cash prizes and certificates. The examinations are held for various levels like Mulamantam and Ghanantam. The TTD conducts annual examinations for the students of Vedas, Āgamas and Śāstras. The Kouta Suryanarayanarao Trust, Vijayawada (presently run by K.L. Manohar) conducts annual examinations for the Vidyaranya Bhasya students and presents cash awards and certificates of merit to the successful. The Saparikaradvaita Vedanta Sabha, the Sringeri Sarada Peetham, Kanchikamakoti and the like conduct Śāstra Sabhās and Vākyārthagoṣṭhīs for promotion of Sanskrit. Thus through examinations and honours, the institutions have helped Sanskrit learning a great deal.

Research and Publications

During the immediately preceding decade, tremendous many achievements were made in the field of research and publication in Andhra Pradesh. The universities, religious institutions and private bodies have played a significant role in this regard. A brief sketch of their contribution is presented hereunder:

SANSKRIT ACADEMY SHODH SANSTHAN, HYDERABAD

As a part of the Osmania University, Hyderabad, the Sanskrit Academy has made wonderful progress in Sanskrit research and publication during 1960s and 1970s. Though established in 1954, later in 2002, this institution was taken over by Rashtriya Sanskrit Sansthan, Ministry of Human Resource Development, Government of India, with the recognition as an Adarsh Shodh Sansthan. This institution has so far brought out nearly 100 publications and has also received an international recognition through its scholarly publications.

Andhra Pradesh State Government Oriental Manuscript Library and Research Institute, Hyderabad, established in 1967 this institution has a collection of thousands of Sanskrit manuscripts. Currently located in Osmania University campus, this institution has published 65 books so far.

S.V. ORIENTAL RESEARCH INSTITUTE

Once under the TTD and now controlled by S.V. University,

Tirupati, this institute is known for its publications and research journal. Besides, there is a big treasure of rare books and manuscripts which is quite useful to Sanskrit researchers. This institution came into existence long back in 1939. Later in 1970s it was relocated in S.V. Univeristy campus along with its collection.

RASHTRIYA SANSKRIT UNIVERSITY

The Sanskrit University, through its research wing, undertook the project of Āgamakośa. The first few volumes are ready. Plans are drawn for the project of Telugu-Sanskrit dictionary. In the last decade, more than a dozen books pertaining to Veda, Nyāya, Sāhitya and Vyākaraṇa were published. These include: collected papers on Hindu astronomy; a study of Sanskrit as spoken in India; Vedic Heritage of India; Vyutpattivādaḥ; Pratyakṣatattvacintāmaṇi Vimarśaḥ; Pauskara Saṁhitā, etc. More than 150 publications are there at the credit of RSV.

TIRUMALA TIRUPATI DEVASTHANAM

The publications brought out by the Tirumala Tirupati Devasthanams are hundreds in number. Just the names of its publications run into dozens of papers. However, some important ones are introduced here. Roughly the TTD publications can be divided into two catagories: original works and translations. The original works published by TTD pertain to various disciplines like the Vedas, Vedānta and other Śāstras, Āgamas, Purāṇas and Sāhitya. Major portion of TTD publications is occupied by the literature of the Bhakti cult and Stotra literature. On the translation side too, TTD has made commendable contributions. It has published the Telugu translations of *Ṛgveda, Yajurveda, Sāmaveda* and *Atharva0veda.* S.B. Raghunathacharya, co-ordinator of TTD Publications, launched a fantastic project to impart Vedic knowledge to the common man. Under this project a Vedic encyclopaedia in

Telugu was planned and the volumes of Saṁhitās, Brāhmaṇas and Āraṇyakas were brought out. Those belonging to the Upaniṣads and Āgamas are yet to come out. Besides, TTD is encouraging enthusiastic writers through its "Aid-to-Author" Scheme.

CONTRIBUTIONS OF SCHOLARS TO THE LITERATURE

Several branches of Śāstric literature have been enriched by various Andhra scholars. In Advaita, we find *Pañcadaśī*. Similarly, we can find prominent works in different branches like *Tarkasaṁgraha* by Annambhaṭṭa and *Rasagaṅgādhara* by Jagannātha, *Prātapaditya-Yaśobhūṣaṇa* by Vidyānātha. This literary tradition has been continued in the present age also by the scholarly community of Andhra Pradesh. All these contributions are recorded in the book *Contribution of Andhra to Sanskrit Literature* written by P. Sri Ramamurty and B. Ramaraju, published in 2002. Very recently, a collection of papers entitled *Sanskrit Literature in Andhra Pradesh (Post-Independent Era)* was brought out by EBL, New Delhi.

This short summary is not sufficient to truly detail the contribution of Andhra Pradesh in the field of Sanskrit studies. However, just a glimpse is presented here for to the benefit of the audience at the global level.

3

Sanskrit in Assam
A Brief Survey

Dipak Kumar Sharma

I

ASSAM, regarded as one of the premier north-eastern states of India, is having a very old tradition of Sanskritic culture. This land was earlier known by the names Kāmarūpa and Prāgjyotijñapura, as can be evidenced in various Śāstras and *kāvyas*, and was ruled over by many kings who were sincere patrons of Sanskrit. A good number of epigraphic records of such kings, namely Bhāskaravarman, Ratnapāla, Vanamālavarmadeva and others, bear testimony to the fact that Sanskrit was treated as a medium of literary expression of the scholars and poets. Assam is known for her tāntric culture and the temple of Goddess Kāmākhyā at the Nilachal hill at Guwahati is regarded as the most revered seat for the tāntric Śāktism. The scriptures like the *Yoginītantra*, the *Kālikā Purāṇa*, the *Dharma Purāṇa* and the *Haragaurisaṁvāda* were composed here. Assamese scholar-writers contributed towards other branches like Smṛti, Jyotiṣa, Āyurveda, grammar and prosody also. Pitāmbara Siddhāntavāgīśa composed a number of Smṛti texts, namely the *Tīrthakaumudī*, the *Pretakaumudī*, etc. Among the scriptures on Jyotiṣa, mention may be made of the *Jyotiramuktāvalī*, the *Varṣakṛtya*, the *Samayāmṛta*, etc. The *Āyurvedakalpataru*, *Āyurvedadarśana*,

Āyurvedasaṁgraha are some valuable texts on medicine. The *Hastividyārṇava* is a famous text on veterinary science, especially on the diseases of elephants. Under the patronage of King Naranārāyaṇa (fifteenth century CE), a famous text on Sanskrit grammar namely the *Prayogaratnamālā* was composed by Puruṣottama Vidyāvāgīśa. Under the patronage of the same king, the *Vṛttamālā*, a book on prosody, was composed by Kavikarṇapūra. Cilārāya, the younger brother of that king, composed a Sanskrit commentary, named the *Sāravatī* on the *Gītagovinda* of Jayadeva. During the rule of the Ahoms, a number of Sanskrit literary works were produced by the scholars of this land. In this context, mention may be made of the *Kāmakumāraharaṇa* of Kavicandradvija, the *Dharmodaya* of Dharmadevadvija, the *Vighneśajanmodaya* of Kavisūrya and the *Śaṅkhacūḍavadha* of Dinadvija. There is a Sanskrit commentary by one Śauriśarman on the *Kāvyadarśa* of *Daṇḍin*, which has since been published. Anundoram Borooah (1850-89), who studied in Kolkata and Britain, and was the first ICS from Assam, was a Sanskritist *par excellence*. Though an administrator by profession in the British regime, Borooah, who had a premature death, contributed immensely towards Sanskrit. Besides the *English-Sanskrit Dictionary*, other text-critical books authored by Borooah are:

- *Mahāvīracarita* (with a self-composed Sanskrit commentary)
- *Sarasvatīkaṇṭhābharaṇa*
- *Nānārthasaṁgraha*
- *Bhavabhūti and His Place in Sanskrit Literature*
- *Ancient Geography of India*
- *Nāmaliṅgānuśāsana*
- *Higher Sanskrit Grammar*
- *Prosody*

"Scholar extraordinary" Krishna Kanta Handiqui (1898-1982) the founder vice-chancellor of Gauhati University, who studied in Cotton College, Guwahati, Calcutta University and in Oxford, comes next to Anundoram Borooah, in terms of chronology. The great contributions of Prof. Handiqui are:

- *Yaśastilaka and Indian Culture*
- *Pravarasena's Setubandha*
- *Śrīharṣa's Naiṣadhacarita*

In this context, mention may be made of Mahāmahopādhyāya Dhīreśvarācārya (1851-1937) an erudite traditional Sanskrit scholar, whose *Vṛttamañjarī* is an exhaustive text on Sanskrit prosody. Cakreśvara Bhaṭṭācārya and Jīveśvara Gosvāmī have to their credit the *Śāktadarśanam* and the *Śrīmaddāmodarīyadarśanam* respectively, both composed in Sanskrit.

II

Assam has produced a number of Sanskrit creative writings as well as critical writings in and on Sanskrit, after 1950, a few of which have already been mentioned in respect of the great scholar K.K. Handiqui. Some of such works are briefly mentioned in the succeeding lines.

Acharya Manoranjana Shastri (1911-88), who had commendable command over Nyāya, Mīmāṁsā, Vedānta and grammar, proved his versatility as a poet also through his poems and dramas. His *Prakāmakāmarūpa*, published in 1990, is a *mahākāvya*, divided into nine cantos called *Ucchavāsa*. This great scholar served as the principal of Nalbari Sanskrit College, and this poetic composition aims at glorifying the land called Kāmarūpa, comprising the north-eastern states of India of the present time. To the credit of the Acharya, there is another minor *kāvya* named the, *Patākāmnāyā* which was published in 1966. This *kāvya* is devoted to presentation of the philosophical significance in poetic style, of the national flag of India, along with the flags of other dignitaries. This exposition is available in the second part of the *kāvya*, which is called the *uttarārdha*, whereas the first part called the *pūrvārdha* bears explanations on the national emblem. The book contains a very lucid gloss entitled the *Janamanorañjanī*, written by the poet himself. The late Shastri wrote a short dramatic composition called the *Utakabhaikṣyam* which was published in 1973. The famous Assamese *kāvya* named the *Keteki* of Raghunath Chaudhary was rendered into Sanskrit by the late Shastri.

The *Śrīkr̥ṣṇalīlāmr̥tam* is another Sanskrit *kāvya* composed by Baikunthanath Chakravarty (1900-76), a traditional scholar having deep-rooted proficiency in *kāvya*, Nyāya, Jyotiṣa, Purāṇa and grammar. This *kāvya*, which was published in 1961, is based on the *Bhāgavata* (X. 5-33). The whole *kāvya*, divided into nine cantos called *pravāha*, is composed in a single metre, i.e. *Toṭaka*.

Bhavadeva Bhagavati (1902-88), the author of the *Satījayamatī*, a Sanskrit *kāvya* in three cantos, which was published in 1933 for the first time, has to his credit another anthology of 229 verses in Sanskrit, called the *Ślokamālā* and it was published in 1952. The poems in this anthology are composed in appreciation of some great personalities like Mahatma Gandhi, Pandit Nehru, Radhakrishnan and so on. It is interesting to find that the late *paṇḍit* composed poems in order to illustrate some grammatical rules also. The late Bhagavati composed a small satirical play called the *Nūtanaṁ Nāṭakam* which aims at pointing out to the malpractices noticed in the society of the time.

Mukunda Madhava Sharma (1934-2009), an internationally acclaimed indologist has a collection of Sanskrit poems named *Stutipraśastimañjarī*, besides his lots of other research-oriented scholarly writings in Sanskrit, English, Assamese and some other languages. As the title indicates, this anthology consisting of 538 verses, is devoted to invocations of various deities and appreciation of some great souls. The book was published in the year 2002. Sharma has to his credit another very valuable book entitled the *Vyañjanaprapañcasamīkṣā*, which is divided into six chapters. This book exhibits Sharma's profound knowledge of Sanskrit poetics and also his flawless spirit as a researcher of comparative symbolism in literature. The book was published in 1979 and appreciated by Sanskritists in India and abroad.

Biswanarayan Shastri (1918-2002), a former member of the Lok Sabha, was another noted Sanskrit scholar of Assam. Shastri wrote extensively on various subjects of Indology, with a keen, critical and analytical perspective. Moreover, he has to his credit a Sanskrit novel named the *Avināśī*, published in the year 1986 and it earned him the prestigious Sahitya Akademi Award. The novel, written in the style of classical Sanskrit prose, is based on a subtle event relating to Bhāskaravarman, a king of Prāgjyotiṣapura of the seventh century CE. It should be stated that the author has successfully resorted to the style of a modern novelist in respect of characterisation, depiction of suspense and conflict, as is evidenced in modern novels of other contemporary languages. Shastri's another collection of articles and short stories in Sanskrit, is the *Hṛdayasaṁvādacayana*. It was published in the year 1989.

Some other Sanskrit scholars of Assam are found attempting successfully to translate some literary works of other languages into Sanskrit. In this context, mention should be made of Pandit Bipin Chandra Goswami (1909-87). The late Pandit translated the *Navamallikā*, an Assamese *Kathākavitā* (poems in prose), composed by Raghunath Chaudhary, into Sanskrit. The original Assamese work was published in 1958, whereas, the Sanskrit version of Pandit Goswami came to light in 1964.

The *Gitāñjalisaṁskṛtaṁ* of Kamini Kumar Adhikari, is the Sanskrit rendering of some select songs from the *Gītāñjalī* of Rabindranath Tagore. This Sanskrit rendering was published in 1961 and it contains 89 songs of the Nobel laureate Tagore. Kaviguru's songs from the *Gītāñjalī* were also translated into Sanskrit by another Assamese scholar. Gauridatta Sarma Shastri translated 157 songs and the said anthology was published in 2002. The same scholar has also translated the *Antarīpa*, an award-winning Assamese novel of Bhabendranath Saikia, into Sanskrit.

The *Pañcatantra* and the *Kādambarī* were translated into Assamese by Prabhat Chandra Sarma Sastri and the two books were published in 1966 and 2000 respectively. The Assamese version of the *Kādambarī* brought the prestigious Sahitya Akademi Award for Sastri. Malinee Goswami translated the *Harṣacarita* into Assamese and it also won her the Sahitya Akademi Award.

Some other scholars have compiled texts on *karmakāṇḍas*. In this context, Pandit Ganganath Sastri, Pandit Mahendra Nath Sastri, Pandit Baikuntha Nath Sastri deserve special mention.

Apart from the Sanskritists having both critical and creative ability, mentioned in the previous lines, some other personalities from Assam, have immensely contributed towards the enrichment of Sanskrit studies in the state through their research oriented works. Resisting the temptation of quoting the detailed list of their works, which are in English, Assamese and also in Sanskrit, the names of only a few of them are mentioned here owing to the paucity of space:

- (Late) Jogiraj Basu
- (Late) Tirtha Nath Sarma
- (Late) Rajani Kanta Deva Sarma
- Apurba Chandra Barthakuria

- Ashok Kumar Goswami
- (Late) Kali Prasad Sinha
- Rajendra Nath Sarma
- Thaneswar Sarma
- Sukhamay Bhattacharya
- Jogeswar Sarma
- Narendra Nath Sarma
- Kiran Chandra Sarma

The humble writer of this article also has a number of books published in English, Sanskrit and Assamese, on various branches of Sanskrit studies to his credit. Moreover, Ranjan Bezbaruah, an alumnus of the Department of Sanskrit, Gauhati University and a singer of appreciable talent, has also compiled Sanskrit versions of the songs of Rabindranath Tagore, Sankaradeva, Bhupen Hazarika, Jyotiprasad Agarwala, Bishnu Prasad Rabha and so on.

III

Sanskrit education in Assam is running in two modes, namely the traditional system based on the *paṭhaśālās* (*ṭol*) and the general system, i.e. through high schools, higher secondary schools, colleges and universities. The Assam Sanskrit Board was set up by the Govrnment of Assam in 1926. Sanskrit and Pāli *ṭols* are affiliated to this Board. The Board prepares the syllabi for the three examinations, namely Praveshika, Madhya and Shastri. Vyākaraṇa (Pāṇini and Ratnamālā), Sāhitya, Veda, Nyāya, Mīmāṁsā, Smr̥ti and Jyotiṣa are there as special subjects for Madhyama and Shastri courses. A candidate qualified in the Shastri course is entitled to be admitted to the Acharya course. At present, there are 82 upgraded and 9 non-upgraded Sanskrit and Pālī *ṭols* in Assam. District-wise distribution of the *ṭols* can be seen from the following table:

District	Upgraded		Non-Upgraded	
	Sanskrit	Pāli	Sanskrit	Pāli
Nalbari	13	×	1	×
Barpeta	8	×	×	×
Cachar	4	×	×	×
Karimganj	6	×	1	×
Hailakandi	1	×	×	×
Golaghat	3	×	×	×
Kamrup	11	×	×	×
Dhubri	2	×	×	×
Goalpara	1	×	×	×
Nagaon	5	×	×	×
Sonitpur	5	×	×	×
Darrang	6	×	1	×
Jorhat	6	1	1	×
Sivasagar	1	1	×	×
Lakhimpur	3	×	×	×
Dibrugarh	×	2	×	×
Tinsukia	1	1	×	×
Kokrajhar	1	1	×	×
Morigaon	×	×	1	×

It may be mentioned here that the two *adhyāpaka*s in an upgraded *ṭol* along with the two other teachers (one for English and the other for science) receive government salary at par with a government high school teacher, while the non-upgraded *ṭol*s receive an annual grant only from the state government. Moreover, the Nalbari Sanskrit College, established in 1938, is also affiliated to the Assam Sanskrit Board and follows the syllabi meant for the *ṭol*s. K.K. Handiqui Government Sanskrit College (called Government

Sanskrit College initially) was established in Guwahati in the year 1970 by the Govt. of Assam. The college is having two tier courses, namely Prag-upadhi and B.A. (Sanskrit). The college is affiliated to the Gauhati University and has Sāhitya, Veda, grammar (Pāṇini), Nyāya, Vedānta and Mīmāṁsā in its Honours (major) course. Moreover, Sanskrit is taught as a compulsory subject in BAMS course of Government. Assam Ayurvedic College, Guwahati and also in BFA and B. Music courses of the State College of Art and Government Music College, respectively, both situated in Guwahati.

Sanskrit as an elective subject, is taught in secondary and higher secondary schools and also in the junior colleges. Of course, as it has ceased to be a compulsory subject in the high schools, it has resulted in an undesirable decrease in the number of students opting for the subject in the succeeding stage. However, Sanskrit is being taught at the degree level at 31 colleges under Gauhati University, 11 colleges under Dibrugarh University and 7 colleges under Assam University. Most of the colleges have two types of syllabi, namely major (Honours) and general (Pass). Except for the Dibrugarh University, the remaining two universities, namely Gauhati University, Guwahati and Assam University, Silchar, have the postgraduate departments of Sanskrit. Besides, Sanskrit is there at the postgraduate level in Cotton College, Guwahati, wherein 20 students are admitted annually for the said course. The two universities are having the provision for M.A. and M. Phil. programmes, besides research work leading to Ph.D. At present, 65 students are admitted every year in M.A. course at Gauhati University. The Department of Sanskrit of Gauhati University, was founded in 1957 and it has since been rendering immense contribution towards Sanskritic studies in the country in general and the north-eastern states in particular. Besides producing hundreds of postgraduate and a score of M.Phil in Sanskrit, more than

100 researchers have obtained the degree of Ph.D. through this department. The department is at present having the services of 14 teachers, three subjects namely Kāvya, Veda and Darśana are taught at postgraduate level as special subjects. The department is publishing an annual research journal and holding two regular annual academic lecture programme. Besides postgraduate, there is provision of M.Phil and Ph.D. course at the Department of Sanskrit, Assam University also. The Sanskrit Department of Assam University is having 6 regular teachers where Kāvya and Darśana, are the subjects of specialisation.

Moreover, the Department of Historical and Archaeological Research, Assam, with its head office in Guwahati, has been preserving manuscripts of Sanskrit and the old Assamese. This government department has already published quite a good number of Sanskrit texts, the manuscripts of which were collected by it. Mention may be made of the Kamrup Sanskrit Sanjivani Sabha at Nalbari, which is also preserving a good number of Sanskrit manuscripts, some of which are already edited and are being published from time to time. The Anundoram Borooah Institute of Language, Art and Culture (ABILAC), instituted by the Government of Assam, also has a Sanskrit cell and it has since published a few important Sanskrit texts.

Contribution of Rashtriya Sanskrit Sansthan, New Delhi, towards the promotion and popularisation of Sanskrit in Assam should be mentioned in this context. Besides sponsoring various institutions to hold seminars/conferences, the Sansthan is at present having 95 centres for imparting Sanskrit education through its non-formal Sanskrit education programme. The districtwise distribution of the centres at present can be shown with the help of the following Table :

District	No. of centres	District	No. of centres
Nalbari	5	Lakhimpur	9
Kamrup	10	Golaghat	2
Nagaon	5	Sonitpur	7
Morigaon	5	Darrang	6
Jorhat	5	Barpeta	5
Sibsagar	3	Dhubri	10
Dibrugarh	6	Cachar	7
Tinsukia	1	Karimganj	5
Dhemaji	1	Total	**95**

It may be stated in this context that there are 8 and 2 numbers of such centres in Manipur and Tripura, respectively. Feedback received from time to time from such centres indicates that a good number of persons, having no formal education of Sanskrit, have been benefited by this programme introduced by the Sansthan. It should be mentioned in this context that over the years, the Sanskrit Bharati has done and is still doing commendable jobs in popularising and propagating Sanskrit in a newer dimension in this part of the country.

Some other organisations have also been to contributing the popularisation of Sanskrit in the state. The Dergaon Sanskrit Sanjivani Sabha, the Bajali Sanskrit Parisad at Pathsala, the Pancakanya Sanskrit Bhasa Pracara Kendra Guwahati, the Lokabhasa Pracara Samiti, Assam Branch are organising spoken Sanskrit conversation camps and other programmes for popularisation of Sanskrit in the state. The Assam Veda Vidyalaya, a Sanskrit *ṭol* affiliated to the Assam Sanskrit Board has been carrying the age-old tradition of recitation of the Vedas with proper accentuation.

Thus, it is felt that Sanskrit in its academic, literary and other popular forms, is receiving proper attention from the academic fraternity of the state. Government of Assam established a new university which is named 'Kumar Bhaskar Varma Sanskrit and Ancient Studies University' in 2011 at Nalbari which is located at a distance of about 50km from the capital city of Guwahati. It is felt by the academics that it is a welcome step on the part of the Government for the promotion and expansion of Sanskrit learning in this north-eastern state of India.

4

Sanskrit Studies in Bihar

Uma Shankar Sharma 'Rishi'

The post-Independence period of Sanskrit studies and its creative literature in the state of Bihar is in a glamorous position in some fields, while in the case of some glorious institutions of the past it is in a pitiable condition. Before Independence the Sanskrit studies here adopted either English medium in the modern colleges or the pure Sanskrit medium in the traditional *pāṭhaśālās*. Thus high standard research articles were published in English in the *Journal of the Bihar Research Society*, which was then a pioneer oriental journal of international fame. Its publication gradually dwindled after 1960s, obviously on account of an apathetic attiude of the assisting government and lack of interest among its officials. The Sanskrit medium institutions depended much on the local landlords for their continuance. The English medium colleges gradually shifted to Hindi medium while the latter still maintained their position even after the Independence.

Government Institutions

The Government of Bihar established five Oriental institutes in 1951 under the Education Department (now the department of human resource development) for encouraging Oriental studies, research and publication (SRP). These were (1) Mithila Sanskrit Research Institute at Darbhanga for carrying on Sanskrit SRP, (2) Nava Nalanda Mahavihara for Pāli SRP, (3) Prakrit Institute of Jainism at Vaiśālī for Prākṛt and Jainism SRP, (4) K.P. Jayaswal Research Institute at Patna for research and publication in ancient Indian history, culture and archaeology, and (5) Bihar Rashtrabhasha Parishad at Patna for Hindi research and publichation. These were provided with very able and energetic directors at the initial stage and, in no time, these institutes proved their worth on the national as well as international level.

Mithila Sanskrit Research Institute under P.L. Vaidya and S.S. Bagchi as its early directors, published about two dozen Buddhist Sanskrit texts like *Avadāna-Kalpalatā* of Kṣemendra, *Laṅkāvatāra-Sūtra, Suvarṇa-Prabhāsa-Sūtra, Daśa-Bhūmika-Sūtra, Jātakamālā* of Āryaśūra, *Divyāvadāna, Aṣṭasāhasrikā, Mahāvastu-Avadāna, Lalitavistara, Mahāyāna-Sūtra-Saṁgraha, Śikṣā-Samuccaya, Saddharma-Puṇḍarīka-Sūtra* and others, which were not available to researchers at that time. Several other original Sanskrit works written by the *paṇḍit*s of Mithilā, were also published subsequently for the first time. A number of doctoral theses of outstanding merit were also published by the institute. Some important publications of MRI are *Pārijāta-Aaraṇa Mahākāvya of Karṇapūra, Kāvya-Parīkṣā of Śrīvatsa* (both ed. A.L. Thakur), *History of Mithila* (Upendra Thakur), *History of Navya-Nyāya in Mithila* (D.C. Bhattacharya), *An Exposition of Vyaktiviveka* (T.N. Jha), *An Exposition of Citramīmāṁsā* (Mangla Pati Jha), *Vācaspatimiśra on Advaita Vedānta* (S.S. Hasurkar), *Liṅga-Vacana-Vicāraḥ* (Pandit Dinabandhu Jha), *Prakīrṇa-Prabandha* (collection of Sanskrit works of MM Ramavatar Sharma), *Upamā-Vivekaḥ* (Kashinath Mishra), *Vaiyākaraṇa-Bhūṣaṇa-Sāra with Dīpikā* (Comm. Pandit Dinabandhu Jha), etc. These publications number about 70.

Apart from its outstanding publications for which the institute is internationally known, it has rendered valuable service in assimilating the traditional Sanskrit-learning with modern methods through its post-graduate curriculum and Ph.D. programmes. Hundreds of scholars received training here and they occupied various dignified posts around the country. For a quite long time it was managed by the Bihar government. But later on it was taken as a constituent wing of the K.S. Darbhanga Sanskrit University. Its glorious days are now part of history. The institute has a rich collection of rare books in Sanskrit and English along with about 12,000 manuscripts all donated by the Mahārājā of Darbhanga at its very inception. Some rare manuscripts have been edited and published too.

Nava Nalanda Mahavihara was established by the Government of Bihar for Pāli and Buddhist studies at Nālandā, near the ancient site of the Nalanda University (fifth – twelfth century) with Bhikhu Jagadish Kashyap as its founder-director. It published the entire *Tripiṭaka* in several volumes in Devanāgarī script for the first time. It gained ground during the directorship of the renowned Sanskrit and Buddhist scholar, Satkari Mookerji (a teacher of the present writer) who edited and translated into English several Buddhist Sanskrit works like the *Pramāṇa-Vārttika* of Dharmakīrti (though only in part). The Mahāvihāra has maintained its worth through postgradute classes, Ph.D. programmes and other standard research publications touching Sanskrit texts too. Besides Pāli and Buddhist texts, it teaches Indian philosophy in general. It has recently been taken over by the Government of India and converted into a deemed university. It is a sort of international centre for Buddhist studies as students from Japan, China, Tibet, Thailand, Sri Lanka and Myanmar have been studying here from the very beginning.

The Prakrit Institute of Jainism and Ahimsa at Vaiśālī is known for the postgraduate studies in Prākr̥t and Jainism along with doctoral research work. It is affiliated to Bihar University for examination purpose. Its research journal containing standard articles, on Indology in general and Prākr̥t and Jainism in particular, is of abiding value even for the Sanskrit researchers. Publications of the institute number more than 50. Some of its significant publications are Indian Logic by K.K.

Dikshit, *Studies in Indian Folk-tales in the Light of Vāsudevahiṇḍī* by Sriranjan Surideva (in Hindi), etc. Sriranjan Surideva edited the *Vāsudevahiṇḍī*, the Prākṛt version of *Bṛhat-kathā* with his Hindi translation, published from Delhi. Many doctoral theses in English and Hindi are other valuable publications of the institute.

The Kashi Prasad Jayaswal Research Institute located in Patna Museum premises is mainly concerned with historical research and publications. Under the directorship of A.S. Altekar, the renowned historian and Sanskrit scholar, it initiated publication of an Indological Research Journal of a very high standard. The Institute has published a *Comprehensive History of Bihar* in six volumes (three volumes with two parts each) in the 1970s. Herein are included the literary pictures (including that of Sanskrit) from different periods of Bihar's history. It is really encyclopaedic in nature. Hemādri's commentary, named *Darpaṇa* on Kālidāsa's *Raghuvaṁśa*, edited by Rewa Prasad Dvivedi, is also an important publication of this institute. One cannot forget the publication of the *Biography of Dharmasvāmin* (1959) in original Tibetan, edited and translated into English by G. Roerich, carrying a long introduction by Altekar. It is noteworthy that Dharmasvāmin, a Tibetan monk, visited Nālandā during the Muslim attack on the monastery and recorded his experiences of his visit to Bihar in his memoirs.

The institute also published several works under the Tibetan Sanskrit Series like (a) *Śrāvaka-bhūmi* of Asaṅga (1973) edited by Karunesh Shukla, (b) *Prātimokṣa-Sūtram* (1975), (c) *Abhidharma-Samuccaya-Bhāṣya* (1976), both edited by Nathmal Tatia, and (d) *Sara-tama* (1979), edited by P.S. Jaini, Professor of Buddhist Studies, University of California, U.S.A. Other important publications of the institute are (1) *Contribution of Bihar to Sanskrit Literature* (1973) by S. Banerjee, (2) *History of Buddhism* by Tāranāth, translated into Hindi by Rigzin Lunup Lama (1971).

Periodical meetings and organising research methodology training for the students of the Oriental subjects are also significant programmes of the institute, which are helpful in encouraging and disciplining Sanskrit researches as well.

The Bihar Rasthtrabhasa Parishad located in Patna is primarily devoted to publication of Hindi books of a very high standard. Besides, it publishes a journal (*Parishad Patrika*) containing outstanding articles in Hindi. Some of the books published by the Parishad during the last 60 years are of enduring value in the field of Sanskrit studies also. We may mention (a) *Kathā-Sarit-Sāgara* of Somadeva (*c.* twelth century CE) with Hindi translation in three volumes, (b) *Kāvya-Mīmāṁsā* of Rajaśekhara (tenth century CE) with Hindi translation by Pt. Kedaranath Sarasvat, (c) *Kāvyālaṁkāra* of Bhāmaha (sixth century CE) with Hindi translation and expositon by Devendranath Sharma, (d) *Saddharma-Puṇḍarīka*, a Mahāyāna text, translated by R.M. Das, and (e) *Bṛhat-Kathā-Śloka-Saṁgraha*, translated by R.P. Poddar and Sriranjan Surideva. These Sanskrit works were translated into Hindi, for the first time.

Besides, the Parishad published some eminent works like several volumes of the Cultural Studies by MM Gopinath Kaviraj under different titles, e.g. *Bhāratīya Saṁskṛti aur Sādhana* (in two volumes), *Tāntrika Vāṅmaya mein Śāktadṛṣṭi* (Śākta View in Tantric Literature), etc. The voluminous research work of P.D. Agnihotri entitled *Patañjali-kālīna Bhāratavarṣa* (India in the Time of Patañjali) is a prestigious publication of the Parishad. Of similar value are the works like *Bhāratīya Bhāṣā-Śāstrīya Cintan kī Pīṭhikā* (Background of Indian Linguistic Thought) by Vidyanivas Mishra and *Bhāṣā-Vijñāna kī Bhāratīya Paramparā aur Pāṇini* (Indian Tradition of Philology and Pāṇini) by Ramdeva Tripathi. Hindi translation of Pischel's *Prakrit Grammar* by Hemchandra Joshi is also quite valuable in the field of Oriental philology. The Parishad has published about 200 books of outstanding merit in the fields of local dialects and their philology, literary criticism and scientific literature.

The above mentioned Bihar Research Society, housed in a big hall of Patna Museum, had seen its glorious days in the stewardship of K.P. Jayaswal and other Orintalists of Bihar. In the 1930s, Mahapandit Rahul Sankrityayan had deposited the entire bulk of manuscripts procured by him during his four adventurous sojourns to Tibet. These were mostly Sanskrit manuscripts. Rahulji was in a hurry to publish the *Pramāṇa-Vārttika of Dharmakīrti* with the Sanskrit commentary he had brought. It was published in 1936 by the Bihar Research Society and it gave him international fame. Although, better editions of the text with English translation appeared later from other publications, but this original edition played a pioneering role. *The Journal of Bihar Research Society* was also a pioneer in the field of Indological studies in Bihar for a long period even up to the 1960s). But the Society with its journal is now in the last stage of survival. Its rich library is also in a ruined state and the old publications of the Society are also not available now.

In 1970s the Bihar government established the Sanskrit Academy on the pattern of some other states, but owing to the lack of infrastructure, it has not been able to function properly. Some initial publications were all that it could do. It is now merged with other academies.

The Bihar Hindi Granth Academy, a government institution (estd. 1970) worked very zealously for publishing over 100 standard books in literary, scientific and miscellaneous fields. Some important works dealing with Sanskrit studies were also published by the Academy such as *Rājaśekhara and His Times* (R.P. Pandey), *Grammatical Categories* (Dipti Sharma), *Kāvya Guṇas and Alaṁkāras* (Shobhakant Mishra), etc. — all in Hindi.

Universities and Colleges

Till 1951 there was only one university (i.e. Patna University) in Bihar having several affiliated colleges both government and private. Of these, Patna College (estd. 1863) located on the bank of the Gaṅgā River taught Sanskrit up to postgraduate standard. (Its postgraduate classes actually started in 1919). Some erstwhile teachers who taught here are still remembered with respect, e.g. Pandit Ambikadatta Vyasa (1900), A.P. Banerji-Shastri (holding Oxonian doctorate degree), Hari Chand and T. Chowdhury. In 1952, Bihar University was carved out having its headquarters at Muzaffarpur with jurisdiction over the whole state except Patna. Patna University became a teaching-cum-residential university having only four colleges teaching Sanskrit and a separate postgraduate department was provided. Bihar University also taught postgraduate Sanskrit in two campuses one in L.S. College, Muzaffarpur and another at Kabraghat, Darbhanga, in the campus donated by the Rājā of Darbhanga. The latter (Mithila Sanskrit Research Institute) opened the doors of postgraduate studies for traditional students having Acharya degrees in Veda, Vyākaraṇa, Sāhitya, Nyāya, Vedānta, etc. for whom admission to M.A. course in Sanskrit was so far forbidden, unless they graduated either privately or through recognised degree colleges. This campus became a centre of learning for Sanskrit studies as it produced a galaxy of Sanskrit scholars in course of time.

In 1961, Bihar University was further divided into four universities, namely, Bihar, Bhagalpur, Ranchi and Magadh, each having a separate postgraduate department of Sanskrit. The headquarters of Magadh University was at Bodh-Gaya, on a wasteland donated by the Mahant of Bodh-Gaya. Soon a university at Darbhanga named L.N. Mithila University was established. In course of time these universities were futher divided owing to increasing workload and the local political pressure. From Bihar University was carved out the J.P. University at Chapra, from Magadha came the Veer Kuer Singh University at Ara, from Mithila came the B.N. Mandal

University at Madhepura, form Bhagalpur came the Siddu Kanu University at Dumka and from Ranchi came the Vinoba Bhave University at Hazaribagh. All the new universities, without taking care of infrastructure and faculty opened their own postgraduate departments in many subjects (including Sanskrit). In such a situation Sanskrit studies suffered a lot in the whole state excepting a few old universities where good libraries and a tolerable number of teachers existed. I have heard that some universities are carrying on postgraduate teaching with a single teacher, resulting into poor admission in the subject there. Its main reason was apathy of the government towards higher education in general and Sanskrit in particular. This is indicated by the poor financial assistance to the universities concerned.

The role of Kameshwar Singh Darbhanga Sanskrit University (KSDSU) towards Sanskrit studies may separately be highlighted here. It was established in 1960 at Darbhanga in the palatial building donated by the then Mahārājā Kameshwar Singh of Darbhanga with exclusive purpose of propagating and expanding traditional Sanskrit-learning. He donated a part of his rich library to the university as well. The function of the old Bihar Sanskrit Association in conducting Shastri and Acharya examinations was merged with this university. The lower examinations of Prathama and Madhyama were entrusted to the newly-formed Bihar Sanskrit Shiksha Board (on the pattern of Bihar School Exam. Board). KSDSU remained only an examining body like its predecessor association till 1974. Ram Karan Sharma joined as its vice-chancellor on 18 April 1974 and he brought the university in the mainstream of teaching and research as well. Post-graduate departments associated with newly-created faculties were established at Darbhanga and the colleges remained responsible for teaching up to the Shastri level. Soon the state government and the UGC showed their benevolence towards financial grants to the university and posts of lecturers, readers and professors (till then unknown to

Sanskrit university) were allowed to be filled up in every department. Posts of principals in its colleges were also raised to the level of readers.

In November 2000 the State of Jharkhand was carved out of Bihar, taking a number of universities with their afilliated colleges. Thus Ranchi, Vinoba Bhave and Siddu Kanu universities were included in Jharkhand. A few colleges of KSDSU falling in the new state became constituent units of the Vinoba Bhave University.

Sanskrit Curriculum

In Bihar, as elsewhere, there are two types of Sanskrit curriculum, viz. general and special. As for the general studies the schools, colleges and universities followed, for a long time, almost the old pattern which was prevalent in British days. The English medium was gradually replaced by Hindi. Sanskrit as a school subject starts now from class VI and textbooks prepared by the SCERT and published by the Bihar State Text Book Publishing Corporation are taught from class VI to XII. The State had no sound policy in place regarding preparation of Sanskrit textbooks for a long lime. But for the last several years these are prepared in the light of the educational curriculum (2005) prescribed by the NCERT, New Delhi. Lessons of the national and local importance are given due emphasis in Sanskrit textbooks so that the learner can express himself in Sanskrit at ease, even when has has to talk about modern subjects.

From the college standard the Sanskrit textbooks are almost confined to old literature of poetry, drama and prose. Only in few places the local modern Sanskrit writing has been introduced. The UGC recently suggested certain changes in the Sanskrit curriculum both at the undergraduate and postgraduate levels which resulted in introducing environmental studies, Indian culture, etc. in some universities. Sanskrit studies in Bihar in fact prospered from 1950 to 1990 and the number of students offering this subject was quite satisfactory. In Patna University there were once 160 students in M.A. (Previous) class. So was the condition in other renowned centres of Sanskrit-learning. But gradually the number came down owing to globalisation, lack of prospects, opening of vocational courses, retirement of good teachers, disinterested teaching, insufficient number of teachers, apathy of the authorities, opening of postgraduate centres without infrastructure, etc.

At the postgraduate level papers of Veda, Vyākaraṇa, Philology, History of Sanskrit literature and a few texts of primary philosophy are compulsorily prescribed while special group of Sāhitya is commonly taught. A few universities teach either Darśana-śāstra, or Linguistics as alternative special group. Research scholars have to engage postgraduate classes as there is dearth of regular teachers everywhere.

As far as the special Sanskrit studies are concerned these are covered by the Sanskrit Shiksha Board (up to Inter-level) and the KSDSU (for graduate, postgraduate and doctoral levels). It is presumed that these institutions produce students with deep devotion to Sanskrit. In 1960s modern subjects were introduced lin traditional Sanskrit examinations, so that the scope of Sanskrit students be widened. In the transitional period examinations of *prācīna* and *navīna* systems were conducted separately. But now only the latter survives. Hence, the students undergoing special training of Śāstras have to pass in modern subjects like English, Hindi, Economics, Political Science, Mathematics, etc. at the graduate level (i.e. Shastri exam.). At the Postgraduate Centre at Darbhanga Acharya classes are conducted in various traditional Śāstras. The medium is Sanskrit. After the Acharya examination in a particular Śāstra some students opt for research work for the Vidyavaridhi (Ph.D.) degree in that Śāstra, if their projects or synopses are approved by the Research Council. The thesis is generally written in Sanskrit except is some cases. Thus the university is doing service to Sanskrit learning in its own way. Despite poor facility for research, some brilliant theses were produced by the scholars at this university. But in most cases, the modern methods of research are not observed because of lake of good infrastructure.

Private Institutions and Magazines

There are several private Sanskrit institutions for the promotion and propagation of Sanskrit among the people. The foremost of these is the Sanskrit Sanjivan Samaj founded by Pandit Ambikadatta Vyasa in 1893 at Patna. It published its magazine *Sanskrit-Sanjivanam* for a long time. After gaps of several years from time to time, it is still surviving with the financial assistance of Jagadish Pandey, its president. Under the editorship of Devendranath Sharma, Kashinath Mishra and the present writer, a journal *Paṭalaśrīḥ* was published for about five years in the 1960s under the auspices of the Sanskrit Natya Parisad. Another magazine, *Sanskrit-Sammelanam* (from Patna) under the editorship of Pandit Chandradipa Shukla was published for a long time, but the demise of its editor resulted in its closure recently. Its several special issues (like Harihar Kripalu Dvivedi number) are of abiding value. The Sanskrit Seva Sangh, founded by Baneshvar Pathak at Ranchi served the purpose of Sanskrit learning by organising periodical meetings and special lectures by specially invited Sanskrit scholars. These institutions prove their worth by celebrating Sanskrit Divas, Gita Jayanti, Guru Purnima, Shastra Sabha, Kavi Sammelan, Vidwat Samman, etc.

Sanskrit Prasara Parishad (Ara) deserves a special mention as it has been publishing a half-yearly research journal named *Araṇyakam* under the editorship of an enthusiastic scholar, Gopabandhu Mishra for the last 20 years. Many other publications of this Parishad along with Vidvat-Sammana are also noteworthy.

Propagators of Sanskrit (Kṣatra-bala)

A.S. Ayengar, the then Governor of Bihar in 1960s was a great propagator of Sanskrit. He encouraged staging of several Sanskrit plays and organisation of Sanskrit Kavi-Sammelans in Raj Bhavan on the occasion of Republic Day, etc. He himself ensured his presence in any Sanskrit meeting, if invited. S.V. Sohoni, ICS, who served the state of Bihar in various capacities and who later became the vice-chancellor of Sanskrit university, Darbhanga and Tilak Maharashtra Vidyapith at Pune, was a profound scholar and lover of Sanskrit and delivered many erudite lectures in the meetings of Bihar Research Society and elsewhere. Rukmini Raman Singh, formerly a landlord of Muzaffarpur was a great lover of Sanskrit and financed the publications of various Sanskrit periodicals. Jagadish Pandey, a retired chief engineer of Bihar patronises Sanskrit Sanjivan Samaj with his benevolent financial assistance and presence in its various meetings

Poets and Writers

In the post-Independence era many poets and writers of Sanskrit in Bihar came to light with their creative and critical writings. The journals and magazines published over these years contain much of their works. A few authors published their own writings while a number of Sanskrit works written by Bihari writers were published by renowned publishers. They include critical as well as literary works. The books thus published are more than 200 in number during the period under review. We are constrained by the limit of space to mention only the well-known writers and their works.

Janaki Vallabh Shastri, the great scholar-poet of Muzaffarpur who has opened the doors of new sensibility in Sanskrit poetry through his *Kākalī* appreciated by Rabindranath Tagore, wrote his *Bandī-mandiram* in Mandakranta metre. Ramnath Pathak Pranai's *Rāṣṭravāṇī* was first published in 1952. It contains

Sanskrit songs in appreciation of nationalism. The book was later edited by R.V. Tripathi and published by the Rashtriya Sanskrit Sansthan in 2010. Bhavanidatta Sharma interpreted the lives of Bharata and Urmila afresh through his *mahākāvyas Bharatacaritam* and *Saumitrisundarī-caritam*. Dinsesh Prasad Pandey wrote many Sanskrit books of which *Mitradūtam* and *Bharatayānam* are well known.

The late Nemichandra Shastri of Ara (who originally hailed from Madhya Pradesh) was a great scholar of Sanskrit, Prākr̥t and Jainism. He edited a half-yearly research journal in Sanskrit, *Magadham* by name. Only after five or six issues it was closed. Its special numbers e.g., Pāṭaliputra Parīkṣitaḥ are of an outstanding value. Shastri was an institution in himself. His contributions are spread in about a dozen books on Indological subjects. He is credited with delivering the first Sanskrit speech in AIOC as sectional president of Prākr̥t and Jainism section at the Ujjain session (1972).

Kashinath Mishra, apart from his *Upamāviveka* mentioned above and his monograph on Udayanācārya in Sanskrit (published by the Sahitya Academy), wrote *Vidyāptiśatakam* (a creative poetic translation in Ārya metre of 100 songs of the Maithilī poet Vidyapati) in 700 verses, *Kamaṭarājataraṅgiṇī* (a versified account of the Karṇāṭa dynasty of medieval Mithilā) in eight *taraṅgas* of Anuṣṭup metre and *Harṣacarita-Mañjarī* (for which he was awarded by the Sahitya Akademy). His eloquent literary style is inimitable in the modern era. Jayamant Mishra wrote *Ārya-Pañcaśati* (a *muktaka kāvya*) besides his earlier critical works *Nibandha-Kusumañjali* (collection of Sanskrit essays on poetics) and *Kāvyātma-Mīmāṁsā* (on the soul of poetry). Munishvar Jha wrote *Veda-Vāg-Vivr̥tti* on the Vedic literature. His Hindi translation of the Whitney's *Sanskrit Grammar* published in two volumes by the U.P. Hindi Sansthan, Lucknow, is well known and shows his linguistic talent. Bechan Jha edited the Kamadhenu Sanskrit commentary on Vāmana's

Kāvyālaṁkāra Sūtravṛtti (published by Chowkhamba Sanskrit Sansthan, Varanasi). His doctoral thesis concept of poetic blemishes was also published by Chowkhamba Sanskrit Series. Satish Chandra Jha is credited for with his work on contribution of Kātyāyana to Sanskrit grammar.

Uma Shankar Sharma 'Rishi' came with his treatise and edition of the *Nirukta* (chapters I-VII) in 1961. His edition of *Sarva-Darśana-Saṁgraha* was published in 1964. Subsequently his edition of the *Ṛgveda-Saṁhitā* (chapter I) with exhaustive treatment appeared in 1973, to be followed by Mīmāṁsā-darśana (Tarkapāda) with *Śābarabhāṣya* (1980), *Kāraka-Tattvānuśīlana* (is doctoral thesis, 1992) and *Sanskrit Sāhitya kā Itihāsa* (1999). His Sanskrit poems were published sporadically in local magazines. Many research scholars under his guidance got their works published through various publishers. Significant works among them are *Pāribhāṣendu-Śekhara: A Study* (Gopabandhu Mishra), *Cultural Studies of Aśvaghoṣa's Works* (Neelam Roy), *Sāṁkhya Philosophy and Pramāṇa* (Madhubala Sinha), *Liṅgānuśāsana: A Study* (Sudha Mishra) and *Philosophy of Aśvaghoṣa* (Mahasveta Maharathi). Veena Sharma's work *Kṣitpratyaya-Vimarśa* was published with the financial assistance of Rashtriya Sanskrit Sansthan.

Kalanath Jha's *Figurative Poetry in Sanskrit* was published by Motilal Banarsidass. Mahesh Jha's *Śataka*s *Śrī Caṇḍikā*, *Saparyā* and *Āryā* are famous for devotional poetry — expressed in chaste style. Ramashish Panday of Ranchi has written more than a dozen Sanskrit books, e.g., *Kāvya-Kādambakam, Mayūkhadūtam, Śikhābandhanam, Karṇārjunīyam* (both dramas), besides *Indirā-Śatakam* and *Pradelikā-Śatakam.* He also wrote a voluminous work on the etymologies of Yāska, published in 1998 from Ranchi. Ram Bilas Chaudhary has written a drama *Adbhuta-Pāṇigrahaṇam* on the institution of marriage.

There is a Sanskrit poetess in Bihar (though she hails from U.P.) named Smt. Mithilesh Kumari Mishra. She wrote a large number of Sanskrit plays, poems and a novel. Among her dramas are *Āmrapāli*, *Tulasidāsa* and *Daśamastvamasi* (satirical one-act plays). Her poems are *Subhāṣitasumanoñjaliḥ*, *Vyāsa-Śatakam*, *Kāvyāyanī* (50 songs) and *Candracaritam* (on Subhas Chandra Bose). She wrote *Jigīṣā* (a novel), *Laghvi* (101 short stories) and *Ādhunikā* (short stories) too. She writes simple Sanskrit in almost spoken style with good fluency.

We cannot forget the two non-residents of Bihar, Ram Karan Sharma and Jagannath Pathak. Sharma settled in Delhi at present is credited with a number of Sanskrit poems like *Pātheya-Śatakam* (1988, on the speciality of Sanātana Dharma), *Sandhyā*, *Śiva-śukīyam*, *Vīṇā*, *Dīpkā*, *Sarvamaṅgalā*, *Gaganavāṇī*, *Mānasī*, *Sumanomālā* (2001), etc. besides two idealistic and utopic novels — *Sīmā* (1987) and *Rayīśaḥ* (1994). His doctoral thesis *Elements of Poetry in the Mahābhārata* was published from California (USA) in 1966. Its second edition was published in 1988 by Motilal Banarsidass. His creativity is still continuing. Jagannath Pathak is settled in Allahabad. His *Kāpiśāyani* (a collection of a variety of Sanskrit poems of new sensibility) fetched the him the Sahitya Akademi Award. His another poem *Āryā-Sahasrānāmam* contains 1,000 verses in Āryā metre. It is written in the form of ancient *muktaka*s but a new philosophical dimension has been drawn upon in its content. Pathak was assigned the task of editing the volume dealing with modern Sanskrit literature by the Uttar Pradesh Sanskrit Sansthan, Lucknow. It was published as volume VII of the *Comprehensive History of Sanskrit Literature*.

Future Prospect

The state of Bihar along with its former part (i.e. Jharkhand) has not lagged behind in Sanskrit studies even in modern age, despite inadequate means. The institutions which moved forward in every respect till recently now suffer from an apathetic attitude of the authorities and consequently they are not in a position of promoting inspiring Sanskrit studies in Bihar.

There are huge manuscript libraries in Sanskrit University and Research Institute at Darbhanga as also in the Bihar Research Society at Patna but they are not utilised and the position is — *jīrṇam aṅge subhāṣitam* (the contents are in a state of destruction in the body itself). The talented poets of Sanskrit in this state suffer from lasiness and dearth of proper appreciation and publication facilities as well. The Sanskrit academies in other states prosper but in Bihar it is still in the initial stage after a period of some 30 years. Universities and private institutions are doing routine work in propagating Sanskrit research and preservation of learning. Sometimes the scholars from outside the state are invited and shown due respect and appreciation which indicates the love for Sanskrit among common the people too. We are still hopeful to revitalise Sanskrit studies in the State of Bihar while boasting of its glorious literary past.

5

Sanskrit Studies in Delhi

Shashiprabha Kumar
Ramakant Shukla

Delhi is not only the political capital of India, but also a hub of the literary, cultural, educational and research activities, although much of these are not widely known through the communication media. There are thirteen universities in Delhi, besides the two deemed to be Sanskrit universities, which are solely devoted to the higher studies in Sanskrit. In the last sixty years or so, Delhi has witnessed a wide interest and steady growth of Sanskrit as well as *saṁskṛti*, reflected through the language. The present write-up aims to highlight a few glimpses of the same.

However, it needs to be clarified at the outset that given the constraint of time and limited availability of information, **the article is only selective and does not in any way claim to be comprehensive.** It is also worth mentioning in this regard that there are at least three prior publications focusing on Sanskrit Studies in Delhi, details of which are given below:

1. "Sanskrit Studies in Delhi" by Prof. Satyapal Narang in *Sanskrit Studies in India,* edited by Dr. K.K. Mishra, Rashtriya Sanskrit Sansthan, New Delhi:1997, pp.75-94.
2. "Sanskrit Studies in Delhi" by Prof. Avanindra Kumar in *Sanskrit Studies in India,* edited by Prof. Vachaspati Upadhyaya, Shri Lal Bahadur Shastri Rashtriya

Sanskrit Vidyapeeth, New Delhi: 2001, pp.145-181.

3. *Dillīsthāh Viṁśaśatābdīyāḥ Saṁskṛta-Racanākārāḥ* authored by Dr. Chandrabhushana Jha, edited by Dr. Srikrishna Semwal, Delhi Sanskrit Academy, New Delhi: 2001.

Since the present article is intended to highlight the status of Sanskrit Studies in Delhi during the last sixty years, hence it has been endeavoured herein to avoid repetitions as much as possible and to elaborate those aspects which were not covered in the earlier works.

It is in the above said background that the following brief sketch is being put forward under seven heads:

1. Department of Sanskrit, University of Delhi
2. Special Centre for Sanskrit Studies, Jawaharlal Nehru University
3. Shri Lal Bahadur Shastri Rashtriya Sanskrit Vidyapeetha
4. Rashtriya Sanskrit Sansthan
5. Delhi Sanskrit Academy
6. Registered /Unregistered societies/trusts
7. Others

Department of Sanskrit, University of Delhi

The Department of Sanskrit, University of Delhi, is as old as the university itself. Having come into existence in 1922, the year the university came into being, initially for two years it had no postgraduate students. In 1924, a student in M.A. was admitted and the department's postgraduate wing came into being. From a small department it has now grown into one of the biggest departments in the university, with some three hundred postgraduate students and one hundred fifty research scholars and about one hundred fifty teachers taking into account teachers, both in affileated colleges and the university department.

The department of Sanskrit has had some of the stalwarts as its members in the past. Prof. Joshi is an internationally acclaimed Sanskritist who has several works to his credit, written in Sanskrit, in English, in French, in Spanish and in Hindi. Having done his D.Litt. from Paris, he introduced modern European research methods in the department. He has been the visiting Professor in the U.S.A. and many other European and Latin American countries. He is a recipient of several awards and gold medals including 'Certificate of Honour' from the President of India and Sahitya Akademi Award.

Prof. Satyavrat Shastri is another world-renowned Sanskrit scholar, who has been Dean, Arts Faculty and Head of the Sanskrit Department. Prof. Shastri is the recipient of seventy-six honours and awards, national and international, including Jnanapith, Padmabhushana and President of India 'Certificate of Honour'. He has authored ten creative works in Sanskrit, six critical works on Sanskrit and two travelogues besides two translated books, five edited books and one compilation of Sanskrit maxims. Over and above these books, he has published more than 150 research articles and contributed foreward to one hundred and twenty-five books.

The department has also had scholars like Prof. S.P. Narang, N.S. Shukla, Avanindra Kumar, Krishnlal, M.I. Khan, Usha Chaudhuri, Vachaspati Upadhyaya, B.M. Chaturvedi, Pushpendra Kumar, M.M. Agrawal on its faculty. At present there are eleven faculty members in the Sanskrit Department of Delhi University:

Name	Designation	Area
Dr. Mithilesh Chaturvedi	Professor & Head	Philosophy of Grammar, Grammar, Literature
Dr. Dipti Tripathi	Professor	Grammar, Linguistics, Poetics & Literature
Dr. Shakuntala Punjani	Professor	Philosophy
Dr. Sharda Sharma	Professor	Veda & Dharmashastra
Dr. Ramesh Bhardwaj	Professor	Grammar, Linguistics, Philosophy & Veda
Dr. Meera Dwivedi	Associate Professor	Poetics & Literature
Dr. Bharatendu Pandey	Associate Professor	Grammar, Linguistics & Philosophy
Dr. Omnath Bimali	Associate Professor	Grammar, Linguistics & Philosophy
Dr. Purnima Kaul	Assistant Professor	Epigraphy, Culture & Literature
Dr. Satyamurti	Assistant Professor	Philosophy, Linguistics & Literature
Sh. Tec Chand Meena	Assistant Professor	Poetics & Literature

The total number of students enrolled in Ph.D., M.Phil. and M.A. courses of the department at present is about five hundred and twenty-five.

Special Centre for Sanskrit Studies, Jawaharlal Nehru Univerity

In 2001, the Special Centre for Sanskrit Studies was set up in Jawaharlal Nehru University. In its existence since the past one decade, the centre has grown in several dimensions. Apart from the seven permanent faculty members, (which is expected to increase very soon), the students' strength in quantity as well as quality is in fact the real achievement of the centre. Eminent, world-renowned Sanskritists like Prof. George Cardona, Prof. M.K. Byrski and Prof. Rama Nath Sharma have come to the centre as visiting faculty while Prof. Ashok

Aklujkar, Prof. Nicholas Kazanas, Prof. T.S. Rukmani, Prof. Subhash Kak, etc. have delivered special lectures at the centre. Every year a Sanskrit Week programme is celebrated in which lectures by invited scholars on the chosen themes are organised and select proceedings are published.

During the Xth Plan research and publication programme, the following five publications are brought out by the centre (besides the individual faculty publications):

1. *Sanskrit Across Cultures*, edited by Shashiprabha Kumar, D.K. Printworld (P) Ltd., 2007.
2. *Sanskrit and Other Indian Languages*, edited by Shashiprabha Kumar, D.K. Printworld (P) Ltd., 2007.
3. *Veda as Word*, edited by Shashiprabha Kumar, D.K. Printworld (P) Ltd., 2006.
4. *Sanskrit Studies I*, edited by Kapil Kapoor, D.K. Printworld (P) Ltd., 2005.
5. *Sanskrit Studies II*, edited by Wagish Shukla, D.K. Printworld (P) Ltd., 2007.

Details of the Projects Completed in the Centre

S. No.	Name of Project	Project Co-ordinator	Funding Agency
1.	*A Multilingual, Multimedia Encyclopaedic Dictionary of Intellectual Terms of Indian Culture (Indian Philosophy)*	Prof. Shashiprabha Kumar	JNU under UPOE programme of UGC
2.	*To Prepare a Reader in Indian Philosophy*	Dr. Ram Nath Jha	UGC
3.	*Database System for Dialects of Hindi*	Dr. Girish Nath Jha	MGAHU, New Delhi
4.	*Online Multilingual Amarakosa*	Dr. Girish Nath Jha	JNU under UPOE programme of UGC
5.	*Bṛhat Vaiśeṣika Kosha*	Prof. Shashiprabha Kumar	UGC

List of Projects Currently Running in the Special Centre for Sanskrit Studies

S. No	Name of Project	Project Co-ordinator	Funding Agency
1.	*Pāli-Śabda-Kalpa-Taruh (A Multilingual Dictionary of Pali)*	Dr. C. Upender Rao	U.G.C
2.	*Indian Languages Corpora Initiative (ILCI)*	Dr. Girish Nath Jha	Department of Information Technology
3.	*Developing Computational Tools for Sanskrit and Sanskrit-Hindi Machine Translation*	Dr. Girish Nath Jha	Department of Information Technology

Faculty: Strength and Specialisation

S. No	Name of the Faculty	Designation	Specialisation
1.	Dr. Shashiprabha Kumar	Professor	Veda, Bhāratīya Darśana: Vaiśeṣika, Vedānta
2.	Dr. C. Upender Rao	Associate Professor	Sanskrit language and Poetics, Pāli and Early Buddhist philosophy
3.	Dr. Santosh Kumar Shukla	Associate Professor	Mīmāṁsā, Dharmaśāstra, Sanskrit Language and Literature
4.	Dr. Girish Nath Jha	Associate Professor	Computational Linguistics, Sanskrit Linguistics
5.	Dr. Hari Ram Mishra	Assistant Professor	Literary theory, Vyākaraṇa, Pāli, Prākṛt
6.	Dr. Ram Nath Jha	Assistant Professor	Indian Philosophy: Vedānta, Principal Upaniṣads and Bhagavadgītā
7.	Dr. Rajnish Kumar Mishra	Assistant Professor	Sanskrit Linguistics, Literary theory , Kashmir Śaivism, Buddhism

Students of the Centre

The first academic programme, i.e. direct Ph.D. was introduced in 2002 when the first batch of nine students was admitted. In 2003, the M.A. programme was initiated and the first batch of 19 students was admitted. From July 2004, the M.Phil/Ph.D. programme has been initiated. The average annual intake of students is 33 for M.A. and 17 for M.Phil/Ph.D. for now, it is likely to change over the years. The total strength of students registered at the centre at present is 145. 54 students of the centre have been awarded Junior Research Fellowship till date.

Besides, there are more than one hundred undergraduate students from other centres who choose Sanskrit as a tool/ optional course.

List of the Students Who have been Awarded Ph.D.

S. No	Name of the Student	Topic of the Thesis	Supervisor	Year of Award
1.	Manju Pandit	The Concept of Puruṣa in Indian Moral Thought with Special Reference to Puruṣa-Parīkṣā of Vidyāpati Ṭhakkura	Prof. Shashi-prabha Kumar	1/12/2006
2.	Devendra Singh	Ancient Indian Therapeutics with Special Reference to Atharvaveda	Prof. Shashi-prabha Kumar	5/12/2006
3.	R. Chandra-sekar	Part of Speech Tagging for Sanskrit	Dr. Girish Nath Jha	12/7/2007
4.	Sudhir Kumar Mishra	Sanskrit Kāraka Analyzer for Machine Translation	Dr. Girish Nath Jha	5/3/2008
5.	Sharda Narayanan	Concept of Jāti and Dravya with Special Reference to Vākya-padīya	Dr. Hari Ram Mishra	11/4/2008

6.	Kaushalya	Dharamshashtra Mein Shudra (Pramukh Panduli-pion ke Vishesh Sandarbh Mein)	Dr. Santosh Kumar Shukla	19/5/2009
7.	Lakshmi Kant Vimal	Śankara Vedānta mein Arthanir-dhāraṇa Siddhānton ka Adhyayana	Dr. Ram Nath Jha	21/8/2009
8.	Renu Kochhar	Śatapatha Brāhmaṇa mein Dārśanika Pratīka: Vijñāna-bhāṣya ke Ādhara Par (Pañcama Kāṇḍa Paryanta)	Prof. Shashi-prabha Kumar	23/11/2009
9.	Kuldeep Kumar	Structure of Vākya in Indian Linguistic Thought	Dr. Hari Ram Mishra	11/2/2010
10.	Priti Bhowmik	Evloving & Learning Methods for Teaching Sanskrit Grammar based on CBSE Syllabus for IX and X: A Critical Study	Dr. Girish Nath Jha	26/4/2010
11.	Anita Swami	Pātañjala Yoga-Paramparā mein Jñānaprakriya kā Swarūpa (Katipaya Ṭīkaon ke Sandarbha Mein)	Dr. Ram Nath Jha	7/7/2011

List of the Students
Who have been Awarded M.Phil

S. No	Name of the Student	Topic of the Dissertation	Supervisor	Year of Award
1.	Anita Swami	Yogasūtra-Vyāsa Bhāṣya Mein Gyānprakriya kā Swarūpa	Dr. Ram Nath Jha	13/10/2006
2.	Yogesh Shama	Hṛdaya Evam Sāhṛdaya: Artha, Srota, Antaḥsam-bandha	Dr. Rajnish Kumar Mishra	30/10/2006

3.	Surjya Kamal Borah	Epistemology in Kaṭhopaniṣad	Dr. Ram Nath Jha	6/11/2006
4.	Abhay Tiwari	Samkālīn Sanskrit Kāvya Sarjanātmakata: Bhāgīrathī ke Viśeṣa Sandarbha mein	Dr. Hari Ram Mishra	22/11/2006
5.	Brijesh Kr. Sonkar	Bhārtīya Darśana me Khyātivāda: Tulanātmaka Adhyayana	Dr. Santosh Kumar Shukla	24/11/2006
6.	Mai Ram	Śaiva evam Vyākaraṇa Tantron me Vāk: Anuvāda, Siddhānta, Darśana	Dr. Rajnish Kumar Mishra	30/11/2006
7.	Subash	Machine Recognition and Morphological Analysis of Subanta Padas	Dr. Girish Nath Jha	9/1/2007
8.	Shruti Rai	Ābhāsa: Its Philosophy and Aesthetics	Dr. Rajnish Kumar Mishra	23/2/2007
9.	Manji Bhadra	Computational Analysis of Gender in Sanskrit Noun-Phrases for Translation	Dr. Girish Nath Jha	9/10/2007
10.	Bhoopendra Singh Parmani	Tarka-Prakāṣinī (Tarka-Saṁgraha kī Aprakāśitaṭīkā) kā Samālocanātmaka Adhyayana	Prof. Shashiprabha Kumar	26/11/2007
11.	Vijendra Singh	Pāṇini Proktakṛt Pratyayon kā Arthavaiśiṣṭya (Śisupālavadha, Navasangaparyanta ke Viśeṣa sandarbha mein)	Dr. Hari Ram Mishra	8/2/2008
12.	Ram Narayan Meena	Bhāratīya Kavi-Pratibhā aur S.T. Coleridge Prātipadita 'Genius (Pratibhā) aur Talent (Prajñā) ki Tulanātmaka Samīkṣā	Dr. Hari Ram Mishra	25/1/2008
13.	Sachin Kumar	Sandhi Splitter and Analyzer for Sanskrit (with special reference to Acsandhi)	Dr. Girish Nath Jha	29/1/2008

14.	Mayank Shekhar	Dhvanyālokalocana Prathamodyota: Dīpa-śikhā kī Dṛṣṭi Mein	Dr. Hari Ram Mishra	4/2/2008
15.	Manju Singh	Bhakti Rasa: Siddhānta Darśana evam Aṇupra-yoga (Utapal Dev Krita Śivastotrāvalī ke Viśeṣa Sandarbha Mein)	Dr. Hari Ram Mishra	3/4/2008
16.	Muktanand Agarwal	Computational Identi-fication and Analysis of Sanskrit Verb-forms of Bhvādigaṇa	Dr. Girish Nath Jha	25/4/2008
17.	Vijay Kumar Meena	Āyurveda Darśana Mein Pramāṇa Mīmāṁsā (Sāṁkhya-Nyāya Darśana ke Viśeṣa Sandarbha Mein)	Dr. Ram Nath Jha	6/4/2009
18.	Diwakar Mani	Online Indexing of Ādi-parva of Mahābhārata	Dr. Girish Nath Jha	9/4/2009
19.	Ramkishor Maholiya	Prasthānatrayī Śaṅkara-bhāṣya Mein Sāṁkhya-Sidhhānta Samīkṣā	Dr. Ram Nath Jha	9/4/2009
20.	Anil Pratap Giri	Rasagaṅgādhara Navyanyāya-Bhāṣā-Pravidhi ke Āloka Mein	Dr. Hari Ram Mishra	20/4/2009
21.	Surjit Kumar Singh	Kridante Recognition and Processing for Sanskrit	Dr. Girish Nath Jha	4/5/2009
22.	Rev. Bakamoone Indaratana	Preventive and Social Medicine with Special Reference to the Caraka Saṁhitā	Dr. Santosh Kumar Shukla	6/5/2009
23.	Shashikant Tripathi	Rasagaṅgādhara evam Rasa-Mīmāṁsā mein Rasavimarṣa	Dr. Hari Ram Mishra	20/5/2009
24.	Monica Kuwar Rathod	Metaphysics in the Philosophy of Ayurveda	Dr. Ram Nath Jha	22/5/2009
25.	Sunita Atal	Sanskrit tathā Greek Raṅgamanca	Dr. Hari Ram Mishra	11/9/2009
26.	Diwakar	Issues and Challenges in	Dr. Girish	8/1/2010

	Mishra	Computational Processing of Vyañjana Sandhi	Nath Jha	
27.	Debashis Ghosh	Erich Frauwallner's Contribution to Vaiśeṣika Studies	Prof. Shashiprabha Kumar	15/1/2010
28.	Sunita Atal	Ekākṣara Śabdon kā Dārśanika Adhyayana	Dr. Ram Nath Jha	27/1/2010
29.	Satyamudita Snehi	Tarkasaṁgraha kā Ārekhiya evam Gaṇitiya Prastutikaraṇa (Navyanyāya-bhāṣā ke Āloka mein)	Dr. Ram Nath Jha	15/2/2010
30.	Sushma Devi	Karuṇa Rasa: Siddhānta, Darśana evam Aṇuprayoga (Kālidāsa evam Bhavabhūti ke Viśeṣa Sandarbha Mein)	Dr. Hari Ram Mishra	26/2/2010
31.	Bipin Kumar Jha	Kashmir Śaiva Darśana Mein Pramāta	Dr. Rajnish Kumar Mishra	17/3/2010
32.	Sarita Singh	Vālmīki Rāmāyaṇa ke Sundarakāṇḍa mein Upamānakṛta Arthavaiśiṣṭya	Dr. Hari Ram Mishra	26/3/2010
33.	Mahendra Kumar Meena	Samsāmayika Sanskrit Kathāsāhitya: Kathā-Vāstu, Śilpa evam Samvedana (Rajasthaniya Pratinidhi Sanskrit Kathākaron ke Viśeṣa Sandarbha Mein)	Dr. Rajnish Kumar Mishra	11/6/2010
34.	Reeta Gupta	'Māyāmatam' mein Vāstuvidyā kā swarūpa	Dr. Ram Nath Jha	10/1/2011
35.	Puran Mal Verma	A Morphosyntactical Analysis of Compounds in Daśakumāracaritam of Daṇḍin	Dr. Hari Ram Mishra	23/2/2011
36.	Vishva Bandhu	Nighaṇṭuparigaṇita Pṛthvivācaka Nāmapada: Eka Pariśīlana (Devaraja Yajvakṛta Nighaṇṭu-Nirvacana Ṭīka ke Āloka Mein)	Prof. Shashiprabha Kumar	24/2/2011

37.	Sapna Jain	Vaiśeṣika Darśana evam Jain Darśana mein Paramāṇuvāda: Eka Tulanātmaka Adhyayana	Prof. Shashi-prabha Kumar	24/2/2011
38.	Manisha Kumari	Vijñānabhikṣukṛta Sāṁkhyasāra kā Dārśanika Adhyayana	Dr. Ram Nath Jha	11/3/2011
39.	Mansingh Kanwat	Yājñavalkya Smṛti ke Sandarbha mein Māna-vadhikāra kī Sankalpanā: Mītākṣara ke Viśeṣa Sandarbha mein	Dr. Santosh Kumar Shukla	29/4/2011
40.	Mukesh Kr. Mishra	Computational Analysis of Sanskrit Homonyms: in the Context of Nānār-thavarga of Amarakośa	Dr. Girish Nath Jha	4/5/2011
41.	Mamta Tripathi	Dhvani Siddhānta: Paramparā Sandarbha evam Aṇuprayoga ('Nirala' Viracita Rāma kī Śaktipūjā ke Viśeṣa Sandarbha Mein).	Dr. Rajnish Kumar Mishra	12/5/2011
42.	Ravi Prakash Singh	Mantrī Pariṣad: Sidhānta evam Vyavahāra (Arthaśāstra evam Śukranīti ke Sandarbha Mein).	Dr. Hari Ram Mishra	23/5/2011
43.	Alok Tripathi	Vakrokti: Theory and Application (A Study of Representative Poems of G.M. Hopkins)	Dr. Hari Ram Mishra	5/9/2011
44.	Sanjeev Kumar	Sanskrit Vāṅmaya Meiṅ Kavi: Avadhāraṇā evam Apekṣāyeiṅ.	Dr. Rajnish Kumar Mishra	12/10/2011

List of the Continuing Ph.D. Students

S. No	Student's Name	Topic of the Thesis	Supervisor	Since
1.	Brijesh Kumar Sonkar	Cārvākīya Avadhāranāon kī Tārkika Samīkṣā	Dr. Santosh Kumar Shukla	2006
2.	Shruti Rai	Śaiva Philosophy of Languages: Issues, Interfaces, Expositions (With special reference to works of Ācārya Abhinavagupta)	Dr. Rajnish Kumar Mishra	2006
3.	Abhay Tiwari	Sanskrit-Kāvyaśāstra mein Saundarya-mīmāṁsā	Dr. Hari Ram Mishra	2006
4.	Yogesh Sharma	Śānta Rasa: Ādhara, Āswāda, Darśana	Dr. Rajnish Kumar Mishra	2006
5.	Subash	Ontological Knowledge Base for Selected Verbs of Sanskrit and Bangla	Dr. Girish Nath Jha	2006
6.	Surjya Kamal Borah	Epistemology in the Principal Upaniṣads	Dr. Ram Nath Jha	2006
7.	Bhupendra Singh Parnami	Vaiśeṣikasūtroṅ kī Pañca Arvācīna Sanskrit Ṭīkāon kā Samalocanātmaka Adhyanana	Prof. Shashi Prabha Kumar	2007
8.	Manju Singh	Rasa: Siddhānta evam Anubhūti (Kāvya ke Sandarbha Mein)	Dr. Hari Ram Mishra	2007
9.	Mayank Shekar	Abhinavgupta kā Kāvyasiddhānta	Dr. Hari Ram Mishra	2007
10.	Manji Bhadra	Knowledge base for Karma Kāraka	Dr. Girish Nath Jha	2007
11.	Sachin Kumar	Named Entities Recognition for Sanskrit: A Hybrid Approach	Dr. Girish Nath Jha	2007

12.	Neelam Yadav	Dharmaśāstriyā Nyāyika Prakriyā	Dr. Santosh Kumar Shukla	2008
13.	Sunita Atal	Nāṭyaśāstra mein Prakriti Vicāra: Siddhānta evam Prayog (Rajasthani Lok Nāṭyoṅ ke Sandarbha Mein)	Dr. Hari Ram Mishra	2008
14.	Bakamoone Indaratana	Bhūtavidyā and its Socio-Psychological Dimensions in the Backdrop of Sinhalese Buddhist Community in Sri Lanka	Dr. Santosh Kumar Shukla	2008
15.	Monika K. Rathore	Philosophical Foundations of Natural Healings in Ayurveda and Taoism	Dr. Ram Nath Jha	2008
16.	Ramkishor Maholiya	Prasthānatrayī Śaṅkarabhāṣya mein Paramātakhaṇḍana Samīkṣā (Bauddha Darśana ke Viśeṣa Sandarbha Mein)	Dr. Ram Nath Jha	2008
17.	Sureswar Meher	Bhārtīya Darśana evam Vigyāna mein Sriṣṭi Saṁracanā kā Anuśīlana (Jagadisa Chandra Hasija kṛta Avināśī Viśva-Nāṭaka ke Viśeṣa Paripreksya mein)	Dr. Ram Nath Jha	2008
18.	Vijay Kumar Meena	Āyurveda aura Pātañjala Yoga mein Mānasika Cikitsā Ka Dārśanika Ādhāra	Dr. Ram Nath Jha	2008
19.	Surjit Kumar Singh	Sanskrit Lexicography Models and Semantic Processing of Sanskrit	Dr. Girish Nath Jha	2008
20.	Sharda Gautam	Jātaka Kathā mein Dharma evam Sādhanā ka Svarūpa	Dr. Rajnish Kumar Mishra	2008
21.	Mohan Singh Rajput	Advaitavedānta mein Gahana Pāristhitikīya Cintana	Dr. Ram Nath Jha	2008

22.	Mahendra Kumar Meena	Sanskrit Kathā Sāhitya: Paramparā, Siddhānta evam Prayoga.	Dr. Rajnish Kumar Mishra	2009
23.	Debashis Ghosh	An Enquiry into Jayanta Bhaṭṭa's Arguments Reflected in the Nyāya-Mañjarī	Prof. Shashi-prabha Kumar	2009
24.	Diwakar Mishra	SAMVĀCAKA: Sanskrit Speech Synthesizer System	Dr. Girish Nath Jha	2009
25.	Nidhi Vedaratana	Pāṇiniyavyākaraṇadiśā Svaraprakriyādhāreṇa Vedārthaparīśīlanam	Dr. Santosh Kumar Shukla	2009
26.	Vakil Ahmad	Social Stratification and Social Mobility in Medieval North India: As reflected in Sanskrit Inscriptions of Rajputs	Dr. C. Upender Rao	2009
27.	Gitesh Nirban	Ethics in the Select-Sub-Narratives of Mahabharata: An Eco-Feministic Study	Prof. Shashi-prabha Kumar	2005
28.	Sushma Devi	Ramayana par Ādhārita Katipaya Nāṭakoṁ mein Strī-Vimarśa	Dr. Rajnish Kumar Mishra	2009
29.	Sarita Singh	Vālmīki Rāmāyaṇa me Upamānakṛta Arthavaiśiṣṭya	Dr. Hari Ram Mishra	2009
30.	Satyamudita Snehi	Mysticism in the Philosophy of Upanishads and Plato	Dr. Ram Nath Jha	2009
31.	Sunita Atal	Vaidika Vāṇmaya mein Ekākṣara Śabdon kā Prayoga evaṁ Unakā Vikāsa	Dr. Ram Nath Jha	2009
32.	Bae Hyang Ok	Individuality and Complementarity of Asaṅga and Vasubaṅdhu in the Development of Yogacara School	Dr. C. Upender Rao	2010
33.	Reeta Gupta	Bhāratīya Vāstuvidyā kā Swarūpa (Viśvakarmā	Dr. Ram Nath Jha	2010

		Vāstuśāstram' ke Viśeṣa Paripreksya mein).		
34.	Sapna Jain	Bhāratiya Darśana evam Vijñāna mein Paramāṇu-vāda (Nyāya-Vaiśeṣika evam Jaina Darśana ke Viśeṣa Paripreksya mein).	Dr. Ram Nath Jha/ Prof. Uttam-pati	2010
35.	Vishva Bandhu	Śuklayajurvedīya-Mādhyandina-Saṁhitāyāḥ Bhāṣika-madhyayanam.	Prof. Shashi Prabha Kumar	2010
36.	Ashutosh Kaushik	Dhātuvihita Kr̥dbhinna Pratyayoṅ kā Artha-vaijñānika Viśleṣaṇa.	Dr. Hari Ram Mishra	2010
37.	Kamini Kumari	Paramahaṁsa Yogā-nanda dvārā Pratipādita Siddhānton kā Adhyayana-Śrīmad-bhagvadgītā evam Pātañjalayoga ke Viśeṣa Praripreksya mein.	Dr. Ram Nath Jha	2011

In addition to the above, Thirty Students Are Continuing Their M.Phil. at the Centre:

S. No	Students Name	Topic of the Thesis	Supervisor Co-supervisor	Year
1.	Anil Kumar	Man Kā Dārśanic Adhyayan: Bhagavadgītā Evam Dhammpad ke Viśeṣa Sandarbha me.	Dr. C. Upender Rao	2011-12
2.	Vikas Singh	Bhāratīya Saṁskr̥ti kā Samīkṣātmak Adhyayana: Milindapañha ke Viśeṣa Sandarbh me).	Dr. C. Upender Rao/ Dr. Vivek Kumar	2011-12
3.	Uma Arya	Soma evam Ayahuaskā: Ek Sāṁskr̥tik Adhyayana.	Dr. C. Upender Rao	2011-12
4.	Satyanarayan	Nirvān kā Sāmājika Mahattva: Suttapiṭaka ke Viśeṣa Sandarbha me.	Dr. C. Upender Rao	2011-12

5.	Pavitra Agarwal	Avyākṛta Praśna: Swarūpa, Prabhāva evam Mahattva: Suttapiṭaka ke Viśeṣa Paripreksya me.	Dr. C. Upender Rao	2011-12
6.	Sarvesh Kumar	Vidhi aura Praśāsana kā Gautama, Baudhāyana evam Āpastamba Dharmasūtron ke Sandarbha mein Samīkṣātmaka Viśleṣaṇa.	Dr. Santosh Kumar Shukla	2011-12
7.	Thakur Shivlochan Shandilya	Pūrvamīmāṁsādarśana mein Jñāna ke Svarūpa evam Prakriyā kā Adhyayana: Prakarana Pañcikā evam Śāstra-dīpīkā ke Vīśeṣa Sandarbha mein	Dr. Santosh Kumar Shukla	2011-12
8.	Rohit Kumar Singh	Kauṭilya Arthaśāstra mein Varṇita Rājya kī Ārthika Nīti kā Viśleṣaṇa: Striyon ke Viśeṣa Sandarbha mein	Dr. Santosh Kumar Shukla Dr. Ashok Kumar	2011-12
9.	Arvind Kumar	Aspṛśyatā kī Avadhāraṇā, Svarūpa evam Manusmṛti, Yajñavalkya Smṛti Nāradasmṛti ke Sandarbha mein	Dr. Santosh Kumar Shukla	2011-12
10.	Chaman Kumar	Kādambaryā Ākathā-mukham Vākyavai-jñānikam Pariśīlanam	Dr. Hari Ram Mishra	2011-12
11.	Mani Shanker Dwivedi	Kāvya Śāstra mein Tātparyavṛtti: Svīkāra evam Parihāra.	Dr. Hari Ram Mishra	2011-12
12.	Kapil Gautam	Ācārya Śaṅkarakṛta Brahmasūtra-Adhyā-sabhāṣya kā Adhyayana: Bhāmatī evam Vivaraṇa Ṭīkāon ke Viśeṣa Sandarbha mein.	Dr. Ram Nath Jha	2011-12
13.	Praveen Kumar Dwivedy	Vīraśaivadarśana mein Tattvamīmāṁsā kā Swarūpa.	Dr. Ram Nath Jha	2011-12

14.	Vandana Yadav	Atharvavedīya Pṛthivī Sūkta evam Gaia Parikalpanā.	Dr. Ram Nath Jha	2011-12
15.	Savitri	Kāvyaprakāśa kī Ṭīkā? Kāvya-pradīpa evam Uddyota kā Tulanātmaka Adhyayana (Dwītiya Ullāsa Paryanta)	Dr. Rajnish Kumar Mishra	2011-12
16.	Devalina Saikia	A Critique of the Congnitive Process in Nyāya Philosophy (With Special Reference to the 1st Āhnika of Nyāyamañjarī)	Prof. S.P. Kumar	2010
17.	Vishvesh	Vaiśeṣikasūtreṣu śabdārtha-Vimarśaḥ	Prof. S.P. Kumar	2010
18.	Anita Meena	Praśastapādabhāṣya mein Pratipādita Padārthasādharmya-Vaidharmya (Nyāyakandali evam Kiraṇāvalī Ṭikaon ke Āloka mein)	Prof. S.P Kumar	2010
19.	Babloo Pal	Kenopaniṣad kā Dārśanika Anuśīlana	Prof. S.P. Kumar	2010
20.	Baldev Ram Kandoliyan	Vanauṣadhivarga of Amarakośa: A Computational study	Dr. G. N. Jha & Prof. Y.B. Tripathi	2010
21.	Archana Tiwari	Automatic Indexing of Caraka Saṁhitā	Dr. G. N. Jha	
22.	Kumar Nripendra Pathak	Challenges in Sanskrit-Hindi Noun Phrase Mapping	Dr. G. N. Jha	2010
23.	Rajneesh Kumar Pandey	Online Indexing of Suśruta Saṁhitā	Dr. G. N. Jha	2010
24.	Paritosh Das	Index Based Search for Bṛhadāraṇyaka Upaniṣad	Dr. G.N. Jha Dr. Srinivasa Varakhedi	2010

25.	Priyanka Pandey	Notion of Politics in Śānti- Parva of Mahābhārata	Dr. S.K. Shukla & Dr. M.N. Thakur	2010
26.	Ashok Kumar	Ślokavārttika ke 'Ātma-vāda kā Samīkṣātmaka Adhyanana	Dr. S. K. Shukla	2010
27.	Chanda Kumari	Madhusūdana Ojha Kṛta Daśavadarahasyam: Samīkṣātmaka Adhyayana	Dr. S. K. Shukla	2010
28.	Nisha Rani	Dravya: Svarūpa evaṁ Bheda Nyāyasiddhanta-muktāvalī evaṁ Manameyodaya ke Sandarbha meiṅ	Dr. S. K. Shukla	2010
29.	Bind Kumar	Application of Vakrokti Theory in Macbeth	Dr. Hari Ram Mishra	2010
30.	Jay Saha	Causatives in Sanskrit	Dr. H. R. Mishra	2010

Shri Lal Bahadur Rashtriya Sanskrit Vidyapeeth

The Vidyapeeth, now a deemed university for Sanskrit, since its modest beginning in the form of a small Vidyapeeth in 1962, has come a long way. It has 5 faculties, 17 departments, 87 teachers and 869 students in all. The medium of instruction in the Vidyapeeth is mainly Sanskrit. Many traditional as well as innovative courses have been started and the vidyāpītha has flourished under the leadership of its two illustrious Vice-chancellors, i.e. late Dr. Mandana Mishra as the founder Vice-chancellor and his successor the late Prof.Vachaspati Upadhyaya, who led the institution for seventeen years consecutively till July 2011.

The Vidyapeeth has its own publication department and regularly brings out a journal titled शोधप्रभा, besides many other publications to its credit. In the year 2001, which was declared 'Sanskrit Year' by the Government of India, Prof. Vachaspati Upadhyaya, along with his colleagues in the Vidyapeeth, organised a World Sanskrit Conference; the proceedings of the conference are already published in five volumes.

Rashtriya Sanskrit Sansthan

Established in 1970 as an autonomous organisation, the Sansthan has been declared as a deemed university w.e.f. 2002. With its headquarters at Delhi, the Sansthan has ten campuses under its aegis in various parts of the country. Several academic programmes are organised by the Sansthan in New Delhi throughout the year, specially the संस्कृत दिवस समारोह and the नाट्योत्सव. The Sansthan is also running correspondence courses for learning Sanskrit besides numerous other schemes for propagation of Sanskrit. The publication department of the Sansthan is bringing out a good number of literary volumes in addition to the quarterly journal *संस्कृतविमर्श* and a quarterly newsletter संस्कृतवार्ता:. The Sansthan is also bringing out an English version of संस्कृत विद्वत् परिचायिका, a *Who's Who in Sanskrit* wherein a brief introduction of all the Sanskrit scholars is being given. The 15th World Sanskrit Conference is being organised by the Rashtriya Sanskrit Sansthan in New Delhi during 5th-10th January, 2012 and many publications including a souvenir as well as the present volume are being published on this occasion.

Many research scholars are pursuing their Ph.D at different campuses of the Sansthan. Some of the topics recently approved by the Central Research Board of the Sansthan are listed below:

List of Continuing Ph.D. Students at the Sansthan

S. No.	Name of the Student	Name of the Supervisor	Topic of the Research
1.	Ms. Kajal Upadhyaya	Dr. Ajay Mishra	*Ācarya Rāmji Upādhyāyakr̥tāyā 'dvāsuparṇā' ityākhyāyikāyā samīkṣātmakamadhyayanam*
2.	Ms. Kavita Sharma	-do-	*Arvācīna Saṁskr̥tmiti-patrikāyāḥ sāhityikamavadānam*
3.	Ms. Kiran Singh	-do-	*Śrī Hariharānandaviracitasya Cāturvarṇyasaṁskr̥tivimarśasya parīśīlanam*
4.	Mr. Gopal Datt Pargai	-do-	*Kālidāsabhārvimā-ghaviracitamahā-kāvyeṣu Alaṁkāra-Yojanā*
5.	Mr. Neeraj Sharma	Dr. Sachidanand Tiwari	*Ādhunikasaṁskr̥tadū-takāvyaparam-parāyām abhirājarājendramiśrapraṇītamr̥gā–kadūtasya samīkṣātmaka-madhyayanam*
6.	Mr. Rajesh Kumar	-do-	*Kālūrihanumantarā-vamahodayānām Gadyakathānāṁ samīkṣātmakamadhyayanam*
7.	Mr. Akshyamani Upadhyaya	-do-	*Ādhunikagītikāvya paramparāyām-Ācarya Haridattaśarmaṇo gītikāvyānām mūlyāṅkanam*
8.	Mr. Ajeet Singh	-do-	*Rasavivekasya samīkṣātmakamadhyayanam*
9.	Mr. Tarun Kumar	-do-	*Kavirāmacandrapraṇītasya vāgbhūṣaṇaśatakasya saṁpādanaṁ samīkṣaṇamca*

A bird's-eye view of the background of the Sansthan is given hereunder —

Prof. Ram Karan Sharma was the founder Director of the Rashtriya Sanskrit Sansthan. At present Prof. Radhavallabh Tripathi is the Vice-chancellor of the Rashtriya Sanskrit Sansthan (deemed university) from 14-8-2008.

NAME OF THE DIRECTORS		
NAME	**FROM**	**TO**
Prof. R.K. Sharma	1970	1974
Sh. P.C. Sharma	1975	-
Sh. S. K. Chaturvedi (IAS)	1975	-
Sh. K. K. Sethi (IAS)	1976	1978
Sh. K. K. Khullar	1978	1979
Dr. R.K. Sharma	1981	1983
Dr. Mandan Mishra	1983	-
Sh. P.K. Pawar (IAS)	1990	1990
Dr. Madhusudan Mishra	Mar 1990	-
Shri P. Thakur (IAS)	Jan. 1991	Feb. 1994
Dr. K. K. Mishra	Feb. 1994	Feb. 1999
Prof. Vachaspati Upadhyaya	Feb. 1999	Nov. 1999
Prof. V. Kutumba Sastry	Nov. 1999	11-5-2003

NAME OF THE PRESIDENTS		
Dr. Murli Manohar Joshi, Minister for Human Resource Development	30-7-2002	10-6-2004
Sh. Arjun Singh, Minister for Human Resource Development	11-6-2004	21-5-2009
Sh. Kapil Sibal, Minister for Human Resource Development	02-6-2009	-

NAME OF THE VICE-CHANCELLORS		
Prof. V. Kutumba Sastry	12-5-2003	11-5-2008
Dr. Anita Bhatnagar Jain	23-5-2008	13-8-2008
Prof. Radhavallabh Tripathi	14-8-2008	-

Prof. Ramkaran Sharma, the founder director of the Sansthan, has recently published two collections of his Sanskrit poems titled शेमुषी and अन्यच्च in addition to several other creative works authored by him earlier.

Prof. Radhavallabh Tripathi, the current Vice-chancellor of the Sansthan, is himself a creative as well as critical writer in Sanskrit besides being a dynamic administrative head. He has recently authored a Sanskrit novel titled *अन्यच्च* which incorporates both the elements: literary delicacy along with serious thought-content. Besides his many other well-known works including the *नाट्यशास्त्र-विश्व*, a special reference needs to be made of the Sanskrit translation *रूमी-रहस्यम्* and *रूमी-पञ्चदशी* of poems and stories authored by Maulana Rumi.

Dr. Ramakant Shukla is pursuing a project of the Sansthan for indexing of all original Sanskrit writings published in various Sanskrit magazines.

Delhi Sanskrit Academy

The Government of Delhi established Delhi Sanskrit Academy in the year 1987, for the propagation of Sanskrit language and literature. Since then the Academy has been actively functioning as an agency for organising several Sanskrit programmes for school, college and university level students of the capital city. Several scholars are invited to deliver lectures and various publications are brought out regularly including the quarterly magazine *संस्कृतमञ्जरी*, besides honouring the Sanskrit writers, young and old.

Registered/Unregistered Societies/Trusts

(I) INTERNATIONAL ACADEMY OF INDIAN CULTURE

Founded in 1933 in Lahore, by Prof. Raghu Vira, the academy is now located in New Delhi and is being directed by its current president, Prof. Lokesh Chandra. Under its *Śata-Piṭaka* series, the Academy has already published more than a hundred volumes. Significantly, the enormously rich library of the Academy is an essential resource-centre for the researchers in Sanskrit and allied areas.

(II) AKHIL BHARATIYA SANSKRIT SAHITYA SAMMELANA

The Sammelana was originally established by stalwarts like M.M. Giridhar Sharma Chaturvedi, Pt. Kedarnath Sharma Saraswat, Pt. Giridharilal Goswami and Dr. Mandana Mishra. The sammelana is privileged in having Dr. Ramakant Goswami as its secretary-general and being located in the beautiful building 'संस्कृत भवन' which provides a platform to several Sanskrit programmes in the city.

(III) DEVAVANI PARISHAD

Established in 1979 by Dr. Ramakant Shukla, the Parishad is serving the cause of Sanskrit in ways more than one. The most notable of its activities is the regular publication of its quarterly magazine *अर्वाचीनसंस्कृतम्*, which has brought to light more than one thousand contemporary creative Sanskrit works besides two hundred critical articles till date. Its founder Dr. Ramakant Shukla has himself authored many Sanskrit works including the popular poem भाति मे भारतम्. Of late he has published सर्वशुक्लोत्तरा, a collection of 63 sanskrit poems which depict the status and aspirations of the contemporary society. He has also brought out a Sanskrit translation of an English novel *Ameena* by Muhammad Umar Kabeer.

(IV) SANSKRIT BHARATI

Samskrita Bharati is a non-profit organisation started by Chamu Krishna Shastry with his 5 friends in 1981 from Bangalore. This paved the way to establish "Samskrita Bharati" — a national level organisation in New Delhi — in 1995. Sanskrit Bharati is primarily a volunteer-driven organisation, with volunteers from all walks of life spending time educating people to speak Sanskrit.

A two week intense residential teaching programme called Samvadashala, is conducted in New Delhi, every summer. Sanskrit Bharati also conducts competitions to encourage Sanskrit learning amongst children.

(V) KALIDASA ACADEMY OF SANSKRIT MUSIC AND FINE ARTS

The academy was initiated in 1994, by the late Prof. J.S. Kulshreshtha for promotion of triple aspects indicated by its name. According to Prof. Sushma Kulshreshtha, its present director, the academy has organised sixteen Kalidasa Mahotsava programmes, fifty national seminars till date and has brought out more than fifty volumes from Sangita Kala Prakashan, its own publication house.

(VI) WAVES

World Association for Vedic Studies was started in the year 1997, by Prof. Bhudev Sharma, professor of mathematics, in the USA. In its fifteen years of existence, the association has been re-christened in India as 'Wider Association for Vedic Studies' and has also opened its chapters in several parts of the country. Till date, the association has organised 14 annual conferences, and brought out four publications. Currently Prof. Ramkaran Sharma is its president and Dr. Shashi Tewari is continuing as its secretary.

(VII) SANSKRIT SOCIETY OF INDIA

In the year 2000, the society was formed by a host of Sanskrit lovers including its young and energetic founder secretary Dr. S. K. Shukla. The society has organised a national seminar on Pūrvamīmāṁsā in JNU and holds several other activites throughout the year.

(VIII) SHRI SHANKARA SIKSHAYATANA KENDRA

Set up in the year 2000 by the wife of the late Sri R.K. Mishra, the Kendra is also engaged in spreading the message of Sanskrit learning as contained in the works of Pt. Madhusudan Ojha and Pt. Motilal Shastri. Dr. S. K. Shukla, the secretary of the Kendra informs us that they organise national seminars and workshops besides monthly lectures on the topics related to Sanskrit learning.

(IX) NISHREYASA

Instituted by Prof. Shashiprabha Kumar and her like-minded friends including Dr. Vedwati Vaidik, Dr. Devkanya Arya and Dr. Kamlesh Garg in the year 2001, the private trust is a modest attempt undertaken at individual level by the trustee members for promotion and propagation of wisdom stocked in Sanskrit sources. In the last one decade, the small organisation has arranged one national seminar, one international symposium and several lecture programmes. Proceedings have been published in its two volumes, titled as follows:

1. *Saṁskr̥ta, Saṁskr̥ti and Saṁskaāra*, edited by Shashiprabha Kumar, Vidyanidhi Prakashan, Delhi, 2009. **ISBN**:81-86700-89-7.
2. *Bhāratīya Jīwana-Dr̥ṣṭi*, edited by Shashiprabha Kumar, Vidyanidhi Prakashan, Delhi, 2009. **ISBN**:81-86700-91-9.

The second series of its bi-annual lecture programmes is in progress on the following two themes:

(a) प्राचीन भारतीय आचार्य Ancient Indian Preceptors.

(b) आधुनिक भारतीय विचारक Modern Indian Thinkers.

(X) GIRDHARILAL GOSWAMI PRACHYA VIDYA PRATISHTHANA

The Government of Delhi has registered this organisation in the year 2002 for the furtherance of Sanskrit learning in the capital. Based in Sanskrit Bhawan, the headquarters of Akhil Bhartiya Sanskrit Sahitya Sammelan, the Pratishthan has started a small library for the use of researchers in Sanskrit.

Others

In addition to the above, there are various other social, cultural and religious bodies which are contributing directly or indirectly to the field of Sanskrit Studies in Delhi. As already stated above, due to limitation of time and space, it is not possible to provide a complete information of all such organisations but still some names may be mentioned as follows: Bharatiya Vidya Bhawan and the school run by it; Chinmaya Mission and Chinmaya Vidyalaya; Akhil Bharatiya Sanatana Dharama Mahasabha and the educational institutes run by it; Arya Samaj and several *gurukula*s being managed by them like Gurukula Gautamnagar, Gurukula, Khanpur, Kanya Gurukula, Narela, and Kanya Gurukula, Rajendranagar; Jaina institutes like Kund Kund Bharati and Bhogilal Leherchand Institute of Indology, etc.

Significantly, various modes of media such as newspapers, magazines, radio, television and e-services have also given a fillip to Sanskrit studies in Delhi. All India Radio and Doordarshan broadcast daily news bulletins in Sanskrit. Several other Sanskrit programmes, prepared by the Rashtriya Sanskrit Sansthan are also being broadcast on DD Bharati. Recently, a Sanskrit poem कवित्वं मे तिरोभूतम् by Dr. Ramakant Shukla was broadcast from All India Radio. A dialogue between Prof. Radhavallabh Tripathi and Dr. Ramakant Shukla was also broadcast. An interview of Professor Satyavrat Shastri was also broadcast under the programme titled संस्कृत-सौरभम् which was started last year.

Last but not the least, there are a host of individuals who are working tirelessely in their own capacity, be it teachers, students, writers, publishers, socio-religious leaders and above all, lovers of Sanskrit. It is, in fact, their steady support and unflinching faith which has kept the spirit of Sanskrit alive in Delhi. In spite of all odds and despite different kinds of denunciations by people with vested interests, Sanskrit studies in Delhi have gained ground and are going to flourish by leaps and bounds in the years to come.

6

The Position of Sanskrit in Gujarat

Gautam Patel

THE position of Sanskrit in Gujarat State is comparatively better than that of in any other state of India. The present government is positively interested in the propagation and popularisation of Sanskrit in the state. For example this is the Golden Jubilee year of the establishment of the separate Gujarat State. During its celebration the state government has given a special grant to the Shri Somnath Sanskrit University for teaching basic speaking Sanskrit to 1 lakh students. It is a matter of pride that the said university has exceeded the target and taught 1,07,000 students the basic Sanskrit with the help of Sanskrit Bharati and the staff of the university as well as some school teachers and college professors. This year, in the budget presented in the State Assembly of Gujarat Rs. 50,00,000 are reserved for International Sanskrit Conference as the State is celebrating the Golden Jubilee year.

On 4 and 5 December 2010, a Maha Kumbha of Sanskrit, a rare event in the history of any university in Gujarat, was inaugurated by Shri Narendra Modi, the Chief Minister of Gujarat State at the Somnath Sanskrit University at Veraval. A national seminar on Sanskrit journalism, *kavi sammelan*, *śalākā parikṣā*, *yuvaka mahotsava* and *bhāsa nāṭya mahotsava* were successfully organised and more than 15,000 peoples were present at the events.

Universities in Gujarat

The following universities in the Gujarat State are having postgraduate departments and students are enrolled for final Acharya or M.A. degree as well as Vidya-Vachaspati or Ph.D. There are many undergraduate colleges and research institutions also which are affiliated to these universities.

SHRI SOMNATH SANSKRIT UNIVERSITY, VERAVAL

It was founded in 2005. The vice-chancellor Pankaj Jani is trying his best to establish certain standards and make the university popular not only in Gujarat but all over India. Narẹndra Pandya, dean of the faculty and Vishubhai Purohita, the registrar and his colleagues are also busy in popularising the subject. Here the P.G. departments of Veda and Sāhitya are imparting knowledge to the students. There are many affiliated *pāṭhaśālās* (given the status of colleges) teaching Vyākaraṇa, Vāstu, Jyotiāṣa, Yoga, temple management along with above-mentioned subjects. There are 57 students in M.A. and a total of 75 students are preparing for their M.Phil. degree in the university and affiliated centre at N.S. Patel Arts College, Anand. This university has confirmed the degree of Vidya-Vachaspati — honorary degree of D.Litt. to Gautam Patel, Bhagwatiprasad Pandya and Rameshbhai Oza (Puj. Bhaishri). The university has published 22 books and a journal named *Somajyoti* is published regularly. There are good number of manuscripts in the affiliated institution of the university. There are 7,000 books in the university. Six students were awarded the Ph.D. degree on 12 April 2011.

K.S.K.V. KACHCHH UNIVERSITY, BHUJ

It was founded in 2007, has enrolled 20 students for M.Phil. and 11 for Ph.D. Moreover, Sanskrit is taught at the affiliated colleges. The former vice-chancellor of this university Kanti Gor is the man of Sanskrit and has written poems and radio plays in Sanskrit. He has tried his best during his office to popularise Sanskrit in the state.

HEMCHANDRACHARYA NORTH GUJARAT UNIVERSITY, PATAN

It was founded in 1986, has a department of "Sanskrit and Bhartiya-Vidya" which is headed by D.V. Rathava. Till now 78 students have obtained Ph.D. and 149 students have been awarded M.Phil. degrees. At present 52 students are there in M.A. Semester-I and II, 35 are in M.A. Part-II and 8 are reading for M.Phil. It organises successfully Hemchandracharya national seminar every year since 1996. Hundreds of students are opting for Sanskrit at the graduate level in the various affiliated colleges of this university. The library of this university has more than 20,000 books on the subject. Along with Sanskrit, Prākr̥t is also taught at graduate as well as postgraduate levels.

SAURASHTRA UNIVERSITY, RAJKOT

It was founded in 1967, has a special Sanskrit Anusnataka Bhavan donated by the Gopalkrishna Trust, Junagarh. Rajendra Chotalia is the head of the department of the P.G. section and M.K. Molia is also working with him along with one more member. It has several affiliated colleges where Sanskrit is taught as compulsory as well as special subject. Till now 28 students have been awarded Ph.D. degree, 15 students M.Phil. and 59 students are at the postgraduate level in Sanskrit subject. The subjects taught are Alaṁkāraśāstra, Vedānta and Purāṇa. Various courses, seminars and lectures are arranged by the department successfully.

BHAVNAGAR UNIVERSITY, BHAVNAGAR

It was founded in the year 1978. There the study of Sanskrit is going on. Numerous students at graduate and postgraduate level study Sanskrit. The subjects like Alaṁkāraśāstra and

Vedānta are taught there. Here various lectures, seminars, etc. are organised regularly.

VIR NARMAD SOUTH GUJARAT UNIVERSITY, SURAT

It was founded in 1967, is not having a special postgraduate department in Sanskrit, even after 40 years of its existence, but Sanskrit is taught at various affiliated colleges and institutions and numerous students are enrolled for M.Phil. and Ph.D. Though there is no special department in this university yet scholars like the late J.T. Parikh, R.G. Asti, Chandratre, D.P. Patel, A.D. Shastri, Arvind Joshi, Vasant Patel and Nina Bhavanagari have contributed to the various branches of Sanskrit literature. More than 17 students have acquired Ph.D. and 13 professors are recognised by the university for teaching M.Phil. and numerous students are working under them.

SARDAR PATEL UNIVERSITY, VALLABHAVIDYANAGAR

It was founded in 1955, has a P.G. department which is headed by Ajit Thakor. There are two more professors. There are 146 students in M.A., 4 in M.Phil. and 12 in Ph.D. Chitraben Shukla, the former head of the department was awarded Gaurava Puraskar by the Sanskrit Sahitya Akademi, Gandhinagar, in 1996. Ajit Thakor has received Katha Award with Katha Foundation, Delhi, in 1995 and First Prize for his writings by Sanskrit Sahitya Akademi (2004) and Guajrati Sahitya Akademi (2006). Gujarati Sahitya Parishad has honoured him with Ramaprasad Baxi Paritoshika. Till not less than 40 students have been awarded Ph.D. degree and numerous students have offered Sanskrit at the graduate level.

GUJARAT UNIVERSITY, AHMEDABAD

It was founded in 1950, has the department of Sanskrit headed by Vasant Kumar M. Bhatt. It was established on 15 June 1954. The late Esther A. Soloman of this department was awarded

Padmashree in the year 1992 and the Certificate of Honour by the President of India in 1983. The late Tapasvi Nandi was awarded the Certificate of Honour in 1996. He was awarded the Shastra Chudamani by Rashtriya Sanskrit Sansthan and Emeritus Professor by the U.G.C. He was also awarded Vachaspati Puraskar by Pujya Morari Bapu. Bhagwatiprasad D. Pandya was awarded the Certificate of Honour by the President of India in the year 1998. He was also awarded Shastra Chudamani and Vachaspati Puraskar by Pujya Morari Bapu. L.V. Joshi was awarded Vachaspati Puraskar by Pujya Morari Bapu. V.D. Pandya was awarded the Certificate of Honour by the President of India in 2010.

Till now 100 students have obtained Ph.D. degree in various branches of learning in Sanskrit. In the current academic years 76 students are reading for final M.Phil., 21 for Ph.D. and 54 students are enrolled in M.A. first semester. Ten thesis, 12 research books have been published and a research periodical *Vidya* (since 1975) is published regularly. More than 50,000 books are there in the library. The department has successfully hosted All India Oriental Conference (1985) and Rashtriya Veda Sammelan in 2010.

THE MAHARAJA SAYAJIRAO UNIVERSITY, VADODARA

It was founded in 1949. The M.S. University of Vadodara is one of the internationally recognised universities of Gujarat. As here the medium of instruction is English only, it has gained proper weightage in the field. This university has a Sanskrit department where Arunodaya Jani, S.G. Kantawala, R.I. Nanavati, all honoured by the President of India have contributed in their field which is recognised at national as well as international level. Till now 52 students have been awarded Ph.D. degree. As of now 40 students are studying for M.A. and 20 for Ph.D. degree. Ravindra Panda of the department has received/won several prizes for his publication and Jayadeva Jani is a recognised poet and novelist of Sanskrit literature.

There are other universities like Gujarat Vidyapeeth (founded by Mahatma Gandhi) at Ahmedabad and Ayurvedic University at Jamnagar where Sanskrit is also taught as per their need.

Sanskrit at the Primary and Secondary Levels

When we survey at the primary and secondary levels at schools, the study of Sanskrit has been made compulsory from standard VIth to IXth. Of course, it becomes optional at Xth standard board exam. The one noteworthy point is that the study of Sanskrit is compulsory in the first year at college level in many of the universities for those who opt for Arts faculty. This system will continue even in the recently introduced semester systems along with elective subjects. Unfortunately, recently Sanskrit has been made optional in the board examination of the Xth standard by the state government.

Institutions in Gujarat

There are certain institutions where the study of Sanskrit or its research work and publications are going on, even better than some other departments of the universities. To name a few of them:

(1) Oriental Institute, M.S. University, Vadodara

(2) Swadhyaya Mandal, Pardi

(3) B.J. Institute of Learning and Research, Ahmedabad

(4) Shri Bruhad Gujarat Sanskrit Parishad, Ahmedabad

(5) Prakrit Text Society, Ahmedabad

(6) Maharshi Veda-Vijnana Akademi, Ahmedabad

(7) L.D. Institute of Indology, Ahmedabad

(8) Chimanlal Gandhi Vidya Bhavan, Surat

(9) Dwarkadhish Sanskrit Akademi and Indological Research Institute, Dwarka

(10) Sanskrit Bharati, Ahmedabad

(11) Sanskrit Seva Samiti, Ahmedabad

(12) Gujarat Rajya University and College Teachers' Association, Ahmedabad

(13) Charutar Sanskrit Vidya Parishad, Vallabhvidyanagar

(14) Anarta Sanskrit Association, Mehsana

(15) South Gujarat University Sanskrit Teachers' Association, Surat

(16) Saurashtra University Sanskrit Teachers' Association, Rajkot

(17) Bharatiya Vidya Mandal, Surat

(18) Arsha, Akshardham, Gandhinagar

(19) Shardaben Chimanlal Educational Research Centre, Ahmedabad

(20) Sanskrit Sahitya Akademi, Gandhinagar

Sanskrit Sahitya Akademi, Gandhinagar, was established to promote Sanskrit studies. It has worked as per its constitution for first 10 years and has published more than 80 books and honoured 20 scholars of the state. Several state level as well as national level seminars and *kāvya-goṣṭhīs* were also organised. After 10 years, the elections, as per constitution of the Akademi was held. But for the reasons best known to them — the government officers — they have not declared the results at all even though more than five years have lapsed. Same position prevails in other Akademis of the state. Now without following the constitution but arbitrarily all the six Akademis of the state are run by one officer-in-charge, which is really painful for many scholars of the subject. Formerly, the Akademi was awarding Gaurava Puraskar of Rs. 21,000 to a Sanskrit scholar, now it is increased up to Rs. 1,00,000 per person per year. R.I. Nanavati and Harshadeva Madhava were awarded this Puraskar last year. Several publications too have been brought out by the Akademi.

Depositories of MSS

There are more than 5,00,000 manuscripts in various institutions of the Gujarat State. Some of the known institutions are B.J. Institute of Learning and Research, Ahmedabad (642 MSS), Gujarat Vidyapeeth, Ahmedabad (535 MSS), Gujarat Vidya Sabha, Ahmedabad (27,107 MSS), L.D. Institute of Indology, Ahmedabad (79,144 MSS), Atmanand Jani Jnana Mandir, Vadodara (7,487 MSS), Oriental Institute, Vadodara (30,211 MSS), Atmanand Jain Sabha, Bhavnagar (1,325 MSS), Shantinath Jain Bhandar, Khambhat (752 MSS), Hemachandra Jain Jnana Bhandar, Patan (14,789 MSS), Sanghvi Pada Bhandar, Patan (1,600 MSS), Chunilal Gandhi Vidya Bhavan, Surat (2,153 MSS) and the Jain Institute at Koba has more than 1 lakh MSS. Names of many small institutions and private collections are not listed here.

[For full details of the names of *bhaṇḍāras* and catalogues of Sanskrit MSS with them, kindly refer to *Contribution of Gujarat to Sanskrit Literature* (*Manibhai Prajapati Felicitation Volume*), General Editor, Gautam Patel, Editors: M.K. Prajapati, Hansa Hindocha, H.R. Patel, published by M.I. Prajapati, Shasthipurti Samman Samiti, Patan.]

Modern Sanskrit

There are numerous modern Sanskrit writers in the state who have contributed in the allmost all the branches of Sanskrit literature, dramas, *kāvyas*, *mahākāvyas*, commentaries, etc. were written in old style. While radio *rūpaka*, television skit, Hyku, Tanka, ballet, sizo *kāvya*, *garbā*, *gha al*, *dohā*, *navalkathā*, short stories, *pravāsa kathā*, *patra-lekhana*, etc. are the modern forms where writers from Gujarat have contributed considerably and commendably. To name a few of them in the last as well as this century: Manishankar Shastri, Badrinath Shastri, Arunodaya Jani, Ghanshyam Trivedi, Bhagwatiprasad Pandya, R.I. Nanavati, Harshadeva Madhava, Gautam Patel, Vasudeva Pathak, Smt. Uma Deshpande, Rita Trivedi, Kanti Gor, K.M. Trivedi, Pankaj Thakar, Shama Dholakia, Jiten Joshi, Swami Satya Prakashji, J.P. Dwivedi, Rushiraj Agnihotri, etc. Some of them have been honoured by the state and the national authorities also. Recently, a Sanskrit daily newspaper was launched and is regularly published by Praful Purohita from Vadodara. The state government also has its website in Sanskrit, which is a unique adventure in the field.

Scholars Honoured by the President of India

There were many scholars of repute who were honoured by the President of India by awarding them a Certificate of Honour. To name few of them are: the late Arunodaya Jani, Pandit Balakrishna Pancholi, Krishnashankar Shastri, K.K. Shastri, Harivallabha Bhayani, Miss E.S. Soloman, Tapasvi Nandi. Following are the living scholars who were honoured by the President of India. Some of them are still contributing predominantly to the various branches of Sanskrit language and literature.

(1) R.S. Betai, Ahmedabad

(2) Gautam Patel, Ahmedabad

(3) S.J. Kantawala, Vadodara

(4) N.M. Kansara, Ahmedabad

(5) Nanavati, Vadodara

(6) Vasant Parikh, Amreli

(7) Vijay Pandya, Ahmedabad

(8) Manibhai Prajapati

Vachaspati Puraskar

Pujya Shri Morari Bapu, world-known saint of Gujarat, has a trust named Shri Sitaram Trust, Mahuva. From this trust every year a national seminar, lasting three days, is held on Ganesh Chaturthi and a reputed scholar of Sanskrit is honoured with Vachaspati Puraskar along with Rs. 1 lakh. The list of the scholars who have been awarded Vachaspati Puraskar till now is as under:

(1) Param Pujya Krishnashankar Shastri (2000)

(2) K.K. Shastri (2001)

(3) Bhagwatiprasad Pandya (2002)

(4) Ester Soloman (2003)

(5) Vasant Parikh (2004)

(6) Tapasvi S. Nandi (2005)

(7) Hariprasad Shastri (2006)

(8) Laxmesh V. Joshi (2007)

(9) Arvind H. Joshi (2008)

(10) Chimanlal V. Raval (2009)

(11) Ramesh S. Betai (2010)

A standing committee of five members to decide the name of a candidate is constituted under the chairmanship of Gautam Patel; other members are Vasant Parikh, Mansukh Savalia, Vijay Pandya and Ajit Thakor.

Some Remarkable Achievements

Swadhyaya Mandal, Pardi, is well known because of Pandit Satvalekarji who has published all the four Vedas, several Brāhmaṇas and Upaniṣads. He has also published the Hindi translation of the critical edition of *Mahābhārata* of BORI, Pune.

The Oriental Institute of Vadodara has brought out most commendable publications; among them the critical edition of the *Rāmāyaṇa* of Vālmīki is well known all over the world. This institution has published Maharaja Sayajirao Sanskrit Series where works like *Nāṭyaśāstra* of Bharata, etc. have attracted the attention of scholars from all over the world. The critical edition of *Viṣṇu Purāṇa* and recently a commentary of Janardana on *Meghadūta* edited by Vadekar are worth noting.

The B.J. Institute of Learning and Research, Ahmedabad has prepared for the first time a critical edition of *Śrīmad Bhāgavata Purāṇa*. The late Padmashree K.K. Shastri, Hariprasad Shastri (winner of Vachaspati Award) and Bhartiben Shelat have prepared this critical edition while consulting numerous MSS collected from India and abroad.

Sanskrit Sahitya Akademi of Gujarat State has also reprinted under the general editorship of Gautam Patel some of the valuable works like *Śrī Bhāṣya* of Rāmānujācārya, translated by the late Anandshankar Dhruva, *Hindu Dharma* by the same author and Kauṭilya's *Arthaśāstra* in three volumes.

L.D. Institute of Indology, Ahmedabad, has published 150 books on various subjects of Indology, most of them are on Jainism.

Shri Dwarkadhish Sanskrit Academy and Indological Research Institute, Dwarka has published more then 35 volumes. From among these *Śaṅkarācārya Pāribhāṣika Kośa* (1, 2, 3, 4, 5) and *Saundarya Laharī* edited by Swami Sadanand and *Kāraka Yojana* by J.P. Dwivedi deserve special mention.

Sanskrit Seva Samiti, Ahmedabad, has published more than 70 works of Sanskrit language and literature. Among them the project of translating *Complete Works of Ādi Śaṅkarācārya* in Gujarati under the general editorship of Gautam Patel has gained popularity. In total 11 volumes are already out in which the major *bhāṣyas* on *Viṣṇusahasranāma*, *Bhagavad-Gītā*, *Brahma-Sūtra* of Bādarāyaṇa and all the 11 Upaniṣads and all the *stotras* as well as some *prakaraṇa granthas* like *Vivekacūḍāmaṇi*, *Sarvavedānta Siddhānta Sārasaṁgraha*, *Ātmabodha*, *Aparokṣānubhūti*, *Śataślokī* and *Prabodha Sudhākara* are included. The plan is going on to complete the project of 15 such volumes. The first three volumes are already out of print and from them the first and the second are republished as revised editions.

Shri Bruhad Gujarat Sanskrit Parishad, Ahmedabad, was established in 1946. This institution has tried its best to popularise Sanskrit in the state. It has held various examinations for school children, students of *pāṭhaśālas* and common man who is interested in Sanskrit. Till now more than 35 lakh of students have appeared in such examination. It has published more than 125 books and the periodical named *Sammansyam* is also published occasionally. It has also published dramas, novels, short stories, *bhajans*, poems, radio plays, etc. By staging Sanskrit dramas and producing them on All India Radio and Doordarshan it has rendered a great service to Sanskrit. The Parishad also organises competitions of *garbā* in Sanskrit, elocution competitions, Sanskrit verse recitations, essay competitions, etc. to popularise Sanskrit. Its present president is Justice M.S. Parikh and exam secretary is Ghanshyam Trivedi who has 100 publications in Sanskrit to his credit.

Sanskrit Bharati has started working in the state from the year 1981. It has arranged more than 500 *saṁbhāṣaṇa śiviras* in the state. Such *śiviras* have created a confidence in the mind of a common man that Sanskrit is not a hard language to learn. They have used modern Sanskrit methods for popularising Sanskrit such as cassettes, DVDs etc. It has created audio-visuals of *garbās*, songs, songs for children, etc. It has published literature like *Vadatu Sanskritam*, *Dhātumañjuṣā*, *Vyavahāra-sahasrī*, Sanskrit dictionary, etc. To enable people learn Sanskrit while remaining at their residences, it has started postal education of Sanskrit also.

The year 2000-01 was celebrated as the "Sanskrit Year" by the nation. During that period Sanskrit Bharati taught more than 12,000 teachers to teach Sanskrit in Sanskrit medium at their schools under the guidance of Rashtriya Sanskrit Sansthan, New Delhi. Sanskrit Bharati of Gujarat State has run successfully 200 Sanskrit *saṁbhāṣaṇaśiviras*.

The year 2010-11 is being celebrated as the Golden Jubilee year of the Gujarat State, a special project in collaboration with Shri Somanath Sanskrit University, Sanskrit Bharati has successfully organised *saṁbhāṣaṇa śiviras* for more than 1 lakh students. In all at 2,000 centres in various districts, 1,07,000 students were trained.

Sanskrit Bharati today runs more than 100 centres for preparing students to appear in Sanskrit Gaurava Pariksha. Moreover, it organises Avasiya Sanskrit Shivirs in summer vacation. It has actively participated along with 162 volunteers in International Sanskrit Book Fair held at Bengaluru in January 2011.

Gujarat Vidya Sabha is a 163-years-old institution, formerly it was known as Gujarat Vernacular Society. The B.J. Institute, affiliated with Gujarat Vidya Sabha, is a recognised institution for postgraduate studies under Gujarat University. More than 100 students in Sanskrit and Culture have obtained Ph.D. degree from here.

It has a very rich library having 80,000 books, 27,107 manuscripts; among them 50 are valuable illustrated manuscripts. It has published seven descriptive catalogues of these manuscripts. This Institute has 5,241 old coins, 1,000 original paintings, 175 sculptures and terracotta objects. It has prepared a critical edition of *Śrīmad Bhāgavata Purāṇa*. It published *Sāmīpya*, a quarterly journal in Gujarati from 1984.

Conclusion

Sanskrit language and literature is like a burning torch which each generation has received from the former and transferred to the next, brighter than ever before. In making this burning torch of knowledge of Sanskrit, the Gujarat State and its inhabitants have contributed more than enough. Sanskrit, to my mind and in the words of my revered Sadgurudeva, the late Swami Gangeshwaranandji, is like the flow of the Gaṅgā, it will never die. The future of Sanskrit is better in Gujarat, in India and thereby in the whole world, also because it has a treasure of knowledge which will never perish but ever enlighten the mankind.

7

Status of Sanskrit Studies in Jammu & Kashmir

Kedar Nath Sharma

JAMMU & Kashmir (J&K) state popularly called the "Crown of India" forms the northern-most state of the Indian Republic. Surrounded by high mountain peaks the state is divided into three regions, i.e. Jammu, Kashmir and Ladakh. The state is blessed with the beauties, glaciers, lakes, lush-green meadows, natural caves and, of course, beautiful people. The three natural regions of the state represent three distinct ethnic groups and their colourful cultural identities. Jammu, popularly known as "Duggar Deśa", is famous for world-renowned Mātā Vaiṣṇo Devī Shrine and other ancient temples which have given it the name "the city of temples". Kashmir or Śāradā Pīṭha is widely acclaimed for its natural beauty, warm hospitality and, above all, as the abode of Śaiva philosophers. Ladakh is quite famous for its high mountains and age-old Buddhist monasteries. Kashmir, in particular, has been a prominent centre of ancient Indian learning and wisdom. Śāradā Pīṭha, Jayendravihāra, Kuṇḍala-vana-vihāra, etc. were famous religious as well as academic institutions which attracted visitors and academicians not only from the different parts of India but also from abroad like Central Asia, Tibet, China, Korea and so on. It was a prominent centre of the Buddhist Sarvāstivāda sect and hosted the Fourth Buddhist Council during the first century CE, during

Kaniṣka's reign, at Kuṇḍala-vana-vihāra. Besides, Kashmir has also contributed extensively to the advancement of almost all aspects of Sanskrit literature like — Indian philosophy, poetics, grammar, Āyurveda and history. Kashmir is famous for its Pratyabhijñā system of Kāśmīr Śaivism which has resulted in radical revision of the Indian philosophy. Śrī Somānanda was the founder of this philosophy. Vasugupta, Bhaṭṭa Kallaṭa, Utpaladeva, Abhinavagupta, Kṣemendra, etc. were some of the most illustrious scholars who gave further boost to this philosophy. Budhism has also a long history in Kashmir. Indian literature cannot be treated as complete without considering the contribution of Kashmir.

Kashmir has produced eminent scholars of Sanskrit Kāvya Śastra. It is a well-known fact that all the six schools of Sanskrit poetics, viz. Alaṁkāra. Rīti, Rasa, Vakrokti, Aucitya and Dhvani originated and developed in Kashmir. It was the scholars of Kashmir again who propounded different theories of Rasa by independent expositions of the celebrated *Rasa-Sūtra* of Bharata. As established by Abhinavagupta, *Rasadhvani* is the soul of poetry. Kashmir was not only a cradle of the schools of poetics, but it also nurtured generations of poets through four centuries or more. Kashmir Valley witnessed different systems in their formative, creative, definitive and scholastic stages.

J&K has to its credit the *Viṣṇudharmottara Purāṇa*, an encyclopedic work compiled near Jammu, the *Vāsuki Purāṇa* written in the hilly areas of Doḍā and Bhadrawāha and the *Nīlamata Purāṇa* of Kashmir which contain a rich treasure of information regarding sacred places, religious rites and festivals and the way of life of the common people of ancient Kashmir. J&K has also produced wonderful Sanskrit literature in the form of historical poems like *Rājataraṅgiṇī* of Kalhaṇa, Jonarāja, Śrīvara, Prajñabhaṭṭa and Śuka, *Pṛthvīrājavijaya* of Jayānaka, *Vikramāṅkadevacarita* of Bilhaṇa and *Rājendra Karṇapūra* of Śambhu. In the field of epics *Kapphinābhyudaya* of Śivasvāmin, *Hāravijaya* of Ratnākara, *Rāvaṇārjunīya* of Bhīma, *Śrīkaṇthacaritam* of Maṅkha and *Kathākautuka* of Śrīvara are worth to mention. Great grammarian Patañjali also belonged to Kashmir and the famous commentary Kāśikā on Pāṇini's *Aṣṭādhyāyī* and the commentaries on Patañjali's *Mahābhāṣya* were also composed here. Cāndra and Kātantra schools of Sanskrit grammar flourished in Kashmir. It is believed that the great sage Caraka, the writer of famous Āyurvedic work *Caraka Saṁhitā* hailed from Kashmir and Dr̥ḍhabala, who revised Caraka's work, also belonged to Kashmir.

Kashmir was famous for its Sanskrit as well as Buddhist studies through the ages. The Chinese travellers, Yuan Chwang and Ou Kong, visited Kashmir in CE 631 and 759 respectively. Both these scholars stayed here for a couple of years to study Sanskrit and Buddhism. Kṣemendra refers to many students who used to come to Kashmir from Bengal and other parts of India to study and achieve perfection in Sanskrit. The high standard of debates and discussions, as indicated in *Caraka Saṁhitā, Pādatāḍitaka, Āgamāḍambara*, etc., are a testimony to this fact.

Unfortunately, we witnessed a dark period for more than five centuries, say, from thirteenth to seventeenth. During this period no creative or scholastic work was produced on this fertile land of J&K. It was only after Mahārāja Ranbīr Singh became the king of J&K in 1857, that Sanskrit writing regained some ground in the state.

Immediately after he ascended the throne of J&K (in 1857) this king being a lover of knowledge in general, and of Sanskrit as well as Persian language and literature in particular, adopted a policy to propagate these two languages. Besides, having faith in religion, the king announced the state of J&K as a centre of religious learning. He established a number of temples and Sanskrit *pāṭhaśālā*s in different parts of the state.

During the post-Independence period, Sanskrit studies suffered due to lack of government patronage except that few institutions that continued to work under the patronage of J&K Dharmartha Trust.

Before January 1990, i.e. the period when militancy gripped the valley, Sanskrit teaching in J&K was quite inspiring and satisfactory. "J&K Dharmartha Trust" which was founded by Mahārājā Ranbīr Singh to promote and propagate Sanskrit language and literature, was playing key role to popularise Sanskrit in the state. Large number of students used to come from various parts of the country and even from Nepal to learn Sanskrit from the *paṇḍit*s of J&K. A large number of students were taught Sanskrit in Sanskrit *pāṭhaśālā*s/*mahāvidyālaya*s of the state. The following were the few institutions established by Mahārājā Ranbīr Singh and his lineage where Sanskrit was being studied in general and research was also being done:

1. Shri Gadadhar Sanskrit Pathashala, Devikātīrtha, Uttarvāhinī.
2. Shri Raghunatha Sanskrit Pathashala (Later on Shri Raghunatha Sanskrit Mahavidyalaya), Shri Raghunatha Temple Complex, Jammu city.
3. Shri Raghunatha Sanskrit Library, Shri Raghunatha Temple Complex, Jammu city.
4. Sanskrit Pathashala at Ranbir Singh High School, Jammu.
5. Dharmartha Vibhaga or Dharmartha Council (now known as Dharmartha Trust), Jammu.
6. Shri Raghunatha Nidhi, Jammu.
7. Sanskrit *pāṭhaśālā*s jointly sponsored by public support and J&K education department in Purmaṇḍala (Jammu) —

i. Sanskrit *pāṭhaśālā* in Jhiri village.

ii. Sanskrit *pāṭhaśālā* in Phalayan village.

iii. Sanskrit *pāṭhaśālā*, Udhampur.

iv. Sanskrit *pāṭhaśālā*, Reasi.

v. Shri Ranvira Pathashala in Jammu city.

8. Shri Vidyadhara Shaivashrama Nidhi or Trust, Karan Nagar, Srinagar.
9. Shri Rupa Devi Sharada Pitha, Srinagar.
10. Shri Rama Shaivasharama, Fatehkadal, Srinagar.
11. Shri Paniniya Sanskrit Mahavidyalaya, Jammu city.
12. Arya Kanya Sanskrit Pathashala, Old Hospital Road, Jammu.
13. Sanskrit Mahilavidyapitha, Jammu city.
14. Kashmir Sahitya Sammelana, Kralkhud, Srinagar.
15. Sanskrit Sahitya Parishad, Srinagar.
16. Sansrkrit Bhasha Prachara Samiti, Srinagar.

— *Viśva Sanskrit Śātābdigrantha*,
Jammu Kashmir Section, Saṁvat 2022.

In these *pāṭhaśālā*s students were provided free meals and boarding facilities along with clothes. Dharmārtha Trust had also been organising various literary competitions and distributed awards in the field of Sanskrit to promote and propagate the Sanskrit studies. But, unfortunately, only three institutions, i.e. Shri Raghunatha Sanskrit Mahavidyalaya, Shri Raghunatha Sanskrit Library and Dharmartha Trust are now functional and the rest do not exist anymore.

Dharmartha Trust had patronised a number of artists, poeticians and scholars who contributed to Sanskrit Literature till 1989.

Some prominent scholars are — Amar Nath Kaul, Ishwar Kaul, Krishna Dutt Shastri, Krishna Pandit, Gurucharan Dass

(Swami), Gopal Rajanak, Govind Kaul (Swami), Govind Bhatt Shastri, Govind Yaksha, Govind Rajanak, Jagdish Shastri, Mahamahopadhyay Jagaddhar Zadoo, Janardan Yaksha, Zinda Kaul, Jiya Lal Kaul, Jiya Lal Dhar, Jiya Lal Pradhyapak, Tribhuvan Nath Shastri, Daya Ram Pandit, Damodar Pandit, Deena Nath Yaksha, Dev Giri Nath, Ram Nath Shastri, Nityanand Shastri, Neel Kanth Gurtoo, Paramanand Pandit, Pushkar Nath Shastri, Prithvi Nath Pushp, Prem Nath Nehru, Badri Nath Nazir, Badri Nath Shastri, Baljinnath Pandit, Badri Nath Kalla, Bhaskar Rajanak, Madhusudan Kaul, Mahtab Kaul (Swami), Mahadev Trik, Maheswar Rajanak, Mukund Trik, Mukund Ram, Mahamahopadhyaya Radha Krishan Kav, Ramkrishna Kavi, Ram Chandra Kak, Ram Chandra Gadroo, Ram Chandra Bhatt, Laxmana Rajanak (swami), Shiv Nath Shastri, Shivopadhyay, Shrikanth Kaul, Sahib Ram, Sukhanand Zadoo, Sudarshan Rajanak, Har Bhatt Shastri, Hari Krishna Mirza, Hriday Nath Kaul, Janaki Nath Kamal, etc.

Present Status of Sanskrit Studies in Jammu & Kashmir

In comparison to past glorious history of Sanskrit teaching, learning and research in the state, there seems no reason to be satisfied with the present status of Sanskrit-learning in J&K. Although Sanskrit-learning is still popular in the state but the fact is that the subject is not a priority for the government as far as its teaching in the schools and colleges is concerned. Still there are some institutions in the state where Sanskrit is taught at the school, undergraduate and postgraduate levels. These institutions or *gurukulas*/*pāṭhaśālās*/*mahāvidyālayas* are run/sponsored either by the private sector or by the state and central governments. These Institutions are:

SHRI RAGHUNATH SANSKRIT MAHAVIDYALAYA

This *mahāvidyālaya* was established at Raghunātha Temple Complex, Jammu in the year 1858 by Mahārājā Ranbir Singh. This *mahāvidyālaya* produced hundreds of *paṇḍits* during the nineteenth and twentieth centuries. This *mahāvidyālaya* is now run by the Jammu & Kashmir Dharmartha Trust at village Birpur (Jammu) and provides teaching of Prajna and Visharada classes under the affiliation with University of Jammu. Presently, the Institution has eleven highly qualified teachers with specialisation in the field of Veda, Vyākaraṇa, Jyotiṣa and Sāhitya. The number of students is more than 100, who are provided free boarding and lodging facilities by Dharmārtha Trust. Three year degree course of Shastri is proposed to be started in the near future.

Some renowned scholar *paṇḍit*s of the *mahāvidyālaya* are:

1. Shri Kaka Rama Shastri
2. Shri Vihari Lala Shastri (author of *Pañcāṅga* and books on *karma-kāṇḍa*)
3. The late Vishnukanta Shastri (former Governor of U.P.)
4. Ganga Datta Vinoda (worked on *Ṛgveda*)
5. The late Kevalakrishna Shastri (expert in Sanskrit grammar)
6. Late Pandit Ramanatha Shastri (Recipient of President's award/Certificate of Honour)
7. Pandit Mula Raja Shastri (Recipient of President's award)
8. Vishvamurti Shastri (Recipient of President's award)

The late Pandit Kaka Ram Shastri of Jammu, a great *paṇḍit* scholar of poetics contributed profusely to the service of Sanskrit language and literature. He would teach and help even the professors of the university to explain the textbooks of poetics (Sāhitya Śāstra).

SHRI GURU GANGA DEVAJI SANSKRIT MAHAVIDYALAYA, SUNDERBANI, RAJOURI (J&K)

This *mahāvidyālaya* was established in 1999 and is run by the

Svāmī Viśvātmānanda Trust, founded by Svāmī Viśvātmānanda Sarasvatī in the Sundarbani area of Rajouri district. The aim of this *mahāvidyālaya* is to provide traditional education to male students. Veda, Vyākaraṇa, Jyotiṣa and Sāhitya along with modern subjects are being taught to the students. The trust provides education, food, uniform, seasonal clothes free of cost. Around 150 students are admitted in Prathama, Madhyama, Shastri (III years courses), Prak-shastri and Acharya (II year courses). The *mahāvidyālaya* offers — Veda, Vyākaraṇa, Jyotiṣa and Sāhitya as fields of specialisation in the said classes. This *mahāvidyālaya* is affiliated to Rashtriya Sanskrit Sansthan, deemed university (New Delhi).

SHRI MATA VAISHNO DEVI GURUKULA, CARANAPADIKA, KATRA (JAMMU)

This *gurukula* was established by the Shri Mata Vaishno Devi Shrine Board, Katra, on 1 July 2010 with the aim to make the students fully equipped with knowledge in the fields of Vedas, Indian culture and religion as well as Sanskrit language and literature. Besides, the students are also provided education in the modern subjects such as English language, mathematics, social sciences and elementary sciences. In the first phase *gurukula* has a proposal to run class 6 to class 12 for its resident students. Six Sanskrit *ācārya*s, having Ph.D degrees in different fields of Sanskrit studies as well as three teachers of modern subjects have been appointed to teach the students. At present 18 students in 6th class and 25 students in 7th class are studying *Śukla Yajurveda*, Jyotiṣa, Vyākaraṇa and Sāhitya Śāstra and modern subjects. Students are provided free meals, books, clothes, medical facilities, etc. by the Shri Mata Vaishnodevi Shrine Board.

STUDY OF SANSKRIT IN GOVERNMENT HIGH SCHOOLS

The implementation of the three language formula in Jammu & Kashmir State does not leave any scope of the inclusion of

Sanskrit as a subject in school curriculum. At the high school level Hindi or Urdu is taught as the first language, English as the second language and Urdu as the third language to those who opt Hindi as the first language and Hindi is taught as the third language to those students who opt Urdu as the first language. As a consequence it has left no scope for teaching of Sanskrit at the school level. The result is that Sanskrit degree holders are forced to teach general subjects and posts of Sanskrit teachers in government schools are either left vacant or merged.

STUDY OF SANSKRIT IN SCHOOLS AFFILIATED TO CBSE (CENTRAL BOARD OF SECONDARY EDUCATION)

Kendriya Vidyalayas, BSF School, Army schools and all other schools which are affiliated to the CBSE (Central Board of Secondary Education) have Sanskrit as a compulsory subject in their curricula from class VI to VIII and as an optional subject from class IX to XII. Thus, the three language formula has created a lack of motivation towards Sanskrit studies at the school as well as college/university levels. Employment opportunities in teaching are becoming lesser and lesser for students of Sanskrit.

STATUS OF SANSKRIT STUDIES AT HIGHER SECONDARY SCHOOLS AND GOVERNMENT COLLEGES

Despite the apathy from the government and the new education policy, Sanskrit is immensely popular among the students and common people of the state, especially of the Jammu region. A large number of students opt for Sanskrit subject in class 11th and 12th and 3-year B.A. course. Thousands of students are learning Sanskrit in around 90 government higher secondary schools and 20 government degree colleges of Jammu region. About 110 lecturers are appointed to teach these students. But, in the government degree colleges of Kashmir, the situation is quite the opposite. No doubt, Sanskrit does exist in the university/college curricula but in reality Sanskrit is not taught in any of the around 35 degree colleges of Kashmir region. The reason is that after migration of Kāśmīrī *paṇḍit*s and Sanskrit teachers from the valley during 1990, the Sanskrit posts have been left either vacant or are merged. Approximately 20 posts of Sanskrit teachers at the higher secondary level and degree college level have been merged in the Kashmir region. The students willing to opt for Sanskrit are discouraged by the authorities by saying that teachers are not available for teaching Sanskrit.

CENTRAL INSTITUTE OF BUDDHIST STUDIES, LEH

Established in 1959 this centre offers standard 1st to Ph.D in Buddhism. The centre lays special emphasis on the study of Buddhism (including language and literature, philosophy, culture, art, architecture and archaeology, etc.) through Tibetan medium. It may be noted here that a vast Buddhist Sanskrit literature was translated into Tibetan, out of which many original Sanskrit texts were lost and have been restored from their Tibetan translations. One Sanskrit teacher, appointed at the centre, teaches the Buddhist Sanskrit subject to the students.

AYURVEDA COLLEGE

Government college of Āyurveda, Jammu, was closed in 1982. A private Āyurveda college came up and has been running in Jammu city since 1998. Sanskrit is a compulsory subject for the degree of BAMS (Bachelor of Ayurvedic Medicine & Surgery). It is giving some incentive to Sanskrit studies in the state.

CENTRAL INSTITUTION

Rashtriya Sanskrit Sansthan (deemed university) Ranbir campus is another major institution at Jammu, providing facilities for teaching/ learning and research in Sanskrit. This Sansthan was established in 1971 under the title of Sri Ranvir

Kendriya Sanskrit Vidyapeeth, affiliated to Rashtriya Sanskrit Sansthan, New Delhi. This campus is one of the 10 campuses of Rashtriya Sanskrit Sansthan situated in different parts of the country. This institution is transformation of 173-year-old Shri Raghunath Sanskrit Mahavidyalaya which was founded by the then Mahārājā Sri Ranbir Singh until it became a deemed university in the year 2002. This Vidyapeeth has been running the following classes.

Course	Duration of course	Equivalent
Prathama	3 years	8th class
Purvamadhyama	2 years	Matriculation
Uttaramadhyama	2 years	10+2 (12th)
Prak-shastri	2 years	10+2
Shastri	3 years	Three year B.A.
Acharya	2 years	M.A.
Shiksha Shastri	1 year B.Ed	
Shikshacharya	1 year M.Ed	

After getting the status of deemed university, only Prak-shastri, Shastri, Acharya, Shiksha Shastri and Shikshacharya classes are being run by the Ranvir campus wherein about 350 students are provided education in the fields of Sanskrit literature, Veda, Vyākaraṇa, Jyotiṣa, Darśana and teaching methodology. Apart from Sanskrit subjects, Hindi, English, Dogri, Political Science, English literature and History are also taught at Shiksha Shastri and Shastri classes. At Shastri and Acharya levels the Sansthan offers various optional subjects like Veda, Vyākaraṇa, Sāhitya, Sāhityaśāstra, Darśana, Jyotiṣa and Arthaśāstra according to choice of the students. Scholarships are provided to help the poor and encourage the meritorious students by the Sansthan.

Now this campus also has become the centre for distance education.

Presently, Rashtriya Sanskrit Sansthan — Sri Ranbir campus is running the following eight *vibhāgas* (departments):

1. Vyākaraṇa Vibhāga
2. Sāhitya Vibhāga
3. Darśana Vibhāga
4. Siddhānta Jyotiṣa and Phalita Jyotiṣa Vibhāga
5. Veda Vibhāga
6. Śikṣāśāstrī Vibhāga
7. Kaśmīra Śaivadarśana Pariyojanā
8. Distance Education Centre

There are 35 professors on the staff role out of which four are on contractual basis.

Research Output

One hundred four research projects leading to Vidyavaridhi (Ph.D.) degree in different fields of Sanskrit have been completed at this campus so far.

Following are some the important publications of the campus:

1. *Kaśmīra Śaiva Darśanam*
2. *Literary Study of Vikramāṅkadevacaritaṁ*
3. *R̥cā-Rahasyam*
4. *The Background of Jaina-jīvana Darśanam*
5. *Nyāya-Sāra-Vicāra*
6. *Grahalaghavakaraṇam* (12 volumes)
7. *Daśa-Padārthī*
8. *Raghunāthaguṇodayāmahākāvyaṁ*
9. *Jyotiṣa-Ratnamālā*
10. *Bījagaṇitam*
11. *Lalita-Stavaratnam*
12. *Paramārthasāra*
13. *Samarasasāra*
14. *Svātantryadarpaṇa*

15. *Bhṛṅgīśa-Saṁhitā*
16. *Śaivācāryo Nāgārjunaḥ tasya Stotrayugalañca*
17. *Tarkapraveśaḥ*
18. *Śaiva-Darśana-Koṣaḥ* (in two volumes), etc.

Śrivaiṣṇavī magazine is also being published annually by the campus.

Library

The library of this campus has nearly 45,000 books on Sanskrit language and literature and 125 rare manuscripts written in Śāradā and Devanāgarī scripts, are also preserved in the library.

Sanskrit at Postgraduate Levels

Presently, J&K has nine universities, namely:

1. University of Kashmir, Hazratbal, Srinagar.
2. University of Jammu, Jammu.
3. Sher-e-Kashmir University of Agricultural Science & Technology, Srinagar.
4. Sher-e-Kashmir University of Agricultural Science & Technology, R.S. Pura, Jammu.
5. Sri Mata Vaishno Devi University, Katra.
6. Baba Gulam Shah Badshah University, Rajouri.
7. Islamic University of Science & Technology, Avantipora, Kashmir.
8. Kashmir Central University, Kashmir.
9. Jammu Central University, Samba (yet to be functional).

Out of these nine universities, provision for teaching and research in Sanskrit exists in Kashmir University and Jammu University only.

KASHMIR UNIVERSITY, SRINAGAR

With the establishment of the Department of Sanskrit in 1983 Sanskrit studies were started in Kashmir University at PG as well as UG levels. M.A. Khan of the Department of Hindi was the founder head (in-charge) of the department. At the time of opening of Sanskrit department. Swami Purnananda Sarasvati was appointed as lecturer and B.K Dembi and B.N. Kalla were as guest teachers. Again, Satyabhama Razdan and Purnima Kaul joined the department as lecturers later. Due to turmoil in the Kashmir Valley, Swami Purnananda Sarasvati and Purnima Kaul migrated from Srinagar in 1989 and since the year 1990, Sanskrit Department of the Kashmir University was affected in the worst possible manner due to terrorism in the valley. It was in the year 2001 that Jalees Ahmed Khan Tareen, the then vice-chancellor of Kashmir University took a keen interest to revive the department and appointed S. Razdan as in-charge head with two teaching assistants. At present the department has one professor (S. Razdan) and two assistant professors.

The Department of Sanskrit, Kashmir University, runs the following courses:

1. 1-year certificate course
2. 1-year P.G. Diploma course.
3. 2-year M.A. programme.
4. M.Phil. Programme.
5. Ph.D. Programme.

Research Activities

Since 2001, the teaching faculty of the department has been seriously engaged in teaching/learning and research activities and students actively participate in the academic as well as extra-curricular activities, including national and international seminars/conferences.

Publications

Four books have been published by the faculty members. Besides, 25 research papers too have been published, in the national research journals.

UNIVERSITY OF JAMMU

Since its birth in 1963, the department of Sanskrit, Jammu University has been contributing extensively towards Sanskrit teaching and research in various fields of specialisation like Veda, Vedāṅga, Indian Linguistics, Grammar, Poetics, Purāṇetihasa, Dramatergy, Vāstu and Jyotiṣa.

The Department of Sanskrit runs the following courses:

Courses	**Duration**
1. M.A.	2 years
2. M.Phil.	1-2 years
3. Ph.D.	

The department of Sanskrit offers 28 courses in M.A. degree, out of which a student has to opt 16 courses in all, spread over four semesters of approx. six months each. The fields of specialisation are — Poetics, Epigraphy, Philosophy and Linguistics. The number of students in M.A. (2-year) course varies from 75 to 80

Research Activities

More than 140 research topics for M.Phil. degree have been completed in various fields of specialisation so for. More than 90 scholars, after working on research topics in Poetics, Philosophy, Kashmir Śaivism, Linguistics, Veda, Vedāṅga, Upaniṣad, Jyotiṣa, Vāstu, Dharmaśāstra, etc. have so far been awarded the degree of Ph.D. At present 20 candidates for M.Phil. and 42 scholars are registered for Ph.D. degrees.

Publications

Since 1963, the Department of Sanskrit of Jammu University has published books and around 200 research papers in different fields of specialisations. The list of some important publications of Sanskrit department is as under:

(A) Ved Kumari Ghai:

1. *Nīlamata Purāṇa: A Critical & Literary Study*
2. *Nīlamata Purāṇa,* vol. II text with English translation
3. *Kaśmīradarpaṇa*
4. *Narendradarpaṇa*
5. *Kaśmīra kā Saṁskr̥ta Sāhitya ko Yogadāna*
6. *Purandhri Pañcakam* (a collection of Sanskrit *rūpakas*)
7. *Studies in Phonetics and Phonology* with special reference to Ḍogrī
8. *Vedāmr̥ta* (Ḍogrī translation of Vedic hymns)
9. *Pāṇḍulipivijñānam* (editing)
10. *Yogadarpaṇa* (Ḍogrī explanation of Yogasūtras). Jointly authored with Ram Pratap
11. *Sāhityika aur Sāṁskr̥tika Nibandha*
12. *Rajendrakarṇapūra*
13. *Bhallāṭa Śatakam*
14. *Mere Gīta Tumhāre Gīta*

(B) Kaushallya Wali:

1. *Concept of Ahiṁsā in Sanskrit Literature*
2. *Concept of Barman and Bhāgya in Sanskrit Literature*
3. *Vijijñāsā* (translation of work of Kaviraj Gopinath)
4. *Jammu Kaśmīra kī Svātantryottara Hind Kavitā: Ek Adhyayana*

(C) Shambhu Nath Shastri:

1. *A History of Vedic Literature*
2. *A New Approach to Some Important Aspects of Indology*
3. *Pāṭhālocana* (textual criticism)
4. *Ādhunikasandarbhe Kālidāsaḥ*

(D) Ram Pratap:

1. *Purāṇaṁ Kāvyarūpataya Vivecanam*
2. *Sāhityasudhāsindhu*
3. *Purāṇavimarśaḥ*
4. *Camatkāravicāracarcā*
5. *Trividha Kāyasamīkṣa*
6. *Kāvyacamatkāra*
7. *Mammaṭottara Yuga ke Bhāratīya Kāvyaśāstra meiṅ Nūtana Avadhāraṇāyeṅ*

   (Five books co-authored with Ved Kumari Ghai)

(E) Mahesh Sharma:

1. *Sacred Idias of East*
2. *Mudrārākṣasanāṭakam: Ek Adhyayana*
3. *Aṁśuka* (collection of poems)

(F) Ramnika Jalali:

1. *Indian Women in Smṛtis*
2. *Kalcuris of Tripurāri*
3. *Status of Women*

(G) Sharda Gupta:

1. *Advaitavedānta aur Śaṅkara Vedānta.*
2. *Viraha* (Hindi poems)
3. *Vedanā* (Hindi poems)

(H) Kedar Nath Sharma:

1. *Rasabhāṣā aur Bhāvabhāṣā* (a literary, psychological, social and religious study of Rasabhāṣā and Bhāvabhāṣā)
2. *Sanskṛta meiṅ Rūpasvanimika Adhyayana*
3. *Kaśmīristotraparamparā Evam Dinakrandanastotra*
4. *Triveṇī* (collection of research papers on linguistics, philosophy, poetics and Indian culture)
5. *Kaśmīra ke Kāvyācārya*
6. *Comparative Study of Centro-Eastern Pahāṛī Languages (Nepālī, Gaḍhwālī and Kumāunī)*

(I) Jagir Singh:

1. *Pratyabhijñahṛdayam aur Vedāntasara ke Sandarbha mein Kaśmīra Advaita Śaivadarśana aur Advaitavedāntadarśana: Ek Paryāvekṣaṇa*
2. *Īśvarapratyabhijñā aur Sāṁkhyakārikā ke Paripreksa meiṅ Pratyabhijñāsiddhānta Tathā Sāṁkhyadarśana: Ek Paryālocana*
3. *Advaita Śaivabhakti Tathā Utpaladeva*
4. *Trikadarśana meiṅ Parāśakti Kālī*
5. *Śaivī Yogarasa.*

(J) Purshotam Sharma:

1. *Īśavāsyopniṣad*
2. *Bhāratīya Jyotiṣa Praveśa*
3. *Laghusiddhānta Kaumudī*
4. *Siddhānta Kaumudī*
5. *Jyotiṣarahasya*
6. *Jyotiṣasāra*
7. *Ṛksūktagauravam*

(K) Sushma Devi: *Bhāratīya Nṛtyakalāyeṅ Evaṁ Nāṭyakalā*

(L) Ram Bahadur Shukla: *Naiṣadhīyacaritam kī Śāstrīya Mīmāṁsā*

(M) Vidyadhar Singh: 1. *Prācīnabhāratīya Purāniveśa*

2. *Bhāratīya Vāstuśāstra kā Itihāsa*

Research Papers

Apart from the above-mentioned 60 books-teachers of this department have also published about 300 research papers.

Major Research Projects Completed/ Undertaken by the Teaching Staff

The teaching staff of the Sanskrit department of Jammu University have been actively involved in their own major research projects. The following major research projects have been completed by the teaching staff:

1. *UGC-Sponsored M/R Project*: A Critical Study of Rasa School. P.I. — Ram Pratap
2. *UGC-Sponsored M/R Project*: The Study of Kaśmīr Śaivism on the Basis of Concerned Original Sanskrit Texts. P.I. — K. Wali
3. *UGC-Sponsored M/R Project*: Status of Indian Women with Special Reference to Smṛties. P.I. — Ramnika Jalali
4. *UGC-Sponsored M/R Project*: A Critical Study of Centro-Eastern Pahari Languages, i.e. Nepali, Gadhwali and Kumauni (2002-05). P.I. — Kedar Nath Sharma
5. *UGC-Sponsored M/R Project*: House Architecture in Ancient India (2009-2011). P.I. — Kedar Nath Sharma
6. *UGC / State Higher Secondary Education Department Sponsored M/R Project*: "Analysis of Sanskrit Phonemes" (Running since 1986). P.I. — Kedar Nath Sharma

7. *UGC Sponsored M/R Project*: A Critical study of Physiognomy (2006-2009). P.I. — Ram Bahadur

Apart from teaching of prescribed syllabi, Sanskrit Department has been staging Sanskrit dramas, holding Sanskrit Kavi Sammelana, elocution contests, Kalidasa Jayanti celebration, Sanskrit *śloka* recitation competition, Sanskrit day celebration, etc. to unfold the latent talent in the student community.

Enovative Programme

A well-equipped computerised phonetic laboratory has been functioning under the principal investigation of Kedar Nath Sharma since 1996 in the department to facilitate teachers, scholars and students working on "phonetics" in particular and on linguistics in general. This scientific approach can help the students to follow scientific trends and meet the demands of the modern development in the society.

Departmental Library

The departmental library of Sanskrit department has more than 17,000 books on different subjects of Sanskrit literature.

SANSKRIT LIBRARARIES OF THE J&K STATE

1. The Research Library of the J&K Government which is now located at the Kashmir University Srinagar, published numerous Sanskrit books under the title "Kashmir Research Series". This Library has 7,000 manuscripts, a large number of which (2,140), are in sanskrit language written in Śāradā script. The MSS section of the library has been reopened about a decade back to for researchers and attempts are being made to microfilm the manuscripts so as to make them easily available for scholars throughout the world.
2. Shri Raghunath Sanskrit Research Institute (previously

known as Shri Raghunath Sanskrit Library) at Raghunath temple, Jammu, is one of the important Sanskrit libraries of northern India. Many important manuscripts are preserved here. The total number of Mss in various categories is 6,079. A descriptive catalogue of these manuscripts was prepared by M.A. Stein in CE 1894 and 1905. The number of Mss in different categories are as under:

(1) Vedic Literature, 202;

(2) Sūtragranthans, 221;

(3) Upaniṣad Sāhitya, 421;

(4) Vedāṅga, 26;

(5) Vyākaraṇa, 279;

(6) Śabdakośa (Dictionary), 70;

(7) Chandograntha, 27;

(8) Saṅgītavidyā (Music), 35;

(9) Alaṁkāra, 106;

(10) Kāvya, 263;

(11) Nāṭaka, 54;

(12) Ākhyāyika, 31;

(13) Dharmaśāstra, 718;

(14) Pūrva-Mīmāṁsā, 158;

(15) Vedānta, 404;

(16) Sāṁkhya, 15;

(17) Yoga, 26;

(18) Nyāyavaiśeṣika, 435;

(19) Jyotiṣaśilpādi, 510;

(20) Cikitsā, 241;

(21) Mahābhāratarāmayaṇādi, 79;

(22) Purāṇamāhātmya, 309;

(23) Bhaktigranthas, 313;

(24) Tantragranthas, 1031;

(25) Jainagranthas, 35;

(26) Tamilagranthas, 68;

(27) Śaradagranthas, 20

— See, Charaka, SDS, *Life and Times of Maharaja Ranbir Singh of Jammu and Kashmir*, p. 273

CREATIVE WRITING IN SANSKRIT

Creative writing in Sanskrit is still going on in the state. *Duggar Stuti* written by Sukh Dev Shastri (1892-1982) is a famous *kāvya* of thirteen cantoes of nineteenth century. This *kāvya* gives a vivid description of the cities and towns of Jammu region. Besides, he has a credit of four other *kāvyas*, which are — *Śrī Jitamālācaritam, Śrī Nehru Śatakam, Śrī Haimamarnāthakathā* and *Bharata Sahasranāma Mahāstotram.*

Another famous creative writer of the state is Kedar Nath Shastri (CE 1892-1980). His *kāvya, Tauṣī Śatakaṁ,* is a collection of 100 verses about the river Tawi which flows by the side of Jammu city. Another work *Sindhu Sabhyatā* is a monograph in Sanskrit prose giving first hand information about the remains of Indus Valley Civilisation as he himself was associated with excavations. His *Bhāratavījaya mahākāvya* deals with the Indo-Pak war of 1965 and is still unpublished. *Rājataraṅgiṇī Pariśiṣṭam* by Kaviraja Bholanath (CE 1905-78) is a continuity of the tradition of *Rājataraṅgiṇī* first written in ancient times in Kashmir. The writer at first describes Jammu and thereafter gives a history of all the Ḍogrā rulers from Mahārājā Gulab Singh to Mahārājā Hari Singh in it.

Shri Ram Krishna Shastri was a prolific Sanskrit poet of post-Independence era and published his Sanskrit *kāvyas*, plays and prose writings on his own. Many of his works were published in the monthly Sanskrit Journal *Suprabhātam*. The eight *Kāvya*s edited and published by him are, *Tārācaritam*, *Vidyānurāgī Raṇvīraḥ*, *Indirāśatakam*, *Śekhaśatakam*, *Caṇḍadevacaritam*, *Neharuśatakam*, *Svatantrottarabharatam*, and *Abhinavaduggaradarśanam*. He has also written two short plays — *Rājaduhitā* and *Duggaroddhāraḥ* and the prose work *Kādambarīkathāsāraḥ*. With the exception of *Caṇḍadevacaritaṁ* and *Kādambarīkathāsāraḥ*, all his remaining works deal with contemporary personalities and events.

Ved Kumari Ghai and Prof. Ram Pratap have jointly brought out *Urmikā* a collection of Sanskrit poems. Ghai has also to her credit *Purandhripañcakam* — a collection of five Sanskrit plays based on the lives of five women. Gangadatt Vinod has to his credit *Vyaṅgoktayaḥ*, a collection of Sanskrit satirical poems. Bihari Lal Shastri has brought out his *kāvya Paraśurāmāyaṇaṁ* in 700 verses. Other writers of Jammu whose Sanskrit poems, essays, plays, etc. have been published in various journals are, Sarva Shri Pandit Kakaram Shastri, Pandit Parashuram Shastri, Ram Nath Shastri, Shambhu Nath Shastri, T.C. Shastri, Priyatam Chandra Shastir, Kewal Krishna Shastri, K. Wali, Rita Jitendra, Yogendra Kumar and Shri Durga Datt Shastri. Of Sanskrit creative writers from Kashmir, we have Baljinath Pandit who has written a philosophical *Kāvya-svātantryadarpaṇa* and B.N. Kalla who has written *Kaśmīrakrandanaṁ*. Shri Jagannath Rivu has written *Śraddhānandacaritaṁ* in 459 verses, parts of which have been published in various journals. Neelakanth Gurtoo an ardent (obedient) disciple of the late Swami Lakshman Joo, a doyen of Kāśmīr Śaivism has edited and translated texts of Kāśmīr Śaivism — (1) *Parātriṁśikā*, (2) *Spandakārikā*, (3) *Sāmba-Pañcaśikā*, (4) *Śrī Harṣeśara-māhātmyaṁ*, and (5) *Amarnātha-Māhātmyaṁ*.

Thus the tradition of creative writing in Sanskrit is still alive in J&K (article by Ved Kumari Ghai, on Sanskrit Studies in India, Published by SLBSRS Vidyapeeth, New Delhi, 2001).

Sanskrit, the original source of Indian culture, is a rich repository of knowledge on the human wisdom, spread over diversified areas of philosophy, spiritual practices, rites and rituals, science, astronomy and astrology, medicine, geography, sociology and so on. People with diverse attitudes and aptitudes studied and wrote on various aspects of life. Obviously it engulfed almost every branch of knowledge. As a result royals too, paid proper attention towards the development of Sanskrit during the ancient and early medieval periods. This trend continued in J&K till the thirteenth century before the introduction of Islam in the Kashmir Valley. We find a decline in the development of Sanskrit, which however, got revived somewhat with the advent of the Ḍogrā rule, especially during the reign of Mahārājā Ranbir Singh. Mahārājā Ranbir Singh gave a boost to Sanskrit studies by establishing various *pāṭhaśālā*s/*mahāvidyālaya*s, research institutes, libraries, etc. The situation again changed by the time of Indian Independence. The priority of the J&K government shifted to the adoption of a new education policy, similar to what we find at the national level. Accordingly, three-language formula consisting of mother tongue, English and regional language got the most prominent place in the academic curricula. Sanskrit was given a back seat. However, the status of Sanskrit in the state is not totally dim and some of the institutions have kept the ray of hope alive. Sanskrit is being taught in the lower classes of CBSE run schools, private *pāṭhaśālā*s/ *mahāvidyālaya*s, Ayurvedic College, Centre for Buddhist Studies, Leh, University of Jammu, University of Kashmir and last but not the least the Rashtriya Sanskrit Sansthan, Ranbir Campus, Jammu. Needless to say, these institutions realise the deep impact of Sanskrit on the day-to-day life of the people of the region, especially its significance in the fields of Āyurveda, Yoga, Hindu *saṁskāra*s, Astrology and Vāstu, etc.; and their intimate relation with the people. It is sad to note that whereas Sanskrit subject is available at the higher education level, it has been removed from the school curriculum. There is serious need to reintroduce the subject at the middle and secondary level so that the gap can be filled up and a continuity of Sanskrit studies can be maintained. The role of Rashtriya Sanskrit Sansthan (New Delhi) becomes more pertinent in such a situation which may be possible in two ways (1) by establishing Adarsh Sanskrit *vidyālayas*, and (2) by persuading the J&K Board of School Education to ensure that Sanskrit gets a proper space in its curricula.

8

Sanskrit Studies in the States of Bihar and Jharkhand

Brahmachari Surendra Kumar

Backdrop

SANSKRIT studies, prior to the arrival of the East India Company of England, had remained confined to the *ṭol*s, i.e. teacher-centric *pāṭhaśālā*s. Usually, a scholar/priest of traditional Sanskrit-learning would start a Sanskrit-teaching centre called *ṭol* and students, mostly from the priest-class, would join them. These *ṭol*s were supported through the munificence of the local *zamīndār*s and wealthy families, as they needed priests who had knowledge of Sanskrit-text-based rituals. The teaching of Sanskrit in those centres (*ṭol*s) focused on the dissemination of religious ritualistic prescriptions of the Dharmaśāstras and their application on the occasion of various festivals, religious rituals or otherwise. During the medieval India, the Purāṇas and other ritualistic literature, and, not the Vedic texts, impacted upon the socio-cultural formations of Bihar and Jharkhand, which were too orthodox to be benefic for the enlightenment of the masses, in respect of the *sāmānya dharma*, enunciated in the Smṛti literature.

In course of time, the East India Company of England gained the dīwānī of Bihar and Bengal. In order to administer these areas they had to be acquainted with the socio-cultural ethos of the people. The Fort William College was established in Calcutta (now Kolkata) and Gilchrist as its principal played a pivotal role in initiating the learning of Indian languages, including Sanskrit. Charles Wilkins (1750–1836), encouraged by Warren Hastings, the then governor-general of the Indian territories acquired by the East India Company with its headquarters at Kolkata, studied Sanskrit at Varanasi, and, in 1785, published a translation of the *Bhagavad-Gītā* (the Song of the Adorable One), and, later on, an edition of the well-known collection of fables called *Hitopadeśa* (or friendly advice). Wilkins, in 1808, also published the first Sanskrit grammar in English. Another English administrator and scholar Sir William Jones (1746-94), a multi-faceted orientalist, during his brief stay of 11 years in India, got founded the Asiatic Society of Bengal, still an institution of national importance at Kolkata, and published in 1789, a translation of the drama *Abhijñānaśākuntala* of Kālidāsa which was highly admired by Herder and Goethe, the German poet. Jones translated the *Manu-Smr̥ti* of Manu and he was the first to publish a Sanskrit text *R̥tusaṁhāra* in Nāgarī script. Jones also encouraged comparative studies of languages like Sanskrit, Latin and Greek. He spoke, at the inauguration of the Asiatic Society of Bengal, of the Sanskrit language to be more perfect and exquisite than the Greek and the Latin and that these three languages appeared to be related and developed from some common source. Consequently, the English, German and French scholars' analytical writings on the Sanskrit language and literature appeared, such as Fiedrich Schlegel's *On The Language and Wisdom of Indians* (1808), Franz Bopp's treatise on "The Conjugational System of Sanskrit in Comparison with that of Greek, Latin, Persian and German" (1816). Later on, a German scholar, F. Rosen, became interested in the Vedic literature and brought out the first eight sections called *maṇḍala* of the *R̥gveda*, in 1838. Rudolf Roth (1821-95) published *On the*

Literature and History of the Veda in 1846. These publications encouraged scholars to take up comparative and analytical studies of Sanskrit texts, Vedic and classical both. In addition to the comparative philological studies of Sanskrit, Kuhn and F. Max Müller both took up the comparative study of Sanskrit and the Greek mythologies. It goes to the zeal and perseverance of Max Müller who, for the first time, published the complete text of *Ṛgveda* with the commentary of Sāyaṇa in the Nāgarī script.

Whatever may be the antiquity of the Vedic texts (approximately 2500 BCE according to M. Winternitz, 2000 BCE by A.A. Macdonell), and despite the history being one weak point in Indian literature, those are the oldest surviving literary documents throwing light on the culture, not only of the Indian people, but also of the human race. It's more probable that the destruction of the ancient libraries like those at Taxila, Nālandā and Vikramaśilā at the hands of the Islamists might have obliterated historical informations as well contained therein.

However, in spite of the successive waves of invasion and conquest by Persians, Greeks, Scythians and Islamists, India shows a remarkable continuity in religious rites and rituals, in domestic and social customs to be equalled by China only, in the whole world.

This brief reference to the contribution of the Western scholars is necessary, as this has shaped immensely the revaluative and analytical studies of Sanskrit.

The English, through the East India Company, founded the Sanskrit traditional learning centre at Varanasi which was upgraded as the Queen's College, and later on, developed into the Sampurnanand Sanskrit University. The English established three universities one each at Kolkata, Bombay (now Mumbai) and Madras (now Chennai) and later on at Allahabad also, and opened the departments of Sanskrit studies. In most of the colleges connected with these universities Sanskrit teaching also was started.

Consequently, socio-cultural contours of Sanskrit literature were explicated and revaluated by the Western and the Indian indologists alike, culminating in the establishment of All India Oriental Conference, with its headquarters at Pune (in Maharashtra) and of the Bhandarkar Oriental Research Institute (Pune), also.

The State of Bihar

The State of Bihar included the region of Jharkhand prior to 2000. The nomenclature Bihar is a variant of the Sanskrit word *vihāra* which means a monastery. This region was called Bihar as it abounded in monasteries.

The State of Bihar has played an important role in the Indian history. Several small kingdoms existed in Bihar. In the great epics, the *Rāmāyaṇa* and the *Mahābhārata* there are references to Viśālapurī, Janakapura, Rājagṛha and Aṅga. Janaka, whose daughter Sītā, the queen consort of the Lord Rāma, was the king of the Videha kingdom in the north of the river Gaṅgā. Jarāsandha, the king of Magadha, had his capital at Rājagṛha, at present in the district of Nālandā. The kingdom of Aṅga which was handed over to Karṇa, the indomitable character of the *Mahābhārata*, by Duryodhana had its capital at Campā near the present city of Bhagalpur. The first republic-state known in history existed at Vaiśālī (a part of the old district of Muzaffarpur) around 700 BCE, which was honoured by the visit of the Lord Buddha. This republic, which followed a policy of respect for all religions and beliefs like *yakṣa*-worship, Buddhism, Jainism and Brāhmanism and believed in the collective wisdom of its inhabitants, was defeated by Ajātaśatru of the imperial Magadha in the south of the river Gaṅgā, through the machinations under the divide-and-rule policy, during the fifth century BCE, and, later on, continued to be a subsidiary of the Mauryan rule founded by Candragupta, till it merged with the Gupta empire in CE 400.

Bihar, against the backdrop of republicanism, gradually showed trends of imperialism and military prowess. Bimbisāra annexed Aṅga-principality and his son, Ajātaśatru, annexed Kāśī and Vaiśālī. His son, Udayabhadra, transferred his capital from Rājagṛha to Patna, which was then called Pāṭaliputra, now the capital of the State of Bihar. Gradually, the Magadha empire with its capital at Pāṭaliputra had become so mighty under the Nanda dynasty that Alexander and his Greek army dare not move towards the State of Bihar.

Candragupta Maurya, the progenitor of the Maurya dynasty, with the help of his mentor Kauṭilya who authored *Arthaśāstra*, the famous treatise on ancient polity, destroyed the Nanda dynasty and extended his empire up to Mysore in the south India, defeated the Greek commander Seleucus and annexed territories up to Hindukush, Baluchistan, Afghanistan, Makrana and part of the the east Iran. His namesake, Candragupta II, was called Vikramāditya as he liberated western parts of India from the yoke of the Śakas in the CE 400.

Bihar lost its glory when the Hūṇas invaded India in the fifth century CE. During the reign of the Pāla dynasty of Bengal (CE 775-1200) the seat of Buddhist-learning at Vikramaśilā (near present-day Bhagalpur) became famous. Nālandā was already a famous centre of Buddhist studies and was visited by the Chinese trader and traveller, Huen-tsang. However, during the Islamic rule that followed, the libraries at Nālandā and Vikramaśilā were destroyed and Bihar remained almost stagnant until the advent of the British by 1765, and after that remained under the governance of Bengal till 1912. It was later separated from Bengal and became the State of Bihar and Orissa till 1936, when Orissa was declared a separate state by the English.

Bihar played an important role in successive phases of the Indian national freedom movement. In the revolt of 1857, Babu Kunwar Singh of Shahabad (Arrah) died fighting the English valiantly. Gandhi's *satyāgraha* was motivated by the miseries of the farmers, when he met them at Motihari, the headquarters of the Champaran district of Bihar. Rajendra Prasad, the first president of the Indian union, Sacchidananda Sinha the first president of the costituent assembly, Jayaprakash Narayan who contributed to the democratic re-formulation, Shrikrishna Sinha, the first chief minister, Anugrah Narayan Singh, the first finance minister, Jagjiwan Ram and Jaylal Chaudhary all those and others, contributed to the progress of Bihar in resurgent India.

In 1912, the region of Bihar became a separate state and the university at Patna was established in 1917. At present, there are six universities of the general category, at Magadha (Bodh-Gayā), Bhagalpur, Chapra, Muzaffarpur, Madhepura (Saharsa) and Arrah (Shahabad). All these universities have opened departments for postgraduate studies and research in Sanskrit. Besides, the Bihar government, at the initiative of the then education secretary, Jagadish Chandra Mathur (ICS), opened institutions for postgraduate studies and research in Sanskrit at Darbhanga, in Prākṛta and Jainology at Vaiśālī and for Pāli language and literature at Nālandā, the latter being famous as the centre of Buddhist studies all over the world in ancient times. In 1960, the Bihar government established the Kameshwar Singh Sanskrit University at Darbhanga, replacing the Bihar Sanskrit Association which was primarily conducting examinations, namely the Prathama, Madhyama, Shastri and Acharya, and supervised teaching of Sanskrit along the traditional lines. Prior to this, the Bihar government had established Sanskrit colleges in 1952 at Ranchi, Bhagalpur, and Patna in addition to the one Sanatana Dharma Sanskrit College, existing at Muzaffarpur, which later on became the constituent unit of the Sanskrit University at Darbhanga. At present, there are more than 100 Sanskrit colleges affiliated to this university. In addition to these, the Government of Bihar established the Bihar Sanskrit Shiksha Board in 1982 for the control and administration of Sanskrit-teaching up to the Madhyama standard. The present chairman of the Board, Siddheshwar Prasad, is a littérateur of repute. Under his editorship the Board is publishing a quarterly literary journal *Vāgvandanā*. He has organised many conferences and seminars of national and state level at Patna, and, in the commissionary headquarters of Bihar for the propagation of Sanskrit studies. At present there are more than 1,000 schools under the Board.

General Characteristics of Sanskrit Studies

Sanskrit studies in Bihar and Jharkhand are characterised by multidimensional trends. The studies carried on in the general universities and colleges are interpretative and more analytical compared to those in the traditional Sanskrit colleges and the university. The latter ones are more concerned with the interpretation and preservation of the Sanskrit texts in the different branches such as scientific literature, phonetics, grammar, mathematics, astronomy, medicine, law, philosophy and poetics, which is appropriate and essential, as the traditional genre of scholarship also need to be preserved and enriched in the face of tremendous innovations and multidimensional advancements in our knowledge.

Scholars in the field of Sanskrit studies since 1950 may be categorised as:

(a) those engaged in creative writing in literature and poetics,

(b) those writing traditional interpretative treatises in Sanskrit, and

(c) those engaged in the dissemination of traditional

Sanskrit-learning through Indian languages, by analysing them in the context of new inventions, technological advancement and socio-cultural formational changes.

The society is not the same today as it was before 1947, as it has changed tremendously in Bihar and Jharkhand in the post-Independence era. The attainment of freedom, widespread literacy, assertion of individuality leading to gradual decline of intra-familial bond, no doubt, a result of industrialisation, have added to the complex social and cultural formations today. The post-independent states of Bihar and Jharkhand, nay, whole of Bhārata (India) from that matter have seen the upward movement of the deprived segments of our populace along the socio-economic and educational ladder; and, consequently, their growing dominance in political dispensation, thus, reducing the severity and disabilities caused by our caste system. These changes have impacted upon the creative writing in Sanskrit. The woman discourse also has added a new perspective to socio-cultural dimension of Sanskrit creative writing.

Sanskrit Studies in Bihar

Sanskrit studies in the state of Bihar belong to an earlier tradition and more systematic expansion when compared with those in the state of Jharkhand which is a nascent one.

There is more than one factor for this difference. One relates to the geographical situation of the State of Bihar. It is not hilly except for some of its southern parts like Bhagalpur and Gaya. Thus the density of population is much more. Beside, with the establishment of the Calcutta University in the eighteenth century, there was wider educational activity in this region. On the other hand, with the establishment of the Patna University at Patna in 1917, teaching of Sanskrit became more widespread. Beside, the establishment of the K.P. Jaisawal

Institute and the Bihar Research Society not only gave impetus to the Indological studies, but also motivated immensely the Sanskrit scholars to take up research work in Sanskrit with comparative and historical perspectives. Scholars like the late Pandit Ramavatar Sharma, Harichand Shastri, A.P. Banerjee Shastri of the pre-Independence era were renowned for their profound knowledge of the traditional texts, as well as of the modern trends of Sanskrit studies.

Another important factor which led to the spread of Sanskrit studies was the deep interest of the rulers of Darbhanga estate, who, through their munificence and love for Sanskrit studies, had contributed immensely in sustaining and supporting the Sanskrit centres known as *ṭols*.

The royal house of Darbhanga was also responsible for the establishment of the Bihar Sanskrit Association, which conducted the Sanskrit studies and examinations up to the standard of Acharya in the Vedic studies, besides Dharmaśāstra, Jyotiṣa, Vyākaraṇa, Vedānta-Mīmāṃsā, etc. The Bihar Sanskrit Association was replaced by a full-fledged Kameshwar Singh Darbhanga Sanskrit University, in 1960.

It may be noted that in addition to the above-mentioned institutions, there are seven universities which teach Sanskrit up to the postgraduate level and allow advanced research work for M.Phil., Ph.D. and D.Litt. degrees.

The region comprising the districts of present Darbhanga, Madhubani, Saharsa and their neighbourhood known under the cover term of Mithilā, has been the seat of renowned scholars in different branches of Sanskrit literature such as Nyāya, Dharmaśāstra, Vyākaraṇa and Sāhitya. The traditional Sanskrit learning was enriched by such leading scholars as Vachaspati Mishra, Mandan Mishra, Ganganath Jha and host of other scholars, who were always engaged in the interpretive study and teaching of Sanskrit texts of the different branches.

Thus, they contributed immensely in the preservation of the traditional learning. A brief account of some of these scholars is given below.

- The late Dharmendra Brahmachari Shastri, a teacher of Sanskrit and later on, head of the Hindi Department, Patna University, was a profound scholar of Sanskrit and Hindi. He was also an acclaimed orator in Sanskrit and Hindi both. His poetic composition *Puruṣa and Prakṛti* is inspired by the Sāṁkhya philosophy. He was the precursor of literary criticism in Bihar. His deep knowledge of Sanskrit poetics and of the trends of contemporary criticism were amazing. His works on the *Bhakti* movement have been published by the Bihar Rashtrabhasha Parishad. D.B. Shastri, as he was usually addressed, occupied myriad positions in the government and the universities of Bihar. His life was cut short while he was engaged in writing a critique of the *Atharvaveda* from the social point of view.
- The late Acharya Devendranath Sharma, a former head of the Hindi department of Bihar and Patna universities, a former vice-chancellor of the Patna and Kameshwar Singh Darbhanga (KSD) Sanskrit universities and ex-chairman of the Inter-University Board, and Sanskrit-Hindi-Bhojpuri Academies of Bihar, dominated the academic expanse of Bihar for a pretty long period. Starting his career as a teacher of Sanskrit in the Patna University, he rose to eminence, both as an academician and an administrator. His *Alaṁkāra Muktāvalī* and the *Mahābhāṣya* on the *Kāvyālaṁkāra* of Bhāmaha, published by the Bihar Rashtrabhasha Parishad, and *Pāścātya Kāvyaśāstra*, are expositors of his profound knowledge of Sanskrit poetics as well as of Western criticism. His book on linguistics *Bhāṣāvijñāna kī Bhūmikā*, is a pioneer work

in Hindi. Prof. Sharma had studied Russian language and literature in the London University. He had visited European countries a number of times on academic assignments .

- The late Ramnarayan Sharma, who died while working as head of the Sanskrit Department, Bihar University was an erudite scholar of traditional Sanskrit-learning and very well acquainted with the modern evaluative technique of research also. His premature death was a great loss to the cause of Sanskrit, as he had devotedly motivated a large number of traditional Sanskrit teachers when he was officer-in-charge of the Bihar Sanskrit Association.
- The late Tarapada Chaudhary, who was head of Sanskrit Department in the Patna University, was a multidimensional scholar. His work on the "Interpretation of Some Doubtful Words of the Atharvaveda" published in the *Journal of the Bihar Research Society*, is highly acclaimed by Vedic scholars both inside and outside India. His books *Avyayavivekaḥ*, "Grammatical Aberrations in the Works of Kālidāsa" are significant contributions to analytical Sanskrit literature and literary criticism.
- The late Bechan Jha's (Head of the Department of Sanskrit of Bihar and Patna universities), book *The Concept of Poetic Blemishes*, and Satyadeva's (Head of the Sanskrit Department, Magadha University) work *A Comparative Study of the Bhāmatī and Vivaraṇa Prasthānas* (1978) are important contributions to the Sanskrit philosophical studies.
- The late Chandrakant Pandey, a former Head of the Department of Sanskrit Patna University was a scholar of Sanskrit grammar and had two publications to his

credit, namely, *Pāṇini and his Aṣṭādhyāyī* and *Patañjalī's Mahābhāṣya.* The late Vidyanand, a former Head of the Sanskrit Department, Patna University, was awarded the degree of M.Litt. for his research-work on Prākṛt by the Cambridge University, UK.

- Pandit Shashinath Jha, attached to the Mithila Sanskrit Institute at Darbhanga, published three books *Tritalāvacchedakatāvādaḥ, Lakṣaṇāvatī Ṭīkā, Vyutpattivādagūḍhārthatattvāloka Vyākhyā* which are sufficient proofs of his scholarship in Nyāya. The KSD Sanskrit University at Darbhanga has published *Śaśinātha Nibandhāvalī* which contains various papers written by him.
- Kavishekhar Pandit Badarinath Jha, also attached to the Mithila Sanskrit Institute, was a renowned scholar who wrote commentaries on different Kāvyaśāstras such as *Surabhi* on *Rasamañjarī, Dīdhiti* on the *Dhvanyāloka, Prakāśa on Rasagaṅgādhara.* His other works include *Kāśyapakulapraśastiḥ, Gaṇeśvaracaritacampūḥ, Āryāsāhasrī* and *Rādhāpariṇayam Mahākāvyam.* He was a recipient of the President's Certificate of Honour.
- Pandit Kulanand Mishra was head of the Department of Darshana, and Pandita Upendra Jha of the Vyakarana Department of KSD Sanskrit University, the latter being the a recipient of the President's Certificate of Honour.
- Pandit Anand Jha was a profound scholar of Nyāya. After his retirement from the Lucknow University, he joined KSD Sanskrit University. He too was a recipient of the President's Certificate of Honour. His works include *Padārthaśāstram, Tarkasaṁgrahavyākhyā, Dhvanikallolinī,* and a detailed commentary on the *Nyāya-Mañjarī.* His *Ānandamadhumandākinī* is an anthology of poems.

- Pandit Ganesh Sharma also attached to the KSD Sanskrit University, and wrote a book *Vijñānaṁ Samājaśca* for which he was awarded a prize of Rs. 10,000 by the Government of India. He was a recipient of the President's Certificate of Honour also. Pandit Brahamadatta Dwivedi, though born in the UP (near Allahabad), spent his entire life in Bihar. He was a renowned scholar of grammar, philosophy and Kāvyaśāstra. He has edited the *Bhagvad-Gītā* with Madhusūdanī commentary. He served as the principal of the Murarka Sanskrit College, Patna till his retirement. He was also a recipient of the President's Certificate of Honour.
- Pandit Namonarayana Jha, a scholar of Sahitya and Vyakarana was also a recipient of the President's Certificate of Honour.
- Pandit Brajkishore Jha retired as the head of the Department of Jyotish of the KSD Sanskrit University. His publications include *Grahaṇamālā*, and *Siddhāntasetuḥ*.
- Pandit Jatashankar Jha, a scholar of grammar, poetics and philosophy, retired as the principal of the Govarernment Sanskrit College under the KSD Sanskrit University.
- Pandit Ramkaran Sharma of Bhojapur, a versatile scholar retired as Head of the Dharmaśāstra Department of the KSD Sanskrit University.
- The late Jayamanta Mishra was head of the Sanskrit Department (BU), vice-chancellor of KSD Sanskrit University, president of the All India Oriental Conference and recipient of the President's Certificate of Honour. His works include *Kāvyātmamīmāṁsā*, *Nibandhakusumāñjaliḥ*, *Saṁskṛtavyākaraṇa* and

anthologies of devotional songs, in addition to a host of ancient Sanskrit texts edited by him.

- Pandit Arjun Jha attached to the KSD Sanskrit University, who was a scholar of Dharmaśāstra and Purāṇas, authored the (*Uṇādikaumudī*).

One notable characteristic of the scholars, noted for their profound knowledge of ancient Sanskrit texts, is their lack of interest in the dissemination of their knowledge through publications. Even some of those scholars who were recipients of the President's Certificate of Honour, were known more for their interpretative study of the Sanskrit texts and their commentaries, than for their innovative publications, with exceptions, of course. The reason may be that they were not much interested in self-propagation.

However, the post-Independence era saw the emergence of a group of scholars well corversant with traditional interpretative Sanskrit texts, and also alive to the sensitiveness of the emerging contemporary socio-cultural and political formulations, as evident in their creative writings in Sanskrit. They also perceived the inquisitveness of the expanding Indian literati in respect of the Sanskrit texts, and, consequently took to writing appreciation of these texts in Indian languages especially in Hindi also.

Among such Sanskrit scholars of the present generation, Ramkarana Sharma and Radhavallabha Tripathi stand foremost.

- Ramkaran Sharma, born in the district of Saran (Chapra), is an erudite scholar of traditional as well as modern trends of Sanskrit learning. He adorned numerous academic and administrative positions within and outside India. He, starting as a teacher of Sanskrit in the Bihar University, Muzaffarpur, rose to be the joint educational advisor and the founder-director of the Rashtriya Sanskrit Sansthana, Government of India, Delhi. He was Vice-chancellor of the KSD Sanskrit University, Darbhanga and the Sampurnanada University, Varanasi. He has been president of the World Sanskrit Congress for 16 years. He worked under the famous linguist B. Emmeneu of the Berkley University under the Fulbright scholarship scheme and his publication *Elements of Poetry in the Mahābhārata* has won worldwide acclaim. His literary works in Sanskrit are 16 in number both in verse and prose. His works have attracted numerous honours. The Sahitya Academy, Government of India, honoured him for his poetry "Sandhyā", Birla Foundation for his "Gaganavāṇī" and the Bharatiya Bhasha Parishad for the *Sīmā* (novel). He is a recipient of the President's certificate of honour. He has founded the literacy society Mandākinī at Delhi.

- Sharma is one of the few creative writers of Sanskrit, who have responded positively to the contemporary and changing socio-cultural dimensions and the decay of value-system in the Indian society. His poems of the Sudharmā, Vīṇā and other poetic compositions, deal with the themes affecting our ordinary day-to-day lives and which pertain to our flora and fauna. His poems on crow, sparrow, rivulet, shrubs are satirical, which are suggestive of the moral decline of our society, with subtlety and sensitivity. His poems delineating historical characters like Ahalyā, Karṇa exude freshness of interpretive rationality.
- Ramdeva Tripathi whose teaching-span extended from 1954 to 1979, was a teacher in the postgraduate Department of Sanskrit, Bihar University, and, later on principal of the Netarhat Public School in the district of Palamu. He combined in himself the traditional

erudition and the analytical research-oriented vision. His work on Pāṇini and the Indian linguistics is highly commended by the Sanskritists.

- Acharya Kishore Kunal of the Indian Police Service, who resigned as additional director-general of police and devoted himself to academics and propagation of Sanskrit and regeneration of socio-philanthropic contents of religious activities, has been a former vice-chancellor of the K.S.D. Sanskrit University. He has guided and edited the important book *Aṣṭādhyāyī-gūḍhārthaprakāśikā* published by the K.S.D. University, which has been acclaimed by the Sanskrit scholars. The Government of India (National Book Trust) has published two volumes of his monumental work *Dalitadevo Bhava* (दलितदेवो भव) which delves deep into the Sanskrit texts and Hindi as well, and propose that the lower castes were treated with generosity and respect in ancient Sanskrit texts (except the Smṛti literature) and during the *bhakti* period of the Hindi literature, and that they contributed significantly toward the expansion of the egalitarian development of our societal formation. He has edited a devotional anthology in Sanskrit, namely *Maruta-Śatakam*. He has been the editor of the *Dharmāyaṇa*, a journal of the Mahabir Religious Trust. At the initiative and under the guidance of Kunal the secretary of the trust, social service schemes like establishment of a cancer institute, maternity hospital have been completed. Kunal, like Swami Vivekananda, has inspired the social contextualisation of religion. As chairman of the Bihar Regious Trust Board he holds the rank of a state minister.
- Kashinath Mishra, a recipient of the President's Certificate of Honour has written *Karṇāṭarājataraṅgiṇī*,

Harṣacaritamañjarī and *Vidyāpatiśatakam,* the first two dealing with the dynasty of the Darbhanga estate and the life of the emperor Harṣavardhana, the third is an eulogy of the poet Vidyāpati in 100 verses in the Āryā metre. Mishra's works are characterised by poetic embellishment of a high order.

- Umashankar Sharma Risi (also a recipient of the President's Certificate of Honour), a former head of the Department of Sanskrits (P.U.) is conversant with a wide range of traditional Sanskrit-learning. His main objective appears to be dissemination of traditional scholarship through the Hindi language. His works include *Nirukta,* a translation of the work of Yāska (chapters I-VII) with an exhaustive analytical preface, an explanatory appreciation of the *Sarvadarśanasaṁgraha,* and *R̥gveda* (first chapter with a critical preface), *Mīmāṁsādarśana, Śābarabhāṣya* (Tarkapādamātra) with a detailed explication, *Abhilekhanikaraḥ* which includes Aśokan and Sanskrit inscriptions and a critical treatise, namely *Kārakatattvānuśīlana* and a *History of Sanskrit Literature.*
- Pandit Adyacharana Jha, a scholar of Sanskrit poetics and literature, was pro-vice-chancellor of the KSD Sanskrit University, and a recipient of the President's Certificate of Honour. His work *Manoramāvivr̥ti* is well known. He has translated the *Rāmāyaṇa* of Kamban into Sanskrit.
- Hariprapanna Dwivedi, a former Head of the Department of Sanskrit, has published "Critique of the Terminology of Pāṇini", which shows his deep study of Sanskrit grammar literature.
- Sureshwar Jha, teacher in the Vyakarana Department of the KSD Sanskrit University, has edited the

Aṣṭādhyāyī of Pāṇini with explicatory notes and illustrations. Vachaspati Tripathi former head of the Dharmashastra Department of the KSD Sanskrit University is known for his incisive knowledge of the Sanskrit literature and the Purāṇas. He has been a recipient of the President's Certificate of Honour.

- Shivavansh Pandey, former vice-chairman-cum-director of Bihar Rashtrabhasha Parishad has made significant contribution to Sanskrit literature, namely *Saṁskr̥t and Saṁskr̥ti* and *Laukika Nyāyakośa*.
- Satish Chandra Jha, former head, Sanskrit Department (BU) and ex. president, All India Oriental Conference, Kurukshetra, has written, *Surathacaritam* which shows his deep knowledge of the Sanskrit literature.
- The late Rammohan Das of Sanskrit Department is known for his work on the status of women in Smr̥ti-literature.
- Pandit Trigunanand Shukla, a scholar of traditional Sanskrit-learning, wrote *Subhāṣacaritam* depicting the contribution of Subhas Chandra Bose to the freedom-movement of India. His critical appreciation of the *Adhyātmarāmāyaṇa* is well known.
- Pandit Gangadhar Sharma and Pandit Yamunadutta Tripathi, teachers of Dharmaśāstra and Sahitya contributed immensely to the propagation of Sanskrit.
- Pandit Kapildeo Sharma, though a teacher of Sanskrit in a high school of Chapra (Saran), wrote *Āśubodhavyākaraṇam* which proved a hit for teaching of Sanskrit. He tried to make the Sanskrit language popular and favoured the Sanskritisation of Hindi vocabulary.
- Ramvilas Chaudhary, a former Head of the Sanskrit

department (P.U.), has written books on grammatical topics such as *kāraka, samāsa,* and *kṛdanta.* His dramatic composition *Adbhutapāṇigrahaṇam* is indicative of his progressive views about social problems. He has organised seminars on varied topics of Sanskrit.

- Kalanath Jha's *Figurative Poetry in Sanskrit,* Ramgulam Mishra's *Bharata-Campu: A Study* are siginificant contributions. The work *Sanskrit Nāṭakoṅ mein Lokajīvana* of Ashok Kumar (professor of Sanskrit, P.U.) explicates the down-to-earth plot-construction of the Sanskrit dramas.
- Brahmachari Surendra Kumar former Head of the Department of Sanskrit (Bihar and Bhagalpur universities), Vice-chancellor of the KSD Sanskrit University, Darbhanga and fellow of the Institute of Advanced Studies, Shimla, has been a recipient of President's Certificate of Honour and UGC Emeritus Fellowship. He had been awarded Commonwealth Scholarship (UK) for the Ph.D. (London University) in linguistics. His works *Coordination in Sanskrit* and *Sanskrit Syntax and the Grammar of Case,* the latter being reprinted in the USA, show his deep knowledge of transformational generative grammar. His two publications in Hindi on theorectical linguistics and Nāgarī script, and the modern Sanskrit literature are indicative of his interest in language and literature and contemporary literary criticism.
- Damodar Mahto, Head of the Department of Sanskrit, (Bhagalpur University) has to his credit a commendable work, namely *Vaidika-Vyākaraṇa.* He is guiding UGC-sponsored projects. His knowledge of Vedic text is deep. He is the only Sanskrit teacher in Bihar with M.A. degrees in Urdu and Persion also.

- Maheshwar Prasad Singh, a Sanskrit teacher under the Bihar University, is an indulgent researcher and has organised UGC sponsorsed national seminars on varied aspects of Sanskrit literature.
- D.S. Chauhan, former Head of the Sanskrit Department (M.U.), has done creditable research work in Sanskrit literature. He is at present working on the Purāṇa literature.

There are a host of teachers of Sanskrit who belong to the comtemporary generation and are expanding the Sanskrit studies on a scale not seen before. Sima Bose, Vyasanandan Shastri, Sangita Agarwal, Nibha Sharma, Chittranjan Mishra, Shriprakash Pandey, Gaurinath Jha, Indranath Thakur (of Bihar University) Lakshminarayan Shah (of the Mithila University), Shripati Tripathi, Shivakant Jha, Madhubala Varma (of K.S.D. Sanskrit University), Mohan Mishra, Tulakrishna Jha (of Bhagalpur University), Aradhana Sinha, Gita Sharma, Priyamvada Gaur, Vibha Mishra (of Magadha University) come under this category.

One sigificiant feature of the Sanskrit studies being pursued in Bihar is the role played by the women teachers who have shown their proficiency in teaching and research activities.

- The late Aditi De, former Head of the Department of Sanskrit, Patna University, was the first woman teacher in Bihar who was awarded the degree of D.Litt. on Advaita philosophy. She organised a UGC-sponsored seminar on grammar and linguistics in 1982.
- Shraddha Mazumdar a senior teacher of Sanskrit at the Bihar University, Muzaffarpur, dedicated to the spread of Sanskrit by encouraging girl students of the colleges to study Sanskrit, died of cancer prematurely.
- Inder Kaur, a Punjabi-speaking teacher of the Bihar University with her in-depth knowledge of Sanskrit

and Hindi, was awarded the doctorate degree for her work on Bāṇabhaṭṭa.

- The late Sudha Rani a former head of the department of Sanskrit (PU), was awarded Ph.D. degree for her work on *The Champu of Bāṇeśvara Vidyālaṁkāra*. She had organised UGC-sponsored national seminar on the Buddhist and Jaina traditions in Sanskrit literature and published the research papers presented therein.
- Dipti Tripathi, born at Patna, and at present director of the National Mission for Manuscripts, Ministry of Culture, Government of India and a former Head of the Sanskrit Department, University of Delhi, started her career as teacher in the Department of Sanskrit, Patna University. She combines in herself the traditional knowledge of Sanskrit grammar and the analytical trends of modern linguistics, as evident from her works *Vyākaraṇika Koṭiyoṅ kā Viśleṣaṇātmaka Adyayana* (1975), *Structure and Meaning* (1982), *Bhāṣāvijñāna kī Bhūmikā* (co-author 2001). Her versatility is also evident from the books she has edited: *Facts of Indian Heritage* (2008), '*Poetic Creativity: Eastern and Western Perspectives* and *Ādhunika Saṁskṛta Sāhitya meṅ Sāmājika Cetanā* (2011). In addition to these, she has more than 32 research papers to her credit.
- Nisha Roy, professor of Sanskrit of the T.M. Bhagalpur University, worked in the field of literature. Her publication *Vālmīkīya Rāmāyaṇa mein Trāsadīya Tattva* has earned appreciation of the literati.
- Minakshi Prasad, professor of Sanskrit of the Magadha University, has written papers published in Sanskrit journals, in addition to two published books on Sanskrit composition for the postgraduate students. She has also authored the book *Kālidāsa kī Kṛtiyoṅ ke Dārśanika Sandarbha*.

- Jayashri Sinha, teacher of Sanskrit in the Bihar University, has produced a critical work *Saṁskṛta-Naṭikā-Vimarśa* known for its excellence in style and her explanatory notes on the *Viveka-Candrodaya*.
- Prabha Kiran, Head of the Sanskrit Department (BU) has two books to her credit *Śrīharṣa ke Rūpaka* and *Nīti ka Ālocanātmaka Adhyayana* in addition to scores of research papers.
- Manjushri, a former Head of the Department of Sanskrit (PU) was awarded Ph.D. for her work on *The Position of Women in the Yājñavalkya-smṛti.*
- Maya Sinha, a former head of the Department of Sanskrit (RU) was awarded the degree of Ph.D. for her work *Saṁskṛtasāhitya meṇ Ṛtuvarṇana.*
- Shanti Jain, a former professor of Sanskrit, of the Magadha University is credited with the publications *Veṇīsaṁhāra kī Śāstrīya Samīkṣā, Kādambarī, Vāsavadattā, Vasantasenā* (based on the *Daridracārudattam* of *Bhāsa* and the *Mṛcchakaṭikam* of *Śūdraka*) and *Ugo he Sūrya*.
- Indu Bala Prasad, a former Head of the Department of the Magadha University, was awarded the degree of Ph.D. (1970) for her critique of the *Mudrārākṣasa* drama.
- Mithilesh Mishra, debuty director, Bihar Rashtrabhasha Parishad has published poetic compositions to her credit such as *Subhāṣa-caritam, Laghvī, Āmrapālī, Tulsīdāsaḥ*. Her interest in creative writing in Sanskrit is laudable.

Non-teaching Organisation

Among the voluntary organisations devoted to the cause of the indological (including Sanskrit textual) studies, the foremost is the K.P. Jaiswal Research Institute, established by the Government of Bihar, with A.S. Altekar as its first director in 1950, for commemorating the contribution of the late Kashi Prasad Jaiswal, the greatest indologist of his time.

One of the objectives of this institute is to produce publications in achaeology, history, Tibetology and Sanskrit. K.P. Jaiswal himself wrote a treatise on "Hindu Polity" and educational and cultural dimensions of the ancient India.

The list of publications of this institute contains 28 volumes in the Tibetan-Sanskrit series, five volumes in the classical Sanskrit series, 15 volumes in the Historical Research text series.

Besides the K.P. Jaisawal Memorial lecture series have also been published in 14 volumes which include D.C. Sarkar's *Aspects of the Cultural History of Bihar* (1983), V.P. Varma's *Eternity and Freedom* (1993) and his *Mahābhāṣya* on the *Bhagavad-Gītā, Samādhi and Prajñā* (1987), and *The Earliest Sakas of Śouth Asia* (1998), by A.K. Narayana. These publications have profusely utilised the related Sanskrit texts.

The contribution of the institute is unique as the works published in the Tibetan series could not see the light of the day otherwise, such as *Pramāṇavārttika Bhāṣya of Prabhākaragupta* (1953) edited by Rahul Sankrtyayana, 2 Indices to the *Pramāṇavārttikabhāṣya* of *Prabhākara Gupta* (1957), Nalinaksha Dutta's *Bodhisattvabhūmiḥ* (1978) P. Pradhan and A. Halden's *Abhidharmakośabhāṣyam of Vasubandhu* (1975).

The Bihar Research Society, established before the state of Orissa, was separated from Bihar, has many ancient rare publications concerning indological studies which are of immense academic significance.

The Sanskrit Sanjivan Samaj of Patna was established more than 100 years ago. It has publications of importance to its credit. It publishes a quarterly magazine also and holds its annual meet regularly with Shivavansha Pandey as its secretary.

Jharkhand: Its Cultural Dimensions and Sanskrit Studies

The state of Jharkhand, carved out of the southern part of the state of Bihar, came into existence in the year CE 2000. It is primarily a hilly region previously called the Chhota Nagpur plateau, and is an extensional part of the Vindhya mountain range. This state is surrounded by the West Bengal in the east, Orissa in the south, Madhya Pradesh and a part of the Uttar Pradesh in the west and Bihar in the north.

As this region is mountaineous, it abounds in luxuriant vegetation and is the richest in mineral deposits in India. Though the land of Jharkhand is not fit for cultivation, yet paddy, wheat, *makkī* (maize), oilseeds, potatoes are produced, but not in sufficient measure. This region of Jharkhand was called Chota Nagpur till its creation as a state in CE 2000. The name Chota Nagpur got currercy, perhaps, during the Mughal period, as this region abounds in snakes and elephants, the word *nāga* meaning snake and elephant both. Another explanation relates this name to Cutā and Nāgo the forefathers of the Muṇḍa tribe. It is also said that the king of the Nāga dynasty ruled over the region with their capital at Chuṭiā on the bank of the river Suvarṇarekhā. The present name of Jharkhand derives from the word "Jhāṛ" meaning shrubs and this region is replete with abundance of vegetation and shrubs.

In the ancient Sanskrit and medieval texts, names like Kokara, Kokaraḥ, Khokhara occur; names like Arkakhaṇḍa, Kīkaṭa, Puṇḍra, Puṇḍrīka are found in Sanskrit texts. *Nirukta* (6/6) says that this region is inhabited by non-Āryans (*kīkaṭo nāma deśonāryanivāsaḥ*).

It is said that this region was called Pulinda, and Daśārṇa also. However, all these probable names went into disuse later on.

This region has significant number of tribes. These tribes

worship the Lord Śiva, the Sun and the flora in the main. They do not believe in the formless Supreme Being. Their gods and goddesses relate more to the flora and fauna of the region. Naturally, large segments of tribes adhere to superstitious rituals. In the Indian constitution they are referred to as scheduled tribes. According to 1971 census their number in Bihar and Jharkhand was a little more than 49 lakh and approximately 9 per cent of the total population of Bihar which comprised Jharkhand region also. The important tribes are Santhals, Muṇḍa, Oraon, and Ho. At present the tribals constitute aproximatly 23 per cent of the population of this newly-created State Jharkhand.

As mentioned above, Sanskrit was taught in *ṭols* in the beginning. As the tribal communities continued to live exclusively in relation to the mainstream of socio-cultural formations and adhered to superstitious ritualistic ways of life, they were not enamoured of the study of Sanskrit texts initially.

However, with the advent of Independence and under the impact of growing literary activities in the region of Jharkhand, they also took to Sanskrit studies. In fact, Sanskrit studies were pursued mostly by the non-tribal population, specially the priest-class, who were needed for performing rituals, under the patronage of landed gentry, big or small, who had settled there long before the independence, i.e. 1947.

Sanskrit Studies in the State of Jharkhand

In the State of Jharkhand, Sanskrit studies were pursued by scholars who fall into three categories. The first category was interested in acquiring ritualistic knowledge for its subsequent application in different festivals, occasions religious or otherwise. However, these ritualistic studies were confined mostly to the Hindu society who had migrated to this region, long back during the medieval period in order to escape from the onslaught of the Islamist invaders, and later on from that of the English as well. The second category of scholars was interested in the interpretive study of the Sanskrit texts in order to preserve them and the commentaries thereon. The third category of scholars, studied Sanskrit in the universities and colleges responding to the contemporary socio-cultural and political dimensions, thus, being more innovative in their writings of the different branches of Sanskrit such as Sāhitya, Dharmaśāstra, Vyākaraṇa and so on.

However, one caution is needed regarding this categorisation which allows overlapping. Thus, the latter two categories, in their ritualistic practices, were acquainted with the ritual texts also, sometimes composing prayers for invoking their deties. Again, the second category which consisted of traditional scholars, did also produce works which responded to socio-political changes like the freedom movement, disabilities emanating from the caste system, untouchability, inter-caste marriage, woman discourse and the like. Similarly, the third category of scholars took to the interpretive study of the ancient Sanskrit texts also.

Now, a brief account of the Sanskrit scholars of this region is given below. As mentioned above, the three categories are not like the watertight compartments.

Of the Sanskrit scholars devoted to the teaching and propagation of Sanskrit in this region, most of them have been and are connected, primarily, with the Ranchi University out of which were created, later on, Vinoba Bhave University (Hazaribagh), Sido-Kanho-Murmu University (at Dumka), Kolhan University (at Chaibasa) and Nilambar-Pitambar University (Daltonganj), with their areal limits redefined.

Some of scholars working in these universities have shown their acumen in their creative dramatic writings, as they have been innovative in their plot-construction and its denouement.

Of such scholars Ayodhya Prasad Singh, former Head of the Sanskrit Department of the Ranchi University is worth mentioning. His one-act play *Nīḍanirmāṇam* is path-breaking in more than one way. It does not contain verses. The dramatic conventions like *Sūtradhāra, Āṅkavibhāga* have been done away with. More importantly, it depicts the life of the lower middle-class parents and their interaction with their son and daughter-in-law. The parents have brought up their son under financial strains but now the son is well employed. The ailing grandma desires to caress and fondle her grandson whose parents have come on a short visit. But, lack of warmth and love, shown by her daughter-in-law and son upsets her. Ultimately, they leave for their place of work and the parents are again left alone. The characters of this one-act play are depicted with intense sensitiveness. The events in the play are the result of cultural decay which has affected our social life.

Professor Singh's work in Hindi. *Bhavabhūti aur Unakī Nāṭyakalā* treats the characters of Rāma and Sītā with utmost poetic sensibility. His compositional dexterity is replete with poetic embellishment like Mādhurya and Prasāda as evident from the prologue of the book quoted below.

ye nāma kecidiha te prathayantyabhijñāṁ
teṣveva prītiparameṣu kave! jano 'yam |
ālocate tava kr̥tiṁ rucirācchabhūṣāṁ
krīto 'smi te guṇagaṇairna samānadharmā | |
kālaḥ kr̥to niravadhirvipulā ca pr̥thvī
jātā paraṁ na pavitāmitasāndravāṇī
śrīkaṇṭhasūnurata eva kathāvatārī
dikkālatīrṇavacasā suchaviṁ tatāna | |
kāvyeṣu nāṭyamadhikaṁ yadi cārurūpaṁ
yāthārthyamasti nitarāṁ tava kāvya eva |
nāṭye kr̥te hi carite niravadyarūpe
bhūmirbhavasya supadā girijeva reje | |

Singh has edited a compendium of the Vedic hymns with his explanatory notes in Sanskrit and Hindi also.

Another scholar of Ranchi University, Dinesh Prasad Pandey was motivated by the heroes of the freedom movement. His *Svatantratā-āndolanam* (1949) is a prose composition, which traces and describes the genesis of the freedom movement and those who fought for the freedom of India such as Vivekananda, Gandhi, Gopalkrishna Gokhale, Madan Mohan Malviya and the like. This prose composition reflects the shift in modern Sanskrit prose writing. His *Bhāratāyanam* is a historical *kāvya* published in 1968 containing 1069 verses and traces the events from the Vedic period to the reign of Harṣavardhana. His *Mitradūtam* is a *Khaṇḍa-kāvya* composition in the *mandākrāntā* metre containing 111 verses and depicting a love-lorn hero.

Ramasisha Pandey, a teacher under the Ranchi University, is well known for his critical evaluation of the *Nirukta* of Yāska. His poems composed in Sanskrit are endowed with poetic embellishment. His *Mayūkhadūtam* (1974) is a romantic composition on the pattern of the *Meghadūtam*.

Chandrakant Shukla, professor in the posgraduate department of the Ranchi University is a versatile writer in both Sanskrit and Hindi. His *Mudrārākṣasanāṭakasya Śāstrīyam Adhyayanam* and its Hindi version are highly acclaimed. He has represented the university in academic conferences inside and outside India.

Vaneshwar Pathak, a Sanskrit teacher under the Ranchi University, published an anthology of select poems of 16 Sanskrit poets (in 1965), one-act play *Kālidāsam* (1961), *Plavaṅgadūtam* (1975) on the pattern of *Meghadūtam*. His social awareness is reflected in his work *Raktadānam*, a two-act play describing the evils of the dowry system in the Hindu society. *Hirocaritam* (1982) is a satirical *khaṇḍa-kāvya* showing the bad effects of West-oriented life on the Indian youth of present times. *Yīśucaritam* (1989) is a translation of the new testament. His other works include *Tvāsmidāsaḥ* (1989), *Vikrāntakarṇam*, a four-act radio-play.

In so far as the first category of scholars, interested in the study of ritualistic texts, is concerned, they edited prayer books. Jagannathashram Swami of Katarasagarh prepared an anthology of Sanskrit devotional songs named *Nirmālyam* is Bangla script in 1968. In fact the Sanskrit scholars, in general, showed their preference for Sanskrit devotional songs in their everyday prayers.

Some of the scholars who were motivated by their study of Hindi and English literature also wrote varied types of books in Sanskrit and in Hindi as they became interested in reaching out to a larger group of readers. In this, they were influenced by the writers of Hindi, English and other Indian languages.

Pandit Ramsundar Sharma wrote textbooks on Sanskrit composition, translation and grammar. He edited a Sanskrit dictionary (pocket edition) in 1954. Pandit Ambika Dutta Mishra, a poet, composed *Dineśābhinandanam* in the honour of Dinesh Prasad Pandey wherein he has eulogised the city of Ranchi, the capital of Jharkhand.

Pandit Suryanarayana Mishra's work (*Nagna-siddha-caritam*), which contains appreciation in 54 verses of a mendicant who stayed naked all his life and an eulogy of the Sun-god in 14 verses.

Pandit Ramadin Pandey, who retired as Head of the Department of Hindi of L.S. College, composed *Devakāvyam*, an anthology of devotional songs. His another composition on *Bāpu-caritam* analyses the life of Gandhi. His *Bhāratanetraprakāśam* is a composition, containing 110 verses which describes the life and contribution of the leaders of freedom movement, such as Gandhi, Rajendra Prasad, Jawaharlal Nehru, Sardar Vallabhbhai Patel, Subhas Chandra Bose, Bal Gangadhar Tilak, Lala Lajpat Rai, Chittaranjan Das, Madan Mohan Malaviya, Lal Bahadur Shastri and the like.

Pandit Badarinath Shastri composed *Navabhārata-nirmātāraḥ*, in prose and verses. Published in 1971, it describes twelve leaders such as Raja Rammohun Rai, Dayanand Saraswati, Bal Gangadhar Tilak, Jagadish Chandra Bose, Gandhi, Sardar Patel, Rajendra Prasad, Jawaharlal Nehru, Subhas Chandra Bose, etc. He has written texts on grammar and translation for the benefit of students.

Pandit Balram Pathak composed a book in Hindi about the rituals like *Śrāddha*, published in 1972.

One migrant from Belgium who settled in Ranchi and taught Sanskrit at St. Xavier's College, Ranchi, is Commile Bulke, famous for his pioneer work named *Rāmakathā* which shows his deep knowledge of the Vedic texts and extensive acquaintance with the story of *Rāmāyaṇa* and its varients, known inside and outside India. He published the first English-Hindi dictionary with the phonetic pronunciation of the English words in Nāgarī script.

Satyanarayana Sharma, teacher of Sanskrit at the St. Xavier's College, Ranchi composed works *Pravacana-cintāmaṇiḥ* (1977), *Pravacanapārijātaḥ* (1977) in Sanskrit prose, and *Prabandhaparāgaḥ* (1981) contain essays on myriad topics in Sanskrit. Sharma had taught in the Mister University of Germany in 1965. He edited the Sanskrit journal *Parmārtha-sudhā* published from Ranchi.

Bhagawan Dutta Mishra, traditional Sanskritist wrote *Pavanadūtam* (300 verses) *Bhārata-vibhūtivarṇanam* (2000 verses) and *Bihāragauravam*. Of these, the former two have been accepted for publication by the Sanskrit Academy, Patna.

Here it is proper to mention the names of the women

teachers of Sanskrit, especially those from non-Hindu sections who have contributed to the propagation of Sanskrit among the girl students.

Scholastica Kuzur, a scheduled tribe member, converted to Christianity, retired as Head of the Department of Sanskrit of the Ranchi University and is still engaged in research work. She has specialised in Sanskrit texts dealing with woman-studies right from the Vedic period.

Anupa Devi, a muslim by faith, Usha Devi of the Orion tribe, Dr Nilima Pathak of the Postgraduate Department of Sanskrit, Ranchi University, Nilam Singh of the Jamshedpur Woman's College, Mina Shukla of the Ranchi University have made significant contribution to the spread of Sanskrit studies, specially among girl students.

Role of Non-governmental Organisations

Of the non-governmental organisations devoted to the spread of the Sanskrit-learning the notables are (i) Sanskrit Seva Sangh, Ranchi (ii) Rashtriya Seva Sangh, Dhurva, (iii) Shivashankar Matha Kanko, Katrasgarh (Dhanabad), (iv) Surbharati Vikas Mandal, Rejo (Palamu).

The above resume, in respect of Sanskrit studies in Bihar and Jharkhand, can't lay claim to exhaustiveness in regard to the research-work undertaken, for the simple reason that there has been constraint of space and time. However, the data furnished above may attract the necessity of preparing the theme under a project. There could be omission of some names which may deserve mention in this limited account. The writer could only seek their indulgence as the saying goes:

kṣamasva mama daurbalyaṁ kṣamāsārā hi sādhavaḥ
sarasvatī mahatī mahīyatām

9

Sanskrit Studies in Karnataka

A.V. Nagasampige

THE State of Karnataka is renowned for its Sanskrit studies and education. The kings and rulers of Mysore province and religious pontiffs have been graciously encouraging Sanskrit language studies, education and research in the state.

I would like to highlight the following ten features of Sanskrit studies in Karnataka —

1. Patronage of kings of Mysore
2. Contributions of the heads of the religious institutions (muṭṭs)
3. Sanskrit *mahāpāṭhaśālā*s
4. Sanskrit *pāṭhaśālā*s
5. University postgraduate study centres
6. Sanskrit newspapers
7. Research organisations
8. Books publishing institutions
9. Universities
10. Individuals' contribution on Sanskrit literature.

I would like to enumerate on the above as follows:

Patronage of Kings of Mysore

Credit goes to King Jayachamarajendra Wadayar for getting

the Kannaḍa translation of the entire *Ṛgveda* in 32 volumes published with the assistance of various scholars during the year 1960. In addition to this, the king was also responsible for publishing *Aitareya Āraṇyaka* and 18 popular Purāṇic texts in Kannada. He was a great patron of Sanskrit learning. King of Mysore has also published many philosophical works in Sanskrit edited by eminent scholars of the then Mysore state.

Contributions of the Heads of Religious Institutions (Muṭṭs)

Various religious institutions, heads of Brāhmins, Vīraśaiva and Okkaliga Muṭṭs have been providing facilities to the students from all communities pursuing Sanskrit studies. Sri Bharatitirtha Swamiji of Sringeri, Sri Vishveshatirtha Swamiji of Pejavara Muṭṭ, Sri Satyatmatirtha Swamiji of Uttaradi Muṭṭ, Sri Shivakumara Swamiji of Siddaganga Muṭṭ, Sri Balagangadharanatha Swamiji of Adichunchanagiri Muṭṭ and many other Swamis of different cult have established Sanskrit *pāṭhaśālā*s in Karnataka. All Swamijis of Karnataka *muṭṭ*s have been always encouraging Sanskrit studies and honouring scholars of Sanskrit every year by organising seminars and workshops.

Sanskrit Mahāpāṭhaśālās

After the reign of *mahārājā*s, the Government of Karnataka has established two Sanskrit *mahāpāṭhśālā*s (postgraduate centres) for the studies in Sanskrit. Further, financial grants are being released to nine recognised Sanskrit educational institutions. Here, Sahitya (SSLC+PUC), pre-Vidvat (graduation) and post-Vidvat (postgraduation) studies are being conducted.

RASHRIYA SANSKRIT SANSTHAN, SRINGERI PARISAR

The Dakṣiṇāmnāya Pīṭha, being the southern *pīṭha* of the four *pīṭha*s established by Śrī Śaṅkarācārya is situated in the serene surroundings of Śṛṅgerī. Students are being taught Sanskrit for several decades and the pontiff of the Śṛṅgerī Muṭṭ is providing suitable facilities for the same. Now, the Rashtriya Sanskrit Sansthan of New Delhi, has established its branch here. This institution is serving in a commendable manner by facilitating Sanskrit studies in all the branches of Śāstras and also by providing hostel facilities to the young students, from various states, seeking studies. Further, the *muṭṭ* is providing admirable service in all the three areas of studies namely, education, research and publication.

SIDDHALINGESVARA VEDA-SANSKRIT MAHAPATHASALA (SIDDHAGANGA MUTT)

Established in the year 1917 (about 94 years ago) in Siddhagaṅge, of Tumkur district, the Veda-Sanskrit Mahapathasala, under the able leadership of the pontiff Sri Shivakumara Mahaswamiji has grown by leaps and bounds. This *mahapāṭhaśālā* is presently imparting education both in Sanskrit studies and Alaṁkaraśāstras along with modern education to about 5000 students, without discrimination of caste and creed, with the help of a team consisting of about 25 teachers.

SRI KALABHAIRVARA SANSKRIT VEDA AGAMA VIDYALAYA

Established in the year 1972, this institution has 25 teaching staff in the faculty of Nyāya, Sāhitya, Jyotiṣa, Dharmaśāstra imparting eduction to more than 2,000 students from all communities along with studies in modern education system.

POORNAPRAJNA VIDYAPEETHA SANSKRITA MAHAPATHASALA

Poornaprajna Vidyapeetha Sanskrit Mahapathasala was established by Sri Vishweshatirtha Swamiji of Sri Pejawara Muṭṭ, Udupi in the year 1956 at Bangalore. This institution has produced eminent scholars of national recognition. It has established branches throughout the State of Karnataka and at various centres in India where hundreds of well-trained scholars are imparting education in Śāstras. Having its main centre in Bangalore, the *vidyāpīṭha* is aided by the state government. It has faculty in Navya-Nyāya Śāstra, Dvaita Vedānta, Alaṁkāra, comprising eleven teaching scholars and imparting education to more than 500 students. Sri Vishveshatirtha of Sri Pejawara Muṭṭ, who is the Kulapati of this educational institution, has provided free education and boarding to the students and about forty teaching faculty members engaged in teaching and *pravacana*s (who are not covered by the state salary scheme), are facilitated with salary schemes. This educational institution is producing well-trained eminent students with deep proficiency in Śāstra. It is noteworthy to mention that this *pāṭhaśālā* is preparing a tool-kit for Sanskrit-Hindi machine translation. Research and publication of various *grantha*s like 1. *Gīta Bhāṣya*, 2. *Gīta Tātparya*, 3. *Seṣacandrikā*, 4. *Pramāṇa Paddhati*, 5. *Nyāyamṛta* are published. Various workshops, lectures and scholars meets conducted by this institution have become popular throughout the country.

CHAMARAJENDRA SANSKRIT COLLEGE, BANGALORE

Established in the year 1953 by the state government, this Sanskrit *mahapāṭhaśālā*, has faculty in the field of Literature, Vyākaraṇa, Dvaita Vedānta, Advaita Vedānta, Viśiṣṭādvaita Vedānta, Jainism and study of all the four Vedas. There are 20 teachers in this institution and more than 300 students.

S.M.S.P. SANSKRIT COLLEGE, UDUPI

This Sanskrit *mahapāṭhaśālā* established in the year 1904. It completed its centenary about seven years ago. It has various divisions consisting of Jyotiṣa, Dvaita Vedānta, Nyāya, Sāhitya and other Śāstras. This institution is equipped to educate more than 200 students with special facility to train in the areas of

Vātulāgama, Tantrasārāgama, Veda and Paurohitya. Having conducted a number of *vidvadgoṣṭhīs*, this institution has contributed to the growth of Sanskrit learning in a unique way.

YOGADIPIKA GURUKULA

Sri Vidyadhisha Tirtha of Palimaru near Udupi, founded this educational institution in the year 1989. Education is being imparted in the areas of Nyāya, Vedānta, Paurohitya, Tantra, Āgama and other Śāstras. Though not aided by any grant from the state government, this educational institution is imparting Sanskrit education to hundreds of students and also providing food and shelter for stay. It has about 11 faculty members. The main stream of strength and activity behind this educational institution is the pontiff Sri Vidyadheesha Tirtha Swamiji of Sri Palimaru Muṭṭ.

SRI MAHARAJA SANSKRIT COLLEGE, MYSORE

Being one of the oldest educational institutions, established in the year 1883, this college is noted for carving out great scholars. Being aided by the state government, this institution has produced many distinguished scholars. It has faculty for the four Vedas, Nyāya, Advaita Vedānta, Vyākaraṇa, Pūrva-Mīmāṁsā, Jyotiṣa and Alaṁkāraśāstras. In addition to the above, it imparts education in the field of Śaivāgama, Vaikhānasāgama, Viraśaivāgama, Tantrasārāgama and Jaināgama. This institution which is noted for creating good scholars, is equipped with 20 teaching faculty and more than 300 students.

SRI RAJARAJESHVARI VIDYASAMSTHE

This institution was started by the pontiff of Svarnavalli Muṭṭ, Sonda, Sri Sarvajnendra Sarasvati, in the year 1929. It is presently headed by Sri Gangadharendra Sarasvati who has made immense efforts for its all round development. It has about 13 teachers educating more than 400 students. Education is imparted in the disciplines of literature, Pūrva-Mīmāṁsā, Advaita Vedānta, along with Āgamaśāstra. This institution has grown and got popularised by the present pontiff through vidwat sabhas and workshops, etc.

SRI JAYATIRTHA VIDYAPEETHA

Sri Satyapramoda Tirtha Swamiji of Sri Uttaradi Muṭṭ established this *vidyāpīṭha* in the year 1989, which presently holds more than 200 students and 15 teaching faculty members. Though not aided by any governmental grant, this *vidyāpīṭha* is run with accredited creative leadership of the present pontiff, Sri Satyatmatirtha Swamiji. Imparting education in the areas of Dvaita Vedānta, Vyākaraṇa, Nyāya and higher studies, this *vidyāpīṭha* is noted for conducting oral examinations for its students in Śāstric texts for testing their mastery of a text, eloquence and memory. Handsome cash awards are given to deserving young *paṇḍit*s. *Nyāyasudhā*, a *magnus opus* of Dvaita Vedānta has been published in six volumes by this institution. It has in its custody vast collection of thousands of palm-leaf manuscripts.

VEDAVIGNANA GURUKULA

This *gurulula* which is in Chenenahalli, near Bangalore was established in the year 1997. Apart from giving education in the field of Nyāya and Vedānta Śāstras, it provides for training in the areas of Yoga and Prāṇāyāma through university system of education. Presently it has about 60 students and 12 teachers. With the able stewardship of Ramachandra Bhatt, Kotemane, this institution is maintaining high standards and has brought out more than 17 publications. It has also conducted a number of seminars on important subjects.

Apart from these educational institutions, the institutions such as Veda Dakshinamurthy Veda Bhavana, Sanskrit Vidyalaya of Gokarna, Sanskrit College of Melkote, Sri Mata

Sanskrit Pathashala of Chamagiri in Yellapura, C.L.Y. Sanskrit Pathashala in Komaleshwaranagara Dharwada, Male Mahadeshwara Sanskrit Pathashala, Gadag, are contributing good service in the field of Sanskrit education.

Sanskrit Pāṭhaśālās

To facilitate studies from Prathama (1st standard level) to Sahitya (SSLC level) 295 schools have been opened in various *tāluka*s and villages. 235 schools are serving the development of Sanskrit studies by obtaining grants-in-aid. These institutions are functioning under the jurisdiction of the newly-commenced Sanskrit University.

University Postgraduate Study Centres

Additionally, the universities in Bangalore, Mysore, Dharwad, Shimoga, Mangalore and Gulburga have postgraduate Sanskrit departments with facilities for higher research. These universities are contributing to Sanskrit education and research in a remarkable way.

Sanskrit Newspapers

The daily newspaper in Sanskrit *Sudharma Patrika*, despite financial constraints, Sri Varadaraja Iyengar and his son Sri Sampath are running with devotion to Sanskrit. *Sambhāṣaṇasandeśaḥ* — the monthly journal of Aksharam is well known in India and abroad and it has more than 5,000 subscribers. The *Dvāsuparṇā* of Dvaita Vedānta Studies and Research Foundation – the half-yearly magazine, *Mādhavī* of Poornaprajna Samshodhana Mandiram are worth mentioning.

Research Organisations

DVAITA PHILOSOPHY RESOURCE CENTRE, MANIPAL

The Dvaita Philosophy Resource Centre is within the Manipal Centre for European Studies of Manipal University.

Manipal Centre for European Studies (MCES) was established in December 2009 with funding from the European Union. The mandate of the centre was to offer a multidisciplinary platform for discussions on various matters that concern human development in general, leading to a mutually beneficial association between Indian and the European academia.

As the strength of India lies in its philosophical traditions, it was proposed that it be offered to the European counterparts, along with other programmes of the centre. Manipal being a part of the temple-town of Udupi, the citadel of Dvaita philosophy, it was natural that special focus is provided for Dvaita studies. It was also the commitment of Manipal University to preserve the spiritual heritage of this region, which led to the establishment of Dvaita Philosophy Resource Centre (DPRC).

This institution was established in December 2009. Ph.D. a research programme (with financial support to select candidates) course is prevalent.

Gītābhāṣya and *Gītātātparya* of Madhva have been translated by Vinay P. into English and are under review before going for print. This will be published very soon by Manipal University.

Pramāṇapaddhati of Jayatirtha has been translated by Srinivas Varakhedi and it is published recently.

ACADEMY OF SANSKRIT RESEARCH, MELKOTE

Melkote is hailed as a major centre of Sanskrit learning. For over 1,000 years it is known as *Jñānamaṇḍapa*. The saint philosopher Śrī Rāmānujācārya, the founder of the school of Viśiṣṭādvaita philosophy had stayed here in Melkote for nearly 14 years. Since then, Melkote has been an advanced centre for Sanskrit learning in Viśiṣṭādvaita philosophy. In the backdrop of this, the Government of Karnataka, way back in 1976, initiated the establishment of a Sanskrit Research Institute in Melkote. Thus, this institution came into inception in April 1977.

Under computer-based Sanskrit teaching tools, a project entitled Śabdārtha has been successfully completed; "Saṁvit" is another computer-based project completed successfully; as a result a Sanskrit learning CD for the beginners has been brought out under the title *Samskritavinoda*.

The Academy has so far brought out more than 100 titles in Kannada, Sanskrit and English. In its research publication programme it has completed Viśiṣṭādvaitakośa project on lexicon of philosophical terms of Viśiṣṭādvaita brought out in 10 volumes and nine works of Śrī Rāmānuja. Other publications of this institute that have been popular are — *Melkote Through the Ages (MTA)*, *Science and Technology in Ancient India*, *Śrībhāṣyam of Rāmānuja* and Kannada editions of Upaniṣads.

RASHTRAKAVI GOVIND PAI SAMSHODHANA KENDRA, UDUPI

Rashtrakavi Govind Pai Samshodhana Kendra was established in 1965. In this institution, 8 teachers are working and 12 students studying. Under the Tulu Lexicon Project (1979-97) an encyclopedic dictionary on the local language — Tulu (which is one of the Dravidian languages) was compiled.

Bunts in History and Culture (2006-10) : This volume was prepared after an elaborate field survey of Guthu houses by Surendra Rao of Mangalore University. Apart from these, more than 63 publications were published by this institution and national as well as International seminars were also organised.

ORIENTAL RESEARCH INSTITUTE, MYSORE

The Oriental Research Institute is a pioneer organisation established in the nineteenth century by the kings of Mysore for preservation, research and publication of oriental manuscripts in different languages. This institute was established in 1891.

More than 210 books in Sanskrit and Kannada has so far been published under the aegis of the institute. An international seminar on "Kauṭilya's Arthaśastra" was conducted from 13 to 16 June 2002. Four days symposium on "Science in India" was organised from 21 to 24 April 2008. Forty-five days workshop for 'Teaching and Training Scholars' in editing of manuscripts was conducted from 25 March to 7 May 2010.

DVAITA VEDĀNTA STUDIES & RESEARCH FOUNDATION, BANGALORE

Dvaita Vedanta Studies & Research Foundation, Bangalore, was established in 1983 to organise advanced study and research in Indian philosophy, particularly Dvaita Vedānta philosophy of Śrī Madhvācārya, Pūrva-Mīmāṁsā, Vaiśeṣika and Sāṁkhya. It also undertakes the collection of manuscripts, digitisation of the same and storing them in C.D. form. It publishes a newsletter called "Dvasuparna". Eight research scholars are working here. Fifty palm-leaf manuscripts and 200 paper manuscripts are collected in its library.

Six students are registered each year for Vidyavaridhi (Ph.D) degree of Sampoornananda Sanskrit University, Varanasi.

More than 50 texts have been published by this institute.

Inter-disciplinary seminars were organised on the following topics:

1. Epistemology of Dvaita Vedanta,
2. Hermaneutics of Dvaita Vedanta,
3. Environment in Purāṇas,
4. Trees and Plants Associated with the Rituals and their Impact on Health,
5. Contribution of Birds and Insects to Human Welfare,

6. Mānasollasā — An Encyclopaedic work on art, architecture and culture.

SAMSKRITA SHODHA SAMSTHANA, SIRSI

Samskrita Shodha Samsthana was established to highlight manifold gems lying in the vast and deep ocean of Sanskrit literature, which is, with its variety and depth, unparalleled in the entire range of world-oriented studies. To achieve this end, Shodha Samsthana is arranging research-based national and state level seminars where young and old scholars assemble and interact with each other. Secondly, the Samsthana is helping research scholars to bring to light their research publications. This Samsthana was established in 1996.

Till now, as many as 17 such research publications have been released. Eight national seminars and one state-level seminar have been successfully organised.

More than 18 texts have been published by the Samsthana. Some of them are: 1. *Madhvācārya's Contribution to Indian thought*, 2. *Vadirāja: The Dvaita Poet: Great but Ignored*, 3. *Tattvamasi in Brahmasūtraśāṅkarabhāṣya*, 4. *Sex Education: Indian View*, 5. *Filial Love in Pratimānāṭaka*.

POORNAPRAJNA SAMSHODHANA MANDIRAM, BANGALORE

The Poornaprajna Samshodhana Mandiram is a brain-child of Sri Vishveshatirtha Swamiji of Sri Pejavara Muṭṭ, Udupi, and was founded and established by him in 1988. This pioneering Sanskrit research institute aims to enable the serious academic study among those interested in Sanskrit literature, as a part of upholding the vision of Swamiji to preserve and propagate the rich cultural and textual heritage of Indian philosophy.

The Ministry of Human Resource Development (MHRD) of the Government of India recognised PPSM as a model research institute, and included it in the prestigious group of the Rashtriya Sanskrit Sansthan (Deemed University) in 1994.

So far, the institution has published rare and valuable unpublished manuscripts on different branches of Indian philosophy. Ninety-five printed works are readily available for sale. These editions have been appreciated by the national and international scholars.

The PPSM organises special lecture programmes of national and international scholars. It also conducted workshop programmes on Advaita Vedānta Paribhāṣā, Viśiṣṭadvaitanavanīta and Dvaitanavanīta in 2007. For the last 4 years workshops on Nyāyāmṛta and Advaitasiddhi were regularly organised.

So far this institution has organised more than 18 seminars on Indian economics, polity,Vedānta, Vāstuśāstra, Āyurveda and other branches of Sanskrit-based knowledge systems and successfully completed Dvaita Vedānta Kośa project.

Prajña — A research journal (annually) and half-yearly newsletter *Madhvi,* are being published regularly every year.

Books Publishing Institutions

VISHVA MADHWA MAHA PARISHAT, BANGALROE

Founded by pontiff of Sri Uttaradi Muṭṭ, Sri Satyatmathirta Swamiji, this institution is striving for more than two decades in the field of publishing the hitherto unpublished texts for the advancement of Sanskrit. Having established units throughout the country, it is imparting Sanskrit education and pravachanas.

AKHILA BHARATA MADHWA MAHAMANDALA

This institution which was established about 50 years ago, by Sri Vishvesha Thirta Swamiji of Sri Pejawara Mutt, published for the first time the Sarva Moola Grantha based on the palm-leaf writings of Sri Hrushikeshathirtha of the thirteenth century, edited by Vidya Vachaspathi Sri Bannanje Govindacharya. This institution is also accredited with the pride of publishing Kannada translation of *Sarva Mūla Grantha* of Madhvācārya. The contribution of this institution towards Sanskrit language and publication is unparallel.

MADHVASIDHANTA SAMVARDHAKA SABHA, UDUPI

Established about 55 years ago by Sri Vidyamanya Thirtharu of Sri Palimaru Muṭṭ, this institution has printed and published the *Daśaprakaraṇa Grantha* of Madhvācārya based on the unpublished palm-leaf writings. It is worth mentioning here that this institution is conducting Vidvat Sabha every year at the national level by inviting various scholars from different parts of the country with the aim of publicising Madhva-thought.

ADHYATMA PRAKASHA KARYALAYA, HOLENARASIPUARA

Founded by Sri Sachidanandendra Saraswati Swamiji of Holenarasipura, about 50 years back, this institution has translated and published various *grantha*s from Sanskrit to Kannada and English. Various Vidvat Sabhas proceedings conducted by this institution have been recorded and the gists have been published along with publishing of research works in a highly commendable manner. Swamiji wrote new commentaries on philosophical texts and translated *Śāṅkarabhāṣya* and *Śrībhāṣya* into Kannada.

TATTVA SAMSHODHANA SAMSAT, UDUPI

Having been founded by Sri Vidyamanya Thirtha of Sri Palimaru Muṭṭ, this institution has published, *Tātparyanirṇaya*, *Upaniṣadbhāṣya*, *Viṣṇusahasranāma* and others with the commentaries of Bennanje Govindacarya and unpublished commentaries. So far, more than 25 research publications have been published by this institution.

SAMSKRITA BHARATI AKSHARAM, BANGALORE

This institution is striving hard to propagate Sanskrit language study not only in Karnataka but also nationally and internationally and has gained immense popularity. With the publication of monthly magazine brought out by this organisation by the name of *Samskrita Sambhāṣaṇa Sandeśaḥ*, which has several thousand readers across the globe, is introducing worldwide the richness of Sanskrit language. At the level of village, *tālukas* and districts, this institution has established Sanskrit language as a medium of communication through speaking and counselling. The publications and CDs brought out by the institution have gained popularity.

Universities

KARNATAKA SANSKRIT UNIVERSITY, BANGALORE

To promote learning of Sanskrit in the state, Karnataka Sanskrit University, Bangalore was founded in the year 2010. Government Maharaja Sanskrit College, Mysore, Sri Chamarajendra Sanskrit College, Bangalore are the constituent colleges and there are 15 affiliated colleges. Prathama, Kavya, Sạhitya, Vidvat-Madhyama and Vidvat-Uttama courses are being taught. 560 *pāṭhaśālā* teachers and 184 college lectures are working under this university. 10263 students in Prathamā, 4212 students in Kāvya, 700 in Sahitya, 342 in Vidvat-Madhyama and 171 students in Vidvat-Uttama are studying here.

Quarterly and half-yearly journals are published by the university. The founder vice-chancellor of this university, Mallepuram G. Venkatesh has taken initiatives for its over-all growth.

VYASA VIVEKANANDA YOGA ANUSANDHANA KENDRA, BANGALORE

This000 institute of Karnataka, known as Vivekananda Yoga Visva-vidyalaya, has gained international fame. This university is not only concentrating on Yoga but also is focusing on Indian knowledge systems. Teaching of *aṣṭāṅgayoga* and conducting workshops at national and international levels are its special features.

VYAASA MADHWA SEVA PRATISHTAANA

Vyaasa Madhwa Seva Pratishtaana is a trust formed mainly for the purpose of disseminating knowledge on Dvaita philosophy. It is a non-profit organisation. Publishing books on Madhva philosophy is its current principal activity. It has published till date eighty-seven books in several languages, including Sanskrit, Kannada, Telugu, Tamil and English. The Trust was founded by Vyasanakere Prabhanjanacharya, an eminent Sanskrit scholar, with many awards and titles to his credit.

Individuals' Contribution on Sanskrit Literature

In Karnataka, many scholars produced creative literature like an institution and it is needless to say that the effort is unimaginable. Jaggu Vakula Bhushana Iyengar, Galagali Ramacharya, Galagali Pandharinathacharya, Shatavadhani R. Ganesh, Vidvan H.V. Nagaraja Rao, Ariyar Rama Sharma, S. Jagannath and many more scholars of Karnataka published valuable books in Sanskrit and highlighted the important contribution of Sanskrit.

10

Sanskrit Studies in Kerala

P.C. Muraleemadhavan

SANSKRIT studies in Kerala had its beginning right from the early centuries of the Christian era. The land, better known as *karmabhūmi* with stress on ritualistic aspect before the emergence of Śrī Śaṅkara, has contributed much to the Mīmāṁsā system both Kaumārila and Bhāṭṭa schools. King Hariścandra of Puraḷi province in the West Malabar is credited to be the promulgator of the system as mentioned by Uddaṇḍa Sāstry (fifteenth century CE) as mentioned in his message poem *Kokila Sandeśa.*

Bhavadāsa, as mentioned in the *Ślokavārttika* of Kumārilabhaṭṭa is one of the earlier writers. The tradition was further developed by the family of Payyūr Bhaṭṭas — six reputed scholars named — Ṛṣi I — Parameśvara I up to Ṛṣi 3 — Parameśvara-3.

Thereafter the period of Śrī Śaṅkara saw a phenomenal growth to the academic aspect of the Vedānta system starting from Advaita and later resulting in the development of various schools of studies and establishment of centres of Sanskrit learning. Other Śāstras too had their firm footings in the land, for instance in the field of Vyākaraṇa. This popular branch saw its culmination in the substantial contribution of Nārāyaṇa Bhaṭṭa, the author of *Prakriyāsarvasva* and *Apāṇinīyaprāmāṇya-sādhana,* wherein he establishes the supremacy of other systems of non-Pāṇiniyan grammar. Then there were several traditional royal families and brahmin houses who promoted the movement further, like the royal family of Zamurin, Kotuṅṅalūr and Kiḷḷimaṅgalam Namboodiri family.

The contribution of Kerala to the connected Sanskrit literature cannot be under rated. The likes of Pūrṇasarasvatī, Śivarāma and others in pure literature, Śabaraswāmī in Vedic literature and the four disciples of Śaṅkara are simply outstanding among the pre-Independence contributors. The works like *Saundaryalaharī* and *Śivānandalaharī* and the rest of Stotra literature and *Kṛṣṇakarnāmṛta* and *Nārāyaṇīya* of Melpputtūr Nārāyaṇa Bhaṭṭa deserve special attention. *Nārāyaṇīya* became very popular because of its charm, in respect of *śabda*, *artha* and *bhāva*.

Even the selection of metres is done with the utmost care and propriety to make them the best *vyañjaka*s of the theme.

In the theatrical aspect, the two dramas of Kulaśekhara — *Tapatīvamvaraṇa* and *Subhadrādhanañjaya* provided a firm footing for the histrionic art and are still surviving through the representation of Kūṭiyāṭṭam dramas whereas, even the Bhāsa plays were adopted to Kerala stage.

The discovery of Bhāsa plays is very significant. It is really a solid contribution of Kerala. Most of the Bhāsa plays were enacted in the Kūṭiyāṭṭam theatre of Kerala.

It is remarkable that the stage manuals, both in the form of *Āṭṭaprakāra* and *Kramadīpika* of Bhāsa plays were unearthed from Kerala only. These facts show the close affinity of Bhāsa plays with the Kerala culture.

The first edition of the *Arthaśāstra* was brought out by Śyāma Śāstry based on the manuscript he discovered from Kerala. The first edition and publication of *Abhinavabhāratī* was also brought to light based on a manuscript unearthed from Kerala.

After the Independence Kerala state saw a substantial growth in all branches of literature arts and Śāstras.

It is K. Kunjunni Raja, who for the first time wrote a work on *Contribution of Kerala to Sanskrit Literature*. It was his doctoral thesis submitted at the University of Madras and prepared under the supervision of C. Kunhan Raja, the illustrious scholar and the great disciple of A.A. Macdonell. Afterwards, several scholars wrote books on the same line, from different states taking K. Kunjunni Raja as the first and the best model in the particular genre. It is clear that Raja paved the way and later writers accepted it wholeheartedly.

It was a fruitful effort made very effectively and seriously and as a result of which we could get very valuable information, even on minor works in Sanskrit, from every nook and corner of India, through the later writers.

Certainly, prior to Kunjunni Raja, there were historians who wrote *Keralīya Sāhitya Caritram* and *Keralīya Saṁskṛta Sāhitya Caritram*. The scholars like Ulloor S. Parameswara Iyer, Vaṭakkumkur Raja Raja Varma and K. Rama Pisharoti, who were in the field, lacked comprehensiveness, proper documentation, in-depth observation, research oriented approach and an eye for important findings. Hence, Raja has been considered as a pioneer of this genre. Later several scholars like Sriramamurthy (Andhra) C.S. Sundaram (Tamil Nadu) S.C. Banarjee (Kashmir, Bengal and Bihar) S. Venkitasubrahmania Iyer (Kerala) etc. wrote some credible works from those states. We got several doctoral theses as a result of much disciplined research after the publication of Kunjunni Raja's book in 1958. The thesis of Raja stands unrevised, simply because of the authenticity of his findings. The later researchers built up superstructures on the foundation laid by him. Among the many centres, where Sanskrit flourished with an increasing enthusiasm, Kerala is one of the most important states. But it is not so well known. We know very well that an intensive study of the development of Sanskrit literature in any particular locality is a prerequisite to the compilation of a complete history of Sanskrit literature of India.

The etymology and the exact significance of the term Kerala is still a matter of controversy. But it is accepted by a majority of scholars that Kera related to Cera by which this region was known in Tamil literature. Thereby history of Kerala like other states in India, is completely shrouded in obscurity. This small state was divided into many tiny kingdoms, but the central political powers rested with three powerful monarchs; that of Travancore, Cochin and Malabar. All these small units finally merged in the Indian Union and in 1956 the United Kerala emerged as an integral political unit of India.

The name Kerala appeared for the first time in the edict of the emperor Aśoka. *Mahābhāṣya* of Patañjalī and *Raghuvaṁśa* of Kālidāsa possess descriptions of Kerala by name. The words Malabar and Malayālam were also used as synonyms of Kerala by several classical writers and historians. Later, Malayālam came to be used for the regional language of Kerala.

According to the popular traditions preserved in words like the Keraḷolpatti, Kerala was reclaimed by Paraśurāma from the sea; and presented to the brāhmaṇas to organise a theocratic government. Whether we believe it or not, it is a fact that Nambūtiris, though numerically small, were at the top of the spiritual and social hierarchy and were well versed in the art of war and peace. The peculiar system of marrying lower caste women by young Nambūtiri brāhmaṇas also helped, unlike in other parts of India, to propagate Sanskrit studies among people of lower strata in the society. The literary patronage of Kerala kings and princes attracted scholars even from outside Kerala. Many scholars and poets like Uddaṇḍa Śāstrī left their birthplaces and came to Kerala and settled down under the patronage of several regional princes. But we could not come across a single instance of scholars going out from Kerala in search of royal patronage. This shows the scholastic fertility of this small state as far as the liteary and intellectual cultivation are concerned.

There were 18 Sabhāmaṭhas established in various parts of Kerala, that were equal to universities. Various Śāstras and Darśanas were taught in-depth, in all these centres.

The women community and the people belonging to the lower castes were allowed to study Sanskrit in Kerala. Many of them matured as authors of several authoritative works in Śāstras, original literary works and even wrote laudable commentaries on Śāstras and Kāvyas.

It is very strange that such a voluminous literature pertaining to Sanskrit and belonging to Kerala is not fully exposed to the outsiders. Hence the endeavours of scholars like Kunjunni Raja are of great help.

Despite the overall fall in the standards especially in the field of śāstraic studies, Sanskrit continued to flourish in Kerala in the literary domain. The influence of the Western literature and the development of the vernacular languages have in a way enriched the Sanskrit literary field during the last four decades. Writers who had imbibed the traditional pattern had begun their writings in the old forms, but have gradually shifted to the modern genres of composition. Even those who began with Mahākāvyas, dramas, lyrics, message poems and Stotras, gradually shifted to more modern genres like short stories, serious essays, metre-free verses and other varieties. This is mainly due to the publication of journals from Kerala as well as from other parts of the country.

After Independence, the people of India became more and more conscious of their own paternal heredity, patriotism and nationalism. As a result of the increasing fertility of these ideals, there have been produced, in the soil of our nation, several original Sanskrit works of repute as well as critical editions and studies of important Sanskrit texts, during the post-Independence period.

Mahākāvyas

It seems that the twentieth-century writers of Kerala took to the composition of Mahākāvyas as a prestigious literary effort. As a result we have quite a good number of standard Mahākāvyas which have won Academy awards for their authors and brought glory to the language. It is a matter of pride that in a single decade that is in 1960s, the state of Kerala could produce five Mahākāvyas in Sanskrit. These are:

1. The *Śrīnārāyaṇavijaya* by K. Balarama Panickar, on the life and teachings of Sri Narayana Guru, the famous philosopher and social reformer of Kerala (published, Trivandrum, May 1971).
2. The *Kṛstubhāgavata* by P.C. Devassia, on the life and teachings of Jesus Christ (published, Trivandrum, in March, 1977),
3. The *Keralodaya* by K.N. Ezhuthachan which is of a historical nature (published in June, 1977)
4. *Navabhāratam* by Mutukulam Sreedhar, which is also a historical Mahākāvya (published, August, 1978) and
5. The *Viśvabhānu* by P.K. Narayana Pillai, on the life and message of Swami Vivekananda (published, May 1979). A brief content of each of these Mahākāvyas is reproduced below, in this context.

ŚRĪNĀRĀYAṆAVIJAYA

This *mahākāvya* in 21 *sarga*s with 1500 *śloka*s deals with the life and teachings of Sri Narayana, an ascetic and social reformer of Kerala who lived in the last part of the nineteenth century and first part of twentieth century. It is a *mahākāvya* which does not strictly conform to the rules of the artificial poem laid down by rhetoricians like Daṇḍin. It may perhaps be called a biographical *kāvya*. The hero of the poem is portrayed in all the solemnity and dignity usually associated with such holy personages. His teachings, especially on the unity of religions and the brotherhood of men, are clearly exposed and expounded in different cantos. Sri Narayana's oft-quoted message — "one community, one religion and one God for all" — has been ably interpreted in canto XIX. As a measure of relief from the tedium characteristic of deductive and philosophic discourses, the author employs natural description abounding in figures of various kinds, thus enhancing the beauty of the work.

The life and teachings of the Gurudeva are well depicted in 21 *sargas* in this *mahākāvya*. In the first two *sargas* the parents of Gurudeva and his holy birth, education, etc. are described. The 20th and 21st *sargas* are fully devoted to depict the theory of one religion, and the establishment of the Sri Narayana Dharmasangha and the *mahāsamādhi* of the Guru.

Though the *mahākāvya* is pervaded by the sentiment of *śānta*, the description of the lamentations of the people on the *samādhi* of the Guru is full of pathos. The author's profound knowledge of the Vedānta and logic entitles him to be the true interpretor of the teachings of the Gurudeva. The simplicity of language, the lucidity of the style and the felicity of expression of the poem make its reading pleasant.

KERALODAYA

K.N. Ezhuthachan composed a historical *mahākāvya* called *Keralodaya* in 21 cantos containing 2500 verses in a variety of classical metres. The history of Kerala from its traditional origin at the hands of the sage Paraśurāma up to the formation of the modern state, covering a period of nearly 2,000 years form the subject matter. The theme — a mixture of legend and history — is significantly arranged into five sections called *mañjarīs* such as *Svapna, Smṛti, Aitihya, Bodha* and *Citra*. The Marxian bias of the author is evident from the last cantos of the work which deal with the history of the last four decades; the struggle for freedom and consequent events. As a poetry the work occupies a high standard and it naturally won an award from the Sahitya Akademi.

KṚSTUBHĀGAVATA

P.C. Devassia, a Christian scholar has composed a *mahākāvya* called *Kṛstubhāgavata,* giving a complete account of the life and teachings of Jesus Christ in 33 cantos commensurate with the life span of the prophet. The familiarity of the author with the Hindu mythology and philosophy has added a rare value to the composition which won him a prestigious award from the Sahitya Akademi. All the important events in the life of Christ are described here in a chaste and lucid style of classical poets. As in other Sanskrit epic poems, one can see, not very long descriptions in *Kṛstubhāgavata*. The holy temple in Jerusalem, Mount Carmel, sunrise and sunset, rivers, beautiful landscapes — all these are portrayed quite attractively and this adds vividity to the general appreciation of the work. The description of the sunset immediately after the famous sermon on the Mount is so touching and relevant that it remains one of the purple patches in the whole poem.

Having drunk deep from the sermon which wanted man to renounce all sorts of mundane pleasures and pursue the path towards spiritual values of life, the resplendent sun felt great satiety and found himself obsessed with the worldliness. He turns out to be philosophical and clads himself in saffron coloured cloaks of humility and then enters a huge cave for meditation and retreat. The poet seems to achieve his purpose by rendering Jesus as the most illuminating person before whom all other manifestations of power, wisdom and knowledge become meek. All seekers of knowledge and truth approach him and remain spellbound wondering at the fathomless depth of his divine insight into the human life. The figure of speech used in the above-quoted lines speaks for the poet's unswerving search for the very meaning of the Christ's life. This gem of a poetic work is embellished very beautifully with similar literary ornaments. We come across several contexts in the *kāvya* where the Christian concepts are moving hand in hand with illustrations from the Hindu texts. It is an unprecedented confluence of the East and the West. The poem makes regular references to Śrī Kṛṣṇa, Śrī Rāma, Vasiṣṭha, Arundhatī, Kaṇva, Buddha, Viṣṇu, Kaṁsa, Rāvaṇa, Brahmā and so on.

VIŚVABHĀNU — DHARMASĀGARA

P.K. Naryana Pillai, has the distinction of composing two great *mahākāvyas*, the *Viśvabhānu* and the *Dharmasāgara*. The first one deals with the life of Swami Vivekananda in 21 cantos and 555 stanzas. The hero is not only portrayed as a great spiritual leader but also the first and the foremost of the *karmayogins* that India had ever produced. The author has drawn his ideas from the authentic accounts of the great saint written by a host of authorities like Romain Rolland. The content of the *Dharmasāgara* is related to the life of the great master *Śrī Rāmakṛṣṇa Paramahaṁsa* in 18 cantos.

NAVABHĀRATA-ŚRĪVIDYĀDHIRĀJAVIJAYA-NĀYAKĀBHARAṆA (1978)

A modern scholar named Multikulam Sridhar has composed three *mahākāvyas* in Sanskrit. His *Navabhāratam* in 18 cantos deals with the story of the modern period of the Indian history. The struggle for independence and the story after the historic event form the central theme. The roles of the architects of modern India, like Mahatma Gandhi, Motilal Nehru,

Jawaharlal Nehru, Subhas Chandra Bose and others are well brought out. The work proves that Sanskrit can very well be an effective medium to deal even with modern events.

His *Śrīvidyādhirājavijaya* in 19 cantos purports to be a biography of Vidyādhirāja alias Caṭṭampisvāmi, philosopher and a modern social reformer of Kerala who joined hands with Sri Narayana Guru. Contemporary dignitaries are also referred to by the poet since they had maintained contacts with the hero of the poem.

The *Nāyakābharaṇa* is the third *mahākāvya* of the poet and it consists of 19 cantos dealing with the history of the state of Travancore. The eighteenth-century ruler of Travancore, King Mārtaṇḍavarma and his exploits form the central theme and his conflicts with the chieftains of the eight prominent families (Eṭṭuvīṭṭil Piḷḷamār) of the state provide ample scope for a dramatic depiction in the poem.

BHĀRATENDU

Bhāratendu is a *mahākāvya* written by Vasudeva Bhaṭṭatiri on the life and message of Mahatma Gandhi with a beautiful style with simple and sweet metres. The poet depicts dramatic scenes from the life of the hero in a most touching manner. The author never followed the traditional style of writing *mahākāvya* as suggested by Daṇḍin. But he never lacks the high flight of imagination and the capacity of flowery depiction.

K.P. Narayana Pisharoti edited and commented the illustrious *mahākāvya* in Sanskrit — *Rāmacarita* in 40 cantos during 1980s. It is a joint authorial work by Vidwan Elaya Tampuran and Cheriya Kochuṇṇi Tampuran that belongs to the nineteenth century CE.

Drama, Dramaturgy and Rhetorics

The twentieth-century dramas differ much from the traditional concepts both in their theme and structure.

About 40 dramas, worthy of being enacted on the modern stage have already been published. Most of them were represented on the stage during the days of the Sanskrit Festival celebrated in different parts of the state. The originality of the theme was always there. Contemporary incidents too found acceptance at the hands of resourceful writers, for instance, there was a tragedy in which several people lost their lives by drinking adulterated liquor. The local government was forced to take action and a public outcry followed. The incident was dramatised under the title *Madirāviṣāda* by Lakshmi Narayana Sharma. Dramas from the local vernacular were also often translated into Sanskrit. Another interesting series of plays was introduced and these could be presented on stage in just 20 minutes duration.

While the traditional rules of dramaturgy are slowly discarded, novel themes from contemporary literature and history are being adopted effectively. Among the modern plays the following may be noteworthy. Krishnachandra (Āttur Krishna Pisharoti) has composed three plays having seven acts each. These are : *Rakṣāpuruṣaka, Samanvaya* and *Yogollāsita*; all drawing their themes from the medieval history of Kerala. V. Krishnan Tampi has composed 8 plays with themes embracing the Indian history, Kerala history and social life in general. Purāṇic themes too are dealt with by him giving a new twist to their outlook. His works are not even generally divided into acts in their strict sense are as follows: *Ajñātavāsa, Dharmāsaya Sūkṣmā Gatiḥ, Draupadīvijaya, Lalitā, Dhruvacarita, Pratikriyā, Vanajyotsnā*, and *Peṭikasaṁnyāsī.* These were written by the author for the purpose of being enacted during the annual Sanskrit College day celebrations. Steeped in the cultural heritage of India, the author has imbibed the Western thoughts and manners sufficiently. This is reflected in his works in a fine socio-cultural blend. The drama *Piñchāñjalam* of P.C. Vasudevan Elayath is a beautiful dramatic piece depicting the story of the origin of the *Kṛṣṇanāṭṭam* theatre of Sanskrit.

T. Ganapati Sastri has composed a short play called *Mahāvivaśāntiyam* based on an English theme. The *Gairvāṇīvijayam* of A.R. Rajarajavarma deals with the progress of Sanskrit education in the state. While the above-mentioned plays show some progressive outlook, stereotyped plays were also composed by some writers drawing on the Purāṇic themes and embracing the genres like *bhāva*s and allegorical plays. The *Ekabhārata* with four acts, composed by Bharata Pisharoti was published during this time. The musical Sanskrit plays like *Santānagopāla* of Devaki Amma, regularly broadcast by the All India Radio appeared during the 1980s. Amaravāṇī programme of the All India Radio, Calicut, after 1950, broadcast of several authentic and creative works in Sanskrit written by veteran scholars of Kerala.

K.P. Narayana Pisharoti translated the *Nāṭyaśāstra* into the Malayalam in three volumes. He has also written several works connected to dramaturgy and Kūṭiyāṭṭam. His work *Kūṭṭampalaṇṇalil* gives valid and authentic information about the Kūṭiyāṭṭam theatre. He has edited several Āṭṭaprakārams and Kramadīpikās which are stage manuals of Sanskrit dramas in Kūṭiyāṭṭam theatre. The *gurukula*s of Kūṭiyāṭṭam known as Ammannūr, Moozhikkulam, Māṇi and Painkulam are still in the mainstream to enact Sanskrit dramas in Kūṭiyāṭṭam styles. Hundreds of students undergo training for several years at all these centres. The founder *ācārya*s of these *gurukula*s are Mani Madhava Chakyar, Ammannur Madhava Chakyar, Painkulam Rama Chakyar and Moozhikulam Kochukutta Chakyar who were doyens in the field of drama. Their great services in the field are being preserved and carried further by their brilliant disciples like Usha Nangiar, Margi Madhu and Cheriya Rama Chakyar. Kerala Kalamandalam became a great centre of classical arts after the inception of Kūṭiyāṭṭam by replanting this temple art from some of the great temples of Kerala.

Literary critics in Sanskrit and Malayalam belonging to this period contributed considerably to the field of studies in Alaṁkāraśāstra and Nāṭyaśāstra. The names of N.V. Krishna Warrier, N.P. Shankunni Nair, P.C. Vasudevan Elyath, K.P. Narayan Pisharoti, M. Leelavathi, M. Sreedhara Menon, N.V.P. Unithiri, K. Kunjunni Raja, C. Rajendran, N. Gopala Panicker, etc. are all worthy of special mention.

The renaissance of Kr̥ṣṇanāṭṭam theatre of Guruvayur Devaswam took place after the intervention of P.C. Vasudevan Elyath, in the form of translation of Kr̥ṣṇagīti and the techniques of Abhinaya of Kr̥ṣṇāṭṭam. A revitalisation of the theatre could be achieved by the scholarly studies of P.C. Vasudevan Elyath in this regard.

Other Significant Works

Apart from the above-mentioned five important *mahākāyas*, certain other poems in the mode of *mahākāvya* came down to us from Kerala, after Independence. Among those works, the most important is *Tīrthapādapurāṇam* by A.V. Sankaran, which is serially being brought out in the *Saṁskārakeraḷam* journal of the cultural department of the Government of Kerala. The work is on the life history of the famous social reformer Sri Chaṭṭampi Swāmikal of Kerala who lived in the last century. A.V. Sankaran's other original work in Sanskrit is the *Maṇikaṇṭhīyam Campūkāvya* which deals with the glory of the god Śāsta of Śabarimala, the famous place of pilgrimage in Kerala.

Among other creative works serially published in the *Saṁskārakeraḷam,* mention may be made of the *mahātyāgī,* on the life of Jesus Christ, written by O.M. Avara and the *Viśudhanabicaritam* on the life and teachings of the Prophet Mohammed, by K.S. Nilakantan Unni, both expounding the teachings of the Christianity and Islam respectively.

The *Vedāntavedana* by Tiruvalla K.G. Kesava Panicker in three *taraṅgas* on the glory of the Vedānta philosophy and the *Saṁskṛtamāhātmyam* by K.P. Narayanan Pisharoti written in the praise of Sanskrit language and containing 110 verses are the two works which are noteworthy because of their peculiar contents. Among the *stotras* published in this journal mention may be made of the *Śrīgaṇeśapañcaka* by Tulasīvanam (R. Ramachandran Nair), *Harinalaya Mahādevapañcaka* by Sāhitya pañcānanan (P.K. Narayana Pillai), on the deity "Śiva of Ettumanur temple". Tulasīvanam has also written and published a beautiful *stotra* called *Sivastavamañjarī* on the god Paramaśiva.

The other works independently published and noteworthy among the original works produced in this period are the *Yeśucarita* which is a prose work in five chapters on the life of Jesus Christ (Ernakulam, 1957) and the *Girigītā* by K.P. Urumeese, a poem dealing with the sermon on the mound (Trivandrum) based on the Holy Bible. The *Nayāgrāprapāṭaḥ* by N.V. Krishna Warrier (N.B.S. Kottayam, 1976) is an interesting short poem on secular theme Niagra waterfall, in 32 beautiful *ślokas* and the *Nāyakopākhyānam* by Girimūlapuram (K. Maheswaran Nair) deals with the social history of the Nair community of Kerala (Service Books, Changanacheri, 1976).

Smt. Sridevikutty Tampuratti of Tiruvaṇṇūr Putiya Kovilakam has four works to her credit, namely *Naiṣadha Bhāmāpariṇaya, Bhāgavatacampū* and *Madurāpurīvilāsa.* V.S.V. Guruswami Sastrikal, has written *Nalodanta* a short *kāvya* on the story of Nala and Damayantī, during the period. Achuta Potuval, a great Sanskrit scholar in Kerala wrote a work called *Mātṛparidevana* which reflects on the past glories of India and laments on the present degeneration (Trippunittura, 1961); V.K.K. Gurukkal in his *Śrīgurugītā,* a short poem of 200 verses gives an account of the life and works of the late Vāgbhaṭānanda, a Swamiyar in Kerala (Tellicheri, 1977);

Devaki Menon wrote a short work called *Śrīśāradādevī-caritasaṁgraha* on the life and teachings of Śrīśāradā Devī (Sriramakrishna Asramam, Madras, 1978); Oṭṭūr Uṇṇi Nambūtiripad, a great devotional poet adds to his contribution to Rāmā-Kṛṣṇa literature with *Śrīrāmakṛṣṇakarṇāmṛta*, *Aghoramaṇi*, etc. From his hundreds of poems, special mention may be made of *Rasamādhurī*. Krishnan Bhattathiri (Murali) extensively wrote devotional poems in Sanskrit, especially on Lord Kṛṣṇa.

The *Śrutyarthamuktāvalī* in Sanskrit authored by N.K. Sundareswaran is a good attempt at summarising the contributions of a great Vedic scholar. V.K. Narayanan Bhattatiri. Similarly, the *Saptaśatīsārasarvasva* in Sanskrit by K. Vishnu Nambutiri, a young scholar in Vyākaraṇa, deserves serious attention of scholars. It is an abridged form of *Devīmāhātmya*. The *Śatarudrīya Bhāṣya* named *Rājalakṣmī* by N.K. Sundareswaran is a good attempt at intrepreting Śatarudra hymns.

The Sanskrit commentary on *Śārikā Sandeśa of Rāmapāṇivāda* by K. Govindan Nambiar, edited and published by C.M. Neelakandhan also appeared during this time.

Dharmaraj Adat has written several studies in classical texts including the *Ṛgveda* in the light of Marxian philosophy. His Ph.D work on *Keralodaya* also deserves a special mention.

The critical edition of *Prakriyāsarvasva* by K.P. Narayana Pisharoti published by Guruvayur Devaswam, has been received with folded hands by the scholarly community. Detailed study on the text has been added by him. *Prakriyāsarvasvavivṛtti*, the unpublished Sanskrit commentary was discovered by P.C. Muraleemadhavan from Killimangalam Nambutiri family. The author Narayanan Nambutiri belongs to this family. The text was edited with a Sanskrit *tippaṇī* by P.C. Muraleemadhavan and K. Vishnu Nambutiri and published in 2006. The authentic introduction of George Cardona adds more seriousness to this work.

Lyrics

At the initial stages of the modern development, lyrics were composed following the well-known models presented by the classical poets. This dependence was visible both in the style of composition and in the selection of themes. Great works were either emulated or translated from regional languages into Sanskrit. Classical poets of the vernacular especially the trio of the present century Malayalam literature, viz. Ullur S. Parameswara Iyer, N. Kumaran Asan and Vallathol Narayana Menon have composed quite a number of lyrics of high standard that suited the Sanskrit idiom. The *Premasaṅgīta* and *Sthaviravicāralaharī*, by N. Gopala Pillai, a former principal of the Sanskrit college, are translations of the originals by Ullur and Asan as mentioned above. P.K. Narayana Pillai translated *Mayūra Sandeśa* of Kerala Varma into Sanskrit under the title *Mayūradūta*. This fancy has really enriched the Sanskrit literature of the modern period. A host of modern writers of different poetic calibre have tried their hands in this direction. But a sense of independence was always there in these compositions. It was only in religious verses called *stotra*s that such writers could express their own sense of devotion. Several poets belonging to the second half of the twentieth century composed many *sandeśa kāvya*s. *Cātaka-Sandeśa* is the one leading among them. Māntiṭṭa Śāstri Sarma, the Nyāya teacher of Sanskrit College, Tripunittura, is the author of the work. The author himself is the hero of the poem in which he sends a message to his beloved, princess Ambālikā of Ananthapuram Palace, at Harippad.

Cātaka-Sandeśa has been published by the present author with his own Sanskrit commentary *Rasikarañjinī* in the year 1992 from Trichur.

There are quite a number of devotional poems composed by the poets of Kerala in praise of different deities of the land wherein gods and goddesses were invoked for blessings. The success of *Nārāyaṇīyam* of Nārāyaṇa Bhaṭṭatiri of Melputtūr, a devotee of the lord of Guruvayur temple, provided the poets with a shining example. The number of poems and the number of writers who composed this typical class of literature could not be easily enumerated.

Vedic Studies

The contribution of Kerala to the Vedic studies is immense both in volume and importance. Scholars from Kerala have written several exegetical works on the Vedic texts. They have also preserved in tact, the oral tradition of the years together. Here, the tradition is authentic and alive, and is not the result of recent revival. *Jaiminīya Brāhmaṇa* is probably the earliest Brāhmaṇa. A complete manuscript of this Brāhmaṇa was discovered by E.R. Srikrishna Sharma from Koṭuntirappiḷḷi near Palghat and was the source of Reghuveera Lokesh Chandra edition in 1954. Three manuscripts were later discovered by Asko Parpola and E.R. Srikrishna Sharma from Pañjāl. Sharma has already prepared a critical edition with the translation of the *Jaiminīya Brāhmaṇa* for the Indira Gandhi National Centre for Arts. The illustrious work of Fritz Stall *Agni: The Ritual Altar of Hindus* was written based on the 12-day prolonged *Atirātra* sacrifice conducted at Pañjāl in Kerala in the late 1960s.

Srikrishna Sharma edited and published from Germany — the Kerala recension of the *Kauṣītaki Brāhmaṇa* and the *Sukhadā Commentary* of Udaya. He used all available manuscripts including the one in the Adayar Library which had been noticed by C. Kunhan Raja.

Kerala has produced yet another elaborate commentary on *Sarvānukramaṇikā*, it is called *Sarvānukramaṇīpadyavivṛtti*. The author though from Kerala, his name is not known. As the title indicates, it is written in the verse form. A rare copy of this manuscript belonging to C. Kunhan Raja was with K.K.

Raja. Parameswara Aithal has edited it at the Heidelberg University in Germany.

Another very important Kerala work on the Vedic exegesis is *Niruktavārttika*. An elaborate metrical commentary on Yāska's *Nirukta*. Its author became a *saṁnyāsin* taking the name Padmapādācārya. Before taking to *saṁnyāsa*, he was Nīlakaṇṭha and belonged to a brāhmin family of Koṇṭayūr on the banks of the Bhratappuzha. On the basis of a manuscript of this work obtained from Kerala, probably from Government Sanskrit College, Tripunitura, C. Kunhan Raja published a paper on *Niruktavārttika* in the Adayar Library Bulletin. Later, the complete text was published by the Ramlal Kapur Trust, edited by Vijaya Pal in 1982, on the basis of this paper manuscript. Recently, the present author has found out two other exemplars of this text from Adayar and Koṭuṅgallūr.

Melpputtur Narayana Bhatta wrote a short poem in nine verses — the *Sukha Śloka* — which is apparently a *stotra* in praise of the goddess, but which gives statistical details relating to the *Aṣṭaka-Adhyāya-Varga* classification of the *R̥gveda* using the *Kaṭapayādi* notation. This has been edited by C. Kunhan Raja. Erkkara Raman Namboodiri, who was an embodiment of the Kauṣītaki tradition, wrote several articles and collected them under the title *Āmnāyamathanam*. He edited the Malayalam monthly journal on the Vedic studies named *Anādi* to popularise the Vedic knowledge. V.K. Narayanan Bhattatiri tried to lay stress on the importance of studying the meaning of the Vedic texts; wrote profusely on the Vedic interpretation based on Yāska and Aurobindo. Mahākavi Vallathol Narayana Menon translated metrically, the entire *R̥gveda* into the Malayalam to popularise the Vedic and Sanskrit culture. The prose translation of the *R̥gveda* by O.M.C. Namboodiripad in the early 1980s, which is considered the most authentic by scholars, cannot be ignored at any level, since he interprets the entire text based on Sāyaṇa.

The name of C. Kunhan Raja deserves special mention in the modern Vedic exegesis. He studied under Macdonnell at the Oxford, and had discussions with Goldner in Germany and Louis Renou in France. Though he was taught that Sāyaṇa was explaining the Vedas without any traditional basis, and the modern research methodology, using comparative and historical approaches was found to help more than Sāyaṇa. Kunhan Raja on his written from the Europe was able to get many pre-Sāyaṇa commentaries on the Vedic text, and published them for the first time. He was convinced that Sāyaṇa was using a continuous tradition, though a ritualistic one. Besides editing commentaries, he wrote several expository volumes like, *Vedas: A Cultural Study; Poet Philosophers of Ṛgveda; Quintessence of the Veda*, etc. His edition of *Asyavāmīya Sūkta* with Ātmārama's Advaitic interpretation together with translation and explaining the riddles, is specially praiseworthy. As a successor in the field, the name of E.R. Srikrishna Sharma has already been mentioned. Kunjunni Raja also contributed several books and research articles on the Vedic exegesis. K.V. Sharma, another scholar in the field also contributed several monographs on the Vedic exegesis. In the first decade of this century a wonderful awakening of the Vedic studies on secular footing came up in Kerala. This mission was championed by the prestigious university of Sanskrit named after Sree Sankaracharya at Kalady, Kerala. This university has started the postgraduate programmes in the Vedic studies admitting students irrespective of caste, creed and gender. Some young, modern scholars also contribute new research articles and have published books in the Vedic studies such as N.V.P. Unithiri, C.M. Neelakandhan, P.V. Ramankutty, K.A. Raveendran and N.K. Sundareswaran. The Sanskrit university at Kalady has undertaken and completed a great task of documenting the entire Kauṣītaki recension of the *Sāmaveda* belong to Kerala. The entire *vikṛtis* like Ūha, Ūṣāṇi are recited by the veteran scholars in the field.

Translations

During this period of post-Independence, several works have been translated into Sanskrit from other languages. Such translations include the literary branches of *mahākāvyas*, *khaṇḍakāvyas* and other such compositions.

Among translations of *mahākāvyas*, K.P. Narayana Pisharoti's Sanskrit rendering of *Keśavīyam Malayala Mahākāvya* by K.C. Kesava Pillai, a famous poet of Kerala of the past generation, is an important and interesting poem (Githa Press, Trichur, 1972). This *mahākāvya* deals with the *Syāmantakamaṇi* and *Satyabhāmāpariṇaya* episodes described in the *Śrīmadbhāgavata Purāṇa*. The famous *Vanamāla* commentary of *Nārāyaṇīyam* by four great scholars like P.C. Vasudevan Elyath, K.P. Narayana Pisharoti, N.D. Krishnan Unni and C.P. Krishnan Elyath brought the work to the common man. The translation from Sanskrit to Malayalam also helped a lot to propagate Sanskrit studies in the state. Several scholars and poets translated classical works into Malayalam both in prose and poetry like Kuttikrishna Marar. The translation of *Śisyanum Makanum* of Mahakavi Vallathole into Sanskrit by N.V.P. Unithiri, P.C. Muraleemadhavan, P.K. Jose, E. Sreedharan and V.R. Muraleedharan was done during the first decade of this century. The translation of *Ujjayinī* of O.N.V. Kurup by N.V.P. Unithiri needs special mention. N.D. Krishnan Unni translated into Sanskrit three famous Malayalam philosophical poems namely, *Jñānappāna* (wisdom in Gāthā) of Pūntānam Namboodiri, *Harināmakīrtanam* (glorification of the names of Hari) of Ramanujan Ezhuttachan, the father of the modern Malayalam and the *Ātmopadeśa-śatakam* of Sri Narayana Guru. Aloor Kesavan Nair also has translated several Malayalam poems into Sanskrit written by great poets of Kerala.

The other noteworthy contribution to this category is the *Kaṇṇakīkovālam Kāvya* by C. Narayanan Nair, Nemmara, which is a Sanskrit rendering of the famous Tamil work *Cilappatikāram* of Inlamkovadikal of the second century CE. This poem contains six cantos and deals with the story of Kaṇṇakī and Kovalan, which is connected with the Madurai Mīnākṣi temple (Salem 1955). Vatakkumkur Rajaraja Varma, the well-known historian of Sanskrit literature of Kerala, has translated the third canto of the *Umākeralam Malayāla Mahākāvya* of Ullur Parameshwara Iyer.

In the *khaṇḍakāvyas* and other literary outputs of this category, some of the poems of Kumaran Asan, Vallathole Narayana Menon and Ullur S. Parameswara Iyer, the three great poets of modern Kerala — who were responsible for the literary renaissance in Malayalam — have been rendered into Sanskrit by scholars like E.V. Raman Nambutiri and N. Gopala Pillai. Thus, we get *Mahākavikṛtayaḥ* and *Keralabhāṣāvivartaḥ* by E.V. Raman Nambutiri which are the two collections of translations of short poems of Ullur and Vallathole (Trivandrum 1947). Kumaran Asan's famous Malayalam poem *Cintāvistayāya Sītā* (Cintavista Sita) has been translated by Gopala Pillai in his *Sītāvicāralaharī*, a good Sanskrit work written in an elegant and lucid style. He has also translated into Sanskrit the *Premasangītam* of Ullur Parameswara Iyer (both published in the name, *Keralapratibhā*; 1965). N. Gopala Pillai has also rendered into Sanskrit the *Gītāñjali* of Rabindranath Tagore in the *gāthā* type. His other Sanskrit translation is the *Daivadaśakam* of Sri Narayana Guru which has also been published in the *Saṁskārakeralam* journal.

Among the other Sanskrit translations from the Malayalam literature, mention may be made of the *Naḷinī* of Kumaran Asan translated by Mahopadhyaya Raman Pillai (Tvm). Another translation by Manan Gurukkal (not published) and yet another one by Ilattur Raghavan, which is serially being brought out in the *Saṁskārakeralam* journal. Kumaran Asan's another famous Malayalam poem *Vīṇapūvu* (fallen flower) has been rendered into Sanskrit by Koyittatta, K.S. Meenambal translated this *kāvya* into Sankrit under the title *Galitakusumam*. The Malayalam poem *Līlā*, another famous *khaṇḍakāvya* of Kumaran Asan has been rendered into Sanskrit by Manan Gurukkal.

A very important and interesting work in this category of *khaṇḍakāvya* translations is the *Mayūradūtam* by P.K. Naryana Pillai, the author of the *Viśvabhānu*. This poem is a Sanskrit rendering of the famous Malayalam poem *Mayūra-Sandeśa* of Kerala Varma Valiya Koyil Tampuran, otherwise known as Kerala Kālidāsa, and it was published recently with the translator's own English translation immediately below the Sanskrit verses. A.V. Sankaran the author of the *Maṇikaṇṭhīyacampū*, etc. has translated into Sanskrit the well-known poem *Śiṣyanum Makanum* (disciple and son) by Vallathol Mahakavi and the *Premasangītam* of Ullur. His another work called *Kanakacandrikā* is a Sanskrit rendering of 15 short Malayalam poems written by Mahakavi M.P. Appan, one of the great Malayalam poets (all of them published, Trivandrum).

Sri Tirunallur Karunakaran, has brought out an excellent Sanskrit translation of the *Candālabhikāukī* (Malayalam work) of Kumaran Asan (Keralakaumudi, 1970). Another important contribution to this field is E.R. Srikrishna Sharma's Sanskrit translation of the short drama *Sandhyā* by Mahakavi G. Sankara Kurup, winner of the first Jñānapītham award. S. Nilakantha Sastri, the author of the *Ujjivini* commentary on the *Dhvnayāloka*, has translated into Sanskrit the Tamil work *Āṇḍāl Tiruppāvai* in the name of *Kātyāyanīvr̥tam* in 120 *śloka*s (Tvm, 1967).

It may be observed in this context that these translations are as important as the original works since these fulfil the double purpose of enriching Sanskrit language and literature on the one side and on the other to encourage national integration and cultural exchange.

N.D. Krishnanunni translated two *mahākāvyas*, *Buddha Carita* and *Saundarānanda* from the Sanskrit into Malayalam. He has also translated some classical works from Malayalam into Sanskrit. K.P.A Menon translated several Sanskrit works into English and brought out some important studies under the label *Nine Gems*. Sudhamsu Chaturvedi, V. Panoli, Sukumar Azhikode and Narendra Bhooshan are some of the scholars who translated and conducted in-depth studies in philosophical texts. Great scholars like Pandit Gopalan Nair and Vaisravanth Raman Namboodiri translated several Purāṇa texts especially the *Bhāgavata*. The ordinary people have been much benefited by these reliable and simple translations. Swami Mṛdānanda translated most of the major Upaniṣads into Malayalam for the first time. It was a great boon to Keralites that they can now follow the hardcore subject of the Vedānta in their simple mother tongue. Ranganathananda, Agamananda, Chinmayanatha and Bhoomanatha Tirtha are chiefly responsible for cultivating great enthusiasm among the Kerala people to study Sanskrit by approaching the original texts.

The original works and translations of Kerala Varma (Kerala Kālidāsa) and A.R. Rajaraja Varma (Kerala Pāṇini) and Kunjikkuttan Thampuran (Kerala Vyāsa) are to be mentioned with great reverence. In the field of the Āyurveda, the contributions of Vaidyaratnam P.S. Warrier, Vaidya Mathom Narayanan Namboodiri and Thykkattu Neelakandhan Moossu, etc. need a special mention. They propagated the Āyurveda along with Sanskrit in a healthy atmosphere. In the Vāstuśāstra, Jyotiṣa and Gaṇita the great scholarship and contributions of Kanippayyur Sankaran Nambudiripad will be remembered for ever.

In Malayalam 75 per cent of the words are from Sanskrit and most of them are *tadbhava*s and *tatsama*s. Hence, from time immemorial the practice in the *gurukula*s is to teach Sanskrit along with Malayalam. Hence up to recent years a Sanskrit degree holder is qualified to teach Malayalam at the high school and college level. In Maṇipravāḷa, a branch of the Malayalam language, we can see a high degree of influence of Sanskrit and only a few Malayalam words can be traced out from such literature.

The translations from Sanskrit to Malayalam also helped a lot to propagate Sanskrit studies in the state. Several scholars and poets translated classical *kāvya*s and *nāṭaka*s into Malayalam both in prose and poetry, like Kuttikrishna Marar.

Significant Editions

Another important contribution to Sanskrit literature during the post-Independence period, is the editions of many ancient texts brought out by well-known institutions and several individual scholars from different parts of Kerala. The Oriental Research Institute and the manuscripts Library of the Kerala University itself has brought out in this period 194 editions of important Sanskrit works in the well-known Trivandrum Sanskrit Series (TSS) which was started by the late famous scholar Mahāmahopādhyāya T. Ganapathy Sastri, who brought out the Bhāsanāṭakas and Kauṭilya's *Arthaśāstra* for the first time. The editions published after 1947 are from TSS No. 160 to 254 and comprise different branches of Sanskrit learning namely (1) Vedic Exegesis, (2) Tantraśāstra and Mantraśāstra, (3) Vedānta, (4) Pūrva Mīmāṁsā, (5) Tarkaśāstra, (6) Vyākaraṇa, (7) Jyotiṣaśāstra comprising astronomy and astrology, (8) Vaidyaka or medicine, (9) Bhojanaśāstra, (10) Mahākāvya, (11) Khaṇḍakāvya, (12) Gadya-kāvya, (13) Campūs and Prabandhas, (14) Stotras, (15) Nāṭaka, (16) Alaṁkāraśāstra and Chandaśāstra. Government Sanskrit College, Thrippunithura has published the Naṭāmkuśam, a treatise on dramaturgy by K.G. Paulose.

The Rama Varma Research Institute, Trichur, the department of Sanskrit and the publication department of the

University of Kerala, the Calicut University's Sanskrit department, Sāhitya Department of Sree Sankaracharya University, Kalady and the Sukrtindra Research Institute, Ernakulam, the Palace Library, Tripunittura and several individual scholars have brought out many important Sanskrit works, during the post-Independence period in Kerala.

Journals of Kerala

Punnassery Nanpi Neelakantha Sharma, the founder of Sanskrit College at Pattambi is considered by Keralites as Gurunātha. He wrote and spoke profusely in Sanskrit. He was the first Sanskrit journalist in independent India. His journal named *Vijñānacintāmaṇi,* was a touch-stone for the scholars with erudition in several Śāstras. Simple and modern way of writing and speaking Sanskrit was patronised by Nanpi. Nanpi is mainly instrumental for the renaissance of Sanskrit in Kerala. His *Raghuvaṁśa* lectures in Sanskrit were published by the Sanskrit College, Tripunittura. There were several journals in Sanskrit published from Kerala. The Government Sanskrit College, Trivandrum, used to issue a journal called *Citra* for several years. But it has ceased to exist for more than 30 years now. Through the pages of these journals, a number of small works were printed.

The Sanskrit journal of the Kerala University Manuscripts Library, mostly published works of a traditional nature like message poems, lyrics, *bhāna*s, *campū*s, etc. But occasionally, some items of modern interest also appeared through its pages. The letters written by T. Ganapati Sastri in Sanskrit to well-known scholars like Sylvan Levi, A.B. Keith, L.D. Barnett, Louis Renou and others are of great contemporary interest. They deal with the situations of the modern times while embracing the horrors of the world war, etc. But such items were rare.

The journal of the Ravi Varma Sanskrta Granthavali,

published from Tripunittura, began its appearance in January 1953. It appeared four times a year and it continued its publication till October 1967 with number 4 of volume XV. In addition to traditional items of publication of old works from the manuscripts it also incorporated modern writings in Sanskrit of varied nature and theme. Some of the items published thought its pages are:

1. An article on temple arts in Sanskrit by K. Rama Pisharoti.
2. A series of articles on the *pañcakarma* mode of treatment by Trkkovil Achuthavarier.
3. A serial on *Jyotiṣa* by Pandit K.N. Subramania Sastri.
4. A short story entitled Pāritoṣikam by P.S. Subbarama Pattar.
5. Well arranged lessons in music.
6. On what is life by P.S. Subbarama Pattar.
7. On Tarkaśāstra by K. Raman Nampyar.
8. On leprosy by Achutavarier.
9. On liberation, etc.

In addition, a host of writers contributed devotional lyrics on the god of Tripunittura called Pūrṇatrayīśa and, on the lord of Guruvāyūr, lyrics of eulogy on the model of *Suprabhāta* too appeared in several issues relating to various deities. Reports on Sanskrit assemblies, homages to patrons, obituary notices, congratulatory stanzas, reviews, etc. filled the pages of these numbers.

The journal is now re-introduced under the name *Pūrnatrayī,* the first issue of which appeared in January 1989 vol. XVI, no. 1) and it is being issued twice a year.

Eranallūr Bharata Pisharoti who has done much for the propagation of Sanskrit in the modern times had issued a journal for about 5 years. His journal *Kāmadhenu* catered to the interests of modern people and successfully propagated contemporary ideas through the Sanskrit medium. It was a bilingual journal as in the case of the other two mentioned earlier.

A bold and successful attempt at launching a pure Sanskrit journal *Bharatamudrā* was made by Aśokan Puranattukara from Trichur as a bi-annual issue from 1979 onwards.

The record of this popular journal is quite envious. It has been already dealing with the contemporary social life, historical events, caricatures of political events, tricks of politicians on the common man, recreations based on some interesting aspects of mythological and Purāṇic themes, etc. Some of the stories introduce the animal world as in the Walt Disney's stories; the intention being to illustrate morals.

More than 200 lyrics have already appeared through this journal; those set in classical metres, vernacular Dravidian metres or metre free verses, it is modern poetry in the true sense of the term. Translations from the other Indian languages too have appeared occasionally. The only form yet to appear is that of a modern full-fledged novel. Nobody has made a serious attempt in that direction. But, a Sanskrit translation of the famous Malayalam novel *Mahāprasthānam* of Matampu Kunjikkuttan was written and published by Aśokan Puranattukara. It has sufficiently proved that Sanskrit language also suits to the modern genre, called novel. He has also translated into Sanskrit *Innalatte Mazhayil* — the Malayalam novel of Mohanan.

Who are the regular contributors to these journals? Retired Sanskrit teachers, of course, do their best. But the most encouraging aspect is that youngsters working as Sanskrit teachers in different schools and colleges, and laymen with some proficiency in the language have taken it up with their heart to contribute to the periodical. The editor claims that he has never experienced any dearth of articles though he is intrigued quite often by the lack of variety. Verses in the form of hymns to local deities pour in at a fast flooding manner at his desk.

The new Sanskrit journals like *Dhīmahī* (CIF Shodh Sansthan), *Kiraṇāvalī* (Sanskrit Research Foundation, TVM), Sanskrit journal of *Sukṛtīndra* and *Sadvidyā* (Sankara College, Kalady) provide an ample opportunity to young Sanskrit researchers to document their research findings in a more attractive manner.

Manuscript, Catalogue and Indices

The other important contribution to the field of Sanskrit research, is the publication of the three volumes of alphabetical index of Sanskrit manuscripts in the Kerala University Manuscripts Library which is one of the famous libraries of the nation. The *Bibliography of the Kerala Sanskrit Literature* by S. Venkitasubramania Iyer, and *Sanskrit Literature of Kerala: Author Index,* by E. Easwaran Nambutiri are very significant works.

Technical and Scientific Literature

Among the scientific and technical works produced in Kerala during the period, the *Sugalārthamālā* on *Vyākaraṇaśātra* by P. Narayanan is an important work as it deals with the variety and complexity of the shades of meanings expressed by definite verbs. A commentary on it called *Dīpikā* has been written by D. Damodara Pisharoti, a great authority on Sanskrit grammar and published along with the text (1964). Āṭṭur Krishna Pisharoti's *Saṅgītacandrikā*, a work on music in 12 sections in Sūtra style; V.G. Nambutiri's *Mīmāṁsānyāyaprakāśakārikāvalī* (1979) and the *Dhavanyālokālocanavyākhyā* called *Ujjīvinī* by Neela Kantha Sastri and Sanskrit commentary on *Vyutpattivādasiddhāntamālā* of Goḍavarma Raja were published during 1990s. It is an abridgement of the theories in Śābda-bodha pertaining to Vibhaktyārtha.

Abridgements

Certain compositions in the form of abridgements of famous Sanskrit works were also produced in this period, and among them mention may be made of the *Kaustubham*, the summary of the tenth Skandha of the *Bhāgavata* by Rama Varma Valiyakoyil Tampuran (1964); *Nārāyaṇīyāmṛta* by C.P. Krishnan Elyath, which is an effective summary of the famous *Narāyaṇīya Stotrakāvya* of Melpputtur Nārāyaṇabhaṭṭa (Trichur, 1976) and the *Megha-Sandeśa Saṁgraha* and *Viśrutacarita* by V.G. Nambuthiri (Trivandrum, 1962 and 1963); the *Mṛcchakaṭi-kakathāsāra* of P.C. Vasudevan Elyath is also significant in this field.

Several *stotra*s and *suprabhātam*s of great literary merit were produced in this period in Kerala. Important *stotra*s among them are the ones produced by Oṭṭūr Uṇṇi Nambudiripad, a scholar devotee of Śrīkṛṣṇa at Guruvayoor temple, who commands a very fluent and lucid style and who is the author of the *Śrīrāmakṛṣṇakarṇāmṛta*. P.K. Narayana Pillai, the author of the *Viśvabhānu Mahākāvya* has several *stotra*s to his credit and among them *Cidātmikāstava* (1960), *Śrīvallabheśasuprabhāta* (1974), *Dharmaśāstrastava* (1974) and *Kanyākumārim Phaje* (1975) are noteworthy creations in this connection. Among the other *stotras Pūrṇatrayīśabhujaṅga-prayāstotram* by P. Narayan Nambutiri, the author of the *Sugalārthamālā* (1967) on the deity of Tripunittura in 43 verses, the Premalahari of K. Bhaskara Pillai in 18 *śloka*s in praise of Devī depicted as knowledge (New Delhi, 1966, with English translation and exposition, 1975), are written in *suprabhāta* style. The *Vātālayeśastavamañjarī* written by V. Ramakumar, a teacher and Sanskrit scholar, in 1000 *śloka*s in the model of Nārāyaṇīya, is an interesting *stotra* work as it deals with several legends (*aitihya*s) connected with the grace of Śrīkr̥ṣṇa at the Guruvayur temple. The *Śabarīśagītāñjalī* a unique *padyagīta* written by P.C. Vasudevan Elyath was a trendsetter as several poems were composed by later writers in that style. It is the first work in Kerala which suits to the rhythm of *Uḍukkukoṭṭupāṭṭu* (Ayyappan Pāṭṭu famous ritual music presentation with *ḍamaru*). Vasudevan Elyath has also composed and published many *stotra-kāvya*s. The style of classical versification in Sanskrit has been continued in Kerala by poets like him.

Many original *stotra*s are even now being composed in Kerala and it is not possible to give an exhaustive account of all such works, because, in many cases such works are not published and so details about them are not easily available.

Institutions and Organisations

RASTRIYA SANSKRIT SANSTHAN

A prestigious campus of the Rashtriya Sanskrit Sansthan under the MHRD, Government of India is situated at Puranattukara in Thrissur district. The Sansthan took over the erstwhile Sanskrit College at Pavaratty which was founded by a great Sanskrit scholar P.T. Kuriakkose in 1911. The great tradition of teaching Sanskrit Śāstra's and Sāhitya was infused by the Sansthan in 1979 by taking over it. In the present scenario of Sanskrit studies in the state, the Guruvayur campus of the Sansthan at Purnattukara plays a pivotal role. Regular courses are conducted by the Sansthan from Prak-Shastri to Vidyavaridhi (Plus two – Ph.D)

Along with preserving the traditional systems of teaching Sanskrit, the Sansthan paved the way for desirable changes in curriculum by modernising the academic programmes and including courses in Information Technology. It is an ideal campus with students endowed with different lifestyles and cultures live together with proper understanding. The Pavaratty Centre of Guruvayur campus was donated free of cost by P.T. Kuriakkose and is worth Rs. 5 crore. This is also preserved well. Various certificate courses and courses under the distance education system have been launched from this centre.

The CIF Shodh Sansthan under the Rasthriya Sanskrit Sansthan at Veliyanadu, the birth place of Śrī Śaṅkarācārya is yet another institution for higher research in Sanskrit. They mostly concentrate in manuscript studies. Several significant publications are brought out by this centre.

Balusscry Adarsa Sanskrit Vidyapeetha imparts education in Sanskrit from Prak-Shastri to Acharya. Apart from these, several private institutions affiliated, Sansthan provides contact courses at various levels in Sanskrit. The Sansthan has further strengthened the informal education in the state. It has opened several centres under the leadership of trained teachers. All these centres are running very well due to the collective participation of people from different stratas of the society.

Institutions like the Chinmaya Mission, Sri Ramakrishna Mission, Bharatiya Vidyabhavan and Amruthananthamayi Mathom have also patronised the Sanskrit studies in the state at the grassroot level. Saraswathi Nikethan Schools have brought Sanskrit as a compulsory component from the 1st standard at school level.

The Sanskrit colleges and the departments of Sanskrit in various universities conduct several courses at postgraduate, M.Phil. and Ph.D. levels. A few Oriental Sanskrit Schools still survive in the state with Sanskrit as their major subject.

SRI SANKARACHARYA UNIVERSITY OF SANSKRIT

Sree Sankaracharya University of Sanskrit at Kalady was established in the year 1993. It has eight centres apart from the main campus at Kalady.

Apart from the preservation of traditional knowledge in

various Sanskrit Śāstras, the university has broken the traditional lines and started several attractive, interdisciplinary and multidisciplinary courses, connecting Sanskrit to the modern streams of education. There are seven departments in the university mainly conducting courses in traditional Śāstras and physical sciences in Sanskrit. Apart from them several other departments in modern streams of knowledge conduct their courses along with Sanskrit teaching. A student of social work or Arabic or Urdu or even English cannot take his postgraduate degree without opting Sanskrit courses from any of the Sanskrit departments; hence non-Sanskrit students also study Sanskrit well with great interest. The university has launched several projects for preserving the traditional wisdom. Under this scheme the Kūṭiyāṭṭam theatre was documented for hundred hours with the assistance of the Government of India. The Government of Kerala too extended financial help to document the entire Sāma chant with a duration of 70 hours. The strengthening of Sanskrit studies in the state — a Government of India project with a total budget of Rs. 7,35,000,00 was implemented successfully at the state level. 36 model schools were started with the help of the directorate of public instruction of Kerala government to implement the scheme.

The Higher Education Council through the Sanskrit University at Kalady, conducted several programmes like "The Erudate" to bring about a healthy atmosphere for Sanskrit research. Intervention by the Higher Education Council has made it possible to improve the situation by inviting veteran scholars from different parts of the globe. George Cardona, Michael Witzel, Maureen P. Hall are few among such scholars who were posted as "Scholar in Residence" in the university. A new vigour, awakening and serious approach is now visible in the field of Sanskrit research due to the effective implementation of the scheme.

KERALA SAHITYA AKADEMI

Kerala Sahitya Akademi has prepared and published the *Kerala Saṁskṛta Sāhitya Caritram* in three volumes. The Akademi also took initiatives in propagating Sanskrit literature besides publishing several classical works.

KERALA SANSKRIT AKADEMI

The Sanskrit Akademi in Kerala was established in 1986. The Akademi has brought a new awakening in the field of Sanskrit studies especially in the field of research. Young researchers are being patronised with sufficient academic and financial support. Several publication projects have been taken up. The Akademi has taken several steps to honour traditional scholars of high repute. They are being provided with suitable financial assistance. Several unpublished manuscripts were unearthed by the Ackademi. It has launched several schemes to patronise the creative writers in Sanskrit. The present author is the founder Secretary of the Akademi.

E. KUNJUNNI RAJA AKADEMI OF INDOLOGICAL RESEARCH

This institute was established in the year 2005. It has several projects in hand to encourage research in various fields of Indology with special emphasis on Sanskrit. It has conducted several research workshops, colloquiums and seminars to provide multiple opportunities to young scholars doing intensive research. It has also instituted several awards like *Rājaprabhā* at the national level. Every year, a prestigious lecture programme under the title Kunjunni Raja Memmorial Lecture is organised and scholars of international repute are invited to deliver lectures. George Cardona, V.N. Jha, Radhavallabh Tripathi are some of the famous scholars who have delivered the said lecture. All the lectures are published immediately after the programme. A south Indian seminar on "New Horizons of Indological Research" was conducted with huge participation of young researchers from various universities.

The present author is the founder chairman of the Akademi.

PRATISHTHANAM

The contribution of Viswasamskrta Pratishthanam for the propagation of Sanskrit is by no means small. The organisation, through young teams of trained teachers, regularly organise very effective Sanskrit *śiviras* which are attended by thousands of lovers of Sanskrit.

Traditional Scholars

The traditional scholars in various Śāstras, who have made a significant contribution to the promotion of Sanskrit in post-Independence era need special mention. Mention to be made of M.H. Sastrikal, R. Vasudevan Potti, V. Venkitaraja Sharma, G. Viswanatha Sharma, K. Govindan Nambiar, D. Damodara Pisharoti, C. Achutha Potuval, C.K. Raman Nambiar, K. Rama Warrier, Moorkkanad Krishnan Nambutiri, S. Venkitakrishnan, N.D. Krishnanunni and P.C. Vasudevan Elyath. A team of young traditional scholars like V. Ramakrishna Bhatt, K.V. Vasudevan, K.P. Babudas, T. Aryadevi, N.K. Sudareswaran, E. Sreedharan, V.R. Muraleedharan, K. Vishnu Numboodiri, K. Muthulakshmi, and P.V Narayanan are expected to contribute to the development of traditional Śāstras in Sanskrit sigificantly in the days to come.

The traditional scholars who lived in the second half of the twentieth century in Kerala, have contributed immensely to the development of various Śāstras. They were masters in different disciplines with noted students under their tutelage. They have thus succeeded in shaping a healthy line of dedicated disciples in their respective fields. Many of them are known through the refined scholarship of their students. They wrote a number of books endowed with several unique features. Among them Mānṭiṭṭa Kuñju Namboodiri the great Naiyāyika and Āsthāna Paṇḍit of the Cochin royal family wrote *Nacaratnamālikā* and its commentary *Nūtanāloka*. It is a *kroḍapatra* on the second definition of *Pūrvapakṣavyāpti,* put forth by Pragadbhamishra in *Caturdeśalakṣaṇī.* 99 *pūrvapakṣa*s raised by the author and their refutation are given in this book. It is a tough work with a complicated style of Navya-Nyāya. The work has been published from Varanasi in 1960.

Modern Scholars

Among the modern scholars in Sanskrit, who have conducted remarkable and authentic studies in various fields of Sanskrit, C. Kunhan Raja's name comes first. K. Kunjunni Raja, E.R. Srikrishna Sharma, K.V. Sharma, P.K. Narayana Pillai, N.P. Unni, T. Bhaskaran, A. Sankaran, A.G. Krishna Warrier, Raghavan Pillai, E. Eswaran Nambutiri Venkitasubrahmani, K. Vijayan, M.S. Menon, N.V.P. Unithiri, C. Rajendran, P.V. Ramankutty, K. Maheswaran Nair, T. Devarajan, C.S. Radhakrishnan, Poojappura Krishnan Nair, Chathanath Achuthan Unni, M. Leelavathy, E.V. Damodaran, P. Ramakrishna Pillai, and the like should be considered with due seriousness.

The Modern Outlook

In spite of the fact that Sanskrit authors who tried their hand at the traditional genres had a progressive outlook it seldom got reflected in their compositions. The medium was not helpful for this. The authors themselves published most of their own works drawing on their own resources. They did not have to obtain the favour of any editor or publisher. Nobody prevented them from publishing their material at their own cost. It is only the emergence of Sanskrit journals that has set a new standard for modernity in Sanskrit literature.

Future Prospect

After a somewhat bleak period of hypernation the future of modern Sanskrit is definitely brightening up for the good. Since the language has a wonderful felicity for adoption to various concepts including modern scientific topics, a resourceful author can always express his thoughts effortlessly. Introduction of loan words from modern Indian and world languages into Sanskrit vocabulary has come to stay and no eyebrow is twisted in modern times when one uses words like "glasnost" and "peristroika", whatever be the medium in which one writes. The rigour of the Pāṇinian grammar which used to worry the puritans does not trouble the modern writers even though they are not at all against grammar as such. In short, Sanskrit writers have awakened to the needs of the changing situations of the modern world. They are no more restricted to their homeland. Before a modern writer the whole world presents itself as a single unit dictum *vasudhaiva kuṭumbakam*, that has once again acquired a true significance.

Conclusion

Though the main portion of the original literary output in Kerala is now in Malayalam, the mothertongue of Keralites, Sanskrit also seems to hold parts of its original influence and popularity. Many original Sanskrit works especially stotras and *kāvyas*, are even now being composed in Kerala by several poets and Sanskrit scholars and it is not possible to give an exhaustive account of all such works, because in many cases such works are not published and so details about them are not easily available. It may be observed, that in Kerala, we see a satisfactory progress in the production of original Sanskrit works as well as in the study and research in Sanskrit, in post-Independence period.

11

Sanskrit Studies in Madhya Pradesh and Chhattisgarh

Radhavallabh Tripathi

MADHYA Pradesh (M.P.) is situated in the heartland of this vast peninsula. Mahakoshal, Bastar and Chhattisgarh, Madhya Bharat and Vindhya Pradesh — these provinces were clubbed with the state of Bhopal to form the state covering largest geographical area in the country in November 1956. However, the enormous size of this state was cut short when the state of Chhattisgarh came into being on 1 November 2000 by separating 16 southern districts from Madhya Pradesh.

Background

The State of M.P. includes cities like, Gwalior, Ujjain, Indore and Raipur (now in Chhattisgarh) where the rulers of princely states in pre-Independence era were favourably inclined towards Sanskrit studies and they patronised *paṇḍit*s and poets of Sanskrit and cultivated the *pāṭhaśālā* system. After Independence, these *pāṭhaśālā*s, however are languishing for want of infrastructure and staff.

Kailash Nath Katju served Madhya Pradesh as its chief minister during 1955-62. He was a lover of Sanskrit and promulgated certain orders in favor of Sanskrit.

Sanskrit Education in Pāthaśālās, Schools and Colleges

Between 1901-62, 278 Sanskrit schools and Sanskrit colleges have been functioning in the state. Apart from them there were two Āyurvedic colleges and three Jyotiṣa schools. Out of these 117 only survived in 1962, and 161 had come to closure. Sanskrit was a compulsory subject in Āyurveda colleges at initial stage, but later was dropped from the syllabi.

There were 129 Sanskrit *pāṭhaśālās* and Sanskrit colleges with a total of 4,703 students in the state when it was formed in 1956. Next year only, the number of these institutions came down to 125, but the student's enrolment went up to 4,822. Most of the schools and colleges of modern education also provided for the teaching of Sanskrit. Sanskrit was introduced as an elective subject in four colleges during 1956-58 at undergraduate level and in one college at postgraduate level. Also it was included as an elective in 13 newly-established colleges during 1957-58. A golden era for Sanskrit studies was ushered in when Kailash Nath Katju became the chief minister of this state and he made Sanskrit a compulsory subject in all schools of the state up to higher secondary level. This naturally led to the multiplication of facilities for teaching of Sanskrit at collegiate level. Such was Katju's interest and enthusiasm for Sanskrit that the Government of M.P. constituted a Board of Sanskrit Education under the Chairmanship of the chief minister himself. The minister of finance, minister of education; eminent scholars like Vasudev Sharan Agrawal, Raghubir, Surya Narayan Vyas, Hiralal Jain, Hariram Mishra and the vice-chancellors of universities of Sagar, Ujjain, Jabalpur and Khairagarh were appointed as members of this board. In the year 1961-62, out of 49 government arts colleges 37 provided for the teaching of Sanskrit.

Sanskrit studies did not prosper in the same ratio during the last decades of twentieth century. The number of students stealthily declined. There are fewer students at collegiate level.

By the end of the seventh decade itself, the number of traditional Sanskrit institutions had come down. The inventory of Sanskrit institutions in India published in 1972 gives the followed note – "In Madhya Pradesh there are 8 Sanskrit Mahavidyalayas, 5 Sanskrit Higher Secondary Schools, and 100 Vidyalayas".

However, the report does not appear to be accurate, because as per the report obtained from APS University Rewa, it used to affiliate as many as 19 Sanskrit Colleges, out of which three are situated at Rewa, five at Satna, two at Sagar and one each at Shahdol, Sidhi, Gwalior, Panna, Katni, Jabalpur, Bhopal, Indore and Ujjain. Apart from these, the university also provided affiliation to 112 Sanskrit *vidyālaya*s that were subsequently taken up by the State Sanskrit Board.

There are more than a dozen state universities in Madhya Pradesh (including the newly created Chhattisgarh). Of these, the universities at Saugar (estd. 1946), Ujjain (estd. 1956) and Jabalpur have postgraduate departments for teaching and research in Sanskrit. There is a provision for teaching of Sanskrit in the departments of Comparative Languages and Cultures of Bhopal and Indore universities. Other universities do not have own teaching departments of Sanskrit, but have affiliated colleges where Sanskrit is taught at undergraduate/ postgraduate level as an elective subject.

There are four state universities in the newly-created province of Chhattisgarh — Pandit Ravi Shankar Shukla University at Raipur, Sarguja University, Guru Ghasidas University (now a central university) at Bilaspur and Chhattisgarh Swami Vivekananda Technical University. None of these have their own postgraduate Department in Sanskrit studies.

Government Dudhadhari Vaishnav Sanskrit Mahavidyalaya in Raipur is one of the biggest Sanskrit colleges in the country. The colleges equipped with a good library and some manuscripts also. Ram Nihal Sharma who served in this college for more than two decades used to bring out a research journal *Medhā* from the institution. Pandit Ravi Shankar Shukla University at Raipur has been running B.A. Classics and M.A. Classics courses through this college. These courses are at par with Shastri and Acharya courses in traditional Sanskrit Institutions. Until the establishment of a Sanskrit Board and subsequently the Patanjali Shodh Sansthan by the state government, the APS University at Rewa used to provide affiliation and conduct the traditional examinations in Sanskrit in the *pāṭhaśālā*s and Sanskrit colleges. Previously these institutions were affiliated to Sampurnanand University, Varanasi.

The Sanskrit Department of Saugar University (re-named as Dr. Harisingh Gour University) is the oldest university teaching department of Sanskrit in the state. It has been actively involved in teaching and research ever since its inception in 1946. V.M. Apte, the founder head of this department specialised in Veda, known for his thesis on the study of Gṛhyasūtras. Ramji Upadhyaya served this department from 1947 to 1980 and also worked as its head after the retirement of V.M. Apte. He has authored several books on Indian culture, Nāṭyaśāstra, modern Sanskrit literature and history of Sanskrit literature in Hindi and Sanskrit. Biswanath Bhattacharya and Vanmala Bhavalkar have served in this department. Bhattacharya is a scholar of Sāhitya and has published several papers and books on drama and dramaturgy. Bhavalkar has worked on women in the *Mahābhārata*. She has also contributed to Sanskrit as a playwright.

Radhavallabh Tripathi served in this department as lecturer from January 1973; he was appointed Reader in 1978 and professor in 1983. He worked as the head of this department from 1980 to 2002 and 2005 to 2008. During his term of headship, the department of Sanskrit at Dr. H.S. Gour University was recognised for DRS (Departmental Research Support) under the scheme of SAP (Special Assistance Programme) by the UGC (University Grants Commission), New Delhi from 1994. It was upgraded as DSA (Department of Special Assistance) from 2007. Tripathi has been running the SAP as Chief Coordinator (1994-2008). He established a Manuscript Library in the Department and discovered a number of rare manuscripts. He also initiated a scheme for publication of rare manuscripts, named as *Prakhyā*. Ten volumes of *Prakhyā* has so far been published. The department published more than 50 books including dissertations, text-books and literary works. The following seminars were organised in the department —

1. All India Level Advanced Institute in Nyāya Darśana (sponsored by the UGC from 24 September 1982 to 14 October 1982. (Discussions published in book-form)
2. All India Level UGC Seminar on "Contribution Islamic Traditions to Sanskrit Literature" during 20-22 September 1984 (Proceedings published)
3. All India Level UGC Seminar on "Kauṭilya's Arthaśāstra" during 16-19 September 1986 (Proceedings published)
4. Re-Orientation Program for College and University Teachers for teaching Sanskrit from 11 to 20 July 1987.
5. All India Level UGC Seminar on "Contribution of Sanskrit to Nation's Integration" from 18 to 21 January 1988. (Proceedings published)
6. National Seminar on Modern Sanskrit Literature from 5 to 7 December 1989.
7. National Seminar on "Tradition of Linguistics in Sanskrit" from 8 to 10 October 1990. (Proceedings published)

8. National Seminar on "Reorganisation of Śāstras with a view to prepare their Computational Data-Base" from 9 to 11 January 1995. (Proceedings published)
9. National Seminar on "Twentieth Century Sanskrit Theatre" held from 22 to 23 February 1996. (Proceedings published)
10. National Seminar on "New Horizons of Sanskrit Poetics" held from 25 to 27 March 1996.
11. National Seminar on "Vedic Foundations of Indian Śāstric Traditions" held from 6 to 8 September 1996. (Proceedings published)
12. National Seminar on "Turning Points in Indian Śastric Traditions" held from 19 to 21 March 1997. (Proceedings published)
13. National Seminar on "Impact of Vedic Traditions on Sanskrit Literature" December 1997.
14. National Seminar on Inter relation between Veda and Itihāsa-Purāṇa (1999)
15. National Seminar on Nāṭyaśātra, Sanskrit Drama and World Theatre, 5-6 January 2000
16. Ātmatattvavivekasatra: A Course on Udayanacarya's text from 6 to 29 February 2000.
17. National Seminar on Modern Sanskrit Literature 25-27 July 2000.
18. National Seminar on Vedic World View and Modern Science 17-18 October 2000.
19. National Seminar on Śāstric Traditions in Twentieth century, 1-2 March, 2001.
20. National Seminar on "Sanskrit Drama and Folk traditions of Indian Theatre" on 2 and 3 January 2005.

The department has been publishing two quarterly research

journals — *Sāgarikā* (in Sanskrit) and *Nāṭyam* (in Hindi). In the Manuscript Resource Centre (MRC) being run under the aegis of the National Mission for Manuscripts in this department around 25,000 manuscripts have been collected and are being digitised. A Hyper-electronic text of *Nāṭyaśāstra, Abhinavabhāratī* has been prepared. Its Hindi and English translations are being prepared. Some manuscripts of *Nyāyakalikā* of Jayanta Bhaṭṭa have been collected and their collation work is in progress.

The Natya Parishad under this department has been actively engaged in staging Sanskrit plays or plays related to Indian culture based on Sanskrit literature for last 31 years since 1973. The Parishad has so far produced and staged about 50 dramas at state as well as national level begging many prizes.

V. Venkatachalam, Harindra Bhushan Jain and Shriniwas Rath have served as lecturers, Readers and professors at Sanskrit Department of the Vikram University at Ujjain. V. Venkatachalam organised a number of national and international seminars on diverse themes related to studies on Kālidāsa and Bhoja. Harindra Bhushan Jain specialised in Jainism. Shriniwas Rath is well known as a Sanskrit poet. Vindhyeshwari Prasad Mishra, Somnath Nene and Murali Manohar Pathak — these three very promising scholars have served this department. Mishra is versatile in Sāhitya, Purāṇa and many other branches and also an eminent poet of Sanskrit. Nene comes from the traditional family of Mīmāṁsakas and he has also worked in the field of Mīmāṁsā. Pathak has also a good command in Vyākaraṇa, Nyāya and Veda. Unfortunately, these three have left Sanskrit Department of Vikram University in recent years to join other institutions. Kedar Nath Shukla (retired) and Balkrishna Shrma are other scholars connected with this department.

Hiralal Jain promoted studies under Prākṛt and Jainism at the University of Jabalpur. He was followed by Vimal Prakash

Jain and Rajendra Trivedi in this area. Krishna Kant Chaturvedi who served this department lecturer, Reader and professor for more than three decades organised a number of national seminars under its auspices. During his regime, the Annual Rajashekhara Samaroha became a regular feature in the university.

In December 2000, the chief minister of Madhya Pradesh made an announcement to constitute the Board of Sanskrit Education. The Board of Sanskrit Education became functional after that and had been affiliating traditional *pāṭhaśālā*s and Sanskrit *vidyālaya*s.

Recently, the Board has been reconstituted and renamed as "Patanjali Shodh Sansthan". Mithila Prasad Tripathi, who has been working as Director of Kalidasa Akademi, was given the responsibility to run this "Sansthan". During 2008-09, the Sansthan has given affiliation to as many as 503 Sanskrit *vidyālaya*s.

Panini Veda-Vedanga Sanskrit Vishvidyalaya — a new university for traditional Sanskrit studies has been established at Ujjain. The university started functioning after its formal inauguration on 17 August 2007 by the Governor of M.P. in presence of the chief minister of the state. Mohan Gupt became its founder vice-chancellor. Very recently Mithila Prasad Tripathi has succeeded him.

17 Sanskrit colleges of M.P. are now affiliated to this university. The university has also started M.Phil. and Ph.D. programmes besides running undergraduate and postgraduate classes in traditional courses. The state government has approved five professors, ten associate professors and 15 assistant professors. The centre is being build up on a 10 hectare land.

In Chhattisgarh, 31 traditional Sanskrit *vidyālaya*s were affiliated to the State Sanskrit Board during 2008-09.

Committees, Commissions and Academies

The old state of Madhya Bharat had a language department. It was established in 1950. This department also made some recommendations for the cause of Sanskrit, particularly relating to purchase of Sanskrit periodicals in the libraries. In the 1955, a 10-member committee was formed to suggest ways and means for promotion of Sanskrit in the state. The committee consisted of stalwarts like V.V. Mirashi, V.M. Apte, S.P. Chaturvedi, Hiralal Jain, S.B. Varnekar and P.D. Agnihotri

Government of Madhya Pradesh constituted an expert committee for Sanskrit studies in the state in 1980. The Secretary of Education was convener of the committee, and members included V. Venkatachalam, Radhavallabh Tripathi and others. Gwalior state constituted Vikramaditya Sahasrabdi Samiti to celebrate the second millennium of Vikrama Saṁvat. The Samiti sponsored two enormous volumes of Vikrama one in Hindi and the other in English. These volumes edited by Rama Shankar Tripathi and Radha Kumud Mukherji respectively, contain valuable articles in 925 and 750 pages by savants like Sampurnanand, Rahul Sanskrityayana, Radha Kumud Mukherji, V.S. Agrawal, B.S. Upadhyaya, S.M. Katre, A.S. Altekar, S.K. Belvelkar, P.K. Gode and others. These volumes have been published by Sindhia Oriental Institute which became an active centre of Indological Research under the direcorship of S.M. Katre.

Sindhia Oriental Institute was established under Gwalior state on 20 October 1931 and functioned for some years under the patronage of the rulers of Gwalior. In 1960, the Institute was handed over to Vikram University. The Institute is equipped with more than 17,000 valuable manuscripts and a rich collection of published books. It has rendered valuable services in the field of Indological research during the directorship of S.M. Katre. Katre brought out the journal of the institute, edited and published a number of manuscripts and initiated the task of preparation of manuscripts catalogues. No full-time director could be appointed after he left this Institute. V. Venkatachalam in honorary capacity remained at the helm of affairs of the institute for some years. He tried to complete the cataloguing of manuscripts. Pracya Niketana Bhopal offered to help the Institute for maintenance of the collection of manuscripts and to open a research centre. As a result Brij Mohan Birla Shodh Kendra was inaugurated on 13 August 1983. Under this research centre, Pandit Rudradev Tripathi edited some of rare manuscripts and published them. The centre has become defunct now.

Pracya Niketana Bhopal has been publishing *Prācya Pratibhā* — a research journal of Indological studies. This institute is basically devoted to the studies in ancient Indian history, archaeology and Indian culture. The journal and the institute both are now in the state of hibernation.

Kalidasa Samaroha, started since 1958 has attained a rare distinction at international level for promotion of Kālidāsa studies and Sanskrit theatre. Kalidasa Academy came into inception in 1977 at Ujjain. This Academi has published a number of books on Kālidāsa studies and Śāstric traditions. It also publishes a research journal — *Kālidāsa*. Adya Rangacharya took over as the founder director of this academy during 1979-80. After him the following persons have served this academy as its directors: Kamlesh Dutt Tripathi from 1981 to 1986; Srinivas Rath from 1986 to 1995; Prabhat Kumar Bhattarcharya from 1995 to 1997; Vinod Semval in 1997-98; C.P. Arora in 1998-99; Krishnakant Chaturvedi from 1999 to 2003, Kamlesh Dutta Tripathi for the second time from 2003 to 2007 and Mithila Prasad Tripathi 2007-10. At present the academy is headed by P.N. Shastri from 6 March 2010.

Madhya Pradesh Sanskrit Academy was established in 1984 by the Government of Madhya Pradesh. Bhaskaracharya Tripathi was appointed as its Secretary. This Academy has been very active until it was merged with Kalidasa Academy. Its regular activities included the organisation of Navodita Pratibha Samagama — a Youth Festival of young *paṇḍit*s and talented artists in Sanskrit at Saugar, Bhoja Samaroha at Dhar, Rajasekhara Samaroha at Gwalior, Bāṇabhaṭṭamahotsava at Rewa. Academi also started its literary journal *Dūrvā*, which has made a mark in the field of contemporary creative writing in Sanskrit.

Maharshi Sandipani Vedvidya Pratishthan (MSRVP) established by the Government of India has been functioning from Ujjain. It works for promotion of Vedic studies in the country by the way affiliating *veda-pāṭhaśālā*s, proving salaries to *vedapāṭhī*s and scholarships to their disciples and sponsoring *veda-sammelans*, conferences and seminars. Vachaspai Upadhyaya, Yugal Kishor Mishra and Shrikishor Mishra have worked as the secretaries of MSRVP. Presently, Roop Kishor Shastri, professor of Veda from Gurukul Kangri University of Hardwar is at the helm of affairs in MSRVP.

Scholars, laureates and authors

Shripada Shastri Hasurkar was not only a great traditional *paṇḍit*, he established a landmark by his *Dvādaśadarśana-sopanāyaliḥ* which is a *saṁgrahagrantha* like *Sarvadarśana-saṁgraha*. Sadashiv Sitaram Musalgaonkar, born in 1886 at Lashkar (Gwalior) composed several Śāstric works like *Vedāntavijñānam*, *Sudhārakaśaṅkāsamādhanam*, *Svakṛta-dharmaśāstrīyavyavasthā-saṁgrahaḥ* and *Sabhrātṛkanyayāḥ Paitṛkarikthe'dhikārosasti na vāḥ*? Prabhudayulu Agnihotri wrote a treatise on modern psychology – *Abhinavamanovijñānam*. Narayan Datta Tripathi had been working as a teacher of Āyurveda in Maharaja Holkar Sanskrit College at Indore. He has authored a text on Kāmaśāstra entitled *Pañcasāyakam* and two works on Vedānta named *Mumukṣusarvasvasārasaṁgrahaḥ* and *Svarūpaprakāśaḥ* along with one work on Mantraśāstra called *Cidambararahasyam.* Virupaksha Swami came from Dharwad. He had also been serving at Indore Sanskrit College. After his retirement from there as the principal of this prestigious institute, he came to live at Ujjain around 1957. He wrote several Śāstric works like *Śāstrabodhaḥ* and *Liṅgidharmaprakāśaḥ*. Pannalal Jain has extensively dealt with various aspects of Jain philosophy and *dharma* in his works like *Dharmakusumodayanam, Ratnatrayī Aśokarohiṇīvrato-dyāpanam, Trailokyatilakavratodyāpanam.*

Amongst some other scholars of Sanskrit from this state, who have been active in the later half of the twentieth century, the names of Hiralal Jain, Prabhudayalu Agnihotri, Prabhakar Narayan Kawthekar, V. Venkarachalam, Ramji Upadhyaya, Krishna Kanta Chaturvedi, Ramnihal Sharma, Rajiv Lochan Agnihotri, Kedar Nath Joshi, Kusum Bhuria, Vindhyeshwari Prasad Mishra, Somnath Nene, Achyutananda Dash, Rahas Vihari Dwivedi may be mentioned. Prabhudayalu Agnihotri worked for his Ph.D. on cultural study of Patañjali's *Mahābhāṣya* at Saugar University. He later on worked on cultural study of *Atharvaveda* and published several volumes on studies in Sanskrit literature. Prabhakar Narayan Kawthekar is known for his work on a text on Dharmaśastra — *Ahalyakamadhenuḥ* and he has also published his studies on Kālidāsa along with his original epic poem *Bājīrāvamastaniyam*. Krishna Kanta Chaturvedi has published his thesis on the history of Dvaita Vedānta.

Madhya Pradesh has produced some of the brightest luminaries in the firmament of contemporary Sanskrit literature. It may be mentioned here that a maximum number of littérateurs having been honoured with prestigious Sahitya Akademi Award for creative writing in Sanskrit have flourished in this state — Shrinath Hasurkar, Radhavallabh Tripathi, Bachchulal Awasthi, Shrinivas Rath and Mithila Prasad Tripathi. Shantipriya Satyadas was given Sahitya

Akademi Award of Sanskrit translation from Urdu poetry. In the first half of twentieth century, Pandit Urvidatta Shastri produced two epic poems *Edavardavaṁśamahākāvyam* and *Sultānajahamvinodakāvyam*. The latter was composed under the patronage of Begum of Bhopal and was completed in 1935. Bhatta Shrinivas Shastri Chakravarthy (1883-1948) worked as *purohita* of the rulers of Gwalior. He composed *Śrīnivāsa-sahasranāmastotra* in 1,000 verses (1928). Other writings by Shastri include *Bhagadviṁśatiḥ, Śrīṣoḍaśī, Gaṅgāṣṭakam, Yamunāṣṭakam, Śrīraṅgarājanakṣatramālā, Rājavivāhavarṇanaṁ, Śrīmanmādhavapraśastiḥ* and *Holotsavavinodaḥ*, Shripadashastri Hasurkar (1882) is also one of the prominent writers of this century, and he introduced new genres in modern Sanskrit writing by his biographies in prose. The other veteran authors of this century born in Madhya Pradesh belonging to pre-Independence era are Sadashiv Sitaram Musalgaonkar, Lokanath Shastri, and Gajanan Karmalkar Shastri.

Pandit Sudhakar Shukla produced a number of epic poems, *khaṭṭakāvyas* and *stotras*. Ramji Upadhyaya has written three novels and several plays in Sanskrit. Pandit Rudradev Tripathi was a versatile author with rare sense of humour and inclination towards satirical compositions. He experimented with the form of parody.

Pandit Suryanarayan Vyas has acquired a legendary fame for his scholarship and study of astrology. He was born on 11 February 1902 at Ujjain and spent all his life there. He was awarded Padmabhusana in 1958 and D.Litt. *honaris causa* in 1963. He published his stray verses composed in Sanskrit under the caption *Bhavya Vibhūtayaḥ* in 1933. Besides he has also composed some *stutis* and songs in Sanskrit and published his studies on Kālidāsa.

Pritamlal Nrisinha Kachchi moved from Kaccha to Indore and served as a school teacher from 1911 there. His poems include *Ārādhanāṣṭakam* (102 verses, 1930), *Śāntiśatakam* (164 verses, 1928), *Unnatiśatakam, Brahmacaryaśataka* and *Bhaktiśatakam*. His *Mātṛbhūmikathā* (in 608 verses, 1932) is an important historical document.

Among post-Independent authors, Sudhakar Shukla was born at Itawa in U.P., and moved to M.P. for serving as a school teacher. After retirement he settled at Datia. He has authored seven books in Hindi and nine of original writings in Sanskrit, which include *Gāndhīsaugandhikaṁ Mahākāvya, Bhāratīsvayamvaraṁ Mahākāvya, Svāmīcaritacintāmaṇih, Devadūtam, Āryasudhākaram* (1500 Ārya-lyrics), *Sūtropaniṣad* (poem on 20-point programme), *Durgādevanam (stutikāvya), Indumatī* (*nāṭikā*) and *Kelikalaśam* (*khaṇḍakāvya*).

Rudradev Tripathi was born at Mandsaur in Madhya Pradesh on 23 September 1925 at Mandsaur. At the age of 21, he started *Mālavamayūra* Sanskrit literary monthly and zealously pursued its publication regularly for 19 years. He has authored around 75 books, out of which 31 are originally in Sanskrit. His major publications in Sanskrit include *Patradūtam, Putradūtam, Gāyatrīlaharī* (in 108 verses), *Badarīśalaharī, Bhairavalaharī, Vinodinī, Hā-Hā-Hu-Huḥ, Ajantādarśanaṁ* (tr. from Gujarati), *Vajramānavaḥ* (travelogue), *Parīksāṇapāṭheyam* (teachers' training), *Bhāratabhāratī* (tr. from Hindi), *Ślokoktilīlavatī* (collection), *Prasaṅgikapadyapiyūṣam* (anthology) and *Citrapadyāvalī*; along with three collections of original Sanskrit songs — *Prenaṇa, Gītigaṅgā* and *Gītāñjaliḥ*; some *campūkāvyas* and Śāstric works. He attempted popular songs in Sanskrit in sequel to Bombay movie songs.

Bachchulal Awasthi was born on 6 August 1919 in Lakhimpurkheri district in U.P. He moved to Saugar University in M.P. in 1967. He retired from there in 1978 and served in a project in the Department of Philosophy in this university for five years. He has been one of the great *paṇḍits* of the century. He published *Pratanini* an anthology of his poems in 1996 for which he received the Sahitya Akademi Award. *Pratanini* is a monumental work presenting a rare fusion of tradition and modernity, of classical idioms and refinement of language and new expressions of imaginations and sensibility.

Premnarayan Dwivedi was born on 5 June 1922 at Saugar and was educated on both traditional and modern systems of Sanskrit education. He has been teaching in schools, in a college and the university at Saugar and settled here after his retirement. He has rendered *Bihārīsatsai* of famous Hindi poet Bihari, which is published. He has also translated the whole of Tulasīdāsa's epic — *Rāmacaritamānasa* along with several poems of Kabīr, Dādū, Rahīm and other saint-poets of Hindi into Sanskrit.

Rewaprasad Dwivedi was born in the village Nandner on the banks of Narmadā near Bhopal and was educated at Varanasi. He served as assistant professor in government colleges of Madhya Pradesh for several years and later on joined Banaras Hindu University. After his retirement he lives at Varanasi. A prolific author, he has made immense contributions to Sanskrit literature. Besides his two *mahākāvyas*, he has published *Revābhadrapīṭham* — a fascinating poem on the river Narmadā; bringing out the echoes of the rural life on the banks of the river, the sheer beauty of its natural surroundings as well as the devotion of the poet. Besides, Dwivedi has published some other collections of his stray verses and poems.

Shrinivas Rath was born on 1 November 1933 at Puri in Orissa, and was educated at Morena in Madhya Pradesh and at Varanasi. He has been serving in the Department of Sanskrit, Vikram University, Ujjain and lives there after his retirement. Rath has exclusively experimented with a Navagīta form very popular in Hindi and his Sanskrit songs have a delightful combination of sound and sense, they also portray the dichotomy and trauma of our age.

Shivsharan Sharma (born 1928) retired as Professor of Sanskrit from M.P. Government Collegiate service. He has published a collection of his Sanskrit songs entitled *Jāgaraṇam* (1963) and has continued this form till now. The songs express patriotism and changing socio-political scene. There is an urge to adopt different norms and outlook.

Bhaskaracharya Tripathi was born on 23 September at Pandar-Jasra near Allahabad and received his higher education at the University of Allahabad. He joined M.P. Government's collegiate service from 1964 and is serving in M.P. till this day. He published hundreds of his poems in *Samskrtapratibhā, Dūrvā, Saṁvit* and other Sanskrit periodicals and two of his collections of poems *Nirjhariṇī* and *Nilimpakāvyam,* besides an original play *Snehasauvīram.* His *Mṛtkūṭam* is a remarkable poem on the destiny of man.

Pushpa Dikshit was born on 12 June 1943 at Jabalpur, and obtained the degrees of M.A. and Ph.D. from the university there. She has been serving in M.P. government colleges from 1965 and presently lives at Bilaspur. She is known as one of the foremost Vaiyākaraṇas in the country, and has attempted a re-organisation of Pāṇinian system of grammar to felicitate teaching. She has also established the Panini Shodh Sansthan at Bilaspur. Besides several poems in Sanskrit periodicals, she has published an anthology of her songs in Sanskrit entitled *Agniśikhā.* Her songs reveal mystic feelings combined with romanticism and tenderness.

Shantipriya Satyadas has been a school-teacher in Grassim, Birlagram (Nagda) near Ujjain. He has established himself mainly as a translator of lyric poetry from other languages into Sanskrit. His *Aśārarasadhāraḥ* was selected for Sahitya Akademi Award for translation. It comprises renderings of 334 *aśāras* (couplets in Urdu) in the same metre. Satyadas also composed some original *ghaẓals* in Sanskrit. The name of Harihar Trivedi may also be mentioned amongst the authors who have devoted themselves to translation of lyric poetry from other languages. In collaboration with L.O. Joshi, Trivedi has brought *Āṅglaromāñcam* translations from romantic poetry of Keats, Shelley and other English poets.

Radhavallabh Tripathi, the present author, has published five anthologies of his poetic writings in Sanskrit *Sandhānaṁ, Laharīdaśakaṁ, Gītadhivaraṁ, Samplavaṁ,* along with three plays, novels and *Sansaraṇaṁ*. He is also known for his contributions to the study of Sahityaśāstra and Nāṭyaśastra.

Vindhyeshwari Prasad Mishra was born in village Pahara of Chhatarpur district in Madhya Pradesh, and received his higher education at Banaras Hindu University. He has been teaching at Saugar and at Vikram University of Ujjain. At present he is working as professor at B.H.U. He has published two collections of his poems and songs — *Sārasvatasamunmeṣaḥ* and *Gītavallarī*. Besides some hundreds of poems published in periodicals. He is a talented and versatile author. He has also experimented in the metres like *dohā, ganakṣarī, kavitta,* etc. which have been prevalent in medieval Hindi poetry. Kamtaprasad Tripathi is retired as Professor of Sanskrit from Indira Kala Sangit Vishvavidyalaya, Khairagarh. He has recently published two collections of his Sanskrit poems.

All of these authors have published the anthologies of their poems in book form, besides contributing to the periodicals Prabhakaranarayan Kawthekar (Indore), Prabhudayalu Agnihotri (Bhopal), Bhagwatilal Rajpurohit (Ujjain), Ila Ghosh (Jabalpur), Rahasvihari Dwivedi (Jabalpur), Kedar Narayan Joshi (Ujjain), Rajaram Tripathi (Bilaspur), Balkrishna Sharma (Gwalior), Dharmendra Kumar (Sagar), Bhagwandas Shastri (Rewa), Sitaram Dwivedi (Chhatarpur) and some other have made their debut through some of the Sanskrit magazines. More than three generations of poets at present are active on the scene.

Notes

1. The data is based on unpublished doctoral thesis of Kanhaiya Dwivedi entitled "Madhya Pradesh meṅ Sanskritādhyayana kā Vikāsa" submitted for award of Ph.D. at Saugar Univeristy.
2. As per the report signed and submitted by the secretary of Patanjali Shodh Samsthan to Rastriya Sanskrit Sansthan, New Delhi.

12

Sanskrit Studies in Maharashtra

Bhagyalata Pataskar

THE progress of Sanskrit in the State of Maharashtra over the past 60 years can be presented in brief as follows:

1. There are some institutions that are solely dedicated to the research work only. They have their own areas to be focused on, e.g. Vaidika Samshodhana Mandala (Adarsh Sanskrit Shodh Samstha) works on the Vedas only. The Bhandarkar Oriental Research Institute, Pune, is known for its *Mahābhārata* project. The progress of these institutes is measured by the number of the books published by them. These institutes also organise seminars and lectures so as to contribute to their main research projects.
2. There are some institutions that are involved in research and teaching, e.g. Deccan College, Pune Apart from the research projects and their publications these institutes also design various academic courses.
3. There are some institutes that bring out the Sanskrit publications only, e.g. Sharada Jnanapeetham, Pune and Ananda Ashrama, Pune. By bringing out old manuscripts into light and encouraging new authors to write, these institutes have really accelerated the progress of popularising Sanskrit in Maharashtra.

4. There are many organisations that have dedicated themselves to popularising and propagating Sanskrit. They have their own methods of functioning. However, each of them have positively contributed to creating a healthy awareness about Sanskrit.
5. There are more than 25 *vedapāṭhaśālās*, preserving the tradition of the oral transmission of the Vedic texts. In addition to those *pāṭhaśālās* there are Vaidikas who are not running the *vedapāṭhaśālās* formally but teaching the students privately (i.e. *Gṛhapāṭhaśālās*).
6. Through these categories of learning centres Maharashtra has produced some versatile scholars, esteemed Vaidikas, dedicated teachers, publishers, writers, readers and above all the faithful supporters for Sanskrit.

The present article elaborates these points as per the discipline of Sanskrit, hereafter.

Veda

The stalwarts of Vedas such as R.N. Dandekar, C. G. Kashikar, S.A. Dange, Sindhu Dange, T.N. Dharmadhikari, G.U. Thite, etc. have substantially contributed to the Vedic studies in Maharashtra. The Centre of Advanced Study in Sanskrit started in 1973, is the institute that accelerated the Vedic study, by making special provision for the Veda studies. The centre has published the translation of *Taittirīya Saṁhitā* (*kāṇḍa* 1 and 2 by V.V. Bhide). R.N. Dandekar was the first director of the centre. K.P. Jog, P.D. Nawathe, G.B.Palsule, G.U. Thite, etc. are the scholars who had led, shaped and strengthened this famous centre of Vedic studies in Maharashtra. R.N. Dandekar's theory of evolutionary mythology, Thite's reflections on several aspects of Vedic rituals, G.B. Palsule's research on Indo-European linguistics added freshness and creativity to Maharashtrian scholarship during the past 60 years P.D. Nawathe is still working on the Kaṭhaka School and so far has published very rare works about this almost extinct branch of *Kṛṣṇa Yajurveda*.

S.A. Dange initiated the course on mythology in the Department of Sanskrit at the University of Mumbai. He correlated the Vedic mythology and the Vedic ritual. The critical edition of the Vedic texts is one noteworthy contribution of Maharashtra, during the years under report.

Vaidika Samshodhana Mandala, Pune, has published the critical edition of *Ṛgveda Saṁhitā* with *Sāyaṇa Bhāṣya*. The edition contains *padapāṭha* also. Only one part of the entire project was published after 1950. The edition is highly recognised by the scholars and due to its perfection and authenticity it is known as the Poona Edition. The *Taittirīya Saṁhitā* with *Sāyaṇa* and *Bhaṭṭabhāskara Bhāṣya* is one of the ambitious projects of this period. There are four volumes, each having two parts. The 5th volume is the index volume, which comprises *pada* and *mantra* indices. This edition also gives *padapāṭha*.

The *Kāṇva Saṁhitā* of the *Śukla Yajurveda* is also critically edited and published by the Vaidika Samshodhana Mandala (VSM). This is the text with *Sāyaṇa Bhāṣya* (on first 20 *adhyāya*s) and *Anantācārya Bhāṣya* (on last 20 *adhyāya*s) as well as *Ānandabodha Bhāṣya* (on the entire Saṁhitā).

Out of Śrauta Sūtras, the Maharashtra scholars worked on the following Śrautasūtras: *Baudhāyana Śrautasūtra* (critically ed. and tr. C.G. Kashikar, IGNCA, 2003), *Āpastamba Śrautasūtra* (text with English tr. and notes by G.U. Thite, NBBC, 2004), the *Bhāradvāja Śrautasūtra* (C.G. Kashikar, VSM, 1961), *Lāṭyāyana Śrautasūtra* (H.G. Ranade, IGNCA, 1998), *Kātyāyana Śrautasūtra* (S.D. Khadilkar, VSM 1974), *Kātyāyana Śrautasūtra* (G.U. Thite, NBBC, Delhi, 2006). VSM has also published the *Kaṭhāraṇyakam* (text with English translation and notes by Bhagyalata Pataskar 2010). All these works proved to be highly rich sources for Vedic studies.

The *Śrauta Koṣa* of the VSM (both Sanskrit and English versions) is the encyclopedic work on the Śrauta ritual. It gives the texts right from the Brāhmaṇas up to the Sūtra texts, regarding one particular ritual. The Sanskrit edition is edited by C.G. Kashikar and the English edition by R.N. Dandekar. The *Śatapatha Brāhmaṇa*, Sanskrit text with English translation and notes (ed. Maitreyee Deshpande NBBC, New Delhi, 2008) gives us text with Eggeling's translation together, for the first time. The informative preface and notes add to the value of this work.

Maharashtra also ranks first among the states for making the authentic recitation available electronically. The Shri Guru Gangeshvara Veda Mandir, Tryambak Road, Nasik, has published the sets of audio CDs of *Ṛgveda*, *Śukla Yajurveda* (Kāṇva and Mādhyandina Śākhās), *Kṛṣṇa Yajurveda* (Taittirīya and Maitrāyaṇī Śākhās), Kauthuma, Raṇayanīya, Jaiminīya Śākhās of *Sāmaveda* and Śāunaka and Paippalāda of *Atharvaveda*.

The VSM has published Saṁhitā and Kramapāṭha of the *Mādhyandina Saṁhitā*. It has also released a film of *Aṣṭavikṛti*, which gives the exact idea of the eight modes of Vedic recitation. The VSM has also released an explanatory film on *Pūrṇamāseṣṭi* and some events from *Vājapeya*, which give us an idea about the Śrauta ritual.

Considering the study of Avesta complementary to the study of the Vedas, the VSM has also published a three volume Devanāgarī edition of Avesta and some other studies on Avesta and comparative aspects of Veda and Avesta.

The VSM research activities are substantially supported by the Rashtriya Sanskrit Sansthana, New Delhi.

Vedic Oral Tradition and Śrauta

Considering the strengthening of the Vedic oral tradition and the revival of the Śrauta, Maharashtra has done remarkable progress. The period under report is really the period of revival of the Vedic and Śrauta traditions.

Maharashtra is specially known for *Ṛgveda* (Śākala) *śākhā* and the Daśagrantha. The Vedacarya Ghaisas Guruji Vedapathasala Vedabhavan, Pune has started a branch in Kelasi (district Ratnagiri) just for the revival of the Ṛgveda Daśagrantha tradition. Recently, two young students completed *ghanapāṭha* of *Ṛgveda*.

In addition to the registered *pāṭhaśālā*s, there is a good number of *gṛhapāṭhaśālā*s, where a teacher privately teaches the students.

Non-residential students or a teacher coming from outside to teach is the new trend in this field.

The real revival and spread has been that of the *Śukla Yajurveda*-Mādhyandina Śākhā. Long back, Vedamurti Shrikrishna Godse Guruji from Benares put in special efforts for strengthening this branch. Now, there is a good number of Saṁhitāpāṭhins and even more than 10 young *ghanapāṭhins*. A number of *Śukla Yajurveda*-Mādhyandina Pāṭhaśālā are now the largest one. The name of Vedamurti Vishvanatha Shastri Joshi be mentioned with great reverence in this regard.

Not only the Saṁhitā or the *vikṛtipāṭha*s but the oral tradition of the Śatapatha also seems to be reviving slowly. A highly revered name in this regard is Vedamurti Manohar Joshi Guruji from Nagpur. Recently, some *Mādhyandinīya*s have also turned to the *upagrantha*s (of this particular Śākhā).

There are also two special Kāṇvaśākhā Pāṭhaśālās in Maharashtra. With the dedicated and enthusiastic teachers these *śakhādhyayan*s will certainly get established. Maharashtra is not that much known for *Kṛṣṇa Yajurveda* (Taittirīya Śākhā) as the south India is known for. However, few *pāṭhaśālā*s here have tried to establish the tradition of Taittirīya Śākhā (comprising of Saṁhitā, Brāhmaṇa, Āraṇyaka, Upaniṣad).

The Maitrayāṇī Śākhā was almost at the verge of extinction. However, the painstaking and continuous efforts of Vedamurti Somayaji Nana Kale have brought about the revival of this *śākhā*. By sending some of his students to Irinjalakuda, he got them trained in Maitrāyaṇī. Similarly, he also revived the tradition of Raṇayanīya Śākhā of *Sāmaveda*. At present there are more than 10 Sāmavedins in Maharashtra, imparting the lore to the new generation of learners.

The past half century or so has really observed the revival of the Vedic oral tradition, in the true sense of the term. The Maharshi Sandipani Rashtriya Vedavidya Pratishthan, Ujjain (Government of India), Kanchi Kamkoti Shankaracharya Peetha, Shringeri Shankaracharya Peetham and Maharshi Vedavyasa Pratishthan, Pune, have played a vital role in this increase and stability of the oral tradition. Maharshi Veda Vyasa Pratishthan has started 18 *vedapāṭhaśālā*s in and outside Maharashtra. Considering the dropout rate of the students from the *vedapāṭhaśālā*s, the visionary founder Swami Govindadeva Giri has started the separate *karma-kāṇḍa* or the *paurohitya* training centre for such students, so that the other *vedapāṭhaśālā*s can concentrate on the sincere students. Swamiji has also started a novel experiment of Vedarthabodha- vidyalaya. Under this scheme the students who have completed the Saṁhitā are further trained in the process of "understanding the Vedic text". It is far more than teaching them just translation.

One more very very new and unbelievable experiment in the field of Vedic recitation is that women, irrespective of caste, are taught the recitation of few Vedic *mantra*s (e.g. Rudrādhyāya, Brahmaṇaspatisūkta, Śrīsūkta and Pavamāna). The recitation of this portion is needed in some rituals. The women priests are very common in Maharashtra. For this particular cross-section, primary Sanskrit classes are also organised privately.

One noteworthy attempt which would certainly confirm the progress of Vedic oral tradition in Maharashtra, is that a young girl from a non- brāhmaṇa family passed the examination of *Śukla Yajurveda* Mādhyandina Saṁhitā recitation. This opportunity was specially brought to her by Kavi Kulguru Kalidas Sanskrit Vishvavidyalaya, Ramtek. She can recite the *sasvara pāṭha* with *hastasvara* of the complete *Mādhyandina Saṁhitā*.

Sati Godavari Mata Kanya Vidyalaya is specially engaged in training the women for recitation at the rituals. The *veda-mantras* which are required in particular rituals are being taught to them at this Vidyalaya.

Presently, there are at least six Śrauta Agnihotrins in Maharashtra. Somayaji Nana Kale has specially tried for the revival of the Mānava Śrauta tradition. He and Somāyajñas Yajñeśvara Selukar had performed advanced Somāyajñas (including Gavamayana Satra) in addition to *haviḥ saṁsthā*. They have specially trained a good number of priests who can perform Śrauta *yajña*s.

Vyākaraṇa

A remarkable work in the field of Sanskrit grammar is 12 volumes of some of the *āhnika*s of *Vyākaraṇa Mahābhāṣya* of Patañjali. The volumes contain the text, its English translation, very informative introduction and exhaustive discussion on the grammatical concepts therein. Moreover, the volumes not only refer to but also discuss the commentaries on *Mahābhāṣya*, i.e. *Pradīpa* and *Udyota*. The first volume of the series is *Samarthāhnika*, published in 1968, and the 12th one is *Sthānivadbhavāhnika* II, published in 1996. (All volumes are edited by S.D. Joshi and J.A.F. Roodbergen and published by the Centre of Advanced Studies in Sanskrit, University of Pune). Equally remarkable work of the same editors is the *Aṣṭādhyāyī* of Pāṇini, with the translation and explanatory notes. There are 14 volumes in this series covering *adhyāya*s I, II, and VII completely and *adhyāya* VI.3, 4. The first one of the series was published in 1991 and the 14th one in 2007. The *Aṣṭādhyāyī* volumes give the Sūtra text with its analysis and the *anuvṛtti*, translation and the detailed explanation with reference to the *Mahābhāṣya*, *Kāśikā* and other important texts of the tradition. The work also gives the detail *prakriyā*, wherever needed. The major theories of the Vyākaraṇa such as *siddha-asiddha*, *kāraka* and the theories about the ordering principles are also discussed elaborately. The *Dictionary of Pāṇinian Grammatical Terminology* (ed. J.A.F. Roodbergen and published by the BORI in 2008) serves very important tool for the study of these works. This carries the index with explanation of the technical terms used in all these volumes of *Mahābhāṣya* and *Aṣṭādhyāyī*, as well as of the expressions and quotations found mainly in *Mahābhāṣya*, *Kāśikā*, *Nyāsa* and other commentaries. The dictionary helps in a very clear understanding of many technical terms of the grammar.

Further, one of the noteworthy attempts is the complete Marathi translation of the *Vyākaraṇa Mahābhāṣya* of Patañjali with short notes by Abhyankar Vasudevashastri (pub. by Deccan Education Society, Pune, further reprinted by Abhyankar Pathashala, Pune, in 2003). This runs into seven volumes and the 8th one is the *prastāvanā khaṇḍa* containing the history of Sanskrit Grammar. The last two volumes of this series fall in the period under review. The Abhyankar Pathashala has also published the Marathi translation of the *Siddhāntakaumudī* with explanatory notes. (M.D. Sathe). Justice Wadegaonkar's Marathi translation of the *Paribhāṣenduśekhara* of Nāgeśa Bhaṭṭa does deserve a respectful mention. This is not only the complete translation but also a very detailed explanation of the *prakriyā*, which reveals almost all the dimensions of the traditional way of studying the subject rather than studying the text only. These three Marathi works are important because they nourished today's students of Vyākaraṇa Śāstra. Though the Marathi translation with explanatory notes of the *Paramalaghumañjūṣā* and the *Vākyapadīya*, Brahmakāṇḍa by V.B. Bhagwat are the students' editions still they give the complete idea of the Darśana tradition of the Sanskrit grammar.

The research works of the Centre of Advance Studies in Sanskrit, University of Pune, has contributed variously to Veda, Vyākaraṇa, Nyāya and Mīmāṁsā. *Anubandh of Pāṇini* (G.V. Devasthali, 1967), *Pāṇini as a Variationalist* (Paul Kiparsky, ed S.D. Joshi, 1980), *The role of the Particle ca in the Interpretation of the Aṣṭādhyāyī* (by S.D. Joshi and Saroja Bhate, 1983), *Fundamentals of Anuvṛtti* (by S.D. Joshi and Saroja Bhate, 1983), *Zero in Pāṇini* (M.D. Pandit, 1990), *Pāṇini's Taddhita Rules* (Saroja Bhate, 1989) are few of the publications without which the study of grammar will remain incomplete.

The Ananda Ashrama is known for the original publications than the translations. The edition of the *Vaiyākaraṇabhūṣanasāra with the Śaṁkarī*, commentary by Sankarashastri Marulkar (1957) and the commentary Suktiratnakara by Shesharatnakara on the *Vyākaraṇa Mahābhāṣya* (V.B. Bhagawat 1999) are the genuine contributions to the grammatical tradition. G.B. Palsule's *Yubhataḥ Saṁskṛtaṁ Prati* gives the thorough view of the Indo-European linguistics in Sanskrit. The BORI has contributed the Marathi translation of the *Vaiyākaraṇasiddhāntakaumudī* (vol 1. Chapters 1-6, V.N. Gokhale, ed. Saroja Bhate) within the period of the survey.

The Deccan Postgraduate College and Research Institute has contributed substantially to the study of grammar and lexicography. The Deccan College publication of *Vākyapadīya of Bhartṛhari* (English tr. and also some portion with commentaries ed. K.A. Subramania Iyer (different parts are published in different years) proves a fundamental source for the study of *Vākyapadīya*. The *Praudhamanoramā* with the commentary *Śabdaratna* (vol. I only, V.L. Joshi, 1986) adds to the list of the publications of the original valuable works. M.A. Mehendale's *Nirukta Notes* (1965, 1978) are just unavoidable study material for the study of *Nirukta*. The Deccan College has started the series of the works on lexicography and accordingly published about 11 rare works on lexicography which really proved a step towards progress of Sanskrit, since, in addition to the help for the historical dictionary, it led to the establishment of the special department of lexicography which is the unique of its kind in Maharashtra. Moreover, the Deccan College has published some very fundamental works, the study of which is inevitable for anyone who wants to be through in Sanskrit, e.g. *A Concordance of Sanskrit Dhatupaṭhas* (G.B. Palsule, 1955) and the most important one is *An Encyclopaedic Dictionary of Sanskrit on Historical Principal* (vol. I part 1 was published in 1976 and till date volumes up to IX part I have been completed).

Yoga

There are some Yoga institutions in Maharashtra, e.g. Lonavala Yoga Institute, Kaivalya Dham (both from Lonavala), Janardan Swami Yogabhyasi Mandal (Nagpur) that are doing research with experiments in the Yoga. The Lonavala Yoga Institute is the one that has specially concentrated on bringing out critical editions of the texts of the Yoga tradition.

I sincerely maintain that it is the large spreading Yoga activities that is attracting a certain class of people to Sanskrit. Taking this situation positively we do need some dedicated system to cater the need of this segment of people.

Traditional Śāstrādhyayana

Revival of the traditional *śāstrādhyayana* is a welcome phenomenon in Maharashtra. The Śāstra Śākhā of Nrisimha Sarasvati Pathashala is training the young, promising students traditionally, who even can debate in Vādasabhā. Devadatta Patil and the Śastra *pāṭhaśālā* in Satara are the names to be noted. Patil has trained students in Nyāya, Mīmāṁsā and Vyākaraṇa. He has completed a scheme for this through which he hopes that Maharashtra would be one of the leading centres for *śāstrādhyayana*.

Literature

During the past 60 years Maharashtra has qualitatively and also quantitatively contributed to the publication of the Sanskrit literature. The fields of the literature to which this contribution is made are, composition of epics (*mahākāvyas*), dramas, poems, other types of writing and translation (from Marathi to Sanskrit).

Mahākāvya (epics) = Maharashtra is proud to contribute 14 epics to modern Sanskrit literature.

The saints Tukarama Maharaj and Jnaneshvara Maharaja; the kings Shivaji, Rana Pratap; the leaders such as V.D. Savarkar, Mahatma Gandhi, Babasaheb Ambedkar, etc. are the personalities that are the heros of these epics. Here is the list for perusal.

Śrī Tukāramcaritam, Śrī Rāmadāsacaritam, Śrī Jñāneśvaracaritam (Kshamadevi Rao), *Śrī Subhāṣacaritam* (Pandit Viswanath Chhatre), *Gaṇapatisambhavam* (Pandit Prabhudatta Shastri), *Tilakayaśo ' rṇavaḥ* (Ane), *Śivarājyodayam* (B. Varnekar), *Yaśodharā-Mahākāvyam, Śrīmatpratāparāṇāyanam* (Pandit Ogeti Parikshit Sharma), *Mahātmāyanam, Svātantryavīragāthā* (Pandit P.G.V. Thekedar), *Śrī Devadeveśvaramahākāvyam* (Pandit Vasant Shevade), *Vaināyakam* (G.B. Palsule), *Bhīmāyanam* (P.S. Joshi), *Kavikaṇṭharamaṇīyam* (M. Penna).

All these epics have maintained the standard of the classical epics laid down by the Sanskrit poetics. These poets have introduced new vocabulary, phrases in Sanskrit.

Apart from the mythical and historical themes, these poets have also handled the contemporary topics in these dramas and lyric poetry. The prose literature in Sanskrit contributed by Maharashtra consists of 15 books. Many of them are biographies, very few are short stories.

In the recent event Vishwa Sanskrit Pustak Mela (in Bengluru, in January 2011), the Nagpur scholars alone came up with 51 published Sanskrit books.

There are some unclassified compositions which are worth mentioning. e.g. *Abhivasubhāṣitavilāsaḥ* (P.N.S. Navre) *Kaṇṭakāñjaliḥ* (*Kaṇṭakārjunaḥ*) *Vidagdha-Kāvyakelī* (Bhausaheb Patankar). These are the collections of independent compositions focusing on modern themes. The *Kaṇṭakāñjaliḥ* is very good example of satire.

Translations

The entire *Dāsabodha* of Saint Ramadas is translated by R.N. Welapure *Saṁskṛtadāsabodaḥ* (Satmaramam) *Jñāneśvarī* is also translated into Sanskrit. G. B. Palsule translated few *abhaṅgas* of Saint Tukārāma. The work is published with the title *Tukā Vkti.* Translations of *Rāmacaritamānasa* (*Tulasīmānasanalinam*) by Nalinee Sadhle) and of *Gondavalekara Mahārāja Pravacane* (*Nāmabhāgavatam*) by Durgaram Upadhye) are major works to be added to the list. The then famous Marathi drama *Śaradā* was translated and also staged under the name *Saṅgitaśāradam* by S.D. Joshi, who also translated Shakespeare's *Hamlet* and also staged under the name *Rāyasenaḥ Durgadeśasya Yuvarājaḥ* *The Wise and Otherwise* of Sudha Murthi is translated with the title, *Utāho Ajñāḥ* (by Asha Gurjar). The recent translations are Śyāmamātā (original *Śyāmacī Āī,* translated by Manjusa Kulkarni). *Bomadilā* (original by Avinash Biniwale tr. D.B. Polkam).

Composition of *ghazal*s is comparatively a new attempt in Maharashtra. In this regard Bhausaheb Patankar's *Vidagdha-kāvya-keli* (ed. Anupama Dongare) is highly recognised collection of Sanskrit *ghazal*s. He is the genius who has tried various modes of composition successfully, e.g. *qawwālī*.

The modern Sanskrit writers of Maharashtra have tried almost all types of literary compositions, and that too with best quality. However, this contribution is too less when compared to the number of scholars and scholarships in Maharashtra. This generation has also become old. Considering the upcoming generation such genius is very rare. The reason might have been that in Maharashtra children are hardly trained in writing Sanskrit. There doesn't seem any such provision in school and college education that would encourage Sanskrit language among the new generation of students.

In order to improve this situation, Asha Gurjar has been sincerely trying to popularise sanskrit by publishing the series of *Samarpaṇam*. The series is in the memory of the late G. B. Palsule. Through *Samarpaṇam* she has motivated, encouraged and guided the students, and the lovers of Sanskrit to write in Sanskrit. Recently the fifth *Samarpaṇam* is released.

Sanskrit Journalism

Girvaṇasudhā is the quarterly magazine published by the Devavanimandiram, Mumbai.

Sharada (founder editor Pandit Vasanta Gadgil) is another journal published from Pune. Recently this monthly journal has celebrated its golden jubilee. *Sharada* is the only monthly journal having an electronic edition and thereby it has reached all over the world.

Sanskrit Bhavitavyam (founder editor S.B. Varnekar, Nagpur) publishes crosswords, interviews, poetry, etc. in addition to other regular columns. Sanskrit *Bhavitavyam* has published more than 50 special issues occasionally.

Bālasaṁskr̥tam (ed. Madhav Badhe) is continuously being published for the past 27 years from Ratnagiri.

Guñjaravaḥ (ed. D.K. Kharawandikar). This is the monthly journal that is engaged in publishing contemporary literature and is published from Ahmednagar.

Saṁvid (ed. Jayantakrishna Dave). This quarterly journal is published by the Bharatiya Vidya Bhavan. Comparatively the issue of this periodical is bigger and comprehensive.

Bharatavāṇī and Sanskrit Dundubhi: These journals unfortunately couldn't be continued.

All these journals and periodicals mentioned above seem to be very sensitive to the contemporary issues. They have tried their best to promote and popularise Sanskrit among masses. They also gave ample scope to the new writers and poets to contribute to the language.

Manuscripts

A few institutions of Maharashtra are engaged in manuscript collection and preservation. They are: Bhandarkar Oriental Research Institute, Vaidika Samshodhana Mandala, Ananda Ashrama, Veda Shastrottejaka Sabha (all from Pune); Pradnya Pathashala (Wai); Veda Shastra Samvardhana Mandir (Karad); Rajwade Samshodhana Mandir (Dhule). In addition to this list, the University departments are also engaged in manuscript collection. Kavi Kulguru Kalidas Sanskrit Vishvavidyalaya, Ramtek, is one of the centres of National Manuscripts Mission Programme. Some Institutes (e.g. VSM) regularly publish the descriptive catalogues of the manuscripts in their collection.

Publication of Some Primary and Fundamental Works

Apart from the *Deccan College Dictionary* the Maharashtra has brought out some outstanding publications which have fundamental value and the study of which is unavoidable for any Sanskrit student or scholar. Here are few of them to support the point. *Śrauta Koṣa* (both Sanskrit and English sections, by VSM, Pune), *Dictionary of Nyaya Terms*, *Concordance of Conceptual Upanisadic Terms*, vols. I to IV (bodh by CASS, Pune), *Dharmakoṣa*, 4 vols. (by Pradna Pathashala, Wai). The CASS has published 12 Bibliographies of several subjects such as Nyāya, Vaiśeṣika,Vyākaraṇa, the branches of Vedānta, etc. *The*

Exhaustive Vedic Bibliography (vol. III up to vol. VII were published during this period. Up to vol. VI by R.N. Dandekar then onwards by G.U. Thite) is the inevitable tool for the Vedic studies since it is the academic googlised attempt. *The Harappan Bibliography* R.N. Dandekar, 1987) is the unique attempt of its own. The truly voluminous and incomparable work is the five volumes of the *History of Dharmaśāstra* by Mahamahopadhyaya P.V. Kane (all these works are published by BORI). Though the major part of the work falls in the previous period, before 1950, its 5th and the final volume came in 1962.

The Institute for the Study of Religion, Pune, has undertaken the mega project of preparing the word index of the *Śāṅkarabhāṣya*. So far, the volumes of the word index of the *Gītaśāṁkarabhāṣya* and *Chāndogya* have been published and the one that of the *Bṛhādāraṇyakaśāṁkarabhāṣya* is in progress.

Sanskrit in Universities

The following university departments carry out the activities about Sanskrit teaching and research. University of Pune, Mumbai University, Shivaji University, Dr Babasaheb Ambedkar Marathawada University, Nagpur University, Amaravati University, Tilak Maharashtra Vidyapeeth. etc. These activities can be grouped under the following heads such as designing the course for Sanskrit for different levels, undertaking research projects, arranging seminars and lectures. The scholars trained in this system have proved to be a real asset for Sanskrit. In addition to that the Kavi Kulaguru Kalidas Sanskrit Vishvavidyalaya, Ramtek, Mumbadevi Adarsha Sanskrit Mahavidyalaya, Bharatiya Vidya Bhavan and K.J. Somaiya Vidyapeetham (last two are granted by Rashtriya Sanskrit Sansthan, New Delhi) are the special Sanskrit universities strengthening and popularising the Sanskrit in Maharashtra.

Some Special Noteworthy Attempts to Promote Sanskrit

There are several small institutes in Maharashtra that specially work for the popularisation of Sanskrit among school and college students as well as among the society by organising competitions, exhibitions, lecture series, workshops, seminars, interviews, stage shows, quiz, etc. It is true that these institutions are not engaged in research, nor are they teaching some serious works. However, their work should not be underestimated since it is this attempt that creates the awareness in the society about Sanskrit. This attempt proves to be inspiring and motivating force through which a good number of mature students turn to advance Sanskrit studies and researches. For example, Maharshi Vyasa Vidya Pratishthana, Mumbai, has arranged a workshop on correct pronunciation of Sanskrit words and recitation of Sanskrit metrical texts. This helps one to enjoy the taste of the Sanskrit. The state-level drama competition (being organised by Fergusson College, Pune, for the past eight years) has continuously succeeded in attracting the students to Sanskrit. The yearly organisation of the state-level Students' Seminars (being organised by the S.P. College, Pune, for the past nine years) succeeded in giving significant research orientation to students in their young days. The real credit of creating Sanskrit-loving and Sanskrit -supporting population goes to the efforts put in by these small organisations and institutes which created a miracle in the Vishwa Sanskrit Pustak Mela held in Bengaluru in January 2011. Few of them are mentioned here just to support my point.

Girvana Vagvardhini Sabha, Pune, is uninterruptedly running Sanskrit *sabhā* fortnightly for the past more than 80 years. The only condition to participate here is to speak in Sanskrit.

Sanskrit Vidya Parisamstha, Pune, and Sanskrit Pracharini Sabha (1984), Pune are promoting Sanskrit at school and college levels through various activities.

Panini Pratishthana, Pune, is encouraging the researchers for higher Pāṇini studies.

Geeta Dharma Mandala, Pune, and Chetana Educational Trust, Pune, are promoting the *Bhagavad-Gītā* only, in the society. After studying *Bhagavad-Gītā* people turn to study Sanskrit out of curiosity.

About 20 organisations are active in Mumbai to promote and popularise and to teach Sanskrit and to do research in Sanskrit. An attempt to be noted is Shrivatsa Bala Mandiram (established in August 1965) which is Sanskrit medium kindergarten school. The school is getting enthusiastic response. The Tilak Maharashtra Vidyapeeth is regularly arranging Vasantik Sanskrit Shikshak Varga (special summer training programme for the teachers). Devavani Mandiram in Mumbai also arranges summer training and orientation camps for the school teachers. Brahmana Sabha, Mumbai, is fully devoted to stage the classical Sanskrit dramas. So far the Brahmana Sabha has staged 24 Sanskrit classical dramas. Sanatana Sabha in Ahmednagar is the organisation, engaged in teaching, arranging various programmes through lectures and popularising the Sanskrit.

The Vedavidnana Mandala, Pune, is continuously arranging lectures and seminars on the scientific issues in the ancient Indian literature. A point to be noted is that its founder, P.V. Vartak (medical practitioner) has succeeded in developing love, zeal and capacity in the society for ancient Indian literature. The research works published by him mainly deal with the dating of the ancient Sanskrit texts.

One more attempt that really gave a new face to Sanskrit langauge in Maharashtra is that of Sanskrit Samvardhan Mandala of Sangamner. Vimal Lele, the visionary founder of the organisation put really tireless efforts to promote and establish Sanskrit in the rural areas around Sangamner (a small town in Ahmednagar district). It is because of her efforts that, that strata of the society which was so far away from Sanskrit has turned to Sanskrit. This effort has yielded the fruit in the form of the establishment of the Research and Postgraduate Study Centre in this small town.

Sangli, Aurangabad and Ratnagiri also have small organisations or groups that work for popularising Sanskrit in the society.

The Indian knowledge system, a small organisation, run by one metallurgy engineer is constantly organising seminars, courses and lectures to establish scientific experiments and scientific truth from ancient Sanskrit literature.

The Prasad Prakashan, Pune, has launched an ambitious project with various schemes. One of them is Apale Veda, Apali Upaniṣade aṇi Apali Purāṇe. Under this scheme four Vedas, 10 Upaniṣads and 30 Purāṇas have been translated into Marathi. These are the authentic translations worked out by a panel of good scholars (the total number of books in this scheme is 17).

Another scheme entitled Devabhāṣece Deṇe: Marāṭhice Leṇe contains 16 books. These books give the complete Marathi translation in lucid style of 30 classics of Sanskrit literature (including the works of Kālidāsa, Bhavabhūti, Bhāsa, etc). These books also contain the Sanskrit text.

The Abhinava Prasanna Darśana comprising of six books gives the detailed introduction to six Vaidika Darśanas and four non-Vaidika Darśanas.

The last scheme under this project is *pañca mahākāvya* giving complete and lucid Marathi translation of five great epics of Sanskrit. (This work is awaited).

Government of Maharashtra's Efforts for Promotion of Sanskrit

The Government of Maharashtra has also taken some steps to

promote Sanskrit. These activities can be classified into three categories —

1. Supporting the research institutes, by giving the grants.
2. Felicitating the Sanskrit *paṇḍits,* teachers and outstanding students.
3. Organising drama competitions, celebration of certain events, e.g. Sanskrit Day. The summer training course, which is run by the Balmukund Lohiya Asiai Abhyasa Kendra, Pune, is being sponsored by the Government of Maharashtra.

Conclusion

This is the satellite view of the activities that have been carried for past 60 years in Maharashtra for promotion of Sanskrit. I don't claim that I have covered each and every activity about Sanskrit promotion in Maharashtra. If something is missing it is just out of oversight. I have sincerely done my best to collect maximum information regarding the issue. However, something missing would still prove the strength and progress of Sanskrit in Maharashtra, I hope. Here is the summary:

1. The research institutes are working in the following fields — Veda, Dharmaśāstra, Vyākaraṇa and Yoga. I mean to say that these have remained the thrust areas of the research in Sanskrit in Maharashtra.
2. However, the publication activity being very strong covers almost all possible areas of Sanskrit studies, e.g. literature, Vedic and ancient Indian sciences, spiritual and religious books.
3. A good number of activities are carried to create, to nourish and to channellise the love for Sanskrit in society in general and to develop research ability among students in particular.
4. Critical editions and translations of original works,

encyclopedic works, bibliographies are the major contribution of Maharashtra to the Sanskrit field.

5. A woman learning traditional Vedic recitation and a lady scholar Pandit Kshama Rao are the real reformative contributions of Maharashtra in the Sanskrit field.
6. The Vedic oral tradition, Śrauta tradition and the *śāstrādhyayana* traditions have been revived in the period under consideration in the true sense of the term.
7. However, I should mention, without fail that sincere and serious scholars of the old generation do worry, for they find that today the scholars with depth and width of the knowledge are very rare. If at all there is anybody, he lacks the modern discipline of research methodology.
8. I personally maintain that the Sanskrit activities in Maharashtra are satisfactory as far as promoting, teaching, researching and publications in Sanskrit are concerned. The people from other strata of the society are turning to Sanskrit; women reciting Vedas (though partly), increasing number of seminars and the participants and inception of new institutions is a welcome phenomenon in Maharashtra and it seems to assure that Sanskrit will not lose its past glory. Now, we need the concentrated efforts to build up the scholarship with traditional depth of knowledge, enriched with modern perspective.

13

Sanskrit Studies in Odisha

Prafulla Kumar Mishra

ODISHA being the first state created on the language basis, quite naturally Oḍiya-speaking people are in majority in Odisha. Oḍiya is the nearest language to Sanskrit. Purī the *sanctum sanctorum* of Lord Jagannātha, known as Puruṣottama-Kṣetra, one among four *dharma*s of the Hindus has the glorious tradition of popularising Sanskrit through centuries.

Background

Orissa as it was known till recently, has beautiful physical surroundings with the Bay of Bengal on one side and a wide range of hills on the other. It has evolved a unique pattern of Indian culture which attracted several saints and savants from various parts of the country. Being the meeting place of north and south India, it accommodates all the features of south and north harmoniously. The food habits, style of living and all other nomenclature of culture is a unique blend of all. Similarly, the saints belonging to different religious sects and philosophical streams, because of its composite culture and mysterious cult of Lord Jagannātha, have flourished here. The state has preserved many of the ancient customs and traditions and made adoptions of other customs in its own way. This, the land of the Lord Jagannātha has contributed a lot to the field of Sanskrit language and literature in different periods, even under the adverse socio-potitical circumstances.

Cultural Heritage of Odisha and Sanskrit

Odisha occupies a significant position on the map of India for its remarkably beautiful golden sand sea-coast, water springs, mountain ranges, forests, historical background of huge temples, Buddhist monasteries, Jaina caves, besides a highly appreciable cultural heritage and worth-mentioning spiritual tradition. Massive construction of temples and worship of different deities have, no doubt, injected a deep faith of religion and spiritualism among the people of this land which had, mainly, generated an atmosphere for learning Sanskrit. After the discovery of Paippalāda recension of the *Atharvaveda* for the first time from a remote area of Mayūrabhañja district of Orissa it is believed that the Sanskrit-learning dates back probably to that period. Most of the scholars and historians are almost unanimous on the fact that the origin of Sanskrit culture in Orissa dates back to fourth century CE prior to which a lot of inscriptions such as rock edicts and the two Separate Rock Edict XII of Aśoka at Dhauli near Bhubaneswar and at Jaugada on the bank of Ṛṣikulya River in the Gañjam district; the famous Hāthīgumphā inscription on the Udayagiri Hill of Khāravela, the emperor of Kaliṅga, in Pāli and Prākṛt testify that the people's language was akin to Sanskrit from an early period (up to CE 1100).

The periods of rise, fall and revival of Sanskrit can be catagorised as under:

(i) Medieval period (Gaṅga and Gajapati kings of Orissa during whose reign Sanskrit had reached its pinnacle of glory from CE 1100 to 1538)

(ii) The period of decadence (from CE 1568 to 1947 during which the Muslims, the Marhaṭhās and the Britishers ruled Orissa)

(iii) The period of revival this continues till date.

Golden Era of Sanskrit Literature in Odisha

Orissa has been home to a number of scholars, poets and rhetoricians in the field of Sanskrit literature among whom the names of Murari Mishra, the author of *Anargharāghavam*; Krishna Mishra, the author of *Prabodhacandrodayam*; Jayadeva, the author of *Gītagovindam*; Visvanatha Kaviraja, the author of *Sāhitya-Darpaṇaḥ*; Kavidindima Jivadeva Acharya, the author of *Bhakti-Bhāgavata-Mahākāvyam*; Raya Ramananda Parnaik, the author of *Jagannāthavallabhanāṭakam*; Narasimha Vajpeyi and Sambhukara Vajpayi both the authors of Smṛti literature, etc. deserve a special mention. Besides literature, Veda, grammar, philosophy, mythology, Dharmaśāstra, music, astronomy, astrology and so on were significantly noticeable during this period. The period of the rule of the Sūryavaṁśī Gajapati kings (CE 1435-1540 = 105 years) in Odisha was a golden era of Sanskrit literature. Mention of the scholars like Kavidindima Jivadeva Ācārya, Kavicandra Ray Divākara Miśra, Kavindra Mārkaṇḍeya Miśra and Raya Ramananda Patnaik may be made in particular.

Gajapati Kapilendra Deva (CE 1435-1458) has authored a drama named *Paraśurāmavijayam*, which provides a lot of material for the reconstruction of the history of this period. His son Gajapati Puruṣottama Deva (CE 1466-79) was a scholar of Sanskrit literature. Regarding his academic excellence, a contemporary poet Kavidindim Jivadeva Ācārya eulogised him in his work. The authorship of the works like *Mukticintāmaṇi*, *Gopālārcanā-paddhatiḥ*, *Nāma-malikā*, *Dasagrīvavadha-mahākāvyam*, *Abhinavagītagovindam*, *Janakapramoda* and *Abhinava-veṇisaṁhāram* are attributed to Gajapati Puruṣottama Deva.

Gajapati Prataprudra Deva (CE 1479-1540) wrote (i) *Sarasvatīvilāsaḥ*, (ii) *Pratāpa-Mārtaṇḍaḥ*, (iii) *Nirṇaya Saṁgrahaḥ*, (iv) *Kautukacintāmaṇiḥ*.

Decline of Sanskrit in Odisha

Sanskrit had to see bad days in the state due to foreign rule. Many reputed families migrated elsewhere for want of patronage. Chauvinism of regional language and influence of Islamic rulers discouraged Sanskrit. British rule gave importance to English education and doyens of Sanskrit learning had to live a very humble life. Popularisation of mystic literature of *pañcasakhās* in Odiya language and their neo religious movement made people turn away from Sanskrit. Industrialisation, urbanisation and job-oriented psychology of the society further discouraged the study of Sanskrit.

Post-Independent Period: An Overview

After receiving a serious setback during the period of foreign rule, Sanskrit-learning started to be revived particularly from the beginning of the twentieth century in Odisha in various ways. This process of revival has been extremely slow and steady because of the advancement of science and technology. Several creative writers, having plunged themselves into the freedom movement, composed patriotic poems in Sanskrit and made serious efforts to give a befitting reply to the disdainful attitude of the British rulers. Those who had underestimated the movement for regional language could not allow the fullest revival of Sanskrit and the system of Sanskrit-learning in the state. In the name of modern educational system designed by Macaulay, the foreigners tried to replace the centres of traditional Sanskrit-learning by high schools, as a result of which the traditional Sanskrit institutions got seriously neglected. Clever and elite people taught their children in high schools. Poor brāhmaṇa boys and only some rare students got interested in reading in Sanskrit in *ṭols*. One *paṇḍit* was telling that during pre-Independent period learning English for traditional elite family was considered as a disgrace. They restrained themselves from learning English in the fear of losing their caste/*dharma*, etc. This was because of ill manners and impure ways of living of the British rulers. In spite of all difficulties, Sanskrit has been occupying a commendable position in educational curriculum designed from time to time for various levels of teaching. Some brāhmaṇa families of Orissa have somehow retained the study of Sanskrit for a considerably long period despite their poor financial condition and other temptations.

Sanskrit as Taught in General Institutions

Sanskrit is taught in different institutions mainly in two streams, i.e. general and traditional. In general institutions, like high schools and colleges, Sanskrit is taught as one of the subjects either as a compulsory or as an alternative subject in language groups.

It may be mentioned that most of these general institutions have been established after Independence. A few colleges and high schools were set up in the last part of the nineteenth century where Sanskrit was introduced as one of the subjects in the curriculum also.

Sanskrit at the Secondary Level

The total number of high schools in Orissa managed by the government, or run on government aid and purely private owned schools for Odiya medium, is about 8,000, which impart teaching to classes VIII, IX and X. In the year 2010, nearly 400,000 students opted for Sanskrit as the third language out of 450,00,000 students who appeared for the high school examination. The syllabus for HSC examination has been designed in the light of the recommendations made by NCERT, and SECRT. From the academic year 2011-12, Sanskrit is being introduced from class VI.

After the formulation of the National Policy on Education by the Government of India in the year 1984, a draft syllabus was designed by the Board of Secondary Education, Orissa, keeping the three language formula in view. The policy makers proposed to make Sanskrit as a part of M.I.L. (1st language), 2. English (2nd language), 3. Hindi (3rd language). Prior to that, Sanskrit was being taught as an alternative subject/language to Hindi for 100 marks. But, in the name of National Policy on Education, the planners wanted to completely ignore the identity of Sanskrit and proposed to include the same as a part of M.I.L. for 20 marks only. Thanks to the sharp reaction of the public and the guardians who could not tolerate this type of assault on Sanskrit language, systematic movements were organised by Sanskrit students and teachers to resist this conspiracy against Sanskrit. It is neither the beginning nor the end; the fight to retain Sanskrit as an important subject is a continuous effort every 10-15 years. During sixties, Sanskrit (paper I consisted of 50 marks) and was taught in high schools as a compulsory subject. But the second paper (50 marks) was optional with Hindi and lower Odiya for non-Odiya-speaking students, except that one could opted for Sanskrit as an optional subject from among physiology, hygiene and mathematics. But there was again a conspiracy to stop teaching Sanskrit during 1970s in the high schools. But the agitation launched by the P.G. Department of Utkal University with the students from Sri Sadasiva Kendriya Sanskrit Vidyapitha and Raveshaw College, from Balasore and other in parts of Orissa could stop this. In the last five years, the champions of agriculture wanted the organisation Saṁskrit Vañcao Samīti to take up the challenge. Again in order to replace agriculture for Sanskrit some officers conspired during 2006-07. Sanskrit Mahāsaṁgha (confederation) was founded to check this mischievous activity of the Board of Secondary Education, Odisha.

The Board of Secondary Education, Orissa, has again changed its syllabus and made Sanskrit as an alternative language to Hindi as one of the third languages for 100 marks, and it may be mentioned, that nearly 80 per cent of the students are offering Sanskrit as the third language.

So far as teaching of Sanskrit is concerned, the lovers of Sanskrit have got many things to say about the present syllabus. Withdrawal of the compulsory status of Sanskrit from the syllabus has degenerated the position of Sanskrit in the secondary education. It is observed that in certain schools, the students managed to ignore Sanskrit completely by taking other alternative languages mainly Hindi. In such a case the students cannot be blamed. It is the teacher who should attract the students to his subject by creating an atmosphere favourable for Sanskrit. It is seen that some Sanskrit teachers are not taking interest in some schools as a result of which the students are not getting attracted towards Sanskrit. This is happening because of want of proper orientation and training of the classical teachers. The Sanskrit teachers are expected to convince the students as well as their guardians regarding the importance and utility of Sanskrit. Moreover, they have to adopt the right devise and proper methodology to teach the students in an attractive manner. Some teachers, mischievous in mind and against the Indian culture and Sanskrit language, discourage and speak ill of Sanskrit. This type of loose brainwashing impresses the immature students.

Sanskrit in Higher Primary

Sanskrit was taught in class VI-VII during the 1970s and 1980s. But it was stopped after introduction for a decade by imitating Kendriya Vidyalayas.

Meanwhile, a decision has now been taken by the authorities to introduce Sanskrit from class VI. After implementation of this decision, a number of students could get more and more interested in Sanskrit language.

Sanskrit in Kindergartens and Primary Schools

(i) There are about 2,000 schools managed by Vidya Bharati Orissa branch known as the Saraswati Sisumandiras of Siksha Vikas Samiti and there imitations in Odisha.

(ii) Again, Odisha is considered as the best place to experiment Sri Aurobindo's Integral Education. Integral schools run by the New Life Education Trust and their imitations are about 1,000 in number.

All of them have introduced Sanskrit from standard one in their own ways. The method of listening, speaking, reading and writing is adopted very skilfully. These students can very successfully speak, read, and write Sanskrit. It appears that students are aptly interested in Sanskrit and enrich their mother tongue with Sanskrit.

Sanskrit Medium Schools/Ṭols

Sanskrit medium schools are styled as *ṭols* (Teaching of Oriental Learning) by British rulers. Formal examination pattern started in India in the year 1912. So also the examination pattern started in Bengal-Bihar-Odisha/Bihar-Odisha for the first time in the year 1912. When in 1936 Odisha became a separate state, Odisha Sanskit Learning and Culture was established as an examining body from Prathama to Acharya degree where Kishorimohana Dvivedi became the first superintendent. Students who completed standard 5 in general schools could take admission in Prathama. Then they would enter Purva-Madhyama and Uttara-Madhyama, then Shastri and Acharya classes subsequently. After introduction of 10 + 2 + 3 pattern, two Madhyamas are now one and a new Upashastri degree has been introduced.

The examinations up to Madhyama are conducted by the Board of Secondary Education of Odisha. Upashastri, Shatri and Acharya examinations are conducted by Sri Jagannatha Sanskrit University. The teaching facilities for Acharya though previously available in different *ṭol*s of Odisha, yet they were all centralised in Sri Jagannatha Sanskrit University. Besides, Madhyama *ṭol*s were separated from Shastri colleges. A person has to study in four types of institutions, such as a primary school, a Madhyama *ṭol*, a Shatri college and then in a university department. On the other hand, a general graduate with Sanskrit can directly be admitted to Acharya class.

There are altogether 442 *ṭol*s or Madhyama Sanskrit *vidyalaya*s out of which 11 are government schools, 187 are government-aided schools and 42 schools are purely recognised private schools.

There are 145 Sanskrit colleges out of which 3 are government colleges, 22 are government-aided colleges, 44 are half aided and 76 colleges are purely private colleges.

Purī being the important religious centre of eastern India there were hundreds of *maṭha*s/convents which were patronising students. Many convents had their own *ṭol*s to teach their pupils and provide them food and lodging up to their end of study. Excepting a few patronised convents at Cuttak, Bhadrak, Balasore, Bhograi, Kendrapara, Jagatsingpur, Bolangir, Sambalpur, Chakapada, Jeypore, Berhampur and Baripada almost all other students were educated at Puri in different *ṭol*s. But gradually most of these *ṭol*s were closed but the institutions are still many. Some of them are mentioned bellow:

- Govardhana Pīṭha of Śaṅkarācārya Maṭha
- Raghunandana Ṭol of Emāra Maṭha
- Uttarapārśvamaṭha Ṭol
- Dakṣinapārśva Maṭha Ṭol
- Mahiprakāśa Maṭha Ṭol
- Badaodia Maṭha Ṭol
- Śri Jagannātha Temple Ṭol

- Girisvami Maṭha Ṭol
- Ādarśa Āyurveda Catuṣpathi
- Vedakarmakāṇḍa Mahāvidyālaya
- Puri Sanskrit College
- Srisadasiva Kendriya Sanskrit College/Srisadasiva Campus of Rastriya Sanskrit Sansthan

Due to the independence movement and Endowment Act the *maṭhas* lost their autonomy and wealth. After wide acceptance of English education, *maṭhas* lost their glamour. The establishment of high schools and colleges in different parts of Odisha discouraged students from coming to Puri. By the end of the 1970s there were only few *ṭols* left at Puri. All other institutions of convents/*maṭhas* had their natural death. But the institutions like Adarsa Ayurveda Catuspathi, Vedakarmakanda Mahavidyalaya and Puri Government Sanskrit College are the main Sanskrit learning centres at Puri. Besides, there are *ṭols* in Girisvami Maṭha, in Govardhana Pīṭha and in Sri Jagannatha temple itself. Even though there is decline in the conditions of *maṭhas*, yet they maintain few students in many convents even today. For traditional Sanskrit learning, Puri is still the centre of Odisha. As has been stated above there are hundreds of Sanskrit institutions in Odisha which are controlled by the Odisha Sanskrit Learning and Culture, Puri, and Sri Jagannath Sanskrit University, Puri. The condition of *ṭols* and Sanskrit colleges is measurable. Buildings are broken and at many places there is no boundary wall. These buildings look like abandoned houses. Nobody could believe that these institutes were, once upon a time, the light houses of traditional knowledge and produced many brilliant scholars. The feudal lords/kings and priestly classes were patronising them. But now the new industrial houses or the government is not patronising them, as a result of which students are not attracted to come to these institutes unless they are very poor.

Sanskrit-learning is somehow connected with poverty in this connection. This is the irony of fate of the traditional ṭols of Odisha.

Sanskrit at Higther-Secondary Level

With a long-drawn effort Sanskrit is accepted as one of the M.I.L. group languages in Odisha. Students not taking Odiya as their M.I.L. paper are taking Sanskrit instead of English. There is a very good response in big colleges. Science students are opting for Sanskrit as their M.I.L. Even if there is resentment from intolerant Odiya teachers, yet the students are determined to study Sanskrit. Besides optional Sanskrit is extended to science students with a view to helping them in future if they study Āyurveda.

Sanskrit in Undergraduate Colleges

Sanskrit (honours) and as an elective subject are generally opted for by the students of the undergraduate level. Honours papers are having 800 mark for 8 papers and elective papers are of two types one is elective-I, having 400 marks for 4 papers, and elective-II, having 200 marks for two papers. The second one is only meant for students of different disciplines interested to know something for their information. But the general students offer elective-I as their major subject other than honours subjects. In Odisha there are "Honours" teaching facilities available in all the government colleges. But the honours teaching facilities in western Odisha and southern Odisha are restricted to government colleges only. In the coastal districts, almost all the degree colleges are having Sanskrit honours teaching facilities excepting a few smaller colleges.

There are about 125 colleges in Odisha where honours teaching facilities are available. They have to appear in an entrance test for taking admission in M.A. (Sanskrit).

Postgraduate Teaching

There are three centres available for postgraduate teaching facilities in Odisha.

(i) Postgraduate teaching department of Sanskrit in Utkal University, Vani Vihar, Bhubaneswar.

(ii) Sailabala Womens' College, Cuttack, under the Utkal University.

(iii) Gangadhara Mehera College, Sambalpur, under the Sambalpur University.

Postgraduate Department of Sanskrit in Utkal University, Bhubaneswar

This oldest Sanskrit department of the state and one of the oldest departments of the university was established in the year 1957.

This department was headed by famous Sanskrit scholars like Artabalhava Mahanty who did monumental work on Prācī Granthamālā and Karunakara Kara who explored *Bauddha Gāna and Dohā,* temporarily. The first regular professor was Prahlada Pradhana (the first vice-chancellor of Sri Jagannath Sanskrit University) an expert in Buddhism and who retrieved Sanskrit form from the Tibetan language Buddhist texts like *Abhidhamma-Samuccaya* and *Abhidhamma-Kośa-Bhāṣyam.* This was his monumental work. He has edited and translated the *Pāli Dhammapada.* His successor did his Ph.D work under Danniel H.H. Ingals at the Harvard University. He has started the tradition of Purāṇic research, as a result of which, a group of Purāṇic scholars among whom U.N. Dhal, a known name in Purāṇic study has made significant contribution to *Goddess Lakṣmī, Śiva Purāṇa, Mahiṣamardinī Iconography,* etc. The successor of Anama Charana Swain was Krishna Chandra Acharya (the formerly vice-chancellor of Sri Jagannath Visvavidyalaya, Puri) who edited *Prākṛt Sarvasva.* He was a scholar of many fields who trained P.K. Mishra, a Sanskrit poet and writer, his successor in poetics and Vedic studies. The able leadership of his disciple could encourage research and creative activities in Sanskrit. Probably nowhere in the country there is *kavi sammelana* at regular intervals and workshops and Sanskrit plays at every annual day celebration. Sri Aurobindo studies and yogic studies were initiated by him. Alekh Chandra Sadangi (the formerly vice-chancellor of Sri Jagannatha Sanskrit Visvavidyalaya) was a Pune trained grammarian who introduced Vyākaraṇa as a special paper. Gopal Krishna Dash, a Purāṇic scholar initially devoted his time in Vyākaraṇa, Veda and literary criticism. Raghunatha Panda has concentrated on Odishan studies especially on *Gītagovinda*. Radhamadhaba Dash as a student of Sarangi devotedly worked on *Kāśikā* and *Harināmāmṛta Vyākaraṇa*. Pratibhanmanjari Ratha did her work on Vedic studies and later joined Subashchandra Dash, a scholar in Indian philosophy. After a long time a young scholar, Parambashri Yogamaya, a Sanskrit story writer, joined the department as a scholar in Vedic studies. Of late, Gopinatha Mahapatra (formerly vice-chancellor of Sri Jagannatha Sanskrit University) has joined this department. There was a very efficient teacher named Sri Sadananda Ramanujadasa, among the first teaching faculty of this department. All of them are well known in their field of research. Teaching facilities are available in Veda, Sāhitya, Vyākaraṇa and Darśana. Besides, there are courses designed on Odishan studies, comparative aesthetics, epics and Purāṇa but these could not be started due to lack-proper teaching staff.

The department, being the only centre of higher studies in Sanskrit, has produced about 160 Ph.D. and 350 M.Phil. scholars. The department has an intake capacity of 64 students for M.A. in the first semester. The alumni of this institute are established in many universities in and outside the country.

The department has two-dimensional activities to train their students in modern research and traditional knowledge of Śāstras, and creative writing. For the former the research journal is *Vāṇījyotiḥ* and the creative writing journal is *R̥tayānī.* Many students are now established poets and writers in the country in Sanskrit. Besides this, yogic study has been added to this department where practical Yoga with Sanskrit yogic texts are imparted to Yoga students.

The university has a treasure of 5,000 palm-leaf manuscripts. Each and every year M.Phil. students are required to make descriptive catalogues of at least four manuscripts each. This activity enables them to read palm-leaf manuscripts, which is useful for their future research.

Besides the regular programme, as many as 150 students join M.A. in Sanskrit through the distance mode under Utkal University. Even after that about 100 students appear annually for M.A. in Sanskrit as private candidates.

Gangadharamehara College and Sailabala College

These two colleges are the government colleges. The postgraduate departments are not separate from undergraduate teaching and the teaching faculties are not appointed for long a period. As a result the teaching departments have limited activities. There is no scope for growth due to discouragement and lack of infrastructure. But those departments still produce good students.

Sri Jagannath Sanskrit Vishvavidyalaya

The Sanskrit-learning again took a leap when in 1981 Sri Jagannath Sanskrit University was established as the third Sanskrit university of the country. Postgraduate teaching, research and other publication works were started. Faculties in Veda, Sāhitya Vyākaraṇa, Dharmaśāstra, Vedānta, Nyāya and Sarvadarśana were opened. Jyotiṣa has been introduced as a part-time study recently. Purāṇa, Mīmāṁsā, Āgama, Sāṁkhya-Yoga like traditional Śāstras and manuscriptology, modern Sanskrit writing, epigraphy, palaeography, tourism, applied Sanskrit, computational Sanskrit, comparative literature, Sanskrit and management study, manuscript preservation, editing and drama-study could also be opened. But they were neglected in course of time. Students and teachers of this university have won laurels and the students and teachers are found to be established in high positions in different universities and colleges of the country.

There are few teachers like Brajakishore Swain and Pyaremohan Pattanaik who are known widely for their scholarship. Keshava Chandra Dash (Sahitya Akademi Awardee) and Harekrishna Satapathy (the vice-chancellor of Rashtriya Sanskrit Vidyapith, Tirupati, and Dalmia Srivani Alamkarana Awardee), are distinguished writers in modern Sanskrit. All others are serious scholars in their field and have guided a number of researchers. They are Adwaitacharana Dhala, Brajakishore Nayak, Kishore Chandra Mahapatra, Nilakantha Pati (vice-chancellor, Sri Jagannatha Sanskrit Visvavidyalaya, Puri), Prabhata Kumar Mahapatra, Kamalesh Mishra, Govinda Chandra Kara, Pramoda Chandra Mishra, Jayakrishna Mishra, Tejapala Sharma, Sathakopa Tatacharya, Harihara Hota, Narayana Pralaya Kumara Nanda, Sarvananda Mishra and Madhava Panda. All of them have produced numerous research scholars with significant works. 226 Ph.Ds and D.Litt. degrees have been awarded over the years.

Most significant study was the publication of Tantra texts like *Mahāpuruṣavidyā* and Sri Jagannatha temple inscriptions. Besides, *Sri Jagannatha Jyotiḥ* is a research journal that regularly publishes research papers of high standard.

Sri Sadasiva Parisara /Campus of Rashtriya Sanskrit Sansthan, Puri

The need for a Sanskrit college was felt by Pandit Sri Harihara Dasha. He travelled all over the country and collected money with his profound scholarship. In this work he was assisted by Mahamahopadhyaya Sadasiva Mishra. Harihara with lots of difficulty could amass the funds and visualised the great institution. But, he had untimely death due to long labour and touring for the above purpose. But, Sadasiva Mishra took up this work. Puri Sanskrit College has seen the light of the day and if gradually became the Government Sanskrit College. There was provision for study of traditional Sanskrit from Parthama to Acharya. Rashtriya Sanskrit Sansthan took it over in 1971. Before that it became the nerve centre of Sanskrit studies of Orissa. There was facility for Ayurveda teaching also in the campus. But Gopabandhu Ayurveda College at Puri was established in 1945 and had its own campus. Pāṇinian study was instituted first in this college at the advent of a teacher called Ramajna Pandey. Scholars like Chintamani Mishra and Prahlada Pradhan and many more became the best exponents among his pupils. Before that Orissa Sanskrit learning and culture was centred on *Candrika Vyākaraṇa Prakriyā Kaumudī* and *Harināmamṛta Vyākaraṇa,* etc. It was Ramajna Pandey who could connect the scholars to the national stream during the early twentieth century.

This institute could not impart Vedic studies even after 100 years and 40 years of management by the Sansthan. The contribution of this institute to Odisha is priceless. This institute intends to create lavish opportunity for its students to compete with other students of the country. Many celebrated scholars have taught and did research here. It has numerous important publications of teachers and erstwhile students. Since this has become a part of an all India organisation, the growth now depends upon the central officers-in-charge.

Sanskrit NGOs of Odisha

Sanskrit movement, prior to 1980 was confined within the four corners of educational institutions in Odisha. Sanskrit *ṭols*, high schools and colleges taught Sanskrit in their course curriculum. Since Sanskrit has submerged in the blood of Odishan cultural tradition, it has come to be performed and recited in rituals, vows and different social ceremonies in Odisha. It was realised that the English education and culture had dominated our social customs and Sanskrit had started to get outdated day by day. The Sanskrit lovers felt that a people's movement can only protect and safeguard the heritage of Sanskrit on the soil. Hence, a number of Sanskrit lovers came forward and started the mass movement for the revival of Sanskrit through different forums and organisations.

Prior to 1980, there was one registered society for Sanskrit in our state, named "Association for Sanskrit Learning and Culture". The same association, represented through its ex-officio secretary-cum-superintendent of Sanskrit studies, Odisha, managed and monitored the academics of traditional Sanskrit institutions. It was a semi-government organisation. Besides, there existed a service association of Sanskrit *paṇḍits* named as "Nikhilotkala Sanskrit Mahamandal". After 1980, the Sanskrit teachers of high schools in Odisha constituted their service association, Odisha Sanskruta Shikshak Mahasangh with its head office at Cuttack. All Odisha Association of College Teachers in Sanskirt was founded in the year 1980 to propagate Sanskrit in the sphere of higher education in the state. The teachers of general colleges and universities have been united through this forum and this association is continuously working for the higher learning and research in the field. The teachers in traditional Sanskrit universities and colleges have got their own service associations.

Once upon a time, Sanskrit was the heart and soul of the

people in India. But the importance of Sanskrit reduced in the socio-cultural environment day by day. Then there started a movement to make Sanskrit the people's language and cultivate the Sanskrit wisdom for strengthening the nation. A number of organisations were established during the last 30 years. Those organisations are being discussed briefly.

ARSHA VIDYA VIKAS KENDRA

This institute was founded by Palasapalli, Bhubaneswar by Swamini Atmajnananda Sarasvati from her own funds. It organises three national-level seminars on Vedas, Upaniṣads, and Indian culture respectively. The *kendra* has a good collection in Indological Research Library for public as well as research scholars. The *kendra* has published valuable publications on different subjects from Veda to *Śrimad Bhāgavata*, literary criticism and creative writings of Modern Sanskrit.

LOKABHASA PRACHARA SAMITI

The Lokabhasa Prachara Samiti was established in March 1983 with its headquarters at Puri. It is an NGO with its motto as easy speaking Sanskrit language for the people. From the date of its inception the Samiti has been organising spoken Sanskrit programmes in different places of India and abroad. It has been performing some one-act plays and dramas on different occasions at different places. As a result of its committed Sanskrit movement, lakhs of the people of our country are being benefited by joining such programmes (i.e. spoken Sanskrit camps).

SARASWATI

Sanskrit Academy of Research for Advance Society through Vedic & Allied Tradition of India has been registered as a society in the year 1997. It aims at the higher research in Sanskrit. The head office of Saraswati is located at Barapada,

Bhadrak. *Lokaprajñā* is the research journal of SARASWATI. This Institute is engaged in different research fields including the preservation of manuscripts. It is also the centre of activities of Lokabhasa organisation at the moment.

ODISHA SANSKRIT ACADEMY

This academy was established on 15 November 1986 at Bhubaneswar to safeguard Indian culture by means of Sanskrit language and literature. It has a research journal named *Sragdhara*. One monthly Sanskrit-Oriya magazine of the academy is also now being published.

AMRUTAVANI SEVA PRATISHTANAM

This organisation has been established in Balasore and is engaged in Simple Sanskrit movement in the country. This organisation has adopted one village near Balasore to be the ideal Sanskrit village. It brings out a regular monthly magazine called *Amr̥tabhāṣā*.

SAMSKRITA BHARATI

Samskrita Bharati has been registered as a trust on 30 August 1999. This organisation has been propagating the Simple Sanskrit movement in the state under the guidance of its central trust in New Delhi.

SANSKRIT SANGEET NATAK ACADEMY

A team of scholars on 10 August 1999 assembled in Banki College Conference hall and decided to establish a national forum for the propagation of dance, drama, songs, etc. in lucid Sanskrit to create a new era of cultural Sanskrit. The organisation was officially established on 15 August 2002 in a meeting at the Postgraduate Department of Sanskrit, Utkal University, and named as Sanskrit Sangeet Natak Academy. Subsequently, it was registered under the Registration of Societies Act XXI of 1860. The academy carries out wide ranging activities that are in tune with the basic objectives: (a) every year two workshops on entertainment and cultural Sanskrit (summer and winter) are being organised since 2006, (b) academy has been organising the national conferences every year in different academic institutions. The first conference of this series was held in Christ College, Cuttack on 22 February 2006, (c) academy awards the personalities, having contributed to and patronised the cultural field of Sanskrit, every year.

SANSKRIT SAHITYA ACADEMY

This Academy was born in the year 2005 out of the "Nikhilotkala Sanskrit Kavi Sammelanam", Cuttack. Sanskrit Sahitya Academy confined itself only to the propagation and preservation of Sanskrit literary heritage and poetic traditions. The academy has been organising national Sanskrit poets conference, Bharata-Bharati Mahotsava every year at Cuttack city and has published *Kāvya-Mahānadī*, *Kāvya-Baitaraṇī* and *Kāvya-Godāvarī*; all these are anthologies of Sanskrit poems. This Academy has been awarding Bharat-Bharati award to a committed Sanskrit literarian, every year.

ACADEMY OF YOGA AND ORIENTAL STUDIES

This academy was established to preserve and protect the yogic tradition of India and the glory of oriental studies. The head office of the academy is located at Bhubaneswar. The academy has been organising Yoga camps, monthly discussions and national conferences every year.

PRACHI VALLEY CULTURAL ACADEMIC AND HISTORICAL RESEARCH SOCIETY, PURI

This organisation was founded in the year 1981 to undertake study and research of inscriptions and copperplates and other Sanskrit hagiologies in and around Puri.

OTHER OLD SANSKRIT ORGANISATIONS

In addition to the above-said organisations there are many regional Sanskrit organisations, i.e. Bhubaneswar Sanskrit

Parishad, Kataka Sanskrit Parishad, Bolangir Sanskrit Parishad and many more.

Out of the above-said NGOs Lokabhasa Prachar Samiti, SARASWATI, Odisha Sanskrit Academy and Academy of Yoga and Oriental studies have been availing the government aid and the rest are self-financed.

Organisations like Lokabhasa, Sanskrit Bharati, Amrtavaniparisad have made history in the country by propagation of spoken Sanskrit. They did spectacular work by retrieving back to the living tradition of day-to-day transaction in Sanskrit. This has helped Odiya students to get jobs elsewhere. Besides, modern Sanskrit writing has been mostly possible with this movement.

Creative Writings

Odisha has kept its tradition of composing poetry and other aspects of literature as in the past centuries. Some of these are mentioned below. The list is only the tip of the iceberg.

MAHĀKĀVYA

1. Harekrishna Satapathy, *Bhāratāyanam*
2. Purnachandra Shastri, *Aparājitā Vadhūmahākāvyam*
3. Dinabandhu Bhanja, *Subhāsitapuṣpakam*
4. Digambar Mohapatra, *Janatantra-vimarśaḥ*
5. Banarjee Patitapavana, *Vrajayuvavilāsamahākāvyam*
6. Prafulla Kumar Mishra, *Dharmapadīyam*
7. Banamali Biswal, *Saṅgamenabhirāma*

KHAṆḌAKĀVYA

8. Acharya Sudarsana, *Jagannāthastottaraśatakam*
9. Acharya Sudarsana, *Kavitāmālā*
10. Bhagirathi Nanda, *Bhāratiyaganatantram*

11. Pramod Chandra Mishra, *Anyoktipañcāśikāśatakam*
12. Govinda Mishra, *Baijayantiśatakam*
13. Digambar Mohapatra, *Rusiaśatakam*
14. Gauri Kumar Brahma, 12 *khaṇḍakāvyas*
15. Kshiroda Chandra Dasa, *Tāruṇyaśatakam*
16. Kshiroda Chandra Dasa, *Cillikā* (translation from Oriya)
17. Kshiroda Chandra Dasa, *Arṇya Śasyam* (translation from Oriya, play)
18. Karunakara Dasa, *Śrīśrī Jagannātha Nakṣatramālā*
19. Karunakara Dasa, *Śrīśrīākhaṇḍalamani Stotram*
20. Suryamani Ratha, *Samasyāpūrtiśatakam*
21. Suryamani Ratha, *Śṛṅgerisa Śatakam*
22. S. Sundar Ranjan, *Hanumat Pañcasat*
23. S. Sundar Ranjan, *Śrī Jagannāthasuprabhātam*
24. S. Sundar Ranjan, *Suraśmi Kasmiram*
25. S. Sundar Ranjan, *Abhāgabhāratam*
26. S. Sundar Ranjan, *Vadarisataraṅginī*
27. S. Sundar Ranjan, *Śaraṇāgataśoḍaṣī*
28. Bharat Chandra Nath, *Śrī Durgā Śatakam*
29. Bharat Chandra Nath, *Śivanadakṛta Upadeśāmṛta* (translation)
30. Bharat Chandra Nath, *Śrīkṛṣṇānanda Kṛta Strotrapuṣpāñjali*
31. Bharat Chandra Nath, *Śraddhāñjali Cayanam*
32. Bharat Chandra Nath, *Daśāvatāraśatakam*
33. Pramod Chandra Mishra, *Utkalgauravam*
34. Pramod Chandra Mishra, *Śrīmandireśatakam*
35. Harekrishna Meher, *Colletion of Poems in Sanskrit*

36. Harekrishna Meher, *Tapasvini* (translation of Gangadhara Mehera's odia *Tapasvinīkāvya*)
37. Braja Sundar Mishra, *Kargilkāvyam*
38. Braja Sundar Mishra, *Candrabhāgā* (translated)
39. Braja Sundar Mishra, *Śonitasvakṣaram*
40. Baikuntha Bihari Nanda, *Kīcakabadham*
41. Baikuntha Bihari Nanda, *Mandadahanam*
42. Bhagirathi Nanda, *Jagannātha Māhātmyam*
43. Umakanta Nanda, V*akulavanam*
44. Umakanta Nanda, *Tapasvinī*
45. Harekrishna Satpathy, *kavisatakam*
46. Harekrishna Satpathy, *Gaṅgājalam Dūṣitam*
47. Harekrishna Satpathy, *Śrīcandraśekharendra Saraswati Śatapuṣpamālā*
48. Harekrishna Satpathy, *Dharmapadam*

DŪTAKĀVYAM

49. Krishnakeshaba Sadangi, *Jimūta Dūtam*
50. Pramod Chandra Mishra, *Candradūtam*
51. Prabodha Mishra, *Dūtakavyagranthāvalī* (collection of nine *dūtakāvyas*)
52. Narayan Ratha, *Kapotadūtam*
53. Narayan Ratha, *Nastavilāsam*
54. Narayan Ratha, *Tīrthavilāsam*
55. Bhubaneswar Kara, *Doṣaśatakam*
56. Bhubaneswar Kara, *Jīvana Darśanam*

GĪTAKĀVYAM

57. Manamohana Acharya, *Gītabhāratam*
58. Manamohana Acharya, *Gītamohanam*

59. Manamohana Acharya, *Gītamilindam*

LAHARĪKĀVYAM

60. Pramodachandra Mishra, *Śrīvimala Laharī*
61. Manamohana Acharya, *Śrīśivānanda Laharī*

MUKTAKA

62. Banamali Biswal, *Vyathā*
63. Banamali Biswal, *R̥tuparṇa*
64. Banamali Biswal, *Priyatamā*
65. Banamali Biswal, *Valentine Day Sandeśaḥ*
66. Banamali Biswal, *Yātrā*
67. Prafulla Kumar Mishra, *Citrakuraṅgī*
68. Prafulla Kumar Mishra, *Brahmanābhiḥ*
69. Prafulla Kumar Mishra, *Tava Nilaye*
70. Prafulla Kumar Mishra, *Koṇārke*
71. Prafulla Kumar Mishra, *Citrāṅgadā*
72. Prafulla Kumar Mishra, *Catvāri Śr̥ṅgāḥ*
73. Prafulla Kumar Mishra, *Kr̥ṣakasya Kathā*
74. Prafulla Kumar Mishra, *Tathāpi Satyasya Mukham*
75. Prafulla Kumar Mishra, *Manojaṅgame*
76. Prafulla Kumar Mishra, *Godhūliḥ*
77. Ravindra Kumar Panda, *pratidhvani*
78. Ravindra Kumar Panda, *Satadalam*
79. Ravindra Kumar Panda, *Urvi*
80. Ravindra Kumar Panda, *Vanaballi*
81. Ravindra Kumar Panda, *Niravajhara*
82. Ravindra Kumar Panda, *Balaka*
83. Keshava Ch. Dash, *Bibhavari*

84. Keshava Ch. Dash, *Praṇaya Pradīpa*
85. Keshava Ch. Dash, *Hṛdayeśvarī*
86. Keshava Ch. Dash, *Mahātīrtham*
87. Keshava Ch. Dash, *Tilottamā*
88. Keshava Ch. Dash, *Śītala tṛṣṇā*
89. Keshava Ch. Dash, *Pratipadā*
90. Keshava Ch. Dash, *Aruṇa*
91. Keshava Ch. Dash, *Madhya Yānam*
92. Keshava Ch. Dash, *Īśa*
93. Keshava Ch. Dash, *Śaśirekhā*
94. Keshava Ch. Dash, *Oṁ Śāntiḥ*
95. Keshava Ch. Dash, *Andhaśrotaḥ*
96. Keshava Ch. Dash, *Urmicūḍā*
97. Keshava Ch. Dash, *Bhinnapṛthivī*
98. Pramod Kumar Nayak, *Savari*
99. Subash Ch. Dash, *Paricayaḥ*
100. Harekrishna Mishra, *Mātṛgītikāñjaliḥ*
101. Banamali Biswal, *Dārubrahma*

SHORT STORIES

102. Banamali Biswal, *Jagannatha Caritam*
103. Banamali Biswal, *Bibhukṣā*
104. Banamali Biswal, *Jijiviṣā*
105. Rabindra Kumar Panda, *Cchinachāyā*
106. Narayana Dash, *Hatyākārī Kaḥ*
107. Narayana Dash, *Ravindrakathākallolinī* (translation from Bengali)
108. Narayana Dash, *Vātyāsāraḥ* (translation from Oriya)
109. Pramod Nayaka, *Uvāca Kandukalyāṇa*

110. Parambashri Yogamaya, *Mṛtyuḥ Candrasyamasaḥ*
111. Parambashri Yogamaya, *Samparkaḥ*
112. Keshaba Chandra Dash, *Ekada*
113. Keshaba Chandra Dash, *Śūnya Nābhi*
114. Keshaba Chandra Dash, *Nimnapṛthivī.*

Other Scholars and Writers

Research papers in English and Sanskrit are enumerated below. Since the vernacular writings though valuable are not enumerated as it does not have circulation among non-Odiya-speaking people. Some of them are quite significant.

1. Patitapaban Banarjee, *Utkaleṣu Saṁskṛta Gītikāvyasyadhārā*
2. Karuna Sagar Behera, *Prācīmāhātmyam:* With Hindi Translation
3. Banamali Biswal, *Niravasvanaḥ Vyathā*
4. Kesaba Chandra Dash, *Research Methodology in Sanskrit*
5. Kesaba Chandra Dash, *Lights on Noncase Relationship.*
6. Pramod Chandra Mishra, *Philosopical Aspects of Naiṣadhīyacaritam*
7. Gangadhar Panda, *Dramas of Kālidāsa*
8. Promodini Panda, *Vedakālīna Nārīśikṣā*
9. Bhagaban Panda, *Śrīgītā Sītā Vallabha Mahākāvyam*
10. Bhagaban Panda, *Vasantotsava Mahākāvyam*
11. Bharata Chandra Natha, *Aristotle's Poetics, Translation and Study.*
12. Ramesh Chandra Panda, *Śabdārtha Sāramañjarī*
13. J.B. Pattnaik, *Sanskrita Bhāṣā*
14. Kishore Chandra Padhy, *Vyākaraṇa Sodhaprabandha*
15. Sadasiva Praharaj, *Bhāratīya Dharmaśāstra*

16. Nilakantha Pati, *A Brief Work of Immanual Kant*
17. Suryamani Ratha, *Rasikaraṅgada Ṭīkā of Gītagovinda*
18. A.C. Sarangi, *Devlopment of Sanskrit from Pāṇini to Patañjali*
19. Braja Kishore Swain, *Narada Smr̥tiḥ*
20. Braja Kishore Swain, *Kālamādhavaḥ*
21. Braja Kishore Swain, *Manusmr̥tiḥ*
22. Braja Kishore Swain, *Nilādri Mahodayaḥ*
23. Braja Kishore Swain, *Dharmaśāstra: an Introductory Analysis*
24. Braja Kishore Swain, *A Link between Tradition and Modernity*
25. Braja Kishore Swain, *The Voice of Verdict*
26. Braja Kishore Swain, *Smr̥timīmāṁsā*
27. Braja Kishore Swain, *Dharmaśāstra Paryālocana*
28. Braja Kishore Swain, *History of Dharmaśāstra in Nutshell*
29. Braja Kishore Swain, *Aspect of Puruṣottamajagannātha*
30. Braja Kishore Swain, *Manu: An Introductory Analysis*
31. Alekh Chandra Sadangi, *Sanskrit Language from Pāṇini to Patañjali*
32. Alekh Chandra Sadangi, *Gleaning of Indian Culture*
33. Prafulla K. Mishra, *Sanskrit Poetics: With Orissan Contributions*
34. Prafulla K. Mishra, *Fresh Lights on Atharvaveda*
35. Prafulla K. Mishra, *Ethics, Erotics and Aesthetics*
36. Prafulla K. Mishra, *An Introduction to Yoga*
37. Prafulla K. Mishra, *The Foundation of Yoga.*
38. Gopala Krishna Dash, *Nārada: A study*
39. Gopala Krishna Dash, *Samskrit Vyākaraṇa*

40. Raghunatha Panda, *Contibution of Orissa to Sanskrit Lyrical Literature*
41. Raghunatha Panda, *Gleaning of Indian Culture and Literature*
42. Radhamadhava Dash, *Idioms from Kāśikāvṛtti*
43. Radhamadhava Dash, *Sanskrit Nibandhāvalī*
44. Radhamadhava Dash, *Tattvadhārā*
45. Pratibha Manjari Rath, *Rudra-Śiva in Vedic Literature*
46. Pratibha Manjari Rath, *Light on Vedic and Purāṇic Studies*
47. Subasa Chandra Dasa, *Gaṅgeśa on yogāruḍhī*
48. Subasa Chandra Dasa, *Bibliography of Pāli and Buddhism*
49. Subasa Chandra Dasa, *Facets of Indology*
50. Subasa Chandra Dasa, *Nyāya Theory of Language*
51. Subasa Chandra Dasa, *Philosophy of Yoga*
52. Svamini Atmaprajnananda Saraswati, *Nomenclature of the Vedas*

This list is also the tip of the iceberg. There are many important publications which are not mentioned here due to fear of prolixity and want of correct information. But this information certainly indicates the continuity of works of Odishan scholars. Sanskrit books are many, but they are not being mentioned here.

Research Journals

1. *Śrījagannātha Jyotih*, published in English and Sanskrit from Sri Jagannatha Sanskrit Visvavidyalaya.
2. *Vāṇijyotih*, published in Sanskrit and English from Department of Sanskrit, Utkal University.
3. *Lokaprajña*, published in both from Lokabhasa pracharasamiti, English and Sanskrit.

4. *Abhivyaktiḥ*, published from Sahitya Vibhaga, Sri Jagannatha Visvavidyalaya.
5. *Sragdhara*, published in Sanskrit and English from Puri by Odisha Sanskrit Academy.

Periodicals

1. *Ṛtayāni*, collection of Sanskrit writings published from Sanskrit Department of Utkal University, Bhubaneswar.
2. *Digdarśini*, published in Sanskrit from Puri for last 35 years.
3. *Amṛtabhāṣā*, published by Amrtavaniparisad in Sanskrit from Balasore, each month.
4. *Mandākinī*, occasional publication from Bhadrak by Lokabhasa Prachar Samitih.
5. *Devabhāṣā*, occasional publication from Cuttack
6. *Utkalodaya*, published from Rourkela.
7. *Priyambada*, was published from Puri.
8. *Devajñānam*, published from Sadasiva Sanskrit College (Dharmasastra Vibhaga) Puri.
9. *Manoramā*, published from Berhampur.

Sanskrit Manuscripts in Odisha

Since Odisha is a coastal state, the writing material for this state was palm leaf. Quite naturally, all the books, accounts, horoscopes, credit transactions, scientific calculations, diagrams and paintings, pictures, etc. were all written by an iron nail and they were preserved in tight binding of bamboo or wooden scale like sticks and tied in threads. They were exposed to sunshine in the autumn and neem leaves were applied to protect them from worm-eating. Those books could remain intact for hundreds of years than any printed or soft material invented so far excepting metal plates. Millions of manuscripts were unearthed in the last decades. But, the super cyclones and floods have consumed them. Besides, the white ants eat them, for they were all kept in cane boxes in thatched houses. The state museum and other educational institutions have started preserving them in late 1950s. The state museum has rare collection of 40,000 manuscripts in 20,000 bundles, in which about 20,000 Sanskrit texts are available. The descriptive catalogues of Sanskrit manuscripts are published subjectwise, accordingly.

Besides, there is a repository of manuscripts in Utkal University Library. The number of Sanskrit texts is about 5,000. Similarly, the preservation of manuscripts in Sadasiva Parisara, Raghunandana Library, Sri Jagannatha Sanskrit University, Jagannathavallabh Matha, Bada Odia Matha, Govardhana Matha of Puri is laudable, with lots of private collection. There are also a good collections of manuscripts in Kapileswarapur, Alarnath Temple, Keonjhara Palace, Brahmagiri, Pipili, Nimapara and in Prachivally, Kakatpur, Avadhut Ashram, Konark, etc. Besides palm leaf manuscripts copperplate manuscripts are available in different parts of Odisha.

Impact of Sanskrit Studies in Odisha

Students who passed out from all the institutes were all engaged till 1995. But because of the ban on appointments as per the DFID programme, the colleges and schools are teacherless. The State Government did not appoint any teachers. For last two years, the government has started contractual appointment of teachers. But before that for the last 12 years students moved outside Odisha and got established outside Odisha. The interaction of scholars outside the state could open their eyes for further progress.

The impact of the Sanskrit on the Odishan language and the way of living is distinctive. The correct pronunciation of vowel ending words and use of Sanskrit words as it is in Sanskrit makes the language chaste. On the other hand, people from other parts de-Sanskritise their language that cuts them off from the national mainstream. It is probably the only state to talk of the interest of the country rather than of any regional bias, because of its strong Sanskrit base.

The nature of the people of Odisha is simple, unassuming, religious and truthful because of the impact of the Sanskrit.

14

Sanskrit Studies in the Puducherry

C.S. Radhakrishnan

TAMASO *mā Jyotirgamaya* (Lead me from darkness to Light). This Vedic prayer from the *Bṛhadāraṇyaka Upaniṣad* being the motto of Pondicherry University, it is the guiding light for the propagation of knowledge. With a view to diving deep into the very ancient language, the department of Sanskrit was started on the 7 August 1988. S.P. Narang was the first head of the department who served for two years (1988-90). After him, the following faculty headed the Department:

- C. Panduranga Bhatta (1990-91)
- V. Kutumba Sastry (1991-99)
- J. Krishnan (1999-2004)
- K.E. Dharaneedharan (2004-07)
- Chakradhar Behera (2007-10)
- C.S. Radhakrishnan (2010-)

The department offers the following programmes:

- M.A. (Sanskrit)
- M.Phil. (Sanskrit)
- Ph.D. (Sanskrit)
- Certificate course in Sanskrit

Faculty

- C.S. Radhakrishnan, Head (obtained Ph.D. from the University of Madras), specialisation: Kāvyaśāstra, Indology, Manuscriptology, Viśiṣṭādvaita.
- J. Krishnan, Associate Professor (obtained Ph.D. from the University of Madras), specialisation: Advaita Vedānta and Nyāya.
- K.E. Dharaneedharan, Associate Professor (obtained Vidyavaridhi from the Rashtriya Sanskrit Sansthan, New Delhi), specialisation: Nyāya, Mīmāṁsā, Advaita Vedānta and Viśiṣṭādvaita.
- Chakradhar Behera, Associate Professor (obtained Ph.D. from the University of Pune), specialisation: Vedānta, Sāṁkhya, Yoga, Linguistics and Literature.
- C. Palaiah, Assistant Professor (obtained Ph.D. from the University of Mysore), specialisation: Kāvyaśāstra.
- Anil Pratap Giri, Assistant Professor (did his M.Phil. from Jawaharlal Nehru University), specialisation: Indian Poetics, Grammar, Navya Nyāya, Language and Methodology, Linguistics.

The department has so far awarded 61 M.Phil. and 22 Ph.D. degrees to its students. Around 30 students are presently doing Ph.D. The intake for M.A. and M.Phil. in Sanskrit is 15 students each, per annum. While the M.Phil. candidates get a monthly fellowship of Rs. 3,000 and the Ph.D. scholars get Rs. 5,000 each granted by the Pondicherry University. For girls and students from SC and ST, and physically handicapped categories the hostels are rent-free. Sanskrit is offered as Part-I Language for the undergraduate courses in Fine Arts and Music in the affiliated College, Bharathiar Palkaikoodam, Pondicherry.

The Sanskrit department of the Pondicherry University has been growing steadily both in terms of the number of students as well as the faculty. While the number of students in major is around 50, there has been a steady growth in the soft-core courses with a total of around 180, students consisting of various other departments. Students of the department have participated in various national and international conferences and presented papers.

Two faculty members have been honoured with titles. Sanskrit Ratna was conferred on C.S. Radhakrishnan in 2008 while K.E. Dharaneedharan was honoured with the titles of Yuvāvipaścit and Śāstraratnākara. Significantly, Kutumba Sastry, the former professor, was elected as the president of the **International Association of Sanskrit Studies** while C.S. Radhakrishnan was elected as member of the Consultative Committee of IASS, at the University of Edinburgh.

The department has conducted the following national seminars/workshops/refresher courses, etc.

1. Veda and Vedṅāga in 1997
2. Workshop on "The Study of Tarkapada of Sastradipika", in 1997
3. "The Relevance of Sanskrit to Contemporary India", in 2000
4. "Mimamsa", in 2006
5. "Relevance of Sanskrit to Modern Age", in 2008
6. A Refresher Course in Sanskrit, of three weeks duration was conducted in 2009.
7. Two-day Workshop on "Scripts and Manuscripts", in 2010.

Visvabharati, the national journal on Sanskrit studies, the first of its kind from the Union Territory of Pondicherry, was launched in January 2011. The journal can be viewed on the website portal of the Pondicherry University.

The **Society for Sanskrit Studies** has been formed and

registered to serve the cause of the Sanskrit studies and the continuity of the journal.

The department celebrates Sanskrit Day every year with speeches by eminent scholars, besides staging Sanskrit dramas and conducting essay writing competitions. The Kapali Sastri endowment lecture is arranged every year. Guest lectures by eminent scholars from other universities and research institutes are also arranged regularly.

Future Plans

The department will be offering diploma in Sanskrit, postgraduate diploma in manuscriptology and palaeography. It also intends to introduce a course on computational linguistics, Navya Nyāya language and methodology. Measures are on to set up a Manuscript Conservation Centre, under the National Mission for Manuscripts. Weekly Sanskrit news and wise sayings will be broadcast on the university's FM radio "Puduvai Vaani".

French Institute of Pondicherry

STATUS

The French Institute of Pondicherry (IFP), UMIFRE 21 CNRS-MAEE, is a financially autonomous institution under the joint supervision of the French Ministry of Foreign and European Affairs (MAEE) and the French National Centre for Scientific Research (CNRS). It is an integral part of the network of 27 research centres connected to this ministry. It is also part of the research unit 3330 "Savoirs et Mondes Indiens" of the CNRS, along with the Centre de Sciences Humaines (CSH) in New Delhi.

HISTORICAL REVIEW

Established under the terms of the Treaty of Cession of French Territories in India, the French Institute of Pondicherry was inaugurated on 21 March 1955. It was initially engaged under the leadership of its first director (Jean Filliozat), in the study of Indian civilisation and culture, and more particularly in the history and the religions of south India.

Indian Society, History and Culture: Sources and Resources

The department of Indology of the French Institute of Pondicherry started at the time of the foundation of this Institute with the Treaty of Cession of Pondicherry by France in 1955. The only European establishment of this type set-up in India, it allows the Western Indologists, primarily Sanskritists, to come and work for long periods with traditional Indian scholars (*paṇḍits*) who are well versed in oriental learning, employed by the institute. IFP has a unique character of being a meeting and exchange place between the Western and the Indian intellectual traditions, at a time when Indian traditional teaching based on transmission from master to disciple is beginning to fade.

Another important originality of the department lies in the richness of its collection of manuscripts and photographs : the manuscript collection is the largest in the world of manuscripts of the Śaiva Siddhānta, a Hindu religious tradition which has flourished in south India for more than ten centuries. There are 8,500 bundles of manuscripts, recently classified as "**Memory of the World" by UNESCO** and the most important available collection of photographs (13,0000) on the religious art and architecture of south India.

The research projects of the department may be grouped into three major areas:

Indian Analysis of Sanskrit Language and Literature

This research axis addresses the need to understand, from within, the concepts in Sanskrit language and literature developed by Indian thinkers and philosophers over the centuries. A close cooperation between Indian scholars and the

Western researchers (possibly at the IFP) is indeed necessary for the study of texts and their commentaries and for the detailed analysis of the complexities of Pāṇinian grammar and of the Indian philosophy of language.

It attempts to understand from inside the conceptions of Sanskrit language and literature developed by the Indian thinkers over the centuries. A major specificity of the Indian intellectual tradition lies in the importance attached to commentaries: in India, all great religious, philosophical or literary texts are subject to commentaries which are intended to clarify it and to supplement them. Far from constituting a minor genre, the commentaries form an essential part of the history of ideas in India, giving place in turn to other commentaries. It is thus logical that the department of Indology devotes great attention to these types of texts. The most significant project of this research orientation, by its extent, its progress and the number of people involved, is *The Dictionary of the Examples of Pāṇinian Grammar*, a joint project between the EFEO and the IFP. In India, Sanskrit grammar occupies a central position, constituting the basis and the origin of other intellectual disciplines; towards the fourth century BCE, Pāṇini described and codified Sanskrit language in a grammar in the form of several thousands of rules, the extreme conciseness of which makes it necessary to take resort to explanatory commentaries. The dictionary of the examples of Pāṇinian grammar brings together and analyses nearly 40,000 examples given in four commentaries of the grammar of Pāṇini (spread over the period from second century BCE to sixteenth century CE) to illustrate and explain the rules of formation of words and sentences; it is divided into eight sections, in accordance with the structure of the commentary which is still in use today in south India for teaching Sanskrit grammar and is thus well known to the *paṇḍits* of Pondicherry. Apart from its value as a reference work for Sanskritists and Indologists, this dictionary, thanks to a system of cross-references between the Sanskrit and the Western grammatical terminologies, will be more largely useful to linguists and philosophers of the language (who have shown a growing interest for several years in the study of the first scientific grammar and its modes of reasoning).

This great "grammatical" project of the IFP is complemented by an ambitious project of bringing out an "*Encyclopaedia of the Doctrines of Philosophy of Language* (*Śābdabodhamīmāṁsā*)" developed in India, dealing with the way in which the meaning of a statement is conceived, expressed and understood. The grammarian starts from words to construct and understand the meaning of a sentence, whereas the philosopher takes the sentence like a significant unit, which he then breaks up into words; two different approaches of language are thus to be found in the dictionary and the encyclopaedia. N.S. Ramanuja Tatacharya, one of the most respected Indian logicians heads this project based on the analysis of several treatises, where the most varied views on these particularly difficult questions are exposed. In this project, attention is also given to the possible applications of some of these Indian analysis of the language for the development and the improvement of natural languages and for computational linguistics, fields of research that are under full development today in various research institutions of India.

History of Religions

The second axis deals with the sources of the history of Śaivism, the most important religious tradition of Hinduism in south India, which grants pre-eminence to God Śiva. It extensively uses the unique collections of the IFP. Work is undertaken in two complementary directions: on the one hand, the cataloguing and digitisation of the manuscripts and photographs, and on the other, edition and analysis of the texts and highlighting of the photo collection.

As a vital tool for the identification of texts and quotations, both while cataloguing and while preparing critical editions, a library of Sanskrit electronic texts, particularly Śaiva texts are made available some of which can be downloaded from the institute's site.

Indology is the study of any old or recent aspect of Indian civilisation that is supported by an analysis of textual sources written in an Indian language, of iconographic sources or of any other relevant document. Historically, since its beginnings in the nineteenth century, the core of Indology has consisted in the study, on strong philological bases, of the very rich existing corpus of texts written in Sanskrit, the classical language of India.

The other major originality of the department of Indology of the IFP lies in the richness of the collection of its manuscripts and photographs gathered since its creation. IFP has 8,600 bundles of palm-leaf manuscripts and 1,150 bundles of transcripts on paper, the majority of the texts being in Sanskrit; the heart of this collection consists in its being the richest collection in the world of manuscripts relating to Śaiva Siddhānta, a branch of Hinduism, which has existed in Tamil Nadu for more than ten centuries. At the iconographic level, the photo library of the IFP has 1,30,000 photographs of temples and sculptures which make it the most significant existing collection of film negatives on religious art in south India.

The richness of the collection of the age-old texts and images and the presence of traditional Indian scholars contribute to make the IFP a preferential place for preserving, transmitting and studying Indian cultural heritage in its material and intellectual forms.

The approximate number of manuscripts in some of the important subjects is as under:

- Canonical texts of Śaivism (Śaivāgama)(1,900)

- Devotional Hymns/Legends of Holy places (*Stotra/ Māhātmya*) (1,360)
- *Mantra*/Ritual manuals (1,890)
- Astrology (435)
- Mythology (Purāṇa) (230)
- Traditional South Indian Medicine (250)
- Vedas (187)
- *Rāmāyaṇa* (192)
- Sanskrit Literature (160)
- Tamil devotional literature (1,350)

The research projects presented here aim at the better use of these exceptional assets of the IFP. The main research orientations are

- Indian analysis of Sanskrit language and literature
- History of Śaivism in south India

This second research orientation uses fully the unique patrimonial resources of the IFP on Śaivism, one of the ancient and powerful branches of Hinduism thriving in south India, which grants pre-eminence to god Shiva.

Most of the personnel employed in this orientation are interested in the sources of the history of the Śaivism in south India. Work is undertaken in two complementary directions: *"the cataloguing and digitisation of the manuscripts"*, on one hand, *"the edition and close study of texts such as the Śaivāgamas"*, on the other. Preservation and analysis of the manuscript collection are thus carried out side by side.

After having published four catalogues of its manuscripts, the IFP began a few years ago, to scan its fragile collection (difficult to preserve in the south Indian climate), and to undertake the electronic cataloguing of manuscripts. This descriptive cataloguing, which represents a first analysis of the contents of the texts, requires specific skills (good knowledge of Śaiva Siddhānta, familiarity with the handwritten forms of the Grantha script, adaptation of the Tamil script being used to note Sanskrit), that nowadays only rare Indian scholars like those employed by the IFP possess; the texts selected on priority for the cataloguing and the scanning, are the Śaivite Āgamas, i.e. the doctrinal or ritual texts of Śaiva Siddhānta tradition, which are the most original in the IFP collection.

Parallel to this work of long-term cataloguing, the department of Indology publishes, presents and translates some of the most important Śaivite texts of its collection: this activity of "*the study and publication of the Āgamas*", which has established the authority of the institute in the world of Indology for over 50 years, by making available the hitherto unpublished fundamental Śaivite texts, goes on even today with several critical editions in progress (*Dīptāgama*, in collaboration with University Paris-III, *Sūkṣmāgama*, . . .). Descriptive cataloguing and editing of texts are the two great sources which will enable researchers to reconstruct the history of Śaivism in Tamil Nadu.

The foundationary research programme of the IFP since its inception remains the critical edition and publication of the unedited Śaiva Āgamas. Under that programme so far ten Śaiva Āgamas (some of them running into more than one volume) have been critically edited on the basis of the manuscript resources available at the IFP as well as elsewhere. The titles of some of them are,

Rauravāgama (3 vols.)

Mṛgendrāgama

Ajitagāma (3 vols.)

Dīptāgama (3 vols.)*Mataṅgaparameśvarāgama* (2 vols. with a commentary written in the tenth century CE in Kashmir), etc.

One of the earliest Śaiva Ritual Manuals, *Somaśambhū-*

paddhati composed by Somaśambhu (tenth century) in central India has also been critically edited for the first time and published along with French translation running into 4 volumes.

Ideas and History Śaiva Siddhānta

ĀGAMAS AND PURĀṆAS

Objectives

Śaiva Siddhānta is a Śaivite school, which, for more than a millennium now, is a major feature of the Indian religious life, especially in Tamil Nadu. It is one of the most complete and strongest religious systems: even today, most of south Indian Śaivite temples follow Śaiva Siddhānta rules. Since its foundation, the French Institute of Pondicherry has been the leading institution in the study and publication of Śaiva Siddhānta texts. Thus scholars attached to the Institute are elaborating the patterns of the complex history of this main current of Śaivite religion. Śaiva Siddhānta studies rely on a wide bilingual textual corpus:

- Sanskrit canonical texts (28 main Āgamas and numerous secondary texts or Upāgamas) describing doctrine, religious practice — either public or private — temple-building, image-making, etc.
- Sanskrit philosophical treatises which elaborate Āgamas' teaching
- Tamil doctrinal treatises, of which Meykandar is one of the main propounders.
- Sanskrit Purāṇas, pertaining to various religious trends; these texts, with a far wider scope, nevertheless include important elements for the understanding of Śaiva Siddhānta ideas and history.

Material and Methods

The IFP manuscripts collection is one of the most complete in the field of Śaiva Siddhānta texts, and thus provides the basic material for all projects dealing with it; the approach being philological, historical and anthropological.

Critical editions of unpublished canonical texts: *Dīptāgama* and *Sūkṣmāgama*

- *Dīptāgama* is one of the 28 Śaiva Siddhānta main canonical texts and deals especially with installation rituals, from the building of the temple to the putting in place of statues, but it also describes general temple rituals as well as lesser known ceremonies such as "the cutting of the leaves" (*patracheda*). Its critical edition, in the line of several others, is not only publishing of a primary Sanskrit source but also focusing on the history of the text marked by successive transformations which are no less than adaptations to the changing religious and social landscape of south India.
- *Sūkṣmāgama*, another Śaiva Siddhānta main canonical text, offers a fairly complete description of temple rituals together with special ceremonies, ordeals of various types or festivals, with a special emphasis on ceremonies involving the goddess. Its critical edition on which work has just started will enhance the place occupied by certain ancient features of the Āgamic tradition in the domain of deities, *mantras* and rituals.
- Historical survey of Śaiva Siddhānta in Tamil Nadu *Śivajñānabodbham*, is the first and the most commentated upon of the doctrinal treatises pertaining to Śaiva Siddhānta. It is translated along with an up-to-now unpublished Sanskrit commentary (sixteenth century). *Pauṣkarāgama*, one of the canonical texts, well known in Tamil Nadu, is critically edited together with an hitherto unpublished Sanskrit commentary, by Jñānaprakāśa, a sixteenth century theologian, who enlightens the

continuity between canonical and later literature, especially in Tamil Nadu.

- *Vāyavīya Saṁhitā*: Śaivite doctrine and ritual in a Purāṇic context last section of *Śiva Purāṇa*, the *Vāyavīya Saṁhitā* is strongly influenced by Śaiva Śiddhānta (see numerous chapters dealing with ritual, Yoga or Śaivite initiation). Most probably written in south India, this Purāṇic text gives new glimpses of the complex position of Śaiva Siddhānta school towards other Śaivite schools flourishing in south India.

BHAIRAVA: ICONOGRAPHY OF ŚIVA

Iconography of the terrible form of Śiva in south India, as a part of "Architectural and Religious Heritage of South India" project.

Objectives

This manifestation of Śiva has induced and inspisred a huge variety of iconographical types. The Indian sculptures of Bhairava show him turn by turn as an untouchable mendicant moving from place to place for his penance or as a glorious god with an aura, surrounded by followers. He can take the appearance of a monster deformed and frightening, dancing in a frenzy on the cremation grounds, brandishing many arms of destruction, or looking young and attractive, or skeletal, incarnation of Time and Death. Some images emphasise the transcendence of this sinful god, showing him as an image of deliverance whom everyone aspires. Many others relegate him to the position of a fearsome guardian, as a *kṣetrapāla* guardian of territory in the temples or in village borders. He is sometimes, in this role of protecting guardian, repeated in eight Bhairavas.

This database offers a vast panorama of images of Bhairava in south India and establishes to what extent certain iconographic particularities are linked to geographical areas, dynasties, and enables the user to see the numerical proportion of images by state, by district, etc.

Ecole francaise d'Extreme-Orient

École française d'Extrême-Orient, EFEO, or the French School of Asian Studies, was founded in 1900 in Hanoi. The mission of the EFEO is interdisciplinary research on the civilisations of Asia, extending from India to Japan. A network of 17 research centres in 12 Asian countries allows its 42 European research scholars (anthropologists, archaeologists, linguists, historians and others) to carry out their fieldwork while maintaining a network of local specialists and Asianists from around the world. The EFEO has played a major role in the discovery and publication of the large corpus of South-East Asian inscriptions in Sanskrit, particularly those now held in Cambodia. One of its largest centres is that in Pondicherry, in which studies of iconography, Sanskrit and classical Tamil are pursued. Research in Sanskrit is conducted particularly in the areas of grammar, Śaiva literature and *kāvya*. The Pondicherry Centre of the EFEO co-publishes the series "Collection Indologie" with the French Institute of Pondicherry, a series which includes numerous critical editions of Sanskrit works.

Its collection of 1,614 palm-leaf bundles of manuscipts are from a single collection in the Tirunelveli district of Tamil Nadu. The digitisation of the manuscripts was undertaken and completed by the Sanmarga Trust India. The manuscripts can be viewed on the website of the EFEO.

Aurobindo Sanskrit Karyalayam

Sri Aurobindo Ashram is a great spiritual centre not only within Pondicherry but across entire India. In fact, devotees of Sri Aurobindo and the Mother and spiritual aspirants from all over the world throng the peaceful and serene Ashram. Attached to the Ashram is the Aurobindo Sanskrit Karyalayam. Its date of inception is 1 July 1984. In consonance with the words of the Mother that "The Sanskrit ought to be the national language of India", the Ashram brings out a Sanskrit quarterly by the name *Lokasaṁskṛtam* consisting of short stories in Sanskrit besides lessons in Sanskrit learning adopting an easy-to-learn methodology. The website of the Karyalayam also has several useful lessons on Sanskrit learning including the metres in Sanskrit prosody. The website is: http://sanskrit.sriaurobindoashram.org.in

There are also several volumes of the book *Surabharati* with easy methods of Sanskrit learning, besides conversational Sanskrit, *Vedapraveśa*, *Stotra*s, popular *śloka*s, dramas and many more.

Srikantha Sivacharya Veda Sivagama Vidyapeetham Karaikkal, Pondicherry Union Territory

What began as "Baala Jnaana Vikasa Kendram" in 1991, later became the Srikantha Sivacharya Veda Sivagama Peetam in 1996. Named after a celebrated Śivācārya who wrote the *Śrīkaṇṭha Bhāṣyam*, the Vidyapeetam was established by Smt. Gnanambal, the wife of Pattu Gurukkal. The institute was started with a view to imparting training to students in the traditional Śaiva Āgamas and in teaching Sanskrit. To start with, it had only four students but gradually the enrolment went up to 75 in about 10 years, The Vidyapeetam was blessed by the pontiffs Nachiappa Gnanadesika Swamigal, of the Koviloor Mutt, Jayendra Saraswati of Kanchi Kamakoti Mutt.

The Vidyapeetam follows the *gurukula* system, providing free boarding and lodging to the students. The admission is open to the traditional Ādiśaiva Śivācārya students only. The syllabus includes Vedas, Śivāgamas, Śilpaśāstra, Sanskrit and astrology besides the Tamil Śaiva canonical texts known as the "Twelve Tirumurais". The duration of the course is six years at the end of which the eligible students are given the certificate and the title "Veda Sivagama Pandita Pravara" at the annual convocation. The first convocation address in 2001 was delivered by H.D. Deve Gowda, the former prime minister of India. Other distinguished dignitaries who have presided over the convocations are K.R. Malkani, the Lt. Governor of Pondicherry in 2003, Subramania Swamy, former Minister of Commerce, Law and Justice, in 2007, A.M.H. Nazim, Leader of Opposition party in the Legislative Assembly, Pondicerry in 2008, P. Shanmugam, former chief minister of Pondicherry in 2009, and V. Vaidyalingam, former chief minister of Pondicherry in 2010.

The Vidyapeetam also publishes a monthly magazine in Tamil and Sanskrit, called *Srikantha Vijayam* focusing mainly on Śaiva philosophy and literature. Annual Conference is also held to provide a forum for scholars to present papers and interact with the experts in the subject. So far, seven batches of students have successfully completed the six-year course. The Vidyapeetam is managed by a Trust looked after by Sarveswara Gurukkal who got his doctorate in Sanskrit from the Pondicherry University. The Trust has also just started the Srimath Srikantha Sivacharya Research Institute in 2009 with a view to publishing rare books and manuscripts pertaining to the Śaiva philosophy.

Sanskrit Vikas Kendram
Karaikkal, Pondicherry Union Territory

The Sanskrta Vikas Kendram was started in 1996 along with the Srikantha Sivacharya Veda Vidyapeetham. It trains students, irrespective of caste, creed or religion to prepare them for the Sanskrit examinations conducted by various organisations such as the Sanskrit Bhasha Pracharini Sabha, Chittor, Andhra Pradesh, the Bharatiya Vidya Bhavan, the Rashtriya Sanskrit Sansthan, Sanskrit Vidyapeetha, Tirupati, etc. Along with the Sanskrit Bharati of Tamil Nadu, this Kendram conducted ten-day "Sibirams" (Spoken Sanskrit Courses) in Karaikkal benefitting around 600 people.

15

Sanskrit in the Punjab

Shankarji Jha

KNOWN as Sapta-Sindhu, the land of seven rivers, during the Vedic age, and Pañcanada — the land of five rivers, during the Purāṇic age, the Punjab has been one of the most prosperous and vibrant states of India. It was here in the Punjab, that the earliest civilisations and cultures of India flourished and the ancient Vedic culture of Indo-Āryans found its cradle. The Punjab is also privileged to have been the land of the Vedas, *Mahābhārata*, and the great grammarian Pāṇini. In the fourth century BCE, the Greeks called it *Pentapotamia* (meaning the land of five rivers). A noted historian I.D. Cunningham opines that the Punjab was known by the name of *Taki*. Hieun Tsang called it as *Tse Kai*. Up to the rule of Maharaja Ranjit Singh, it was known as Lahore province or the Kingdom of Lahore. In 1849, the Britishers named it the province of Punjab. Right from the India's Independence, it is called East Punjab or the Punjab.

The region of Punjab has all along been the stronghold of pure Indian or Vedic culture. So pervasive was the impact of Sanskrit language and learning in this region that towards the close of the nineteenth century, a great western Sanskrit scholar, A.C. Woolner came all the way from the University of Oxford to join as a faculty member and to head the Department of Sanskrit at the newly-established Panjab University at Lahore, the capital city of the then undivided Punjab. Lahore (presently in Pakistan), was a great seat of learning especially in the field of Sanskrit studies. In the pre-Partition days, the Panjab University, Lahore, boasted of great Sanskrit scholars like Lakshmana Swaroop, Vishvabandhu, Mangal Dev Shastri, Suryakant, Pandita Bhagavaddatta, Pandit Parameshvaranand Shastri and others. After the Independence, the reputed Panjab University was finally shifted to Chandigarh in 1953. It is presently functioning gloriously imparting education in many disciplines, including Sanskrit.

Right from its inception at Chandigarh in 1953, the Department of Sanskrit of Panjab University has a grand tradition of scholarship. While the late D.N. Shukla, has done very valuable work on Vāstuśāstra, Ram Gopal has worked on the Vedic grammar and Kalpa-Sūtras. After his retirement from the Department of Sanskrit, Panjab University, Chandigarh, he was made the vice-chancellor of M.D. University, Rohtak (Haryana). Presently residing at Chandigarh, an octogenarian, Ram Gopal is still engaged in the serious research work on Vedic studies. Jagannath Agrawal and Hem Raj Basta, the noted teachers of the department, have produced valuable works on epigraphy and philosophy respectively. Ram Murti Sharma has served the Sanskrit department and brought laurels for himself and the Panjab University both, by contributing enormously in the field of Advaita Vedānta. After his retirement, he was made the vice-chancellor of Sampurnanand Sanskrit University, Varanasi. Devi Datta Sharma has enriched Sanskrit research in linguistics. Ramakant Sharma Angiras has rendered distinct service to the Department of Sanskrit as a scholar of Vedānta. Veda Prakash Upadhyaya has produced work on Vedic *iṣtis* (sacrifices). The department of Sanskrit of the Panjab University is presently headed by Shankarji Jha who has produced an exegetical translation of the *Rasa-Gaṅgādhara* of Panditaraj Jagannath and a work on the linguistic philosophy of Sanskrit grammar. Vikram Kumar has produced works on Vedic studies while Virendra Kumar Alankar has produced works on Sanskrit and Vedic Etymology (*nirvacana*).

Prior to the Indian Independence, the Punjab had about 200 Sanskrit institutions running on the traditional pattern of Sanskrit education. In the course of time, the states of Himachal Pradesh and Haryana came into existence, and now the state of Punjab has become a small state in terms of area. Sanskrit, however, has been deep-rooted here and at present there are 10 to 12 Sanskrit institutions running on the traditional pattern in spite of facing apathetic attitude from the government.

In the field of Sanskrit-teaching and research the city of Hoshiarpur deserves mention. Hoshiarpur located Vishvesvaranand Visvabandhu Institute of Vedic Research and Indological Studies (VVIR&IS; now a regional centre of the Panjab University, Chandigarh) which is an important and time-honoured Sanskrit institution of the Punjab. The late Padmabhusana Visvabandhu was instrumental in establishing this institution at Hoshiarpur during the chaotic condition of the Indo-Pak division in 1947. Visvanbandhu's famous work *Vedic Padānukramaṇikā* (Vedic Concordance) has been published from the VVIR&IS Hoshiarpur in several volumes. This institute has a good manuscript library also. Besides, it has taken care of another manuscript library owned by the Dayanand Anglo-Vedic (DAV) organisation. This manuscript library is now shifted to the DAV College, Sector 10, Chandigarh. It has a large collection of Sanskrit manuscripts attracting researchers from all parts of the world. The scholars like Acharya Visvabandhu, Munisvardeva, Siddhesvar Verma, etc. and recently Braj Bihari Chaube, Damodar Jha, etc. who have produced a galaxy of research works on Vedic studies and allied subjects have served this Institution. At Hoshiarpur, there is another important institution — Visvesvaranand Vedic Research Institute devoted to research works and publications.

Some of the noted research publications of VVIS&IS, Hoshiarpur, are as follows:

(i) *Vaidika-Padānukrama-kośa* (16 volumes)

(ii) *Ṛgveda-vaiyākaraṇa-padasūci*

(iii) *Atharvaveda-vaiyākaraṇa-padasūci*

(iv) *Caturveda-vaiyākaraṇa- padasūci* (2 vols.)

(v) *Taittirīya-vaiyākaraṇa-padasuci*

(vi) *Upaniṣad-vaiyākaraṇa-padasūci*

(vii) A critical edition of the *Śaunakaśākhā of the Atharvaveda*

(viii) *Ṛgveda-mantrānukramaṇī*

(ix) *Ṛgveda-padānukramaṇī*

(x) *A Comparative and Etymological Dictionary of Vedic Interpretation*

(xi) K.K. Dhawan: *Upaniṣadoṅ meṅ Kāvya-tattva.*

(xii) *Mahāsubhāṣita-saṁgraha*

(xiii) V.R. Sharma (ed.): *Gāyatrī-vidhāna-sūtra,* and *Kṣudrakalpa-Sūtra*

(xiv) K.V. Sharma: *Vāk-Saptatī, Candrodaya-Nāṭaka*

xv) Siddheshvar Verma: *Etymologies of Yāska*

xvi) B.B. Chaubey : (i) *Treatment of Nature in the Ṛgveda,* (ii) *Vādhūla-Śrauta Literature* (in 6 vols. published between 1993 and 2010)

(xvii) Munishwara Dev: *Aitareya Brāhmaṇa*

(xviii) Damodar Jha; (i) *Āpastamba-Śulva-Sūtram* (with four major commentaries), (ii) *Maitrāyaṇī-Śulva-Sūtram, Āśvalāyana-Śrauta Sūtram* (published from the Rashtriya Sanskrit Sansthan, New Delhi), (iii) *Devībhāgavata-sadukti-maṇimālā* (2010), *Bhaganasamīkṣā*. Presently, the following prominent projects are underway in the Hoshiarpur based Sanskrit Institute:

Critical edition of *Āśvalāyana-Śrauta Sūtra.*

Critical edition of *Aitareya-Brāhmaṇa* with Sanskrit Commentaries of Sāyaṇa and Govindaswāmin.

Critical edition of *Taittirīya-Brāhmaṇa,* with Sanskrit commentaries of Sāyaṇa and Bhaṭṭabhāskara.

Sanskrit teaching and research are being carried out in the Sanskrit departments of the three state universities, i.e. Panjab University, Chandigarh, Guru Nanak Dev University, Amritsar and Punjabi University, Patiala. In the Panjab University, there is "Dayanand Chair for Vedic Studies" devoted to Vedic research in the light of the teachings of Swami Dayananda Saraswati. The scholars Ramnath Vedalankar and Bhavani Lal Bharatiya have rendered their valuable service to this Dayanand Chair of the Panjab University. Dharmendra Kumar Gupta, Abhimanyu, Bhim Singh (presently with the Kurukshetra University, Kurukshetra), Ravinder Kaur, Indra Mohan Singh, etc. are noted Sanskrit scholars at the Department of Sanskrit, Punjabi University, Patiala, while Krishna Lal Sharma, Shukadeva Sharma, Lekh Ram Sharma, etc. have taught and researched at the Department of Sanskrit, Guru Nanak Dev Universiy, Amritsar. In the Punjabi University, Patiala, there is a newly-established Valmiki Chair for promoting research on Maharṣi Vālmīki and his works. Sanskrit is also taught in the degree colleges of the state. Besides, there is a "Bhasa Vibhaga" under the Punjab government where the translation work of Sanskit texts is also promoted.

One of the premier Sanskrit institutions of the Punjab is Sri Sarasvati Sanskrit College, at Khanna (Punjab) that is following the syllabus of the Rashtriya Sanskrit Sansthan, New Delhi, while the other Sanskrit institutions located in almost all parts of the Punjab follow the syllabus prescribed by the three state universities for the traditional degrees of Prak-Shastri, Shastri and Acharya in different subjects like Vyākaraāṇa, Sāhitya, Darśana, etc. Acharya Visvanath Sastri, Acharya Yasodeva Sastri, etc. were noted Sanskrit teachers at Sri Sarasvati Sanskrit College, Khanna. This is a brief overview of Sanskrit institutions in the Punjab, most of which provide traditional Sanskrit education, and are run mainly on donations by private managements. The financial support from the government is meagre, and the Sanskrit teachers working in such institutions are experiencing bad employment conditions. Some of the privately managed Sanskrit institutions provide free lodging and boarding to the students. The main Sanskrit colleges of the Punjab are listed below:

(i) Sarasvati Sanskrit College, Khanna
(ii) Sanatana Dharma Sanskrit Mahavidyalaya, Hoshiarpur
(iii) Government Sanskrit College, Nabha
(iv) Multanimal Sanskrit College, Patiala
(v) Durgyana Sanskrit Mahavidyalaya, Amritsar
(vi) Sanskrit Mahavidyalaya, Hadiabad
(vii) Sharada Sanskrit College, Abohar
(viii) Sanskrit Vidyalaya, Fazilka
(ix) Sanskrit Vidyalaya, Sirhind
(x) Dandi Svami Sanskrit Mahavidyalaya, Ludhiana
(xi) Sanskrit Vidyalaya, Mai Hiran Gate, Jalandhar
(xii) Sanskrit Vidyalaya, Datarpur
(xiii) Ranavir Government Sanskrit College, Kapurthala
(xiv) Sanatana Dharma Sanskrit College, Sector 23, Chandigarh
(xv) Sri Rishikul Sanskrit Vidyapeeth, Sector 47, Chandigarh
(xvi) Jind Baba Sanskrit Mahavidyalaya, Sector 20, Chandigarh

Although the condition of Sanskrit studies in the Punjab has been worsening during the last 60 years, still, it has been the place of scholars and poets devoted to the service of Sanskrit. Hoshiarpur has been the home of several Sanskrit scholars and poets among whom one was Acharya Vidyanidhi who wrote two prose-works (*gadya-kāvya*), *Dayānandacaritam* and *Bhaktaphūlasinghcaritam*. In the glorious tradition of Sanskrit scholarship, we also have the late Acharya Charudeva Shastri, a resident of the village Tanda under Hoshiarpur district of the Punjab, who has produced several works on Sanskrit grammar. His worthy son, Satyavrata Shastri is a well-known Sanskrit scholar and poet, now based in New Delhi. In fact, the land of Punjab is very proud of being the birthplace of the worthy son and the worthy father. Satyavrata Shastri has produced several works, prominent among which are *Bṛhattara-bharatam* (a lyric: *khaṇḍakāvya*), *Bodhisattvacaritam* (an epic in 14 cantos depicting the life of *Gautama Buddha*), *Śrī Gurugobindsinghcaritam* (an epic in 25 cantos), *Indirāgāndhī-caritam* (depicting the life of Indiṛa Gandhi, the former prime minister of India), *Rāmakīrti-mahākāvyam* (an epic in 25 cantos), etc.

Another prestigious poet of Hoshiarpur is Shyamadeva Parashar who has produced as many as 36 poetic pieces in Sanskrit. Very recently, he passed away. Prominent among his works are : *Anyoktiśatakam, Śṛṅgārabhāratī, Ṛtucakram* (all lyrics); *Cārucaritacarcā* (consisting of 31 stories in a blend of prose and verses), *Kaśmīra-Kāmanīyakam* (a lyric in 150 verses), *Paramāṇuastram* (a lyric on the atomic weapon in 100 verses), etc. His last work is an epic *Triveṇī* in more than 20 cantos.

In the tradition of Sanskrit creative writers, there is an important figure named Mathuradatta Shastri, a Sahitya Akademi prize winner who has served the Punjab as Sanskrit teacher and enriched Sanskrit by writing beautifully stageable one-act plays in Sanskrit and other poetic pieces. His masterpiece *Ekāṅka-Pañcadaśī* was published in 2001. This work has three sections, *Pallavapañcakam, Dyāvāpṛthivīyam,* and *Kālagiriḥ*. The first two sections of this combined work have been published earlier also. Each of these sections contains five one-act plays. In the *Kālagiriḥ* the heroism of Indian soldiers during Indo-Pak war in the Kargil region of Jammu & Kashmir has been eulogised. Now his *Sanskrit-Gītāvaliḥ,* has also been published. Presently, this poet-cum-dramatist is based at Panchkula near Chandigarh.

Another celebrated poet from the Punjab is Shiva Prasada Bharadwaja. His poetic work *Bhārata-Sandeśaḥ* is published in two parts containing 320 verses. In the first part, the Indian ideals and culture are eulogised, while the second part contains the peaceful messages of Rajendra Prasad, the first president of India in versified form. His *Abhinava Rāga-Govindam* is an anthology of Sanskrit songs. In 1980, his poetic work *Matkurāyaṇam* was published. His other works are, *Śrī Guru Ravidāsa-Śatakam, and Paṭela-Caritam,* an epic in 52 cantos. He has served as a teacher at VVIR&IS, Hoshiarpur.

Shashidhar Sharma, an eminent Sanskrit scholar and retired teacher of Panjab Unviersity, Chandigarh, has made some noteworthy contributions to Sanskrit poetry. His epic *Vīra-Taraṅgiṇī* is based on the heroism of Indian soldiers during the Indo-China war. His other poetic works are *Gauravaṁṛtam* and *Bhuvaneśī-stavaḥ.*

Jagdish Prasad Semawal of VVIR&IS Hoshiarpur has produced a good number of Sanskrit poems, such as : *Śrī Rāmacaritāvalī, Śrī Durgā-Mahāstotra, Śrī-Śivastutiḥ, Candropalambhaḥ,* etc.

Devadatta Bhatti has contributed important lyrics — *Irā* and *Sinīvālī.*

Jagadram Shastri from Hoshiarpur has produced beautiful prose poetry *(gadya-kāvya), Chatrasālavijayam.* Nigamabodha

Tirtha has published *Kṛṣṇam Vande Jagadgurum* — a lyric in Sanskrit. Pandit Pashupati Jha, a Sanskrit teacher at VVIR&IS, Hoshiarpur, has published *Nepālasāmrājyodayam* depicting the glory of the Hindu kingdom of Nepal. His another work is *Śṛṅgāracaritāvalī* a poem expressing erotic sentiment. Sudarshan Sharma has *Śrīgurunānakacaritam* to his credit. Svayamprakasa Sharma has *Indra-Yakṣīyam* and *Bhagatsiṁhacaritam*, both poetic works, to his credit. Virendra Kumar Alankar of Punjab University, Chandigarh, has published three poetic pieces — *Devapraśasti-kāvyam, Apūrvalokaḥ Khalu Lokitaḥ saḥ* and *Padmacandrodayam*. For his work *Padmacandrodayam*, he was awarded the Banabhatta prize by Haryana Sahitya Akademi.

I, too, have made some humble contributions to Sanskrit poetry. One work *Bhāvakadambakam*, an anthology of short poems in traditional Sanskrit metres *Mandakrāntā* and the like is published and others are awaiting publication.

Lekharam Sharma, GND University, Amritsar, is presently engaged in a research work on contemporary creative writing in Sanskrit. He has provided me with some information which is reproduced below:

- Shyamdev Parashar, *Cārucaritacarcā*, 1986.
- I.M. Singh, Patiala, *Gurunānakadevasaṁstavaḥ*, 1991.
- Sridhar Prashad Baluni, *Daśameśacaritam*, 1994,
- Sudarshan Kumar, *Vīragauravacaritam*, 1995.
- Shiva Prasad Bharadwaj, *Śrī Indirāgauravam*.
- Dalbir Singh, *Pūrṇasardhaśatakam*, 2005, Amritsar.
- Swayamprakash Sharma, *Indrayakṣīyam, Amṛtamanthanam Mahākāvyam, Japajī-Śatakam, Bhagatasiṁhacaritam*.
- Jit Singh Khokhara, *Yautukam, Prītiḥ, Gurunānaka-bhagavatpādaḥ*.
- Arvind Mohan, *Upaniṣad-Pañcakam, Kutragatā sā Santiḥ*.
- Om Prakash Sharma Subandhu, *Sandeha-Sandohaḥ, Sā bālikā*.

- Shukadeva Sharma 'Munu',*Vetālaparājayam, Maṅgala-Nakṣatram.*
- Mathuradatta Pandeya, *Pr̥thvīrājavijayam.*
- Charudeva Shastri, *Śrīgandhicaritam.*
- Bahadur Chand Chhabara, *Puṣpahāsaḥ.*
- Chunni Lal Sudan, *Kaśmīra-Vihāraṇam, Hutātmā-Bhagatasiṁha-Caritāmr̥tam, Gaṅgālaharī, Hindusamdarśa-Sopānam.*
- Hamsaraj Shaili, *Haṁsamuktāvalī.*
- Lakshminarayan Gautam, *Tavaiva Gītāni.*
- Jagadram Shastri, *Madanacaritam, Saṁsakr̥ta-Saṅgīta-Rāmāyaṇam, Dharmacarcā.*
- Vedaprakash Vidyavacaspati, etc. *Jalam Praṣṭarādapi Kaṭhorataram, Dr̥ṣṭibhedaḥ, Ānandabhavanat Śāntivanam, Tamisra Śphuliṅgaśca.*

In short, it may be said that the stream of scholarship and creative writing in Sanskrit is still flowing in the state of Punjab, although not with the same vigour as in the past. If appropriate support from the administration or the government is secured, it will be of great help in the promotion of Sanskrit language and its wider learning in the state.

16

Status of Sanskrit Studies in Rajasthan

Devarshi Kalanath Shastry

RAJASTHAN has had a long-standing tradition of cultivating the Sanskrit learning and literature. Just as the Princely States of Rājpūtānā have created history through the zeal of their rulers for protecting *dharma* from the onslaughts of foreign conquerors, in the same way they have made a mark in preserving and fostering the ancient heritage of the Śāstras, the Vedas, philosophy, religion, astronomy, indigenous medicine (Āyurveda) and other branches of Indian wisdom by rescuing them from extinction. One of the factors responsible for profuse sprouting of different learning disciplines of Sanskrit in these states was the tradition that the rulers here used to vie with one another for bringing top-ranking Sanskrit scholars and poets from different parts of the country to their courts, giving them patronage and getting them settled in their states as court-poets *rājagurus*, priests or writers or even as state astronomers or *vaidyas*. These scholar-families were given enough facilities to live in comfort and pursue the tradition of their family disciplines of cultivating a particular Śāstra.

That is why the history of development of Sanskrit literature here can be traced back to the time of Māgha, one of the three most eminent poets of Sanskrit. Māgha flourished in the court of Varmalata or Dharamalata the ruler of Gujarat (eighth century CE) under whose rule was Bhinmal, the town which now forms a part of Jalore district of Rajasthan. His famous epic *Śiśupālavadha* is one of the most celebrated classics of Sanskrit poetry occupying the highest rank in the history of Sanskrit. Dhanapāla, writer of *Tilakamañjarī* belonged to Sanchor (Jalore district, Marwar) and Vāgbhaṭa, writer of *Kāvyānuśāsana* belonged to Mewar, Hari Sūri and Nayabhadra Sūri of Chittor and Jinadatta Sūri of Mewar are also recorded in the literary history as scholars of good eminence. That Dharmaśāstra, Tantra, Jaina philosophy, etc. were studied, taught and pursued in these states of Rajasthan vigorously is evidenced by the availability of thousands of such manuscripts in the old libraries and collections in different states. The Jaisalmer collection has thousands of such Sanskrit, Pāli, Apabhraṁśa and some other text manuscripts. It deserves a special mention here that Dr. Bühler, the famous German orientalist had discovered the manuscripts of Bilhaṇa's *Vikramāṅkadevacarita* (a historical Sanskrit epic) and Vākpatirāja's *Gauḍavāho* (a historical Prākṛt epic) in the same collection at Jaisalmer and got them published from these copies.

Patronage to Sanskrit by the Riyāsats

In all the *riyāsat*s the rulers and also some philanthropic organisations and individuals took it as their sacred duty to establish Sanskrit *pāṭhaśālā*s where the Vedas and the different Śāstras were taught by the *paṇḍit*s to pupils free of charge. The founding of Jaipur city also synchronised with the event of the ruler's (Sawai Jaisingh's) invitation to many eminent Sanskrit scholars from different parts of the country to come and settle down in Jaipur. This patronage to the Sanskrit learning and the Śāstric disciplines later earned a name for Jaipur in the field of Sanskrit eduation and the ancient literary heritage next only to Banaras; that is why until a few decades ago inquisitive students from different parts of the country and even abroad would come to Jaipur to learn Sanskrit from some eminent scholars.

The rulers of small Princely States of Rajasthan as also the rich and devout businessmen, wealthy priests and chiefs of religious endownments and temples, monks of Jaina religious sects, etc. promoted the Sanskrit Śāstras and learning in various ways, e.g. by establishing, managing or financing Sanskrit *pāṭhaśālās*, providing proper facilities to preserve manuscripts in their libraries, temples and the Jaina *upāśraya*s. Rajasthan is well known for its collection of ancient Sanskrit manuscripts, throughout the literary world. The libraries and *granthāgāra*s of Bikaner, Jaisalmer, Nagaur, Jaipur, Bundi, Jodhpur, Udaipur, Chittor, Nathdwara and Kankroli have been centres of attraction for many Sanskrit scholars from all over the country and abroad.

Education of Sanskrit

There was hardly any state in Rajasthan where due importance to Sanskrit learning was not given or due respect to Sanskrit scholars was not paid. The rulers of Jaipur in particular showed their loyalty to the Sanskrit by inviting selected and renowned scholars of Sanskrit from other states of the country and providing them with all facilities to run their *gurukula*s, *pāṭhaśālā*s or *upāśraya*s where pupils had facilities of residing while learning under their *guru*s. The rulers of smaller principalities like Sikar, Khetri and Shahpura also patronised and encouraged the learning of Sanskrit by establishing Sanskrit teaching institutions. Similarly, the Mahārāṇā of Udaipur founded Maharana Sanskrit College, Udaipur, and offered gold in the form of *tulā dāna* to *paṇḍit*s for its finance. It shows his great love for Sanskrit education. The rulers of the states or the "temple boards" also established Sanskrit *pāṭhaśālā*s in Nathdwara, Kankroli, Begun, Dungarpur,

Chittorgarh, Kota, Bundi, Jhalawar, Bhawani Mandi, Dholpur, Bharatpur and Karauli. The ruler of Alwar built a grand institution and a separate hostel building for a Sanskrit school at Alwar to be run on the system of *gurukula*. Anoop Singh, the then *maharājā* of Bikaner was himself a scholar of Sanskrit. He preserved Sanskrit manuscripts for his personal library which is now famous as the Anoop Sanskrit Library. The rulers of Jodhpur also patronised and promoted the learning of Sanskrit by establishing Sanskrit *pāṭhaśālā*s, one of which is now known as Darbar Sanskrit College, Jodhpur. No doubt, the number of students in these schools was very small but the learning and teaching was profound and of the highest quality. The traditional way of teaching Sanskrit aimed at thorough learning of the subject by the students. The students in these different institutions in the last few centuries prepared themselves well for the examinations conducted by the Queen's College, Banaras or the Bengal Sanskrit Association, Calcutta.

After the Merger of the States

After merging the *riyāsat*s the State of Rajasthan was formed in 1949. In this state Sanskrit continued to be a subject in the universities and colleges and also the Sanskrit *pāṭhaśālā*s continued to flourish. One post of deputy director for Sanskrit education was created in the directorate of education department, Rajasthan at Bikaner to supervise the running of the Oriental Sanskrit Institutions of the state. There was a demand from the Sanskrit scholars that there should be a full-fledged department of Oriental Sanskrit Institutions. Thereupon, a committee was formed to discuss the problems of Sanskrit education and suggest steps for the upliftment of the same. This committee recommended the establishment of a separate directorate of Sanskrit education. It would give recognition to Sanskrit examinations as equivalent to other boards/universities; provide for separate teacher-training facilities for the candidates passing the Sanskrit exams, improve hostels and look after the overall development of Sanskrit education, etc.

Establishment of Directorate of Sanskrit Education

As per recommendations of the Joshi Committee, a separate directorate for the Sanskrit education was established by the state government in 1958. It was empowered to have administrative control over the Sanskrit institutions and take responsibility of promoting Sanskrit in all the Sanskrit institutions and colleges of the state.

Today, Rajasthan is the only state in the country which has a separate portfolio of minister for Sanskrit education and also a separate Sanskrit directorate for the development and promotion of Sanskrit. The revival of Sanskrit education and its planned gradual development started from here. This directorate is directly under the administrative control of the education secretary of the Rajasthan government.

Sanskrit Examinations

The graduate and postgraduate level examinations of oriental stream (Shastri and Acharya exams) are conducted by the Jagadguru Ramanandacharya Rajasthan Sanskrit University. It has teaching facilities also. Before 2000 these examinations were conducted by the universities of Jaipur, Jodhpur, Ajmer and Udaipur. All these universities had established faculty of Sanskrit. Similarly, the Sanskrit 'praveśikā' and 'upādhyāyā' examinations are being conducted by the Rajasthan Board of Secondary Education, Ajmer, since 1962.

Sanskrit in the Universities

In the university education system, Sanskrit is a subject at the degree as well as the postgraduate levels (B.A. and M.A. examinations). Research for the doctoral degree (Ph.D.) is also conducted in Sanskrit. There is provision for post-doctoral research also (D.Litt.). There are six multi-faculty universities in Rajasthan having facilities for such education and research including the residential facilities and also in the affiliated colleges situated in different districts. These universities and colleges have Sanskrit departments comprising professors, readers, lecturers, etc. teaching a large number of students. They are all affiliated to the J.R.R. Sanskrit University. Sanskrit colleges are administered and looked after by the directorate of Sanskrit education.

Even in the pre-Independence period the colleges run by the Princely States had a brilliant record of Sanskrit education and scholarship. In these colleges eminent Sanskrit scholars who had also studied English and other languages and subjects held the posts of scholarship in Sanskrit and used to come to these colleges from all parts of the country. It would be of interest to note here that the celebrated scholar of Varanasi Mahamahopadhyay Gopinath Kaviraj had come to Jaipur state's Maharaja's College to study Sankrit and other subjects here in the beginning of the twentieth century. Pt. Chandradhar Sharma Guleri, a renowned scholar and creative writer of Hindi, Sanskrit, etc. was a product of this college. Renowned scholars like Madhusudan Ojha, Vireshwar Shastri, Soorya Narayan Shastri and Mathura Nath Shastri have been some of the eminent teachers in this college.

Similar was the case of other colleges run by other Princely States like Jodhpur, Alwar, Udaipur or Bikaner.

Traditional Sanskrit Education

As indicated earlier, these states had their own Sanskrit *pāṭhaśālā*s the history of which can be traced to the ancient times or the mediaeval period. These were financed largely by the royal houses or the philanthropic millionaires.

Many such traditional Sanskrit institutions running on the system of *gurukula* are continuing even today at Chittorgarh, Ratangarh, Laxmangarh and other places. The local Sanskrit institutions that were run by different smaller states before the merger have been classified, rated, graded and recognised by the state government. Today there are about 2,100 students of 'acharya', 9,000 students of 'shastri', 8,500 students of senior 'upadhyaya', 15,000 students of 'praveshika' and about 66,000 students of pre-'praveshika' classes studying as regular students in 23 'Ācharya' colleges, 26 'shastri' colleges, 42 Senior 'upadhyaya' (higher secondary) schools and 91 'praveshika' (secondary) schools of the *gurukula* stream.

Recognition of Exams and Employment Opportunities

The state government has recognised the oriental examinations of 'praveshika', senior 'upadhyaya', 'shastri' and 'acharya' as equivalent to secondary, senior secondary, B.A. and M.A. exams, respectively for all purposes including recruitments. It has resulted in better employment opportunities for the candidates passing Sanskrit examinations. They are also eligible for Rajasthan civil and police service and other competitive examinations.

Sanskrit at the Secondary Stage of Education

Sanskrit is taught as a compulsory subject from class VI to VIII by the department of primary and secondary education, Rajasthan. In the three-language formula Sanskrit along with Urdu, Sindhi or other Indian languages is recognised as the third language for the secondary stage of school education. The number of students appearing at the secondary exams of R.B.S.E., comes to more than 5 lakh each year. Out of this many students opt for Sanskrit as their third language. Thus, Sanskrit has been given due importance in the main stream of education also. Rajasthan is the first state in the country which started providing teacher-training facilities of S.T.C. to 'praveshika' and 'upadhyaya' pass candidates. Separate training schools have been opened for them. Such 'praveshika' and 'upadhyaya' pass candidates can also seek admission in general S.T.C. schools. Such teachers take jobs in the primary schools of Sanskrit.

Candidates obtaining 'shastri' or 'acharya' degrees of the oriental examination scheme are admitted to 'shiksha shastri' (B.Ed.) training with Sanskrit as their teaching subject in the teacher training colleges of Rajasthan. A large number of 'shiksha shastri' (B.Ed.) degree holders take up teaching jobs in secondary and senior secondary schools of Sanskrit. 'shikshacharya' is equivalent to M.Ed.

Manuscript Libraries

According to a survey there are more than 1 lakh Sanskrit manuscripts preserved in Rajasthan. More than 30,000 of them are present in the personal collections of princes like the Pothīkhānā of Jaipur or the Anoop Sanskrit Library of Bikaner. The third biggest collection of manuscripts in Rajasthan is in Jaisalmer. Besides Sanskrit, manuscripts of historical importance in other languages and ancient paintings are also available in these collections.

The rare manuscripts of Jaisalmer library date back to twelfth and thirteenth centuries. Palm-leaf manuscripts are also available here.

The Oriental Research Institute of the Government of Rajasthan also called Prachya Vidya Pratisthan is situated at Jodhpur. It has been organising collection, studies and publication of the manuscripts in Rajasthan for the last 57 or 58 years. Till date it has collected about 1,25,000 manuscripts. Most of them are published, while the unpublished manuscripts are being edited and taken up for publication. Prachya Vidya Pratisthan has also preserved the manuscripts in Prākṛt, Apabhraṁśa, Hindi, and Rajasthani languages. Amongst rare manuscripts, *Dhvanyālokalocana* and *Janaka Kalpa-Sūtra* of CE 1428 are worth mentioning. Seven branches of this institute are working in different cities of Rajasthan.

Sanskrit Advisory Board

The state government has constituted an advisory board to advise the government from time to time on the development of Sanskrit language. Renowned Sanskrit scholars of Rajasthan are its members. The director of Sanskrit education is the member-secretary whereas the education secretary is also a member of the Board.

Contribution to Śāstras

As a result of continuous efforts by different princely states and the Rajasthan government to promote Sanskrit learning the study of all the Śāstras in Rajasthan has been flourishing for long.

Learned Sanskrit scholars of different branches of studies were called from the south, from Maharashtra, Bihar, Bengal, Kashmir and other regions and settled here. Their writings under the patronage of the rulers brought them world fame. In astronomy Jagannāth Samrāṭ and Puṇḍarīka Ratnākara of the eighteenth century and Pandit Kewal Ram, M.M. Durga Prasad Dwivedi, etc. of the twentieth century have been the glorious figures of their field. Vidya Vachaspati Madhusudan Ojha was a luminary of the Vedic and Śāstric wisdom whose lectures on Veda and Dharma in May 1902 in London had dazzled the Western scholars of that time.

Shri Bhai Nath Maithail, Pt. Kanhaiya Lal Dadhimath, Nand Kishore Sharma, Govind Narain, Yugal Kishore, etc. are well known in the field of philosophy.

These scholars of the esteemed Sanskrit College of Jaipur have been a perennial source of inspiration for the study of philosophy, specially the Nyāya. Pandit Pattabhiram Shastri, one of the greatest authorities on Mīmāṁsā had also worked here from 1945 to 1951. The names of Shri Laxmi Nath Shastri Dravid, Shri Chandra Dutta Ojha, Pandit Chandra Shekhar Dwivedi, Pandit *Giridhar Sharma Chaturvedi* and Kedar Nath

Ojha are the well-known figures in the field of grammar. Pandit Dwivedi later on occupied the position of the Puri Peetha Shankaracharya from 1962-92.

The famous scholars and writers of the *Sāhitya Śāstra* were Shri Krishna Shastri, Mathura Nath Shastri, Hari Shastri and others.

Study of Vedic Literature

Rajasthan has contributed remarkably to the study of Vedic literature. Pt. Madhusudan Ojha, a scholar of international repute has earned a name for his revolutionising exposition of the Vedas delineating the astrophysical, astrobiological and other scientific secrets underlying them. He has written some 200 scholarly works on the Vedic science and history. Vedic Tattva Shodh Sansthan, founded by Pandit Moti Lal Shastri is a leading research centre of India regularly publishing the valuable Vedic literature. The *Rajasthan Patrika,* a leading Hindi newspaper of Jaipur, is also doing remarkable service to the Vedic learning by publishing Vedic literature written by Pandit Ojha and Moti Lal Shastri. The University of Jodhpur has also founded a research cell in Jodhpur for the publication and research of Vedic *vijñāna*.

Sanskrit Academy and other Voluntary Organisations

The state government has established a "Sanskrit Academy" to preserve and promote Sanskrit language and literature. The academy publishes learned creative writings of literary writers of Sanskrit and also gives them awards. It also honours them with all-India awards on writings related to Veda, Vedānta, Sanskrit prose, drama, science and other Śāstric writings. It also provides financial relief to needy Sanskrit scholars or the widows of Sanskrit scholars. It is an autonomous (semi-government) body with its headquarters at Jaipur.

Besides the academy, many other private institutions are also contributing in their own way valuable services for promoting Sanskrit. Such institutions include Rajasthan Sanskrit Bhasha Parishad, Jaipur; Rajasthan Sanskrit Sahitya Sammelan, Jaipur; Vedic Shodha Sansthan, Ajmer; Mahamahopadhyaya Giridhar Shodh Sansthan and Manju Nath Smriti Sansthan, Jaipur; All India Sanskrit Parishad, Udaipur; Vishwa Bharati, Bikaner and Jaina Vishwa Bharati, Ladnu.

Catalogues

Hundreds of manuscripts of the famous *granthāgāras* of Rajasthan have been brought to light by different catalogues published by different institutions. These manuscripts include many valuable, still unknown original works on Kāvya, Tantra, Drama, Dharmaśāstra, Astrology, Nyāya and other branches. Details of these manuscripts can be found in catalogues published by the State Palace Libraries of Jaipur and Jodhpur, Rajasthan Prachya Vidya Pratisthan of the Rajasthan Government (Jodhpur), Anoop Sanskrit Library, Bikaner and some other Jain collections.

Kendriya Sanskrit Vidyapeetha, Jaipur

The Government of India started the postgraduate and Research Institute for Advanced Sanskrit Studies at Jaipur in 1983 under the scheme of setting up higher institutes in different parts of the century. It was the eighth such institute in the country. It has distinguished itself in the field of Sanskrit studies. It is a campus of the Rashtriya Sanskrit Sansthan, a deemed university under the Government of India now.

Establishment of Sanskrit University in Rajasthan

In 1998 the state government of Rajasthan passed an Act in the Legislative Assembly that a Sanskrit university would be established in the state to promote Sanskrit studies and research. The Act envisaged the conduct of various Sanskrit examinations — 'shastri' and 'acharya' by the proposed Sanskrit university. The university started functioning in 2001. Dr. Mandan Mishra took over as its first vice-chancellor. Subsequently, Satya Dev Mishra (2002-05), K.V. Ramakrishanamachariyalu (2005-08), Yugal Kishor (2008-10) have been the vice-chancellors of this university. Presently renowned scholar Ramanuj Devanathan is heading this university as its vice-chancellor. The university was re-named as Jagadguru Ramanandacharya Rajasthan Sanskrit Vishvavidyalaya on 27 June 2005. The university has 6 faculties — Veda-Vedāṅga, Sāhitya, Darśana, Śramaṇa Vidyā, Adhunik Gyān-Vigyān and Education (Shiksha). There are arrangements for faculty teaching for degrees like 'acharya', 'shastri', 'shiksha' shastri, 'shikshacharya', etc. Research for Ph.D., D.Litt. degrees is also conducted here. There is a composite advanced course of 'sanyukta acharya' also for higher oriental studies. Diplomas in jyotiṣa, vāstu, computer applications, library science, etc. are awarded.

There are 9 chairs for specialised research in designated fields like Jyotiṣa, Vedic science, Vyākaraṇa, Mīmāṁsā, Vedānta, modern Sanskrit, religion and culture, Jainology and Sāhitya. Eminent senior scholars specialising in these respective fields designated as chairpersons are working to guide research, publication activity and higher studies in the concerned subjects. There is a research centre also. Astronomical observatory, *yajñaśālā*, etc. are being constructed. A rich library is available in the vast campus, recently developed in Madan village. Hostel and other buildings have also come up very well.

Besides faculty teaching, research and other cocurricular activities the university has 25 postgraduate colleges, 26 degree colleges and 17 education (shiksha shastri) colleges affiliated to it. Some 15,000 students appear every year for the oriental degrees of the university.

Sanskrit Sansthan Campus (Deemed Universiry)

Besides the State Sanskrit University there is another Sanskrit university working in Jaipur by way of a campus of the Rashtriya Sanskrit Sansthan which is a deemed university and has its headquarters in Delhi with more than 10 campuses all over India. Such campuses have all faculty teaching facilities as well as research facilities for oriental examinations. The Oriental College now entitled Kendriya Sanskrit Vidyapeeth was started in Jaipur in CE 1983. It is now called the Jaipur campus of the said deemed university which has its own building, hostels and other branches. It has also some publications to its credit.

In this way Jaipur which has been styled as another Kāśī for Sanskrit education can claim housing two oriental universities in its ambit.

There are, of course, Sanskrit departments working in all the universities of Rajasthan (multi faculty universities) which have faculty teaching facilities for Postgraduate classes and affiliated colleges teaching Sanskrit at degree and postgraduate level and awarding degrees such as B.A., M.A., Ph.D., D.Litt., etc. as differentiated from 'Shastri', 'Acharya', 'Vidya Vachaspati', 'Sahitya Varidhi', etc. awarded by the oriental universities. Quite a good number of students offer Sanskrit as a subject for B.A. or M.A. degrees as it is a scoring subject for different competitive examinations like I.A.S., R.A.S. and other allied services.

Creative Writing

Creative writing in different genres in Sanskrit has also been flourishing in Rajasthan over the centuries. Sanskrit authors of Rajasthan have given new directions to Sanskrit poetry and prose. A brief account of such literary activity over the last two or three centuries is being presented here.

HISTORICAL EPICS

In almost all the earlier Rājpūtānā states historical epics in Sanskrit were composed by the court-poets. They provide first-hand evidences for tracing the history of Rājpūtānā in different ages.

Even before the founding of Jaipur city the rulers of Amber had been patronising Sanskrit scholars. In the court of Raja Mansingh I (CE 1550-1613) poets like Muraridasa, Harinatha and Mohan Kavi had composed historical poems and plays and cultivated traditions of scholarship. Scores of Sanskrit epics are available on the history and chronology of Jaipur, some of which are *Rāmavilāsa* by Viśvanātha Rānāḍe (c. 1680), *Īśvaravilāsa* by Śrī Kr̥ṣṇa Bhaṭṭa (CE. 1740), *Jayavaṁśamahākāvya* by *Sītā Rāma* Parvaṇīkara (c. 1830) and *Kacchavaṁśamahākāvya* by Krishna Rama Bhatta (nineteenth century). Annals of Pr̥thvīrāj Cauhān of Ajmer were recorded in a Sanskrit epic *Pr̥thvīrājavijayam* by his contemporary Jayānaka which is regarded an authentic source of history. History of Mewar is available in epics like *Amarasāra* of Jīvandhara, *Rājaratnākara* of Sadashiva Nagar, *Saṁgrāmamahodaya* of Bihārī, *Vīravaṁśavarṇanam* of Nagaji Ram and in scores of *praśasti*s and *vaṁśāvalī*s contained in elegant poetic compositions inscribed on stones and pillars of temples and forts. The epic *Rājapraśasti* by Raṇchhoṛa Bhaṭṭa was inscribed on 25 stone slabs and is still preserved on the shore of the lake Rajsamand near Kankroli. History of Jodhpur state is preserved in Sanskrit epics like *Ajitodayam* and *Abhayodayam* by Bhaṭṭa Jagjīvana and *Durgāvijayakāvyam* by Haridvija (composed for Rathor Durga Das). History of Bundi is preserved in an epic *Surjancarita* of Candraśekhara, a court-poet of Rao Surjan Singh of Bundi (sixteenth century). In the modern times also Sanskrit poets have carried on the tradition of recording contemporary events in Sanskrit poems and plays. Krishna Ram Bhatta (ninteenth century) and Mathura Nath Shastri (twentieth century) have written poems

Jayapuravilāsam and *Jaipurvaibhavam* respectively, describing Jaipur of their days, Ambika Datta Vyas (originally of Jaipur who had settled in Banaras) had written a historical novel *Śivarājavijayam* on Shivaji.

DRAMA

Sanskrit plays had been composed and performed at the royal courts of the rulers over the last 5-6 centuries. This tradition made it possible to have some original Sanskrit dramas by eminent dramatists. Someśvara, the author of *Lalitavigraharāja* and *Vijayaśrī* (Ajmer CE 1153-63), and Mohan Kavi, the author of *Damana Mañjarī Nāṭikā* (CE 1600), Kṛṣṇa Datta, the author of *Rukmiṇīmādhavam*, Harijīvanamiśra the author of *Palāṇḍumaṇḍana*, Ghṛtakulyā and other plays (seventeenth century), Vishvanath Ranade, the author of *Śṛṅgāravāpikā* (CE 1976) (all from Jaipur) are authors of the old stock whose Sanskrit plays constitute valuable landmarks in the history of Sanskrit drama.

POETRY

Besides the dramatists, Sanskrit poets of Rajasthan continued to adorn the edifice of poetry with their precious jewels throughout these 5-6 centuries. Poets like Rudrakavi (author of *Bhāryāśataka*, CE 1620) of Jaipur, Śrīkṛṣṇa Bhaṭṭa of Bikaner (seventeenth century), author of three *śataka*s published in *Kāvyamālā*; Sītārāma Parvaṇīkara (eighteenth century), Kṛṣṇarāma Bhaṭṭa and Harivallabha Bhaṭṭa (nineteenth century whose works were published by Nirnaya Sagar Press) of Jaipur, Śrīghrakavi Nanda Kishore Shastri, Ramanath Shastri and Manilal Bhatt of Nathdwara, Giridhar Sharma "Navratna" and Giridhari Shastri of Jhalawar, Ganesh Ram Sharma of Doongarpur, Nityanand Shastri and Vidyadhar Shastri of Bikaner, Mathura Nath Bhatt, Hari Shastri, Soorya Narain Shastri, Hari Krishna Shastri, Navalkishor Kankar, Dinanath Trivedi and Ramgopal Shastri, etc. of Jaipur, Madan Sharma

"Sudhakar" of Shekhawati, Madhukar Shastri of Kota, Kantha Mani Shastri, Lakshmi Narain Purohit, Giridhar Lal Shastri, Gangadhar Shastri, etc. of Udaipur and among the younger ones Hari Ram Acharya, Padma Shastri, Radhakrishna Shastri and Girija Prasad of Jaipur are some poets among many who have written poems which were published in individual anthologies or various periodicals of Sanskrit. The Rajasthan Sahitya Academy has also brought out a selection of representative poems of prominent poets of Rajasthan. These poetic writings include poems on old and new themes, in old and new metres including *ghazal*s and songs. Mathura Nath Bhatta is known for writing Sanskrit poems in Braja *bhāṣā* metres and Urdu *ghazal* metres also. His poetry has the freshness and variety coupled with the learned idiom of classical writing. He inspired many a Sanskrit poet to break new paths in Sanskrit poetry. He wrote in all the genres of prose, fiction, essays, skits, etc., profusely revolutioned the creative writing scene in Sanskrit, edited the journal *Sanskrit Ratnākara* and started a new era. He aimed at proving Sanskrit as a living language vibrant with freshness and capable of imbibing new idioms. The literary historians of Sanskrit have called him an epoch-maker of the 1930-60 era.

This is an elaborate testimony to the fact that a remarkable feature of contemporary Sanskrit poetry of Rajasthan is the wide canvas of themes and the variety of metrical and linguistic vehicle. Kala Nath Shastri's panegyric of the soap in *Phenakaśatakam* along with poems in different styles of songs, *ghazals*, *samasyāpūrti*, lyrics, parodies, etc. have been published in his *Kavitāvallarī* (anthology).

Equally gratifying is the diversity of metrical vehicles employed by the modern Sanskrit poet of Rajasthan. Ranging from the classical metres common in Sanskrit, Prākṛt and Apabhraṁśa, the poets here have written with felicity in Urdu and Persian metres, in song forms, *qawwālī*s, blank verse and all that the like of which is found in the modern poetry of other languages. Nursery rhymes of Dr. Hari Ram Acharya, songs of Girija Prasad and Radha Krishna Shastri set to music are a common face in the poetic symposia of Sanskrit in Rajasthan which still attract the audience just as the *kavi sammelans* of Hindi or *muśairā*s of Urdu do. A glance at the Sanskrit publications of the last four decades and the material published in Sanskrit periodicals over the last 50 years will evidence the Rajasthan Sanskrit poets' awareness of the modern context, the socio-political changes taking place on the national scene, the struggle of the nation for Independence and other important events. Padma Shastri has written an epic on the life of Lenin. Mohan Lal Pandey of Jaipur has written *Patradūtam* on the theme of Saddam Hussein of Iraq, the Gulf War and the US troops. He has written a historical novel on Padminī set against the background of Rājpūt medieval history. The story of Gandhi in Sanskrit verses written by Madhukar Shastri was published by the Rajasthan Sahitya Academy. Poems and plays on the life of Nehru or on the Bangladesh liberation or on the passing away of a national dignitary are a usual face we come across while glancing through the Sanskrit periodicals of Rajasthan of the last few decades.

FICTION AND RADIO PLAYS

Besides poetry, the authors from Rajasthan have also produced a rich variety of prose writings and fiction in its various genres. Udayacandra of Bikaner (seventeenth century CE) wrote *Pāṇḍityadarpaṇam* in prose and verse. Haridevavyāsa (seventeenth century CE) wrote travelogues in letter form entitled *Ajitavijñaptiḥ*, Mathura Nath Bhatta (twentieth century CE) has written novels like *Ādarśaramaṇī* and over 100 short stories in Sanskrit both on historical and social themes. Other fiction writers of Rajasthan are, to mention a few, Ganesh Ram Sharma, Narain Kankar, Kala Nath Shastri, Lakshmi Narain Purohit and Hari Krishna Goswami's Sanskrit plays have been written by Govind Prasad Dadhich of Jaipur and Satya Narain of Ajmer. Credit of reviving the intense activity of original playwriting in Sanskrit should go to the Jaipur station of All India Radio which started broadcasting a series of original Sanskrit plays in 1956 which went up to 1962. Radio plays on historical and social themes written by AIR Jaipur during this period include Mañjulā by Mathura Nath Bhatta, *Cittorasiṁhaḥ* by Kala Nath Shastri, *Bhartṛhariḥ* by Hari Ram Acharya. Sanskrit plays of Kala Nath Shastri are collected in *Saṁskṛtanāṭyavallarī* and those of Dr. Hari Ram Acharya in *Pūrvaśākuntalam*. Dr. Indu Shekhar of Jaipur too has written radio plays. A collection of Sanskrit one-act plays written by Dr. Narain Kankar has been published by the Rajasthan Sahitya Academy. A collection of Pt. Ganesh Ram Sharma's short stories has also been published by this Academy. Recently, the Academy has brought out a collection of Sanskrit fiction. Short stories, novels personal essays of Kala Nath Shastri have been published under the titled *Ākhyānavallarī*. A selection of stories of the same author was published by Rajasthan Sanskrit Academy under the title *Kathānakavallī*.

EDITING

It deserves a special mention here that the paṇḍits of Jaipur were the most prominent among those who contributed to the revival of Sanskrit literature in the beginning of the nineteenth century by way of intense publication activity by Nirnaya Sagar Press, Venkateshwar Press and Gita Press. The *Kāvyamālā* series brought out by the Nirnaya Sagar Press deserves a special mention. It was for the first time in this series that hundreds of valuable poems and works of hundreds of poets were collected, edited and published in 14 "clusters" (called *gucchakas*) with short notes on the authors. In all 150 poetic works were published in these 14 collections. Besides this, 100 other volumes of literary works and works on poetics were published in this series. This had brought a veritable renaissance in the Sanskrit world in the nineteenth century As editors of this series eminent Sanskrit scholars of India had lent their services. Most prominent among these was Mahāmahopādhyāya Durga Prasad Sharma of Jaipur (nineteenth century) who edited a large number of these titles. M.M. Shivadatta Sharma Dadhimat and Kedara Nath Sharma (son of M.M. Durga Prasad) of Jaipur also edited some volumes of this series.

A number of books like *Mañjunātha Granthāvalī* and others have been edited by present author in collaboration with Ramakant Pandey.

TRANSLATIONS

A remarkable trend in the Sanskrit literature is a long tradition of translating important works from other languages into Sanskrit. Rajasthan also has contributed to this tradition just as the poets of the eighteenth and nineteenth centuries translated into Braja *bhāṣā* the classics of Amaruka, Bhartṛhari, etc., the Sanskrit poets of later days made effective and successful attempts at translating works of Persian, Hindi and other languages into Sanskrit. Giridharī Sharma "Navaratna" of Jhalawar had translated and published some *rubaits* of Omar Khayyām. Mathura Nath Bhatta of Jaipur translated *dohās* of the classical Braj *bhāṣā* poet Bihārī's "Satasai" and also *gāthās* of *Gāthā Saptaśatī* in the same metre into Sanskrit. Bhagwan Datt Shastri Rakesh of Bhilwara has translated Jaya Shankar Prasad's Hindi classic — *Kāmāyanī* epic in Sanskrit verses. Dharmendra Nath Acharya of Bharatpur has translated and published the Persian *Gulistān* of Sheikh Sādi in Sanskrit verses and prose styled as *Puṣpālokaḥ* and Guru Govind Singh's *Zafarnāmā* from Persian into Sanskrit styled as *Vijayapatram*. He has also translated all the *rubaits* of Omar Khayyām in Sanskrit verses. Kala Nath Shastri has translated some *ghazals* of Ghālib in the same metre. Vishveshvar Nath Reu of Jodhpur (twentieth century) has done a commendable work by writing the Hindu law in Sanskrit verses styled as *Āryavidhānam*, Mathura Nath Bhatta translated novels and short stories from Bengali into Sanskrit and also stories of Prem Chand and some other leading Hindi writers. Goswami Hari Krishna Shastri translated a Bengali novel and a Hindi novel. Madhukar Shastri of Kota is translating the holy Quran into Sanskrit. Dr. Shiv Kumar Shukla has translated *Rāmacaritamānasa* of Tulsīdās into Sanskrit.

LITERARY JOURNALS

With the rise of Sanskrit periodicals in India like *Vidyodaya* (CE 1873) and *Saṁskṛtcandrikā* (CE 1893) an era of profuse creative activity of literary journalism had set in by the end of the nineteenth century Rajasthan, especially Jaipur, contributed to this trend most admirably, *Saṁskṛtaratnākara* a long-lived and celebrated Sanskrit monthly was started in Jaipur in 1904, was later adopted as its chief organ by the All India Sanskrit Sahitya Sammelan (a leading organisation of Sanskrit) and continued to be published from Jaipur till 1949 when its office was shifted to Banaras. Its editor Mathura Nath Shastri of Jaipur created many landmarks in the history of Sanskrit journalism by introducing modern trends in it like regular columns of book reviews, news and notes, fun and frolic, views' forum and so on. After transfer of its headquarters, Jaipur started another Sanskrit monthly *Bhāratī* in 1950 which is continuing to date. The Rajasthan Sanskrit Academy has instituted a Sanskrit quarterly *Svaramaṅgalā* which is being published regularly. All these Sanskrit periodicals have contributed richly to the development of creative genres of recent varieties in Sanskrit. Rajasthan Sanskrit Academy has published an account of the modern Sanskrit writers in five volumes.

Many Sanskrit scholars of Rajasthan have been honoured

by the president of India with certificate of honour. When such honour was instituted in 1958 M.M. Giridhar Sharma Chaturvedi was the first to be honoured. Since then Dr. Mandan Mishra, Dr. R.C. Dwivedi, Pandit Jagadish Sharma, Pandit Nawal Kishore Kankar, Pandit Gangadhar Dwivedi, Dr. Narain Kankar, Pandit Khadga Nath Mishra, Pandit Kalyan Datta Sharma, Devarshi Kala Nath Shastri, Dr. Shiv Datta Chaturvedi, Mohan Lal Pandey, Prabhakar Sharma Shastri, Gopal Narain Bahura, Hari Ram Acharya, Dayanand Bhargava and Badariprasad Shastri of Jaipur, Pandit Vishwa Nath Mishra of Bikaner and Satya Narain Shastri of Ajmer have also received this honour. Thousands of Sanskrit teachers and hundreds of devoted Sanskrit scholars are still pursuing reading, writing and teaching activity of the Sanskrit language and literature here in the state of Rajasthan.

17

Sanskrit Studies in Tamizh Nadu

Sundari Siddhartha

SANSKRIT studies have come a long way from the days of the Renaissance. The study of it has been recorded in the publication of the Rashtriya Sanskrit Sansthan in 1996 (*Sanskrit Studies in India*). Therein, studies in Tamil Nadu are recorded at pp. 245-51. We proceed ahead from there.

Tamil Nadu has the unique honour of being the one state which has its own ancient, classical language Tamizh, and still it promoted the even more ancient, classical language Sanskrit for thousands of years, recognising in it a rich repository of culture and heritage, similar to its own. Most of the kings of the dynasties that ruled here, patronised both the languages as if they were their two eyes. But, it is evident that Sanskrit began to languish here during the last century. So, the revival of Sanskrit Studies gains all the more importance.

Sanskrit study covers both, the study of the "language" and the study of the "literature in that language". Both are important and need to be retained.

Study of the Language

As of now, (i) Sanskrit Bharati with its various branches all over Tamil Nadu; (ii) Sura Bharati of Egmore, Chennai; (iii) Sanskrit Education Society, and numerous other agencies are fully dedicated to the propagation of the language, with

Spoken-Sanskrit camps and correspondence courses, regular classes and online teaching, with or without exams. Thus, both technical and human websites are spreading all over Tamil Nadu, attracting people of all ages and from all streams and professions. It augurs well for inter-disciplinary study and research. We eagerly await concrete results.

Study of the Literature

The Institutions, the Projects and the Publications are the three main segments under which this information is arranged.

Institutions

We will dwell on the Study Centres in the capital city of Chennai. Besides them, there are centres in other cities and towns too, namely Madurai, Tiruchy, Kumbakonam, Tiruvaiyaru, Thanjavur, Coimbatore, Kanchipuram, Srirangam, Salem, Tirunelveli and so on.

In the past few years, the following centres too have started offering Sanskrit studies:

1. Shastra University (near Tanjavur) — Postgraduate course and Ph.D.
2. Periyar University at Salem — B.A. (Undergraduate course).
3. Manonmaniyam University at Tirunelveli — M.A. (Postgraduate course).

TRADITIONAL INSTITUTIONS

Besides the B.A. (undergraduate course, etc. of the Western system), we have Veda Pāṭhaśālās, Oriental Schools, and Sanskrit Kalāśālās. The first teaches Vedas in the traditional way. (Rajasaheb Govinda Dikshitar Pathasala at Kumbakonam; Vedapathasala at Thiruvanaikka.) In the Oriental School, students from the 6th to the 10th class, have extra papers in Sanskrit, Arabic or Persian. After studying Sanskrit, they get

Oriental School Leaving Certificate and can join Prāk Siromani +2 course. Oriental schools started in Tamil Nadu in 1960s at Mylapore, Mambalam, Kanchipuram, Kumbakonam, Tanjavur, Vizhuppuram, Madurantakam and Pudur. The Sanskrit Kalāśālās are institutions like the Madras Sanskrit College (1906) at Chennai, teaching Sanskrit at the higher level and covering all sections of Sanskrit grammar, literature, philosophy and other Śāstras. To name a few: Sri Ranganatha Paduka Vidyalaya (1967) and Sri Andavan Pathasala at Srirangam; Sri Ahobila Matham Sanskrit Kalāśālās at Madurantakam; Raja's College (1880) at Tiruvaiyaru; and others. [In the Madras Sanskrit College and Ranganatha Paduka Vidyalaya, Senior Sastra Cudamani professors conduct special courses on *Udgrantha*s or terse advanced texts (like *Śāstra-Dīpikā* in Mīmāṁsā and *Citsukhi* in Vedānta) in the field of their specialisation to senior students and junior teachers]. At Chennai, female students are being admitted to the Siromani courses, from 1989.

> [From 1980-81 onwards the Siromani syllabus includes a study of English and the regional language also. This gradual process of bringing in the traditional and modern subjects into the curriculum is going to prove to be the major thrust area in bringing depth and substance into our research projects.]

MODERN INSTITUTIONS

The universities in Tamil Nadu having Sanskrit teaching colleges are: Madras University, Chennai; Bharathidasan University, Tiruchy; Madurai Kamaraj University, Madurai; Bharatiyar University, Coimbatore; Alagappa University, Karaikudi; and Annamalai University, Chidambaram. Many of the colleges are autonomous. A fairly recent university is the Sri Chandrasekharendra Sarasvati Visva Mahavidyalaya at Enathur, Kanchipuram.

As a major subject along with allied subjects like history, culture, music and philosophy, Sanskrit is offered in two colleges — Queen Mary's College for Women and RKM Vivekananda College for Men. Sanskrit is studied in the first two years at the B.A. level in many colleges — Queen Mary's, Presidency, Stella Maris, Loyola, Madras Christian College, D.G. Vaishnava, Anna Adarsh, Dr. MGR Janaki, SIET, MOP Vaishnava, SRM, Gurunanak, A.M. Jain, SDMB Vaishnav, Kumararani Meena Muthiah, at Chennai; and in about 10 or more other colleges outside Chennai. In the past fifteen years, Sanskrit studies have attracted, besides brahmins — muslims, non-brahmins and other backward communities, specially in the Chennai city. This may, in the future, prove helpful in filling up the reserved posts with well-qualified students of our own.

Institutions having facilities for M.Phil., and Ph.D. along with post-graduate teaching, are mainly in Chennai. They are — Sanskrit Department, University of Madras; Presidency College (autonomous) and Vivekananda College of Ramakrishna Mission (autonomous). There is also one college in Tiruvaiyaru (Thanjavur district). Besides these, three very prestigious private institutions in Chennai also offer Research Courses in Sanskrit. These include (1) The Kuppuswami Sastri Research Institute, Mylapore; (2) Sathya Nilayam, Thiruvanmiyur; (3) Adyar Library and Research Centre. (Kuppuswami Sastri Research Institute, when it was affiliated to the Rashtriya Sanskrit Sansthan used to award Vidyavaridhi degree which is the traditional equivalent to the Ph.D. degree.)

Major Projects of the Central Government

After Independence, four research projects were sanctioned by the Central Government. *Rāmāyaṇa* was given to Gaekwad University, Baroda; *Mahābhārata* to BORI, Pune; Dictionary to Deccan College, Pune; and Madras was asked to bring out the

New Catalogus Catalogorum (NCC) for Sanskrit, Pāli and Prākṛt texts. To date, 18 volumes have been completed, till the letter "vai".

Under the UGC scheme, spoken Sanskrit classes were conducted at 300 centers in 2003–04.

"Epoch Making Social Thinkers" is a UGC-sponsored project. Under that, "Adi Sankaracharya Study" is being conducted in Kanchipuram at the Enathur University.

National Manuscripts Mission project for preserving the Sanskrit and Tamizh manuscripts is going on at the Government Museum, Chennai, with nodal assistance from the Sanskrit and Tamizh departments of the Madras University.

Propagation of Sanskrit Studies through Translations

Tamizh is the state language of Tamil Nadu. A sizeable number of intellectuals are at home with it.

Quite a number of Sanskrit texts (specially on Vedānta, like *Pañcadaśī*, *Gītā* with commentary of Madhusudan Sarasvati, Śrīdharī commentary and others) were and are being translated into Tamizh to facilitate the accessibility to all those inclined towards Sanskrit studies.

Mathams engaged in such work are:

1. Vira Subbiah Swamigal Matham
2. Koviloor Madalayam, Karaikudi

Libraries (having Sanskrit related Books and Journals, etc.)

1. Government Oriental Manuscripts Library, Chennai.
2. Adyar Library and Research Centre, Chennai.
3. Kuppuswami Sastri Research Institute, Chennai.
4. Sanskrit Department, University of Madras.

5. Philosophy Department, University of Madras.
6. Connemara State Central Library, Chennai.
7. U.V. Swaminatha Iyer Library, Chennai.
8. Presidency College Library, Chennai.
9. Thanjavur Maharaja Serfoji's Saraswati Mahal Library, Thanjavur.
10. Sri Chandrasekharendra Sarasvati Visva Mahavidyalaya, Enathur, Kanchipuram.

Publishers of Works in Sanskrit and/or dealing with Sanskrit Studies

Sanskrit study needs books — original, secondary, critical, comparative and so on. Some of the Sanskrit publishers are listed here:

1. Adyar Library and Research Centre, Adyar, Chennai — 600 020.
2. Kuppuswami Sastri Research Institute, Mylapore, Chennai — 600 004.
3. Sanskrit Academy, Mylapore, Chennai — 600 004.
4. Madras Sanskrit College, Mylapore, Chennai — 600 004.
5. Government Oriental Manuscripts Library, Marina Campus, Chennai — 600 005.
6. University of Madras Publications, and the New Cata-logus Catalogorum, Marina Campus, Chennai — 600 005.
7. The Sanskrit Education Society, Old 212/13-1, new 11, St. Mary's Road, R.A. Puram, Chennai — 600 028.
8. The Saṁskṛta Raṅga, 54 Thiru Vi Ka Road, Mylapore, Chennai — 600 004.
9. Dr. V. Raghavan Centre for Performing Arts, 1, Third Street, Bhaktavatsalam Nagar, Adyar, Chennai — 600 020.
10. Krishnamacharya Yoga Mandiram, 31, 4th Cross Street,

Ramakrishna Nagar, Chennai — 600 028.

11. Sri Ramakrishna Math, 31 Ramakrishna Math Road, Mylapore, Chennai — 600 004.
12. Sri Nrisimhapriya, 30, Venkatesa Agraharam, Mylapore Chennai — 600 004.
13. Lifco Publishers Pvt. Ltd., New no. 36, North Road, C.I.T. Nagar, Chennai — 600 035.
14. Sree Sarada Education Society, East Coast Flats, Adyar, Chennai — 600 020.
15. Adi Sankara Advaita Research Centre, Chennai — 600 004.
16. Uttamur Publications of Uttamur Viraraghavachariar, Nadamuni Street, T. Nagar, Chennai — 600017.
17. Samata Publishers, Personal Bookshop, Teynampet, Chennai — 600 002.
18. Vedanta Desikar Research Centre, Mylapore, Chennai — 600 004.
19. "Andavan Ashramam at Srirangam", Desikachari Road, Alwarpet, Chennai — 600 018.
20. Saraswati Mahal Library, Thanjavur.

Journals promoting Sanskrit Studies

IN ENGLISH

1. *Journal of Oriental Research*, Madras (published by Kuppuswami Sastri Research Institute, Mylapore, Chennai — 600 004) {Started in 1927}.
2. *Brahma Vidya* — The Adyar Library Bulletin (published by Adyar Library and Research Centre, The Theosophical Society, Adyar, Chennai — 600 020) {Started in 1937}.

IN SANSKRIT

1. *Samskrita Sri* (published by The Sanskrit Education

Society, 11 (old 212/13-1), St. Mary's Road, R.A. Puram, Chennai — 600 028.

Projects, Seminars

TRADITIONAL DEBATES

Vakyartha Sadas are regularly arranged on various topics and conducted in the traditional way, in the following institutions:

1. Madras Sanskrit College, Mylapore, Chennai.
2. Sankara Matham, Mambalam, Chennai.
3. Sankara Matham, Kanchipuram.
4. Andavan Ashramam of Srirangam.

PROGRAMMES ORGANISED AT MADRAS SANSKRIT COLLEGE

1. 2006 — Vidvat Sadas on Sahitya and Jyotisha.
2. 2006 — Nine Day Conference on "Samskritam and Samskriti".
3. 1994-95 — Vakyartha Vidvat Sadas.
4. 1990-91 — Workshop on "Comparative Rituology".
5. 1990 — Seminar on "Phaladipika".

PROJECTS UNDERTAKEN AT KUPPUSWAMI SASTRI RESEARCH INSTITUTE

1. 2011-12 — Tamil translation of "Paduka Sahasram" (Sri Kesava Iyengar Endowment).
2. 2010-11 — Caturyuga Calendar (Ramanandha Adigalar Foundation).
3. 2007-09 — Preservation of the rare and ancient books through the Photolam system.
4. 2009 — Caturyuga Calendar (Dr. N. Mahalingam Endowment).
5. 2009 — Sanskrit Literature (Dr. V. Raghavan Centenary Celebrations).

6. 2008 — Religion and Philosophy of Vaishnava Agamas (National Seminar sponsored by Rashtriya Sanskrit Sansthan, New Delhi).
7. 2008 — Amritanadopanisad (Shri G.R. Nataraja Iyer Endowment).
8. 2005-08 — Encyclopaedia of Numerals (B. Venkataramani Endowment).
9. 2006-07 — Advayatarakopanisad (Sri G.R. Nataraja Iyer Endowment).
10. 2006 — Preventive Conservation of Manuscripts (jointly with Government Museum, Chennai).
11. 2007 — Tattvānusandhānam (Critical edn. & tr.) (Prof. R. Sankari Endowment).
12. 2005-06 — Digitisation of rare and ancient books (more than hundred years old) by the TTD (Tirumalai-Tirupati Devasthanam) under the Million Book Project initiated by Dr. A.P.J. Abdul Kalam, the then President of India.
13. 2004-05 — Computer Cataloguing of the Library Books.
14. 2004-05 — Darśanopanisad – Translation project (Smt. Kanthimathi Ammal Endowment).
15. 2004 — Sri Nandikeśakārikā – Critical edition (Dr. S. Jayashree Endowment).
16. 2000-04 — Sadratnamala (An Astro-mathematical text) [under INSA].
17. 2003 — Ancient Indian Scientific Knowledge, Ancient Indian Polity (jointly with Samskrita Academy, Chennai).
18. 2001 — Aṣṭāṅga Nighaṇṭu (Prof. G. Masti Subramaniyan Endowment).

19. 1999-2000 — Bhagavad Gita Bibliography (Suryakumari Dwarakadas Endowment - vols. 1 & 2 published).
20. 1999 — Women in Epics (A.C. Kamala Endowment for Women Studies).
21. 1997-99 — Women in Vedic Age (A.C. Kamala Endowment for Women Studies).
22. 1996 — Sanskrit and South Indian Languages (Golden Jubilee Valedictory function).
23. 1995 — Sanskrit and Medical Science (Golden Jubilee Seminar).
24. 1994 — Sanskrit and Science (Golden Jubilee Symposium).
25. 1992 — Saiva Rituals and Philosophy.
26. 1990 — Vedic Sammelan (sponsored by Rashtriya Veda Vidya Pratishthan, New Delhi).
27. 1989 — Vaiṣṇava Āgamas.
28. 1988 — Symposium on Temple Arts.
29. 1988 — Umāpati Śivācārya, His Life, Work and Contribution to Śaivism.
30. 1983 — Colloquium on "Interpretation of Mīmāṁsā Sutras".
31. 1982 — Seminar on Domestic Vaishnava Rituals, Siva Temple and Temple Rituals.
32. 1981 — Seminars on Art, Archaeology, Ayurveda, Literature, Yoga and Sastras.
33. 1967 — Seminar on Arthashastra.

AT RKM VIVEKANANDA COLLEGE

1. 2000 — Conference on "Wisdom of India".

2. 1999 — National Level Conference on "Art and Architecture – Sanskrit Sources".
3. 1998 — UGC State Level Conference on "Gṛhya Sūtras".
4. 1997 — Seminar on "Rasa and Dhvani in Sanskrit, Tamizh and Hindi literature".
5. 1996 — Seminar on "The Cultural Heritage of India".
6. 1995 — Seminar on "The Technical Sciences in Sanskrit".
7. 1994 — Seminar on "Research Methodology".
8. 1993 — Seminar on "Comparative Study of Sanskrit and English Literature".
9. 1988 — Seminar on "The Ramayana".
10. 1982 — Seminar on "Golden Age of Sanskrit" (Proceedings have been published).

AT DEPARTMENT OF SANSKRIT, UNIVERSITY OF MADRAS

1. 2011 — One-day Seminar on Shri Anandamurtiji's Contribution to Philosophy, Language, Literature and Science (in collaboration with "Renaissance Universal" (RU), Chennai).
2. 2010 — Eleven days National Workshop on "Strategies of Linguistic Description adopted in Paniniyam and Tolkappiyam" [sponsored by the Central Institute of Classical Tamil (CICT), Chennai].
3. 2009, March — UGC National Seminar – "Vedangas and their Modern Relevance".
4. 2009, January — National Seminar on Agamas – in Theory and Practice (jointly with "Art of Living", Bangalore).
5. 2008, August — Symposium – "Punarunmeshah – Resurgence of Sanskrit Studies".

6. 2008, April — One-day Seminar on "Influence of Sanskrit on English & vice versa (in collaboration with Madras English Association, Chennai).
7. 2008, February — Refresher Course in Sanskrit and other Indian Languages (sponsored by UGC).
8. 2006, April — Advance Level National Workshop on Manuscriptology and Paleography (in collaboration with the National Manuscripts Mission, Ministry of Culture, Government of India).
9. 2006, February — International Seminar on "Kriti Rakshana —Manuscripts and Indian Knowledge Systems" (with the National Manuscripts Mission, Government of India).
10. 2005 — Three-day Seminar on "Yoga & Positive Health" (sponsored by UGC).
11. 2004 — One-week National Workshop and Seminar on "Manuscriptology, Palaeography & Technical Sciences (in collaboration with IGNCA, New Delhi).
12. 2000 — Science and Technology in Sanskrit Writings (with financial help from the Ministry of Human Resource Development, Government of India).
13. 1999, May — Minority Language (Reference Course).
14. 1999, February – Vedangas—Import and Off-shoots.
15. 1997 — Silpa and Agamas.
16. 1991 — The Philosophy of Visistadvaita.
17. 1985 — All India Level Seminar on "Post Sankara Advaita" (sponsored by UGC).
18. 1982 — Classes in Indian Philosophical Systems (refresher course).

Publications

AT KUPPUSWAMI SASTRI RESEARCH INSTITUTE (KSRI)

[Note — The *Journal of Oriental Research* was started in 1927. Eighty-two volumes have been published till now.]

1. 2011 — Siva Linga Worship – Authentic documentary (in VCD).
2. 2011 — *Sāṁkhya Saṅketa Kośa*, vol.1.
3. 2011 — *Sad Ratnamālā* of Sankara Varman (a mathematical and astronomical text), ed. with English translation and notes.
4. 2010 — *Lectures on Patañjali's Mahābhāṣya*, vols. IX & X.
5. 2010 — *Sanskrit and Saṅgīta*.
6. 2009 — *Lectures on Patañjali's Mahābhāṣya*, vols.VII & VIII.
7. 2009 — *Nandikesa Kasika* with Upamanyu's Commentary and with English translation.
8. 2008 — *Advayatarakopaniṣad* with English translation.
9. 2009 — *Amṛtanadopaniṣad* with English translation.
10. 2009 — *Sanskrit and Science* (revised with index).
11. 2008 — *The Concept of the Beautiful in Sanskrit Literature* (re-edited).

AT ADYAR LIBRARY AND RESEARCH CENTRE (ALRC)

ALRC publishes books in three categories : (a) Adyar Library Series, (b) Adyar Library General Series, and (c) Pamphlet Series.

1. 2009 — *Pratyabhijña Hṛdayam* with translation.
2. 2009 — *Studies on Some Concepts of Alaṁkāra Śāstra*.
3. 2008 — *Yoga Upaniṣads*, translation.
4. 2008 — *Śākta Upaniṣads* (text).
5. 2004 — *The Thirty-two Vidyās*.

6. 2004 — *Mānameyodaya.*
7. 2004 — *Nāgārjuna's Mūlamadhyamakakārikāḥ.*
8. 2003 — *Vaiṣṇava Upaniṣad.*
9. 2003 — *Vedānta Paribhāṣā.*
10. 2002 — *Vaiṣṇava Upaniṣad*, translation.
11. 2001 — *Madhyamakahṛdayam* of Bhavya.
12. 2000 — *Varivasyā Rahasya* (reprint).
13. 2000 — *Lakṣmī Tantra.*
14. 2000 — *Indian Theories of Meaning.*
15. 2000 — *Amarakośa* with South Indian commentaries.
16. 2000 — *Caturdaśalakṣaṇī*, part 2.

Pamphlets

1. 2007 — The Spiritualscape of the Upaniṣads.
2. 2007 — Vedic and Mesopotamian Interactions.
3. 2007 — Tarap-tamap-augha-sūtra — Krodarthavāda of Ramabhadra Dīkṣita.
4. 2007 — Tapas in the Bhagavad-Gītā.
5. 2005 — Dialogues of Plato and the Upaniṣads.
6. 2005 — Bādārayaṇa and Vyāsa as authors of the Brahma-Sūtra.
7. 2005 — Anyapadeśa Pañcasat.
8. 2003 — Vaiśeṣika Catuḥsūtrī.
9. 2001 — Patañjali's Metaphysical Schematic: Puruṣa and Prakṛti in the Yoga-Sūtra.
10. 2001 — Bhavya on Mīmāṁsā (Bhavya's Madhyama-hṛdaya Ch.IX, introduction and English translation).

In Bulletins of Government Oriental Manuscripts Library

1. 2004 — Kaṭākṣaṣoḍasī (Vaiṣṇavism) XXXI.

2. 2003 — Ganeṣadarśanam (Philosophy) XXX.
3. 2002 — Ganeṣadarśanam (Philosophy) XXIX.
4. 2001 — Agnihotra Yajña (Religion) XXVIII.
5. 2000 — Agnihotra Rakṣāmaṇi (Śrauta) XXVII.

At the Sanskrit Department, University of Madras

1. 2010 — *Pure Soul and its Infinite Treasure.*
2. 2007 — *Essays on Indian Philosophy* (N. Vasupal).
3. 2006 — *Environmental Awareness in Jainism* (Geetha Ramanujam).
4. 2006 — *Jaina Ethical Works* (N. Vasupal).
5. 2005 — *Facets of Jainism*, Series 1 (N. Vasupal).

The Saṁskṛta Raṅga

1. Bibliography of Modern Sanskrit Plays — 1998 to 2002

Dr.V. Raghavan Centre for Performing Arts

1. Punarunmeśaṇa — Centenary Publication 2008 (Collected presentation by young scholars) funded by Sangeet Natak Akademi, New Delhi.

Sree Sarada Education Society (SSES)

1. 2008 — Directory of Doctoral Dissertations on Sanskrit by the Indian Universities, K.V. Sharma, Rashtriya Sanskrit Sansthan, New Delhi.
2. 2008 — *Bṛhat-Saṁhitā* with Commentary of Utpala Parimala Yogin, Part-1 (50 chapters), ed. K.V. Sharma, Rashtriya Sanskrit Sansthan, New Delhi.
3. 2008 — *Gaṇitayuktibhāṣā* — Rationales in Mathematical Astronomy (text in Malayalam with English translation and explanatory notes) published in two parts by Hindustan Book Agency, New Delhi.
4. 2007 — *New Lights on Manuscriptology*, ed. Prof. Siniruddha Dash, Sree Sarada Education Society.

5. 2006 — *Gaṇitayuktibhāṣā of Jyeṣṭhadeva* (part 1 in Sanskrit) by Prof. K.V. Sharma, Indian Institute of Advanced Studies, Simla.
6. 2002 — *Scientific Texts in the Manuscript Repositories of Kerala and Tamil Nadu*, ed. K.V. Sarma, Rashtriya Sanskrit Sansthan, New Delhi.

Institutional Pillars Supporting Sanskrit Studies

MADRAS SANSKRIT COLLEGE

It is recorded that in 1882, Madras had 12,498 indigenous schools. So, rightly has it been said that from the time of King Aśvapati of the Upaniṣads, who said that there was none in his state who was not learned, to the time of the British administration, the tradition of learning had been maintained in India by a network of Agrahāras, Tols and Pāṭhaśālās. The British started three Sanskrit institutions — the school at Poona in 1821 and the colleges at Banaras and Calcutta in 1791-92 and 1824. If nothing else, it exposed them to Sanskrit, resulting in the government orders dated 3 September 1814 and 31 June 1836, enunciating the intrinsic value of Sanskrit, its usefulness to enrich the vernaculars and its richness in scientific, philosophical and other material which could be correlated to corresponding branches of modern study. Among the English-educated Indians, it resulted in the awakening of an awareness of the rich heritage of India. Noted luminaries of the day, who were ably led by Sri V. Krishnaswami Iyer (who went on to become the judge of the Madras High Court), noticing the fast deteriorating standard of Sanskrit, started the Madras Sanskrit College in 1906.

Thanks to the vision of the founders, the basic preliminary works of Sanskrit in Vyākaraṇa and other Śāstras were compulsorily taught to the students. English was taught, as also comparative and critical studies. With the first principal being Mahāmahopādhyāya Prof. Kuppuswami Sastri, the college progressed very well. In 1948, Sanskrit lost importance in schools and this resulted in the decrease in the number of students seeking admission to the college. The Golden Jubilee of the College was celebrated in 1957. Recognition came from the Madras University and the central government. The college was recognised as "Adarsh Sanskrit Mahavidyalaya" and the government grants started coming in. The salary of the lecturers was hiked accordingly. Women were admitted from 1989. At present there are nearly 130 students and 13 staff on the rolls. This may be because of the extension of the hostel facilities with free boarding and lodging. In the academic year 2004-05, the syllabus of the Sanskrit Siromani was revised by the University of Madras — Prak-Siromani — 2 years; Sanskrit Siromani Madhyama (B.A.) — 3 years; and Sanskrit Siromani (M.A.) — 2 years. In this seven years' course, English, Hindi/Tamil, and Computer Science have been made compulsory to meet the present-day needs and to help develop communication skills among the students. In 2006 this great Institute completed 100 years of fruitful work in the field of Sanskrit studies, marked by year-long celebrations including conferences, Vidvat Sadas, honouring of scholars and so on. The college continues its services to the cause of Sanskrit.

Kuppuswami Sastri Research Institute

A Private Registered Body; voluntary, public, non-profit, non-governmental organisation KSRI was founded in 1944, to conduct and continue high-class Sanskritic and Indological research as initiated by Prof. Kuppuswami Sastri. Renowned personalities like Dr. S. Radhakrishnan, Prof. M. Hiriyanna and others were actively associated with the institute as presidents, secretaries and members. Dr. V. Raghavan, the Sanskrit scholar of international repute, was the founder-secretary and mainstay of the institute.

In 1983, the Institute was recognised as Adarsh Shodh

Sanstha (Ideal Research Institute), by the Government of India. It was also officially affiliated to the University of Madras and the Rashtriya Sanskrit Sansthan, New Delhi, for carrying on postgraduate and post-Siromani research by scholars from India and abroad. Assistance from the Government of India gave a fillip to the activities of the institute. The staff set-up was enlarged and remarkable progress was made under the directorship of Dr. S.S. Janaki. In 1995 the institute opted out of the financial aid of the government. From then on, it has been raising funds to maintain its ever expanding activities and the necessary infrastructural facilities.

The present director is Dr. V. Kameswari. The projects are many and varied. From 1960, there has been a steady inflow of scholars from different parts of the world. They worked under the supervision of Dr. V. Raghavan, till his demise in 1979. Dr. S.S. Janaki continued the good work thereafter. Diverse categories of research — traditional, modern, interdisciplinary, and specially Āgamic studies — started in 1983 and the momentum is on, to this day.

SARASWATI MAHAL LIBRARY

The Thanjavur Maharaja Serfoji's Saraswati Mahal Library is one among the few medieval libraries that exist in the world today. This inexhaustible treasure house of knowledge was built up by the successive kings of the dynasties of Nāyaks and Marāṭhās of Thanjavur. It contains valuable collection of manuscripts, books, maps and paintings on a variety of subjects from cooking recipes to the elephant study. The *Encyclopedia Britannica* describes it as "the most remarkable library in India". The Sanskrit collection, with about 40,000 manuscripts is unique in many aspects. The manuscripts here date back to the sixteenth century CE. The catalogue of palm-leaf manuscripts was first prepared in CE 1801 during the reign of King Serfoji II. As of now, 24,432 books, 8,818 palm-leaf manuscripts and

3,076 paper manuscripts have been catalogued. The scripts used for the Sanskrit texts are — Grantha, Devanāgarī, Nandināgarī and Telugu. A few are in Malayalam, Kannada, Oriya, etc. The 27th volume of the *Sanskrit Catalogue* was published in August 2008. The Department of Culture of the Government of India granted the funds. The project staff of the National Manuscripts Mission put in their hard work, along with the Sanskrit professors of Rajah's College, Tiruvaiyaru. The library directors Smt. S. Rajalakshmi and Dr. A. Veeraraghavan have made a sincere appeal to the public to donate manuscripts that may be with them to the library and earn fame like Raja Serfoji.

Their publications are in Sanskrit and also in Tamizh and Marathi. With modern technology and scholars coming from all over, it serves as a strong base for Sanskrit studies.

ADYAR LIBRARY AND RESEARCH CENTRE

This library was founded in 1886 by the founder-president of the Theosophical Society, Colonel H.S. Olcott. Referred to as the abode of ancient wisdom, it is a non-sectarian centre of research in Eastern civilisation, philosophy and religion. It was founded "for the revival of oriental literature, the rehabilitation of the true paṇḍit in public esteem, the promotion of a higher moral sense and spiritual aspiration among Asiatic youth, and a stronger mutual regard between the learned of the East and the West".

The valued possessions of the library are many — 18,600 manuscripts of palm-leaf and paper, 1,75,000 printed volumes and journals — old and new, from all parts of the world. Books are in Sanskrit and in many languages from the East and the West. Modern technology and friendly facilities are appreciated by scholars coming for research. This great centre of Indological research has established itself as one of the best maintained and service-motivated oriental libraries in India.

It is also known for academic excellence in its scholarly publications.

CONNEMARA PUBLIC LIBRARY

This library came up way back in 1890. It was the biggest in Tamil Nadu, till the new "Anna Centenary Library" came up in Kotturpuram (South Chennai) in the year 2010. As per the agreement with UNESCO, all the UN publications are available here. Also, a copy of all books published in India have to be given here. For Sanskrit researchers in Chennai, if they don't get an old important book in any other library or as a reprint in a book shop, there is a fair chance that they can get it here. They also have books for the youth to prepare for civil services and other exams. It believes that while teaching is time bound, library learning is timeless.

THE SAṀSKṚTA RAṄGA, CHENNAI

This private registered organisation was founded in 1958 by the vibrant scholar Dr. V. Raghavan. It can be said that it is a continuation of the work that had already been going on in Madras in the presentation of Sanskrit plays, by organisations like the Madras Sanskrit Academy and Suguna Vilas Sabha. Besides the ancient plays like *Mālavikāgnimitram*, modern plays authored by V. Raghavan himself, were also staged. More than 50 plays have been presented on the stage, T.V. and the Radio by the Raṅga. It also publishes the journal *Saṁskṛta Raṅga Annual*, with articles on traditional theatre, South-East Asian theatre, and other subjects connected with Sanskrit drama. After the demise of the mentor, Dr. S.S. Janaki took it up and now V. Raghavan's daughter Nandini Ramani is running it successfully. In 1989 the symbolic "Naṭyaśālā" was prepared for the Raṅga, by Sri Goverdhan Panchal of Ahmedabad, at the suggestion Dr. S.S. Janaki. The "Imaginary Theatre" was a modification of Bharata's prescriptions to suit the exigencies of the present-day proscenium theatre.

SANSKRIT ACADEMY, CHENNAI

This academy was inaugurated in 1927 at the Senate Hall of the Madras University by Pandit Madan Mohan Malaviya. The academy's main concern is to bring together all the scholars, paṇḍits and lovers of Sanskrit and to promote and propagate the Sanskrit language and literature among the different strata of people by conducting Pandit Parishad, honouring eminent scholars, etc. But the most remarkable work is the attempt made to retain Sanskrit in schools and colleges by making representations to the government and putting up a strong fight for the same, as recently as in 1989 and 1998. With two of its offshoot organisations blossoming fully (KSRI from 1944 and Saṁskṛta Raṅga from 1958), the academy is concentrating on getting the younger generation to realise the importance of Sanskrit studies. The present secretary of the academy is Prof. K. Srinivasan, Professor and head of the Sanskrit department, RKM Vivekananda College.

QUEEN MARY'S COLLEGE

The college was set up as early as 1914. It is the only government college for women which offers Sanskrit as a major subject. Autonomy was granted to the college in 1987 and then as under the semester system new courses on Āyurveda, epigraphy, etc. were introduced and computer science is in the process of being started. Seminars are regularly conducted as also plays, debates and other extra-curricular activities, etc. The students of the department have presented variety programmes over All India Radio, and have enacted scenes from Sanskrit dramas on the television.

PRESIDENCY COLLEGE

Presidency College too is an autonomous college since 1987. It was the first college in Madras and its Sanskrit department started in 1856. The Honours course came in 1911. This degree was equal to M.A. and covered the same syllabus. The exceptionally intelligent students thus got the M.A. degree in three years and saved a year. This course was discontinued in 1960. Sanskrit as major and at the postgraduate level preserves a high standard of the curriculum which compares favourably with that of any other leading university in our country. Most of its alumni are serving/have served in different colleges and many have won the president's awards and other honours. Also, many of the old students have served and are serving the cause of Sanskrit studies in various educational institutions spread all over India.

The department successfully conducted UGC-sponsored "Spoken Sanskrit Classes" for 12 months with 70 students attending every month. More than 800 students (both Sanskrit and non-Sanskrit) benefited from it. Yearly seminars and special lectures are also arranged. The first lady to take a doctorate in Sanskrit at the University of Madras was one Dr. D.C. Saraswathi. She passed her M.A. examination from this College in 1958. In 1981, the department got recognised by the University of Madras for carrying on research for M.Phil. and Ph.D. degrees, though the latter is still granted by the university only.

RKM VIVEKANANDA COLLEGE

The Ramakrishna Mission Vivekananda College is one of the premier institutions in India. The college was established in 1946 with a view to propagating the ideals of Swami Vivekananda by imparting man-making and character-building education to the youth of India. The dept. of Sanskrit was there from the beginning. This college (autonomous from 2004) offers Sanskrit as a subject at four different levels: (i) Language for B.A., B.Sc., B.Com. students, (ii) B.A. major Sanskrit, (iii) M.A. Sanskrit, (iv) M.Phil. and Ph.D. research degrees.

The department conducted "Spoken Sanskrit Classes" and Workshops on "Communication and Language Skills".

Conferences and seminars are held as also competitions organised for the students in speech, recitation, etc. The present head of Sanskrit department is Prof. K. Srinivasan.

DEPARTMENT OF SANSKRIT, MADRAS UNIVERSITY

The Madras University started in 1857. In 1914, the first batch of students in Sanskrit honours was examined by the university. Prof. S. Kuppuswami Sastri, head of the Sanskrit department at the Presidency College (1914-43), played the most significant role in the history of Sanskrit studies in this university. The university adopted at his instance, many regulations to encourage Siromani students of Sanskrit to gain proficiency in the modern methods of study. The Oriental Learning Course included a study of comparative and historical methods of criticism and comparative philology. Correspondingly, in the modern honours course in Presidency College, representative texts in the eight Śāstras (Mīmāṁsā, Vedānta, Sāṁkhya, Yoga, Nyāya, Vaiśeṣika, Alaṁkāra and Vyākaraṇa) were incorporated with a grounding in Comparative Indo-European philology with special reference to Sanskrit. This was a laudable effort of the Madras University to conserve a language, the learning of which enshrined much of the cultural heritage of the country.

The present head of the department of Sanskrit is Professor Siniruddha Dash. Besides research work, there are seminars, conferences and part-time courses on Yoga, study of Grantha script, etc.

New Catalogus Catalogorum

This is a major project of the university. Between 1891 and 1903, the German orientalist, Theodor Aufrecht published a catalogue of Sanskrit manuscripts. In 1935, it was decided to revise the three volumes of Aufrecht and bring it up to date. Dr. V. Raghavan, as the senior assistant started the work. The first volume of the *New Catalogus Catalogorum* was printed in 1949.

Eighteen volumes have come out since then. The utility of the information available in these volumes is widely accepted.

The departments of philosophy (Vaiṣṇavism and others), music, history and others have inter-disciplinary studies with the help of the Sanskrit department.

RAJAH'S COLLEGE, THIRUVAIYARU, THANJAVUR DISTRICT

A long-standing pioneer institution, it is now affiliated to the Bharatidasan University at Tiruchy. Having courses in both arts and science, it offers B.A., B.Sc. and B.Com. degrees. All infrastructural facilities are available, including hostel, library, computer labs, etc. The teaching faculty of the Sanskrit department have been assisting in the cataloguing work in the Saraswati Mahal Library.

AHOBILA MUTH SANSKRIT VIDYALAYAS,
WEST MAMBALAM, CHENNAI

This organisation is rendering yeoman's service to the cause of Sanskrit studies, by training the students in the Vedas and other Sanskrit texts, even while making them well prepared for further global studies and jobs. This has become possible as, along with the academic and religious studies in Sanskrit, modern subjects are also taught. Major financial assistance is received from Rashtriya Veda Vidya Pratishthan, Ujjain, which is a wing of the HRD Ministry. This helps to provide nearly free education along with boarding and lodging facilities. While awards and huge financial assistance are given for specialisation in the Vedas, some students are also able to go for studying engineering and chartered accountancy. Nearly 760 students from here are studying or working in the US at present.

Sri Ahobila Muth Oriental Higher Secondary School (SAMOHSS) was established in 1952. To date, more than 1000 students have graduated from here. It serves as the feeder institution to the Madhurantakam College, for higher studies in Sanskrit. The Ahobila Matham is said to have been founded in CE 1398 for Sanskrit studies. It has been preserving the Vedic tradition for more than 600 years. There clarion call is — *vidyā vindate amṛtam* and *vedo rakṣati rakṣitaḥ*. They are planning to launch the "Association of Friends and Alumnae of Ahobila Muth School". It is indeed an institution working from the grass roots without discrimination of caste, creed, gender or social standing.

Conclusion

This report, by itself, is only an appendix, that is, *per se*, listing the facilities that exist for Sanskrit studies in Tamil Nadu. The relevance of all this effort lies in the fruitful results that periodically emanate from these infrastructures. So, all we can do is to keep up the momentum and go ahead (*caraiveti, caraiveti* = keep going on).

Annexure I

Research Work Record

(A few drops in the ocean of Sanskrit literature)

At Kuppuswami Sastri Research Institute

From 1983 onwards . . .

SASTRA CUDAMANI (GOVERNMENT OF INDIA) — EQUIVALENT TO D.Litt. OR POST-DOCTORAL RESEARCH

(i) Dr. C. Panduranga Bhatta — Critical Study of Arunagiri's Commentary on Kalidasa's Raghuvamsa.

(ii) Dr. N.S. Satagopan — Critical edition from manuscripts study of the life of Ramanuja Mahadesikan.

(iii) Dr. V.L. Sethuraman — Edition and Study of Dattatreya Campu.

[All three were awarded the degree in February 1990]

VIDYAVARIDHI (EQUIVALENT TO Ph.D.) THROUGH AFFILIATION TO THE RASHTRIYA SANSKRIT SANSTHAN, NEW DELHI

1. Critical Study of Sambu Bhatta's Pūrvamīmāṁsā views.
2. Ayurdayam in Jyotiṣa.
3. Critical Study of *Hāthasaṅketacandrikā* of Sundaradeva.
4. Critical edition and study of manuscripts of Amarananda's *Svātmayogapradīpa.*
5. Critical edition and study of manuscripts of *Vidhibhūṣaṇa* by Venkatanarayana.
6. Critical edition and study of *Tantranītilaharī* of Ramanujadasa from manuscripts.
7. Critical edition and study of *Dārukavanavilāsa* by Ratnaradhya.
8. Critical edition and study — *Alaṁkāraśirobhūṣaṇa.*
9. Critical edition and study of *Dhanyakumāracarita.*
10. *Śrītattvavicāraḥ* in Śrī Vaiṣṇava Sampradāya.
11. Nalladhvari's *Advaita Rasa Mañjarī.*
12. Dr. V. Raghavan's contribution to research in Sanskrit literature.
13. Lasyaṅgas.
14. Bhūta Śūddhi in Śaiva Āgamas.

Ph.D. (AFFILIATED TO UNIVERSITY OF MADRAS)

1. Critical study of *Nyāyavivaraṇa* of Ānandatīrtha.
2. Critical edition and study of *Tattvaguṇadarśa* of Annayarya.
3. *Vyāyoga* — A type of Sanskrit Drama: Theory and practice.
4. *Yoga Yājñavalkya* — A critical study.
5. Saṁnyāsa Dharma — An evaluation.

6. Contribution of Cakra Kavi to Sanskrit literature.
7. *Bījagaṇita* — A critical study.
8. *Vidhitraya Paritrāṇa* — A critical study.
9. *Puruṣa Parikṣā* — A socio-cultural study.
10. Women's rights in Dharmaśāstra.
11. Dream motif in Sanskrit literature.
12. *Amogharāghava Campū* — critical edition.
13. Kṣīraswāmin's commentary on *Amarakośa*.
14. Sthalavṛkṣas and their ecological value.
15. *Nītiprakāśikā* — A critical study.
16. *Bṛhat-Saṁhitā*.
17. *Jīvānandanam* — A critical study.
18. Critical study of *Jīrṇoddhāra Daśaka*.
19. Contribution of Śrīdhara and Śrīpati to Indian mathematics.
20. *Parijātahara Nāṭaka* — A critical study.
21. Critical analysis of *Śiva-Saṁhitā*.
22. Yogic elements in Mahākāvyas.
23. *Viveka Mārtaṇḍa* — A critical study.
24. Musical elements in Sanskrit drama.
25. *Yoga-Sūtras* and Sahajamārga.
26. Contribution of Nalladvarin to Sanskrit literature.
27. *Karmavipāka*.
28. *Ātmajñāna Vivaraṇa* — A critical study.
29. Contribution of Rājacūḍāmaṇi Dīkṣita.
30. *Śataśloki* with commentary — A critical analysis.
31. Socio-cultural study of Kṣemendra's works.
32. *Adbhuta Darpaṇa* — a study.

33. Commentaries of Dakṣiṇāvartanātha.

At Presidency College

1. *Naṭeśavijaya* — A critical study.
2. A therapeutical approach to Kāma-Śāstra.
3. *Saṅgīta Muktāvalī.*
4. *Sudarśana* — A study.
5. *Sundara Rāmāyaṇa* — A study.
6. Śāstras in Kāvyas.
7. Contribution of Y. Mahalinga Sastri to Sanskrit literature.

At the University of Madras — Department of Sanskrit

HERITAGE RESEARCH (DURING 1921–54) Ph.D. or M.Litt.

1. A. Sankaran — Some Aspects of Literary Criticism in Sanskrit or theories of Rasa and Dhvani.
2. T.R. Chintamani — A Short History of Pūrva-Mīmāṁsā Śāstra.
3. V. Raghavan — Bhoja's Śṛṅgāra Prakāśa.
4. P. Subrahmanya Sastri — A Study of the Literary Aspects of the Ṛgveda.
5. H.G. Narahari — Ātman (Soul) in Pre-Upaniṣadic Literature.
6. K. Kunjunni Raja — Contribution of Kerala to Sanskrit Literature.
7. C.R. Swaminathan — A Critical Study and Edition of the Unprinted Cantos of the Jānakīharaṇa of Kumāradāsa.
8. S.S. Janaki — A Critical Study and Edition of the Alaṁkārasarvasva Vimarśinī of Vidyācakravartin.

9. V. Swaminathan — A Critical Study of the Mahābhāṣya-ṭīkā of Bhartṛhari and Edition of the first 3 Āhnikas.

TITLES OF Ph.D. THESIS SUBMITTED

- 1999 — Valliparinaya by Bhāskara Yajvā - A Critical Edition and Study.
- 1999 — Nāmasiddhānta — Doctrine of the Divine Name (Texts, Traditions and Trans-religious Approaches).
- 1999 — Concepts, Contexts and Connotations in the Kṛtis of Śrī Muthusvāmi Dīkṣita.
- 1999 — The Concept of Samanadhikaranya — Its Syntactic and Semantic Aspects.
- 1999 — On Perception.
- 1998 — Advaita and Dvaita.
- 1998 — Aspects of Nyāya-sudhā.
- 1997 — The Nyāyasiddhāñjana of Vedānta Deśika — A Critical Study.
- 1996 — Studies in the *Adhikaraṇasārāvalī* of Śrī Vedānta Deśika.
- 1996 — Pūrva-Mīmāṁsā and Viśiṣṭādvaita — A Comprehensive Study of the Mīmāṁsāpādukā of Śrī Vedānta Deśika.
- 1995 — Vedānta Cūḍāmaṇi (Text with an Introduction, English Translation and Notes).
- 1995 — Word Formation in Sanskrit (with Special Reference to Taddhita-Formation).
- 1995 — Nītimālā — A Critical Study.
- 1995 — Alaṁkāraratnākara of Sobhākaramitra — A Critical Approach.

- 1994 — Henry David Thoreau in the Light of Sanātana Dharma.
- 1993 — Nominal Compositions in Sanskrit and Tamil — A Comparative Study.
- 1993 — Vasumanala Nāṭaka of Perusuri — A Critical Edition and Study.
- 1993 — Prolegomena to Advaita Vedānta.
- 1993 — Gleanings from the Śrībhāṣya.
- 1991 — The Tattvānusandhāna of Śrī Mahādevānanda Saraswati — A Critical Edition and Study.
- 1988 — A Critical Edition and Study of the Vedāntaratnakośa of Nṛsiṁhāśrama.
- 1987 — The Concept of Praṇava – Its Meaning and Significance in Hindu Religion.
- 1987 — The Siddhāntatattva of Anantadeva — With the Auto- commentary the Sampradāyanirupaṇa — A Critical Edition and Study.
- 1987 — Subhadrāpariṇaya of Nalla Dīkṣita.
- 1987 — The Jijñāsādhikaraṇa of the Śrībhāṣya — A Study.
- 1986 — Three Little-known Advaitins.
- 1986 — The Advaitamoda — A Study.
- 1985 — A Critical Edition of the Anubhūtiprakāśa of Vidyāraṇya (With An Introduction and Appendices).
- 1985 — The Bhāgavata Campū of Cidambara Kavi.
- 1984 — Yādavābhyudaya — A Study.
- 1984 — Parāśarabhaṭṭa's Contribution to Viśiṣṭādvaita.
- 1984 — The Pratyaktattvacintāmaṇi of Sadānanda — A Study.
- 1983 — Some Aspects of the Philosophy of Bhartṛhari.

- 1983 — The Pādukāsahasra of Śrī Vedānta Deśika — A Study.
- 1983 — Contribution of Atiratra Yajvan to Sanskrit Literature.
- 1982 — A Study of the Īṣṭasiddhi of Vimukti in the Light of the Īṣṭasiddhi-vivaraṇa by Anubhūti-svarūpācārya.
- 1982 — Yatraprabandha of Samarapungava Dīkṣita — A Critical Edition and Study.
- 1982 — A Critical Edition of the Yogamaṇiprabhā of Ramananda Sarasvati with the Gloss Svasanketa.
- 1981 — Saundaryalaharī — A Study.
- 1981 — Dice Play in Sanskrit Literature — A Study.
- 1981 — Vedānta and Yeats.
- 1981 — Saṭhavairivaibhavaprabandha — A Critical Edition and Study.
- 1980 — Ramabhadra Dīkṣita and His Works — A Study.

At RKM Vivekananda College

- 2011 — Vaiṣṇava Āgamas and Viṣṇu Images in the Government Museum.
- 2011 — Ethical Values in Upaniṣads Pertaining to Education.
- 2010 — Vidagdhabodha of Śrī Mishrabhupati — A Study (in Sanskrit).
- 2010 — The Rama stories of Thai Ramakien — A Comparative Study with the Rāmāyaṇa of Vālmīki and Kamban [Research Scholar — Waradat from Thailand].
- 2009 — Śrī Vadulaveeraraghavasuri's Sanskrit Works — A Study (in Tamil).

- 2009 — Buddhist Epistemological Critique by Jayanta Bhaṭṭa in Nyāyamañjarī.
- 2009 — Jyotiṣaśāstre Vāstuvicāraḥ (in Sanskrit).
- 2008 — An Aesthetic Enjoyment of Kālidāsa's Works.
- 2008 — Musical Instruments in Sanskrit Literature.
- 2007 — Nyāsavidyā Pariṣkṛti of Vādhula Varadadāsa — A Critical Edition and Study.
- 2006 — Elements of Dharmaśāstra in Mallinātha's Commentaries on Kālidāsa's Works.
- 2005 — Aghoraśivācārya Paddhati — An Edition and Study.
- 2004 — Sūryaśataka — A Critical Edition.
- 2003 — The Principles of Management Found in Sanskrit Literature.
- 2002 — Vivekavijayam — A Critical Edition and Study.
- 2001 — Tatakaparinaya Campu of Gaṇapati Śāstrī — A Critical Study.
- 2000 — Śabdavyāpāraḥ — A Study on Sound and Sense — An Indian Approach.
- 1997 — The Place of Arthāntaranyāsa in Sanskrit Literature.
- 1996 — Concept of Nāṭyābhinaya in Sanskrit Literature.
- 1996 — Vaikhānasa Gṛhyasūtra Bhāṣya — Critical Edition and Study.
- 1996 — Gaṅgāvataraṇa — A Study.
- 1995 — Rukmiṇīpariṇaya — Critical Edition and Study.
- 1993 — Alaṁkāramuktāvalī — Critical Edition and Study.

- 1989 — Alaṁkārarāghava of Yajñeśvaradīkṣita (Alaṁkāraprakaraṇa) — Critical Edition and Study.
- 1988 — The Concept of Conceit as a Poetic Device.
- 1987 — Rahasya-traya-sarartha-saṁgraha of Kumāravaradācārya — A Study.
- 1980 — Śivalīlārṇava — A Cultural Study.
- 1979 — Prahasana in Sanskrit Literature — A Study.

Annexure II

Foreign Scholars

Scholars from Abroad

At the Sanskrit Department of Madras University:

1955 — Prof. Norman Brown — Saundaryalaharī

1955 — Klaus Comman — Sāṁkhya

1956 — Heinz Titelbach — Sanskrit literature, grammar, drama

1957 — Artola — Rājanīti in Mahābhārata

1957 — M. Biardeau — Vākyapadīya and Brahmasiddhi

At the Kuppuswami Sastri Research Institute

From 1960, there has been a regular inflow of scholars from different parts of the world. This includes Fellows from the American Institute of Indian Studies, Indo-Canadian Institute, Fulbright and Smithsonian Fellows, etc. The institute provides facilities for them to meet other experts in the field and hold discussions with them, and also to learn Sanskrit and study specific texts. Names of a few such scholars are: Dr. Robert Lister, Daniel Smith, Nariko Mayeda, J. Ensink, Patricia Butterfield, F. Wilson, James Bruce Long, George Hart, Walter Neeval Jr., K. Kamimura, M. Watase, Peter Khoroche, David

Nelson, Michael Font, Melodie Doherty, David Iglehart, Nadine Verardi, Wayne Surdam, V.K. Chari, Keith Jefferds, Robert Gottlieb, Fabrizia Baldissera, Tessa Wilcox, Francis Clooney, Any-Claude Medioni, Armelle Choquard, Julie Hiebert, Michael Nixon, Mecille Josephine, Geenens Phillppe, Richard Karin, Leon Hannotte, John Taber, Alyette Degraces, Robert Brown, Nienke Kruger, Indira Peterson, Bruce Perry, Martha Ann Selby, Ginnette Ishimatsu, Annie Christine Couturier, Steven Hopkins, Denise Hanusek, Karen Pechilis, Stephen Jenkins, Lawrence McCrea, Janet Shea, Tara Michael, Yigal Nronner, Katherine Zubko, Ute Husken, Rupa Roberts, Daud R. Ali, Ajay K.Rao, Richard Davis, Vena Ramphal, Whitney Cox, Devan Patel, Sucharita Adluri, Blake Wentworth, Ronit Ricci, Timothy Lubin, Swamini Hamsananda.

Other Facilities Include Classes For

- Basic Tamizh/Conversational Tamizh.
- Basic and Conversational Sanskrit.
- Specific texts for graduate/postgraduate students.
- Research methodology for Ph.D. scholars.

And

- Affiliation as long-time/short-time scholars with fees and recommendation from their house universities.
- Student visa, academic assistance, library, translation facility.
- Opportunity to attend lectures and seminars in the Institute.
- Traditional and modern type of teaching.
- Vedic chanting.

18

Sanskrit Studies in Uttar Pradesh

Hari Dutt Sharma

UTTAR Pradesh is the biggest state of India. Its area and population were bigger, before it was divided and a separate state named Uttarakhand was established in 2000. If we observe thoroughly, we find that Sanskrit studies have flourished in this state in the post-Independence period. The state situated along the catchment area of two mighty and pious rivers the Gaṅgā and the Yamunā that flow incessantly, in the same way Sanskrit education in Uttar Pradesh is flourishing in two streams, the traditional as well as the modern.

Traditional Sanskrit Education

In Uttar Pradesh Varanasi is an important seat of traditional Sanskrit learning, with its famous Sampurnanand Sanskrit Vishvavidyalaya, that was established earlier as Banaras Sanskrit College and recognised as university in 1956. It is the oldest seat of learning traditional Sanskrit Śāstras. It possesses an ancient library known as Saraswati Bhawan Library, which is a treasure house of ancient manuscripts, more than 1 lakh in number. Subject-wise catalogue of these manuscripts has been published. Microfilming of manuscripts has also been completed. There is a research institute named Anusandhana-Sansthanam, which is involved in huge work of research and publication of traditional Śāstras. It also publishes the literary magazine Śodha Patrikā *Sārasvatī Suṣamā* regularly. More than 1,000 Sanskrit *pāṭhaśālā*s are affiliated to this university. Some of these are as old as 200 years and have been celebrated their second centenary. It is a fact that this *paṭhaśālā* based traditional Sanskrit education is diminishing day by day.

Uttar Pradesh is the only province, privileged to have two campuses of the Rashtriya Sanskrit Sansthan, one at Allahabad and at the other one at Lucknow. Earlier known as Ganganath Jha Anusandhan Sansthan and Ganganath Jha Kendriya Sanskrit Vidyapeetha, these institutes have been doing tremendous work on Sanskrit research. This research institute was inaugurated on 17 November 1943 by the late Pandit Madan Mohan Malviya. Great scholars like Aryendra Sharma, Pandit Mandan Mishra and Gaya Charan Tripathi have been principals of this institute. Vidyapeetha has a big library containing a huge collection of the books authored by Pandit Ganganath Jha and several other famous scholars. It has a huge collection of Sanskrit manuscripts, a number of which have been published now. A descriptive catalogue of Sanskrit manuscripts has also been published. Besides publication of hundreds of books this campus has been publishing a research journal of international repute, namely *Journal of the Ganganath Jha Kendriya Sanskrit Vidyapeetha*. A magazine named *Uṣatī* is also being published from the premises of this *parisara*. Teachers of this campus have launched a new *patrikā* named *Dr̥k*, which is a critical journal on the modern Sanskrit literature. Twenty-two volumes of this journal have been released till now. It has proved to be a strong platform for criticism on contemporary Sanskrit literature. Lucknow campus of Rashtriya Sanskrit Sansthan is also imparting traditional Sanskrit education from Prak-Shastri to Acharya level and conducts research on various branches of Sanskrit learning. It also organises M.M. Gopinath Kaviraj memorial lectures every year. Besides Adarsh Sanskrit *vidyālaya*s run by Rashtriya Sanskrit Sansthan, in Uttar Pradesh, there are several *veda pāṭhaśālās* run by Maharshi Sandipani Rashtriya Veda Vidya Pratishthan.

The faculty of Sanskrit learning and theology, Banaras Hindu University, Varanasi, is a great centre of traditional Sanskrit learning. It has eight departments with large number of specialisations in Veda, Vedic Darśana, Vyākaraṇa, Bauddha and Jain Darśanas, Dharmaśāstra, Mīmāṁsā, Dharma-Āgama, Jyotiṣa and Sāhitya. A galaxy of renowned Sanskrit scholars have been professors in this faculty. To name a few, Rewa Prasad Dwivedi has edited and published complete works of Kālidāsa by the name *Kālidāsa-Granthāvalī*. He has recently published a monumental work *Bhoja's Śṛṅgāraprakaśa* in two volumes. Kamalesh Datta Tripathi, who has done work on *Vākyapadīya, Rasagaṅgādhara* and *Nāṭyaśāstra,* is still with the faculty as emeritus professor. The faculty publishes a research journal also. Some other institutions like Gurukul Kangri Vishvavidyalaya, Hardwar (before bifurcation), Central Institute of Higher Tibetan Studies, Sarnath, etc. are rendering good services for the cause of Sanskrit learning. Saral Sanskrit-speaking courses run widely by Rashtriya Sanskrit Sansthan have done good work among new learners of Sanskrit.

Sanskrit at Primary/Secondary Level

Sanskrit is being taught at the primary stage from class 3 and somewhere from class 6 onwards as a compulsory subject in the government and private schools. Sanskrit is an optional subject at high school and intermediate levels in the colleges under the Uttar Pradesh Board of Secondary Education and the CBSE. But it is not a good sign. Actually Sanskrit should have been taught compulsorily at least up to 10th class in higher secondary education.

Sanskrit in Higher Education

In Uttar Pradesh Sanskrit studies are flourishing in a better way at the higher education level. There are departments of Sanskrit in the universities and the post-graduate/degree colleges. Among the central universities the department of Sanskrit at the University of Allahabad is the oldest such department in U.P. It has nourished great scholars and academicians like Pandit Ganganath Jha, P.K. Acharya, Baburam Saxena, Kshetresh Chandra Chattopadhyaya, M.M. Umesh Mishra, Saraswati Prasad Chaturvedi, Adya Prasad Mishra, all stalwarts in their respective fields. Adya Prasad Mishra, who was head of the department for a longer time, has contributed a lot in the field of Indian philosophy, specially Sāṁkhya philosophy. He has produced a monumental work on *Viṣṇusahasranāma*. Chandika Prasad Shukla of this department achieved fame in the field of poetics by writing Sanskrit commentary *Dīpaśikhā* on *Dhvanyāloka*. Pandit Lakshmi Kant Dikshit, Suresh Chandra Pandey and Suresh Chandra Shrivastava also contributed to the effort for upgradation of Sanskrit teaching in the department. The department has earned good reputation due to tremendous writings of Prof. Rajendra Mishra, who had served the department for more than two decades. The department got wider international recognition and acclaim through frequent foreign visits of Hari Dutt Sharma, present head of the department and for organising of three National seminars and one International seminar in the recent past on "Sanskrit in the Context of Western Criticism".

The department of Sanskrit at Banaras Hindu University, Varanasi was founded along with the foundation of the university itself. A number of scholars like Siddheshwar Bhattacharya, Bishwanath Bhattacharya, Shri Narayana Mishra, etc. have been the leading figures of this department. Aligarh Muslim University also had a department of Sanskrit for a long time, in which stalwarts like Ram Suresh Tripathi, Parmanand Shastri, C.T. Kenghe worked for decades. Lucknow

University possessed a high profile department of Sanskrit, where K.A.S. Iyer, Kanti Chandra Pandey, Satyavrat Singh, etc. were quite popular for their works and teaching. The Gorakhpur University had a Sanskrit department having deep attachment with great names such as Pandit Vidya Niwas Mishra its founder and Atul Chandra Benarji its nourisher. Mahatma Gandhi Kashi Vidyapeetha was also a fine seat of Sanskrit learning, where Pandit Vayu Nandan Pandey and Amar Nath Pandey were in the forefront of Sanskrit teaching and tradition.

A great number of postgraduate and degree colleges are running all over Uttar Pradesh, which are affiliated to different state universities like those at Agra, Gorakhpur, Kanpur, Meerut, Ruhelkhand, Bundelkhand, Awadh, Purvanchal, etc. postgraduate and undergraduate level teaching is going on there in the departments of Sanskrit. Researches are also being conducted mainly for Ph.D. degrees, by the young scholars but the standards of research have come down too much and control on sub-standard research is the need of the hour. Only few researchers are exploring the scientific subjects and bringing out scientific elements hidden in the ancient Sanskrit texts.

Creative Sanskrit Literature

Sanskrit language in the modern age is passing through a phase of its vast production of creative writing. As in the old times and pre-Independence days, in this post-Independence age also Sanskrit writing has flourished a lot. We can see the incessant flow of *mahākāvya*-writings flooding the treasure trove of Sanskrit literature, such as *Rukmiṇīharaṇam* by Kashinath Dwivedi, *Pārijātaharaṇam* by Umapati Sharma Dwivedi, *Śrī-Nehru-Caritam* by Brahmanand Shukla, *Janavijayam'* and *Cīraharaṇam* by Paramanand Shastri, *Āryodayam* by Ganga Prasad Upadhyaya, *Jānakī-Caritāmṛtam* by Ram Sanehi Das, *Saulocanīyam* by Vishnudatta Shukla, *Jayadeva-Kīrtilatā-*

Mahākāvyam by Ram Balak Shukla, *Mālavīya-caritam'* by Ram Kuber Malaviya, *Karṇārjunīyam* and *Maharṣi-Jñānānanda-Caritam* by Vindhyeshwari Prasad Shastri, *Bhūbhāminī-Vibhramam* by Ram Sewak Malaviya, *Svarājya-vijayam* by Dwijendranath Shastri, *Urmilīyam* by Narayana Shukla, *Nehru-yaśaḥsaurabham* by Balabhadra Prasad Shastri, *Jawāhara-Jyotir-Mahākāvyam* by Raghunath Prasad Chaturvedi, *Neharūdayam* by Ayodhya Prasad Shastri, *Haripreṣṭha-Mahākāvyam* by Vanmalidas Shastri, *Jhāṁsīśvarī-caritam* by Subodh Chandra Pant, *Guru-Nānakadeva-caritam* by Vishnudatta Sharma, *Dvārikādhīśa-Mahākāvyam* by Vasudevakrishna Chaturvedi, *Śumbhavadhm Vindhyavāsinī-caritam* by Vasant Tryambak Shewde, *Vidyottamā-Kālidāsīyam* by Ram Kishor Mishra, *Hariṣcandra-Mahākāvyam* by Balvir Datta Shastri, *Lauhapuruṣāvadānam* by Shiv Prasad Bhardwaj, *Tulasī-Mahākāvyam* and *Pārvatī-Pariṇayam* by Raghunanadan Sharma, *Mahāvīrābhyudaya-Kāvya* by Ratinath Jha, *Digdeśa-Varṇanam* and *Rāmāmara-Caritāmṛtam* by Tripurari Sharan Pandey, *Sītā-Caritam* and *Svātantrya-Sambhavam* by Rewa Prasad Dwivedi, *Jānakī-Jīvanam* and *Vāmanāvataraṇam* by Abhiraja Rajendra Mishra, *Bhīṣma-Caritam* by Hari Narayana Dikshit, *Śivavīra-Caritam* and *Bhagavān Paraśurāmaḥ* by Krishna Datta Sharma, *Sudāma-Carita* by Indradev Dwivedi, *Ātmavijñāna* by Kapildev Dwivedi, *Rādhā-Caritam* by Kalika Prasad Shukla, *Hari-Caritāmṛtam* by Hari Padmanath Shastri, *Vāmana-Caritaṁ* by Kapildev Dwivedi, *Bhārgava-Rāghavīyam* by Swami Rambhadracharya, and *Gosvāmi-Tulasīdāsa-Caritam* by Hari Prasad Dwivedi, *Rakṣata Gaṅgām* by Kamala Pandey etc.

We can observe here that vision and imagination of the contempory poet has undergone a sea change in the modern age. Poets have written *mahākāvya*s on the Purāṇic episodes, but the old concept of theme and characters has changed, as we see the new ideas in *Sītā-Caritam* and *Jānakī-Jīvanam* about the banishment of Sītā. Starting from the later half of the twentieth century, we find that Sanskrit poems were mostly written on themes like patriotism, freedom heroes, social problems, and Purāṇic characters, etc. Composition of *carita kāvyas* became prevalent. Actually post-Independence period is the golden age of the language, as creative Sanskrit writing has gained the real momentum. In Uttar Pradesh also Sanskrit literature was produced in various forms of poetry, such as, *mahākāvya, laghukāvya, gītikāvya, upanyāsa, kathā sāhitya*, drama, one-act plays, reports, essays, etc. On one side Pandit Batuknath Shastri Khiste came with the *Kāvya-kallolinī*, full of alliterations and difficult words, on the other side Bachchulal Awasthi came up with his *Pratāninī*, containing fresh wine of *ghaẓal*s and lyrics in the old pot of Sanskrit language. While Jagannath Pathak introduced a new type of lyrics having the taste of Urdu/Aṛabic poetry in his lyrics — *Kāpiśāyanī, Mṛdvīkā, Pipāsā, Vicchittivātāyanī*, etc. He has absorbed the essence of the poetry of Umar Khayyam in his poetry. Pathak was awarded the Sahitya Akademi and Birla Foundation awards. Bhaskaracharya Tripathi wrote a collection of lyrics *Nirjhariṇī* and a *khaṇḍakāvya* named *Mṛtkūṭam*. He also received the Sahitya Akademi award. Abhiraja Rajendra Mishra is really a great hero in the field of lyrical poetry. He has composed a great variety of Sanskrit *kāvya*s, out of which eight may be called as purely *gītikāvyas*, e.g. *Vāgvadhūtī, Mṛdvīkā, Śrutimbharā, Madhuparṇī, Kaumāram, Mattavāraṇī, Araṇyānī, Śālabhañjikā, Havirdhānī*. Mishra has given the Sanskrit *gīti-gaẓal* a new name *galajjalikā*. Later two *kāvya*s are declared as Sanskrit-*ghaẓal kāvya*s' by his pen, as he writes on the main front of *Śālabhañjikā* — 'An anthology of *galajjalikā*s bearing fresh social emotions'. A separate collection *Kanīnikā* has been declared as 'An Anthology of *ghaẓal*s'. All the lyrics of the poet Abhiraja are sweet, melodious, having variety of rhythms and as a spontaneous overflow of imagination and feelings. He has written a number of *laghukāvya*s, *śatakakāvya*s and many other varieties of poetry. He has been honoured with the

Sahitya Akademi award, Birla Foundation award and many other awards. All his compositions are published from Allahabad, as he calls himself a *Triveṇīkavi*. Ichchharam Dwivedi Praṇava, resident of Mainpuri in Uttar Pradesh, is a great poet of sweet songs. His collection of songs is *gīta-mandākinī*. *Mitradūtam* and *Dūtaprativacanam* are two of his messenger poems, which have dealt with social problems and some natural phenomena. Nalini Shukla of Kanpur is a composer of lyrical poems. Her *Nirjhariṇī* is a *gītikāvya* and *Bhāvāñjaliḥ* a *muktaka kāvya*. Hari Dutt Sharma is also a celebrated Sanskrit lyrist, who has been given the surname *Kavipuṁskokilā* for the emotional melody seen in his songs. His lyrical poems are, *Gītakaṇḍalikā*, *Utkalikā*, *Bālagītālī* and *Lasallatikā*. He won the Sahitya Akademi award for his *Lasallatikā*. He also represents the modern Sanskrit poetry or *navagītavidhā*. Janardan Prasad Pandey Mani, a promising young poet and recipient of "Bādarāyaṇa Vyās Sammān" is reputed for composing sweet lyrics on human emotions. His *kāvya*s include *Rāgiṇī*, *Niḥsyandinī* and *Nīrājanā*. Acharya Baburam Awasthi, resident of Lakhimpur Khiri, is also a known name among the writers of Sanskrit folk songs sung on different social or family occasions like birth, marriage, etc. and known as *bhaktigīta*, *prabhātagīta*, *holīgīta*, *vasantagīta*, etc. All such songs can be presented in the rhythm of local folk songs. His compositions are *Lokagītāñjaliḥ* and *Gītagaṅgā*. Maharajdin Pandey, resident of district Gonda, has developed a new style of songs in Sanskrit poetry, i.e. Sanskrit songs based purely on Urdu *ghazal* in style and metre. His collections are *Maunavedhaḥ* and *Kākṣeṇa Vīkṣitaṁ*.

Uttar Pradesh has seen composition of Sanskrit *kāvya* on large scale, which may not come under the sphere of lyrical poetry, but it is no doubt, high level poetry mostly in traditional metres. Most of them are *muktaka kāvya*s, composed on one theme or a variety of themes on different aspects of life, society and the world. In this particular category we may recognise the poetry of Govind Chandra Pandey, whose collection *Bhāgīrathī* was felicitated with the Sarasvatī Sammān of K.K. Birla Foundation. *Bhāgīrathī* is a collection of poet's experiences of different aspects life and society. Pandey translated a number of English poems in Sanskrit, which were published in one single collection named *Astācalīyam*. Banmali Biswal, the editor of the famous journal *Dṛk*, is also a prolific writer of modern Sanskrit poetry. His *kāvya Saṅgamenābhirāmā* is in the traditional way. He is one of the exponents of free metre style. His collections *Vyathā, Ṛtuparṇā, Priyatamā, Yātrā* are composed in *muktachanda* style, adopted by some poets in Sanskrit. *Valentine Day Sandeśaḥ* and *Dārubrahma* are lyrical forms of poetry. Om Prakash Pandey of Lucknow has also contributed to the Sanskrit writing. He received the Sahitya Akademi Award for his poem *Rasapriyā Perisa Rājadhānī*, a description of Paris, the capital of France. Prashasya Mitra Shastri, popular poet of humour and satire has written several poems in this style and received huge applause from the audiences at Sanskrit *kavi-sammelanas*. His *kāvyas* specifically are *Hāsyavilāsaḥ, Vyaṅgyavilāsaḥ, Komala-Kaṇṭhakāvaliḥ, Vyaṅgyārtha-kaumudī*, etc. In the field of *hāsya-vyaṅgya Tīrthayātrā-Prahasanaṁ* by Ram Kuber Malviya, *Navoḍhā Vadhūrvaraśca* by Pattabhiram Shastri and *Narmasaptaśatī* by Vagish Shastri are also some notable compositions.

There has been a trend of writing poems on contemporary and international topics and also on foreign visits in this period. While Shivadatta Sharma Chaturvedi wrote *Kārl Mārx-śatakam* and *Sphūrtisaptaśatī*, Raghunath Prasad Chaturvedi composed *Marxim-Gorkī-Pañcaśatī*. Abhiraja Rajendra Mishra wrote *Vimānayātrā-Śatakam'* and *Bālī-pratyabhijñāna-śatakam*. Rewa Prasad Dwivedi wrote description of America in his *kāvya Amerikā*. Many poets in Sanskrit wrote a series of poems on terrorism, when it spread awfully all over the world, e.g.

Ātaṅkavādaśatakam by Vagish Shastri. Some more worth noticing and valuable *kāvyas* of this period are: *Rāṣṭraratnaṁ* by Yagyeshwar Shastri, *Gāndhigauravam* and *Baṅgaladeśaḥ* by Ramesh Chandra Shukla, *Subhāṣa-Candrodayaḥ* by Raj Narayana Prasad Mishra, *Subhāṣacaritam* by Dharmavir Kumar Shastri, *Bharatasiṁhacaritāmr̥tam* by Chunnilal Sudan, *Jawāharacaritam* by Mijazilal Sharma, *Ahaṁ Rāṣṭrī* by Uma Shankar Sharma and Vyomshekhar, *Kavitā* and *Saundaryavallī* by Amarnath Pandey, *Ādyācatuḥśatī* by Adya Prasad Mishra, *Gītālī* by Chandrabhanu Tripathi, *Kāvyakiraṇāvaliḥ* and *Vasantatilakam* by Ram Kishor Mishra, *Saṁskr̥ta-Varṣābhiyānam* by Ram Narayana Mishra, *Kūhā* by Uma Kant Shukla, *Taraṅgadūtam* by Kriparam Tripathi, and *Tīrthabhāratam* by Rahas Bihari Dwivedi, *Dharā Kampate* by Kamala Pandey etc.

Uttar Pradesh can be proud of having generated a profound stockpile of creative writing on Sanskrit dramas, fiction, *laghukāvyas*, one-act plays, etc. The significant achievements in prose-writing during the last 60 years can be presented in the following way: *Tripuradāhakathā* by Ram Swarup Shastri, *Sauprabham* and *Kaumāram* by Vedavyas Shukla, *Dvāsuparṇā* and *Satya-Hariṣcandrodayaḥ* by Ramji Upadhyaya, *Daridrāṇāṁ hr̥dayam* by Narayana Shastri Khiste, *Cakravat Parivartante* by Vidyadhar Dwivedi, *Aravinda-Darśanam* and *Guhāvāsī* by Satya Prakash Singh, *Udayana-Caritam* and *Tapovanavāsinī* by Krishna Kumar, *Gopālabandhuḥ* by Hari Narayana Dikshit, *Kaumudīkathā-Kallolinī* and *Vyākr̥ti-Vatsarājam* by Ram Sharan Tripathi, *Antardāhaḥ* by Ram Kishor Mishra, etc. As far as story-writing is concerned, we see that trend of writing short stories is prevalent these days. Some collections may be mentioned here, e.g. *Kathāsaptakam* by Nalini Shukla, *Kathāsaṁvārtikā* by Bhagirathi Prasad Tripathi, *Kathākaumudī*, *Śvetadūrvā*, and *Antardhvaniḥ* by Prabhunath Dwivedi, *Ikṣugandhā* and *Rāṅgaḍā* by Rajendra Mishra, *Nīravasvanaḥ*, *Bubhukṣā* and *Jijīviṣā* by Banmali Biswal, *Āṣāḍhasya prathamadivase* and *Anabhīpsitaṁ* by Prashasya Mitra Shastri. He has received the Sahitya Akademi Award for *Anabhīpsitam*, a selection of modern Sanskrit stories. Like other parts of India, Uttar Pradesh also has produced dramatic literature in Sanskrit. Several dramatic rules have withered away over time. Short plays, one-act plays and radio plays have replaced the bigger plays. Collections of plays have also been published from time to time such as *Nāṭyapañcagavyam*, *Nāṭyapañcāmṛtam*, *Catuṣpathīyam*, *Rūparudrīyam*, *Nāṭyanavaratnam*, etc. by Rajendra Mishra, *Ekāṅkāvaliḥ* and *Ekāṅkamālā Dhruvam* by Ram Kishor Mishra, *Laghunāṭikāvaliḥ* by Krishnadatta Sharma, *Tripathagā* and *Ākrandanam* by Hari Dutt Sharma.

Critical Sanskrit Literature

Like creative literature, critical literature in Sanskrit has been written in abundance by scholars of different Śāstras in Uttar Pradesh. Gaya Charan Tripathi, Maan Singh, Satya Prakash Singh, etc. have done a great work on the Vedic literature. Work of G.C. Tripathi *Vedic Devatā: Udbhava evaṁ Vikāsa* got much recognition. *Bhaktirasārṇavaḥ* by Swami Hariharanand Saraswati 'Karapatrī' is a valuable philosophical work on *bhakti*. Govind Chandra Pandey has also produced a great work *Bhaktidarśana-Vimarśaḥ* on *bhakti*. He has contributed a book *Saundaryadarśana-Vimarśaḥ* on aesthetics and *"ekaṁ sad viprā bahudhā vadanti"* on philosophy. A great scholar, Kanti Chandra Pandey wrote an authentic book *Comparative Aesthetics* in two volumes. While Pandit Ramagya Pandey and Pandit Ram Prasad Tripathi of Varanasi have done valuable work on Sanskrit grammar, Rajaram Shukla has been handling a great project on Navya-Nyāya philosophy in terms of science and technology. While Priyavrat Sharma has done much work on Āyurveda, Girija Shankar Shastri has contributed a lot in the field of Jyotiṣa. Shivji Upadhyaya worked on Sanskrit poetics and wrote a book *Sāhitya-Sandarbhahm* whereas Acharya Rewa Prasad Dwivedi wrote the original works *Kāvyālaṅkārakārikā* and *Alaṁ Brahma* to his credit. Other important works on Sanskrit poetics are *Abhirāja-yaśobhūṣaṇam* and *Śāstrālocanam* by Rajendra Mishra. The work on dramaturgy *Nāṭyśāstrīyānu-Sandhāna* is a remarkable achievement of by Ramji Upadhyaya. The celebrated writer, Pandit Baladev Upadhyaya has contributed a series of books on the History of Sanskrit literature. The finest of them are *Purāṇa-Vimarśa, Bhāratīya Vāṅmaya meṅ Śrīrādhā, Saṁskṛta-śāstroṁ kā Itihāsa*, etc. Sudyumna Acharya, whose workplace has been Balia in Uttar Pradesh, has done valuable work of interpreting Indian philosophy in terms of modern science. He has produced the books *Adhivijñānaṁ Darśanaśāstram* and *Rājantāṁ Darśanāṁśavaḥ*. *Manovijñāna-Mīmāṁsā* by Vishweshwar Siddhant Shiromani is a great work on psychology. *Vāstuśāstram* by Dwijendranath Shukla is a good work on architecture. *Saṁskṛta-Vāṅmaya-Manthanam* by Vagish Shastri is a collection of highly-rated essays. *Vyākaraṇatantra kā Kāvyaśāstra par Prabhāva* by Hari Ram Mishra, *Later Sanskrit Rhetoricians* by Anand Kumar Shrivastava and *Glimpses of Sanskrit Poetics and Poetry* by Hari Dutt Sharma are some notable books on poetic criticism.

Uttar Pradesh Sanskrit Sansthan

Uttar Pradesh Sanskrit Sansthan, earlier known as the Sanskrit Akademi, a recognised body of the Uttar Pradesh government, is also rendering its great services for promotion of Sanskrit. Its big annual functions are "Vālmīki Samāroha", "Vyāsa Samāroha", "Sanskrit-Divas Samāroha", "Puraskāra Samāroha", etc. Every year Sanskrit Sansthan distributes several glorious awards to deserving authors, poets, Veda *paṇḍit*s and scholars. Among the awards important ones are "Viśvabhāratī Puraskāra", "Maharṣi Vālmīki Puraskāra", "Maharṣi Vyāsa Puraskāra", "Veda Paṇḍita Puraskāra", etc. This Sansthan has already released several standard publications. The greatest monumental work of the Sansthan is *Saṁskṛta-Vāṅmaya kā Bṛhat Itihāsa*, with Pandit Baladev

Upadhyaya as its chief editor. Its 17 volumes have come out so far. The Sansthan also publishes a half-yearly magazine titled *Pariśīlanam.*

Sanskrit Organisations

Some voluntary Sanskrit organisations are also rendering good services for the propagation of Sanskrit. Among them Akhil Bharatiya Sanskrit Parishad, Lucknow, an autonomous body having a rich library, is rendering good services in the field. It has been publishing Sanskrit journals named *R̥taṁ* and *Ajasrā* for a long time. It has also come out with special volumes of *R̥tam* such as *Prof. K.A.S. Iyer Felicitation Volume* and *Prof. Ludwik Sternbach Felicitation Volume,* etc. Some voluntary organisations like "Puran Shodh Sansthan" at Ram Nagar Fort, Varanasi, "Puran Shodh Sansthan" at Naimisharanya, Bhagavata Prachar Samiti, Mathura, Sarvabhauma "Sanskrit Prachar Karyalaya", Varanasi, "Sanskrit Bharati", etc. are active in popularising and preserving old traditions of Sanskrit. Sudhakaracharya Tripathi has been organising annual "Vyāsa Samaroha" function in Meerut for several years. Abhinay Bharati, Varanasi; Kalidasa Akademi, Allahabad; Sanskrit Department, University of Allahabad; Ganganath Jha Kendriya Sanskrit Vidyapeetha, Allahabad; Prachya Vidya Sansthan, University of Lucknow, etc. are some venues, where Sanskrit plays have been produced regularly for several years with a missionary zeal.

Sanskrit Journals/Magazines

Some Sanskrit journals and magazines have contributed a lot to the cause of Sanskrit in Uttar Pradesh. These are 'Saṅgamanī', Allahabad, edited by Pandit Prabhat Shastri, *Viśvabhāṣā,* Varanasi, edited by Kashiraj Trust; *Sarvagandhā,* Lucknow, edited by Virabhadra Mishra; *Vrajagandhā,* Mathura edited by Vasudevakrishna Chaturvedi; *Pārijātam,* Kanpur, edited by Prakashmitra Shastri; *Gāṇḍīvam* and *Sūryodayaḥ* from

Varanasi; *Anusandhāna*, Meerut, edited by Durga Prasad Mishra; *Prācyavidyānusandhānam*, Baraut, edited by Vedapal, *Surabhāratī*, Mainpuri edited by Ichchharam Dwivedi *Vākovākyam*, Varanasi, edited by Vivek Pandey, etc.

Sanskrit Publishers

It is highly remarkable that the state of Uttar Pradesh is home to big publishing houses, which is a positive factor for propagating Sanskrit studies. Motilal Banarsidass, Chaukhambha Orientalia, Chaukhambha Vidya Bhavan, Chaukhambha Sanskrit Series, Chaukhambha Surabharati, Bharatiya Vidya Prakashan, Indica Books, etc. have their establishments in Varanasi. Gita Press, in Gorakhpur is also rendering appreciable services by bringing out religious Sanskrit texts.

Conclusion

We thus observe that Sanskrit studies in Uttar Pradesh have been flourishing in various forms and formats during the post-Independence period of just over 60 years. There has no doubt been a deep decline in the standard of traditional Sanskrit education. Sanskrit subject has been very popular in the provincial competitive examinations in Utter Pradesh and candidates offering Sanskrit as one of the subjects are coming with flying colours. As regards research projects and publications, some research projects mainly funded by the UGC as the major or minor projects are being conducted in the university departments. Research works are also being conducted for doctoral degrees in the universities, deemed universities and postgraduate colleges, though high standard works are very few in number; some of theses have been published in the book form. Master works have been produced by some scholars in different branches of Sanskrit and Indology, such as Vedic studies, Purāṇic studies, grammar, philosophy, poetics, linguistics, religion, history, culture, arts, sciences, etc. Some institutions and individuals have done tremendous work to explore scientific elements in Sanskrit. Sanskrit department of the Allahabad University organised a national seminar on this topic in 2005 and has published its proceedings under the title "Science and Scientific Elements in Sanskrit". Banaras Hindu University in Uttar Pradesh hosted the "Fifth World Sanskrit Conference" in 1981. Proceedings of the same were published by the Rashtriya Sanskrit Sansthan in 1985. "All India Oriental Conference" was also hosted by some universities in Uttar Pradesh; the latest one was organised by Sampurnanand Sanskrit University, Varanasi in 2004. Uttar Pradesh has been one of the pioneering states in producing high level creative and critical literature in Sanskrit in abundance during the last 60 years. The flow of literary works is appreciable and the prospects are encouraging. One can hope for a brighter future for Sanskrit studies in the large state of Uttar Pradesh.

19

Sanskrit Studies in West Bengal

Somesh Kumar Mishra

Backdrop

When a retrospective journey is done through the corridors of history to refresh our memories of the origin, evolution and development of Sanskrit studies in Bengal then we come across vicissitudes of images. References about Bengal are drawn from various ancient sources. *Baudhāyana Dharma-Sūtra* (1.1.25), the epics (*Rāmāyaṇa* and *Mahābhārata*), *Aṣṭādhyāyī* (6.2.100), etc. In course of time, especially during Gupta and Pāla period, concrete literary sources came into existence. The Gupta period also saw the emergence of certain new dimension of technical Śāstras like the elephant lore called Hastyāyurveda. Candragomin developed the Gandea School of Sanskrit Grammar. During the Pāla period, Nyāya and Vedānta developed new degrees of maturity. Dharmaśāstra of Bengal, especially with its proposition of Dāyabhāga, was a new milestone and became a treatise *par excellence.*

The evolution and development of Sanskrit studies in Bengal in British and post-British period witnessed the parallel currents of university system as well as the traditional system represented by *ṭols* also known as *catuṣpāṭhis*: On one hand the University of Calcutta with a rich department of Sanskrit, established by Sir Ashutosh Mukherjee, who was the vice-chancellor of the university, fondled the saplings of Sanskrit, and on the other hand, Government Sanskrit College, Calcutta, developed on the fertile ground prepared by the great academician and philosopher Ishwar Chandra Vidyasagar.

The period under our preview witnessed the coming up of many prominent universities in Bengal.

Jadavpur University: Jadavpur University came into existence in the year 1955. The department of Sanskrit was started in the very next year, i.e. 1956. The university offers graduate, postgraduate and research facility for the Sanskrit students. In order to disseminate the treasure of knowledge embedded in the Sanskrit texts' the university started evening courses for Sanskrit studies. The University Grants Commission, acknowledging the potential and efforts of the university in the field of Sanskrit learning identified the department for special assistance with thrust area of literature and literary criticism as well as philosophical studies. The university has to its credit large number of publications of Sanskrit works.

Rabindra Bharati University: In 1960 Rabindra Bharati University was established to offer undergraduate, postgraduate and research programmes for the students of Sanskrit. In 1989, this university could develop the School of Vedic Studies with the approval and financial assistance of the University Grants Commission. The School of Vedic Studies was finally inaugurated in July 1990. The objective of this school is to sponsor lectures, hold seminars and help in conducting doctoral and post-doctoral research in the thrust area. The school also has taken up the responsibility to collect and preserve manuscripts, publish journals and bring out other publications.

University of Burdwan: University of Burdwan was established in 1959 with a strong Sanskrit department. It can boast of a large volume of publications in the field of Sanskrit.

Viswa Bharati University: The only central university in the state runs a very strong Sanskrit department along with a Pāli and Prākṛt department.

Sanskrit Studies in the Last 60 Years

In order to make an assessment of the period covering last six decades it would be advisable to study the contribution of the scholars associated with the university system in the state of West Bengal.

The most voluminous work in the Sanskrit literature in the last 60 years in Bengal has been done in the field of *kāvya*. The prominent names in this field in the period of our consideration, are Pandit Srijiva Nyayatirtha (1893-1992), Gourinath Shastri, Siddheswar Chattopadhyay (1918-83), Nityananda Smrititirtha (1923-2008), Ramaranjan Mukherji (1926-2010), Anantalal Thakur, Dr. Dhyanesh Narayan Chakraborty, Dipak Ghosh (1941-2005), Karuna Sindhu Das, Samiran Chakraborty, Tarapada Bhattacharya and many others.

The study of Sanskrit studies in Bengal could be conducted in two ways. First method is to prepare a list of scholars and then their respective works, while another way is to classify the works as per their category and then the names of the respective authors or editors.

Gaurinath Shastri was a renowned professor and administrator. He was a rare blend of scholarship and administrative competence. He was an academic giant and a prolific writer. Some of his notable publications deserve to be mentioned as under:

1 *Philosophy of Word and Meaning* (1959)

2 *A Study in the Dialects of Sphoṭa*

3 *Concise History of Classical Sanskrit Literature*

4 *Kiraṇāvalī* (vols. 1, 2, 3)

5 *Sanskrit Sāhitya kā Itihāsa.*

6 Critical edition of *Saṅgītadāmodara*

7 Critical edition of *Anumiter Manusatvavicāra*

8 Critical edition of *Tattvacintāmaṇi-Mayūkha*

9 Critical edition of *Kāvyaprakāśaṭīkā of Paramānanda Chakravarti* (vols. I & II, 1976)

10 Critical edition of *Maṅgalavāda* — with the editors own commentary *Prabhā* (*Tattvacintāmaṇi*); The Asiatic Society, 1974

11 *Kiraṇāvalī* — with Hindi translation (1976)

12 Critical edition of *Kiraṇāvalīrahasya* (1980)

13 Critical edition of *Nyāyakandatidarpaṇa* (in press)

14 Critical edition of *Usaragadaya* (1979)

15 Critical edition of *Vyomavati* (in press)

Srijiva Nyayatirtha : Srijiva Nyayatirtha, son of the famous Sanskrit scholar Pandit Panchanan Tarkaratna belongs to Bhatpara, in 24-Parganas. He has to his credit one *mahākāvya* in more than 3000 *ślokas*, four *khaṇḍakāvyas* and 29 *dṛṣyakāvya*, one *citrakāvya* with *citrālaṁkāra*, 30 *rūpaka* and an edition of major Purāṇa in Sanskrit. The *dṛṣyakāvya* produced by him could be enlisted as below:

Nāṭakam

1 *Mahākavi Kālidāsa* (1963).

2 *Śaṇkarācāryavaibhavam* (1968).

3 *Vivekānandacaritam.*

4 *Nigamānandacaritam*

5 *Raghuvaṁsam* (1962)

6 *Kumārasambhavam* (1965)

7 *Śrīkṛṣṇakautukam* (1969)

8 *Nāgānistāram* (1974)
9 *Samayasāgarakallolam* (1970)
10 *Svatantrasandhikṣaṇam* (1957)
11 *Mādhurī*
12 *Vidhiviparyāsam*
13 *Puruṣapuṅgavam* (1960)
14 *Vivāhaviḍambanam* (1961)
15 *Candatāṇḍavam* (1955)
16 *Bhaṭṭasaṅkaṭam*
17 *Puruṣaramaṇīyam*
18 *Kṣutakṣemiyam*
19 *Śatavārṣikam*
20 *Cipitakacarvaṇam*
21 *Rāgavirāgam*
22 *Vanabhojanam* (1959)
23 *Daridradurdaivam* (1968)
24 *Cauracāturyam* (1952)
25 *Nastahāsam*
26 *Sindhusauvirasaṅgrāmam*
27 *Kailāsanāthavijayam*
28 *Giridharasavardhanam* (1960)

Several works of Bhāsa, Śūdraka, Kālidāsa, Śrī Harṣadeva, Bhavabhūti, Viśākhadatta, Diṅgnāgācārya, Rūpa Goswāmi, etc. were re-studied during this period by various scholars and numerous *dṛṣya kāvyas* were created. The notable ones are as follows:

Dṛṣya Kāvya — Mahākavi Bhāsa

1. *Cārudattam,* Kumud Ranjan Roy (1967).
2. *Pañcarātram,* Krishna Gopal Goswami (1972).
3. *Pañcarātram,* Kumud Ranjan Roy (1972).
4. *Pañcarātram,* Dilip Kumar Kanjilal (1973).
5. *Madhyamavyāyoga,* Vamapada Basu (1973).
6. *Pratimā Nāṭakam,* Jagadish Chandra Tarka Tirtha (1377 Baṅgābda).
7. *Pratimā nāṭakam,* Vāmapad Basu (1371 Baṅgābda).
8. *Svapna-vāsavadattam,* Pandit Ashok Nath Shastri and Saroj Nath Bhanja (1956).
9. *Svapna-vāsavadattam,* Anil Chandra Basu (2004).
10. *Svapna-vāsavadattam,* Shanti Bandopadhyaya (2004).
11. *Svapna-vāsavadattam,* Madhava Das Chakravorti (2004).
12. *Svapna-vāsavadattam,* Niranjan Mishra (2004).

Mṛcchakaṭikam — Śūdraka

1 *Mṛcchakaṭikam,* Udaya Chandra Bandopadhyaya and Anita Bandopadhyaya (2006).

Abhijñānaśākuntalam — Kālidāsa

1. *Abhijñānaśākuntalam,* Satya Narayana Chakroborti (1988).
2. *Abhijñānaśākuntalam,* Ramendra Mohan Bos (1960).
3. *Abhijñānaśākuntalam,* Vidhu Bhushan Goswami (1960).
4. *A Reconstruction of the Abhijñānaśākuntalam,* Dilip Kumar Kanjilal (1980).
5. *Abhijñānaśākuntalam,* Anil Chandra Basu (2006).
6. *Abhijñānaśākuntalam (Eka Viśleṣita Adhyayana)* Pranava Kumar Datta (2006).

7. *Abhijñānaśākuntalam*, Ashok Kumar Bandopadhyaya (1412 Baṅgābda).

Mālavikāgnimitram — Kālidāsa

1. *Mālavikāgnimitram*, Pratap Chandra Sankhya Tirtha.

Ratnāvalī — Śrīharṣa Deva

1. *Ratnāvalī*, Madhava Das Chakravorti.
2. *Ratnāvalī*, Sharda Ranjan Roy (1963).
3. *Ratnāvalī*, Sri Ashok Kumar Bandopadhyaya (2008).

Uttarāramacaritam — Bhavabhūti

1. *Uttararāmacaritam*, Sita Nath Acharya and Dev Kumar Das (1998).
2. *Uttararāmacaritam*, Vidhu Bhushan Goswami (1998).
3. *Uttararāmacaritam*, Shyamapad Bhattacharya (2007).

Mudrārākṣasam — Viśākhadatta

1. *Mudrārākṣasam*, Udaya Chandra Bandopadhyaya (2008).

Kuṇdamālā — Diṅgnāgācārya

1. *Kuṇdamālā*, Kali Kumar Datta (1964).

Dānakelikaumudī — Rūpa Goswāmī

1. *Dānakelikaumudī*, Jayasree Mitra (2003).

Śrī Hanumāna (Mahānāṭakam)

1. Śrī Hanumāna, Jivanand Vidyasagar (1969).

While studying the other literary creations produced in Bengal during the period of our consideration it was noticed that the Sanskrit creation had accommodated, to a greater extent, the styles and patterns which could be termed occidental. While studying the *śravyakāvya* of the period, we come across a psychology of the literary artists of this period that majority of them preferred to re-study and represent the new versions of the old literary giants like Bāṇabhaṭṭa, Daṇḍī and Subandhu. The notable creations of the period are:

Gadya — Kāvya
Kādambarī — Bāṇabhaṭṭa

1. *Kādambarī*, Ramapada Battacharya (1976).
2. *Kādambarī*, Dilip Kanjilal (1977).
3. *Kādambarī*, Ashok Nath Battacharya (1977).
4. *Candrāpīḍasya Mahāśvetādarśanam*, Krishna Gopal Battacharya (1977).
5. *Candrāpīḍasya Mahāśvetādarśanam*, Prabodh Chandra Lahidi (1977).
6. *Śukanāsopadeśa*, Niradvarana Bhattacharya (1976).
7. *Kathāmukham tathā Śukanāsopadeśa*, Ashok Kumar Chattopadhyaya (1415, Baṅgābda).
8. *Kādambarī* (*Kathāmukham Tathā Śukanāsopadeśa*), Udya Chandra Bandopadhyaya (2005).
9. *Kādambarī Antargata Śukanāsopadeśa*, Smt. Kripamayee Kanjilal (2004).

To the important ***gītikāvya*** belongs the ***dūtakāvya*** which are both the edited works as well as original compositions. The notable ones are as given below:

Dūta-kāvya

1. *Meghadūtam*, Ramaranjan Mukherjee.
2. *Meghadūtam*, Guru Nath Vidya Nidhi.
3. *Meghadūtam*, Jitendra Vimal Choudhari (1951).
4. *Meghadūtam*, Dhyanesh Narayana Chakravorti (2003).
5. *Meghadūtam*, Varada Charan Mishra.

6. *Meghadūtam Paricaya,* Parvati Charan Bhattacharyaya (1376 Baṅgābda).
7. *Candradūtam,* Madhu Sudan Vedanta Shastri (1990).
8. *Bhṛṅgadūtam,* Gopika Mohan Bhattacharya.
9. Vāṇidūtam, Lakshmi Kant Mishra (2004).

Some other *lokopayogī gīti kāvyas* (*gīti kāvyas* considered beneficial for the society) at large were created in abundance. Few popular ones could be enlisted as below:

Pañcatantra-Śrī Viṣṇu Śarmā

1. *Pañcatantra,* Jaysree Chattopadhyaya, Sanskrit Pustak Bhandar, Kolkata.

Subhāṣita-Kāvya

1. *Sadukti Karṇāmṛtam,* Sridhar Das/ Suresh Chandra Banerjee (1965).
2. *Udbhaṭasāgara,* Purna Chandra Kavi Bhushan Kavya Ratna (1851 Śakābda).
3. *Nītimuktāvalī,* Sri Himanshu Prasad Bhattacharya.
4. *Kavitākorakam,* Sri Avinash Chandra Chakraborti (1980).
5. *Hitavāṇī,* Praphulla Chandra Chakravorti Smriti Tirth (1408 Baṅgābda).
6. *Udbhaṭaślokasaṁgraha,* Manvendu Bandopadhyaya (1995).
7. *A Book of Treasure from Sanskrit Literature,* Dhirendra Nath Banerjee (2004).
8. *Meghadūtam Paricaya,* Parvati Charan Bhattacharyaya (1376 Baṅgābda)
9. *Candradūtam,* Madhu Sudan Vedanta Shastri (1990).
10. *Bhṛṅgadūtam,* Gopika Mohan Bhattacharya.
11. *Vāṇīdūtam,* Lakshmi Kanta Mishra (2004).

Śataka-kāvya

1. *Śāntiśatakam*, Satya Narayana Chakravorti (1996).

Bengal, under the period of our consideration also witnessed the editing of several *campū-kāvyas*, as for instance the *Gopāla Campū* of Śrijīva Goswāmī was edited by two renowned scholars Nityaswarup Brahmachari and Dileep Kumar Kanjilal. The *Campū Rāmāyaṇa* (Araṇya) of Bhojrāja was again edited by two scholars, viz. Anil Chandra Basu and Ashok Kumar Bandopadhyaya. Some other important *campū-kāvya* which were created and handed down for the benefit of succeeding generations could be listed as follows:

Campū-kāvya

1. *Śrīgopālacampū* (Pūrva Khaṇḍa), Jiva Goswami/Nitya Swarup Bramhachari (1961).
2. *Śrīgopālacampū* (Uttara Khaṇḍa), Dilip Kanjilal (1961).
3. *Campūrāmāyaṇa* (Araṇya Kāṇḍam) Bhojraj, Sarwabhoum/Anil Chandra Basu (1961).
4. *Campurāmāyaṇa* (Araṇya Kāṇḍam), Bhojraj Sarwabhoum/Sri Ashok Kumar Bandopadhyaya (1961).
5. *Citracampū*, M.M. Vaneshwar Vidyalankar/ Janki Nath Shastri (1982).

Sanskrit studies in our period of consideration cannot be complete without the name of Ramaranjan Mukherji. His scholarship and administrative capabilities had transcended the boundaries of the state of Bengal and in turn the geographical boundaries of the nation. Mukherji was known for his command over Sanskrit, English and Bengali. He was a prolific writer and wonderful orator. He took the message of Sanskrit far and wide, beyond the frontiers of the country. His literary creations are both edited work as well as original creations. Some of his memorable works apart from editing of *Meghadūtam* are:

1. Elements of Literary Criticism in Ancient India
2. Comparative Aesthetics
3. Imagery in Poetry
4. Vyaktiviveka (vol. I)
5. Sri Aurobindo on Vedic Dieties
6. Global Aesthetics and Sanskrit Literature
7. Rasasamīkṣā

It is noteworthy at this juncture to take note of the contributions of Sitanath Acharya and Dipak Kumar Ghosh in the field of Sahitya. Dipak Kumar Ghosh received the Sahitya Academy award for his poetic creation called "Rabindra Sangeetam". It is a translation of Rabindra Sangeet in Sanskrit.

Bhāvavilasitam, which is a collection of 25 poems, and *Kāvyanirjharī* are beautiful examples of the poetic creation of Sitanath Acharya. The concept of his social lyric took the shape of *Śiśuyuvādurdaivabilasitam* while his imagination of love lyric took shape of *Kā Tvam Śubhe*. His *Gourinath Praśasti* which contains 250 *śloka*s is yet to be published while his short story *Bāndhabi Rakṣitā* was published in the Sanskrit Sahitya Parisad Patrika.

On the works of grammar several literary projections have surfaced which belong to our time frame. Pandit Gaurinath Shastri, Pandit Vishnupada Bhattacharya, Karuna Sindhu Das and many other have contributed richly to the field of grammar. A list of the works produced during this period could be given as follows:

Vyākaraṇa (Text only)

1. *Mahābhāṣya* (Paspaśāhnikam), Kumud Ranjan Roy (1963).
2. *Mahābhāṣya* (Paspaśāhnikam), Dandi Swami Damodar Ashram.

3. *Mahābhāṣya* (Paspaśāhnikam), Sanghamitra Das Gupta.
4. *Mahābhāṣya* (Paspaśāhnikam), Gangadhar Kar Nyayacharya.

Miscellaneous Works on Sanskrit Grammar

1. *The Philosophy of Sanskrit Grammar,* Pranat Chandra Chakraborty (1930 and 2001).
2. *The Philosophy of Word and Meaning,* Gaurinath Shastri (1959).
3. *A Study in the Dialectcs of Sphoṭa,* Gaurinath Shstri (1980).
4. *Word and its Meaning — A New Perspective,* Drishna Nath Chattopadhyaya (1979).
5. *Logic, Language and Reality,* Bimal Krishna Matilal (1985).
6. *The Word and the World,* Bimal Krishna Matilal (1990).
7. *The Philosophy of Language,* Pradip Majumdar (1977).
8. *The Meaning of Nondenotative Words : A Study on Indian Semantics,* Pradip Majumdar (1985).
9 *A Study in Language and Meaning,* Vishnupada Bhattacharya (1962).
10. *Yāska's Nirukta and the Science of Etymology,* Vishnupada Bhattacharya (1980).
11. *Vākyapadīyam* (Brahmakāṇḍa Prathama Khaṇḍa), Vishnupada Bhattacharya (1971).
12. *Vākyapadīyam* (Brahmakāṇḍa, Dvitīya Khaṇḍa), Vishnupada Bhattacharya (1985).
13. *Śabdaśaktiprakāśikā* (Prathama Khaṇḍa), Madhusudan Nyayacharya (1980).
14. *Śabdaśaktiprakāśikā* (Dvitīya Khaṇḍa), Madhusudan Nyayacharya (1982).

15. *Śabdārthavādasamīkṣā*, Gangadharkar Nyayacharya (2003).
16. *A Pāṇinian Approach to Philosophy of Language* (Kauṇḍa Bhaṭṭasya Vaiyākarṇa Bhūṣaṇasārasya Vistṛtālocana Āṅgānuvādaśca), Karuna Sindhu Das (1990).
17. *Semantic-Syntactic Relations: A Philosophical Approach* (Abhirāmvidyālaṁkārsya Kārakṭippni), Karunasindhu Das (1994).
18. *Paribhāṣās in the Pāṇinian System of Grammar*, Karuna Sindhu Das (1984).
19. *Prācīna Bhāratera Bhāṣā Darśana*, Karuna Sindhu Das (2002).
20. *Vyākarṇadarśane Vāgarthaprasaṅga*, Karuna Sindhu Das (2003).
21. *Prācīna Bhāratera Śāstraracanā o Vyākhyāner Rīti Paddhati*, Karuna Sindhu Das (2002).
22. *Śabdaratna*, Satyendra Bhattacharya (2001).
23. *Siddhāntadīpa*, Satyendra Bhattacharya (2001).
24. *Pāṇinidarśana*, Chinmayee Chattopadhyaya (2001).
25. *Vararūca Saṁgraha*, Alapna Chaudhuri (2001).
26. *Govind Bhaṭṭer Samāsavāda*, Tulika Chakrabarti (2001).
27. *Concept of Asiddhatva*, Rabisankar Bhattacharya (1984).
28. *A Handbook of Sanskrit Philosophy*, Satyaranjan Banerjee (1987).

Bengal has always been a strong centre of Darśana, especially Nyāya and Vedānta. In earlier days the different regions of Bengal were known for specific branches of Sanskrit studies, but the scholarship of the present days has blossomed in all branches in all regions of Bengal.

Vedānta Paribhāṣā edited by Mohan Bhattacharya (1963, Kolkata) and *Upaniṣad Pañcaka* by Chitrita Devi (1964) are important creations of this period. Other notable works of the period on Vedānta, mostly Advaita Vedānta, are as follows:

Advaita Vedānta

1. *Vedāntaparibhāṣā*, Mohan Bhattacharya (1963).
2. *Vedāntadarśana-Advaitavāda*, Ashutosh Bhattacharya Shastri (1962).
3. *Advaitavedānte Pratyakṣapramāsvarūpavicāra*, Minatikar (1966).
4. *Bhārtīyadarśane Muktivāda*, Vijayabhushan Bandopadhyaya (1361, Baṅgābda).
5. *Advaitavedānte Avidyā*, Shitanshu Shekhar Vagachi (1962).
6. *Advaitavedānte Avidyānumāna*, Yogendra Vagachi (1968).
7. *A Doctrine of Māyā*, Anil Kumar Roy Chaudhari (1950).
8. *Modern Polity and Vedānta*, Satkari Mukherjee (1972).
9. *Brahamasūtra and Śrīmadbhāgavata*, Anilhari Chattopadhyaya (1978).
10. *The Advaita Concept of Falsity: A Critical Study*, Nirad Baran Chakroborty (1967).
11. *Amalānanda, Bhāmati-o-Vivaraṇaprasthāner Yogasūtra*, Himansu Narayan Chakraborty (1971).
12. *Brahmasūtramālā* (Śaṅkara, Rāmānuja Bhāṣya), Vani Bhadra Pushpa Devi (1976).
13. *Advaitamatasamīkṣā*, Sri Mohan Bhattacharya (1975).
14. *Advaitavedānte Prācīnakahini*, Swami Vidyaranya (1972).
15. *Vākyārtha Nirūpaner Dārśanika Paddhati*, Amritanshu Shekhar Vagachi (1981).
16. *Advaitatattvamīmāṁsā*, Abhedanand Bhattacharya (1994).

17. *Veda-Vedānta* (Pūrva Khaṇḍa Brahmasūtra), Mahanamavrat Brahmachari (1402, Baṅgābda).
18. *Advaitacintaya Ācāryaḥ Maṇḍanaḥ*, Rama Prasad Bhattacharya (1382, Baṅgābda).
19. *Śaṅkaravedānte Tattvamīmāṁsā*, Kalipad Singh (1982).
20. *Śaṇkaravedānte Jñānamīmāṁsā*, Kalipad Singh (1983).
21. *Advaitavedānte Jñāna*, Minati Kar (1988).
22. *Bhāratīya Sādhanar Dhāra*, M.M. Gopinath Kaviraj (1965).
23. *Jīvanmukti Tattva, Pramān-o-Sadhan* (Minti Kar, 2000).
24. *Praṣnottarī Vedānta Sopān*, Swami Mahadevanand Giri.
25. *Vedāntajijñāsā*, Anirwana Satya (1386 Baṅgābda).
26. *Vedāntasaṁjñāvalī*, Ramkrishna Adhikari (1996).
27. *Vedāntadarśane Advaitavāda*, Ashutosh Shastri (1961).
28. *Bhāratīya-o-Pāścātya Darśana*, Satish Chandra Chattopadyaya (1963).
29. *Bhāratīyadarśanakośa* (Tṛtīya Khaṇḍa Prathama Bhāga), Mohan Bhattacharya and Dinesh Chandra Bhattacharya (1981).
30. *Bhāratīya Sanskṛti aur Anekānta Vedānta*, Kalidas Bhattacharya (1982).
31. *Vedānta-o-Advaita Vāda*, Swami Vidyaranya (1982).
32. *Bengali Manase Vedānta*, Bhavatosh Datta (1986).
33. *Vyāsa Darśana*, Swami Vidyaranya (1988).
34. *Advaitavedānte Ajñāna*, Chandrodaya Bhattacharya (1994).
35. *Advaitavedānte Pratikarmā Vyavasthā*, Nirmal Kumar Panigrahi, (1994).
36. *Vedāntapraveśa*, Ramapad Bhattacharya (1996).
37. *Upaniṣader Sandeśa*, Shashanka Bhusan Bandopadhyaya (1998).

38. *Vedānta Mahāvākyārthavicāra*, Tapan Kumar Chakraborty (2000).
39. *Sāṁkhyadarśaner Vivaraṇa*, Vidhubhushan Bhattacharya (1984).

It is also to be noted that the faith groups like the charitable and religious trust like Ramakrishna Math and Mission, Mahamilan Math and others have contributed richly in terms of publication of books and journals on Vedānta. Ramakrishna Mission Institute of Culture runs courses on Sanskrit studies — both traditional and modern. It organizes lectures on topics of Veda, Vedānta and Epics regularly. Veda, Vedānta and Epics are the life blood of Indian culture. Any and every attempt to restore the greatness of Indian culture is a service of Sanskrit.

Ramkrishna Mission is one of the leading publishers of books and journals on Vedānta. Its publications are all available on the Internet.

In the field of Veda and Vedāṅga School of Vedic studies, Rabindra Bharati University has made a remarkable contribution under the leadership of Samiran Chandra Chakraborty and Nabanarayan Bandopadhyay. The Valuable contribution of the School of Vedic Studies of Rabindra Bharati University is the publication of the following books, journals, CDs, pamphlets, etc.

1. *Some Aspects of Vedic Studies: Retrospect and Prospect*, ed. Samiran Chandra Chakrabarti (1996).
2. *Buddhism and World Culture*, ed. Samiran Chandra Chakrabarti (1998).
3. *Bhārata Itihāse Vaidika Yuga*, Narendranath Bhattacharyya (1998).
4. *Gopatha Brāhmaṇa*, tr, Beng., Tarak Nath Adhikari (1999).

5. *Ancient Indian Views in Truth and Falsity*, Nabnarayan Bandyopadhyay (2002).
6. *Indian Etymologists and their Etymologies*, Dipak Bhattacharya (2002).
7. *Prācīn Bhārater Dharma, Samaj-o-Darśana*, Hemanta Kumar Ganguli (2003).
8. *Schools of Vedic Interpretation: Eastern and Western*, Bhabani Prasad Bhattacharya (2006).
9. *Laghu-Yajñapārśva-Pariśiṣṭa and Mahad-Yajñapārśva-Pariśiṣṭa*, Nabnarayan Bandyopadhyay (2006).
10. *Proper Names of Persons in Vedic Literature*, Samiran Chakraborti (2008).
11. *Bengal's Contribution to Vedic Studies*, ed. Nabanarayan Bandyopadhyay (2010).

Actually, Veda and Vedāṅga are the fields in which Bengal has shown special interest. Scholars in the subject are from all parts of Bengal. Some of the notable works that deserve to be mentioned here are:

Veda and Vedāṅga

1. *Śrutisañcayanam*, Gobindagopal Mukhopadhyay (vol. I) (1977).
2. *Śrutisañcayanam*, Ayodhyanath Sanyal (vol. II), (2008).
3. *Vaidika Bhabnai Soma*, Biswanath Mukhopadhyay (1979).
4. *Vaidika Sāhitya Saṅkalana* (1965).
5. *Gopatha Brāhmaṇa*, Taraknath Adhikari (1999).
6. *Bhārata Itihāse Vaidika Yuga*, Narendranath Bhattacharya (1998).
7. *Some Aspects of Vaidic Studies*, ed. Samiran Chandra, Chakraborty.

8. *The Gr̥hya Rites vis-à-vis the Arthavanik Tradition.*
9. *Dictionary of Vedic Ritual*, Chitrabhanu Sen (1983).
10. *Indian Culture and Society in the Vedas*, Priti Mitra.
11. *Lifestyle and Technical Occupation in the Vedic Age*, Pradyot Kumar Dutta.
12. *Medical Science in the Veda*, Pradyot Kumar Dutta.
13. *Socio-Economic Life of India in the Vedic Period*, Haripada Chakraborty.
14. *Vedic India: Political and Legal Institutions in Vedic Literature*, Haripada Chakraborty.
15. *Vedic Grammar* (Text, notes, English Translation), ed. Bhabani Prasad Bhattacharya.
16. *The Biological and Historical Significance of Vedic Mythology*, A.K. Bhattacharya.
17. *Mythology and Ritual Symbolism: A study with Reference to the Vedic and Tāntric Agni*, Dipak Bhattacharya.
18. *Origin and Development of Scientific Treatment in the Veda*, Pradyot Kumar Dutta.
19. *Studies in the Śrautasūtra's of Āśvalāyana and Āpastamba* (vol. I), Bhabani Prasad Bhattacharya.
20. *Studies in the Śrautasūtra's of Āśvalāyana and Āpastamba* (vol. II), Bhabani Prasad Bhattacharya.
21. *Studies in the Śatapatha Brāhmaṇa*, Santi Banerjee.
22. *The Paribhāṣās in the Śrauta Sūtras*, Samiran Ch. Chakraborti.
23. *Pāṇini and Prātiśākhya*, Pradyot Kumar Dutta.
24. *Gopatha Brāhmaṇa : A Critical Study* (An analysis of the topics and a comprehensive critique of the Brāhmaṇa text of the Atharvaveda), Tarak Nath Adhikari.
25. *R̥gveda-Prātiśākhya*, Bhabani Prasad Bhattacharya.

26. *Sāyaṇa's Methodology in Interpreting the Ṛgveda,* Indrani Kar.
27. *A Critical and Comparative Study of the Pratiśākhyas,* Chhya Banerjee.
28. *New Selections from the Brāhmaṇas,* Samiran Ch. Chakraborti.
29. *The Vedic Heritage,* ed. Mnanbendu Banerjee (2010).
30. *Āpastamba Sāmānya-Sūtra or Yajñaparibhāṣa-Sūtra,* ed. Amar Chattopadhyay (2006).
31. *Āśvalāyana Śrautasūtra,* ed. Amar Chattopadhyay (2002).
32. *Caṇḍasūtrabhāṣyam-Yādavaprakāśakṛtam,* ed. Haridas Sinha Ray (1977).
33. *Śrautasūtra of Aśvalāyana,* reprint version (1989).
34. *The Gṛhyasūtra of Āśvalāyana,* ed. Ramanarayan Vidyaratna and Annadachandra Vedanta Vagish (reprint), (1986).
35. *The Paippalāda-Saṁhitā of the Atharvaveda* (vol. II), ed. Dipak Bhattacharya (2008).
36. *The Ṛgveda-Saṁhitā* (vol. I), Translation in English, ed. Basanta Kumar Ganguli (2004).
37. *Vedacarcai Baṅgabhūmi-o-Samasrami,* Amar Kumar Chattopadhyay (2005).
38. *Sampratīka Kāle Baṅgālir Veda Gabesanā-ebam-Prasaṅga-Anusaṅga,* Sambhunath Chakraborty (2006).
39. *Vaidika Sāhityer Rūparekhā,* Santi Bandyopadhyay (1993).
40. *Ved-Mīmāṁsā* (vol. I), Anirban (1975).
41. *Veder Parichaya,* Yogiraj Basu (1980).

Vijñāneśvara's *Janmasvatva-Veda* (Right of sons to the paternal property by virtue of birth) and the *Aṣṭaviṁṣatitattva* (28 *tattvas*) 8 Raghunandan made the ground of Bengal so fertile with the percolation of Dāyabhāga to the blood stream of Bengal that it still happens to be one of the strong centre of *karma-kāṇḍa*. Some of the scholarly creations of this period in the field of Dharmaśāstra and Purāṇa are as follows:

Dharmaśāstra

1. *Dharmaśātras: A study in their Origin and Development*, S.C. Banerjee (1962).
2. *A Glossary of Smṛti Literature*, S.C. Banerjee (1963).
3. *Samāja Saṁskāraka Raghunandana*, Bani Chakraborty (1964).
4. *Studies in Some Aspects in Hindu Saṁskāras in Ancient India*, Heramba Chatterjee (1965).
5. *The Early Hindu Civilization*, Ramesh Chandra Dutta (1963).
6. *The Law of Debt in Ancient India*, Heramba Chatterjee (1971).
7. *The Social Background of the Forms of Marriage in Ancient India* (vol. I, II), Heramba Chatterjee (1974).
8. *Studies in Some Aspects of Hindu Saṁskaras in Ancient India in the Light of Saṁskāratattva of Raghunandana*, Heramba Chatterjee (1967).
9. *Varṇāśrama Dharma*, Baradakanta Majumdar (2005).
10. *Hindu Narioṅ ke Kartavya*, Hemant Kumari (1977).

Purāṇa Miscellaneous

1. *Studies in the Upapurāṇas*, vol. I : *Saura and Vaiṣṇava Upapurāṇas*, R.C. Hazra (1958).
2. *Studies in the Upapurāṇas*, vol. II : *Śākta and non-sectarian Upapurāṇas*, R.C. Hazra (1963).
3. *Sāhityaratnakośe*, vol. II : *Purāṇa Itihāsa Saṁgraha*, ed. S.K. Dey and R.C. Hazra (1959).

4. *Padma Purāṇa : A Study,* Ashoke Chatterjee (1967).
5. *Purāṇa Paricaya,* Ashoke Chatterjee (1977).
6. *Mother Goddess Caṇḍī (Its Socio-ritual Impact on the Folk Life)* Sibendu Manna (1993).
7. *Economic Life in the Great Epic,* S.K. Banerjee (1990).
8. Brahmavaivarta Purāṇe Samāja-o-Saṁskṛti, Haradhan Manna (2009).

The scientific temper of the scholars of Sanskrit surfaced not only in the study of ancient medicine but also in the fields of Jyotiṣa and the sciences related to art, architecture, music, painting, warfare and aeronautics. The categorized table of publications done during this period (as given below) throw good light on the proposition that Sanskrit studies in Bengal actually flourished in all branches:

Sciences: General

1. *A Concise History of Science in India,* D.M. Bose (1971).
2. *The Positive Sciences of the Ancient Hindus,* Brajendranath Seal (1985).
3. *Science and Technology in Ancient India,* Manabendu Banerjee (1993).

Jyotiṣa: Astronomy, Astrology, Mathematics

1. *History of Astronomy in India,* S.N. Sen and K.S. Shukla (1985).
2. *A Bibliography of Sanskrit Works on Astronomy and Mathematics,* S.N. Sen, (1966)
3. *Prāthamika Jyotirvidyā,* Apurba Kumar Chakraborty (1990).
4. *Prācīna Bhārate Trikoṇamiti Carcā,* Pradip Kumar Majumdar (1989).

5. *Pracīnabhārate Jyāmiticarcā*, Pradip Kumar Majumdar (1992).
6. *Gaṇitāvalī*, Completed by Bibhuti Bhusan Bhattacharya, eds. Manabendu Banerjee and Pradip Kumar Majumdar (2005).
7. *Gaṇitaśāstre Smaraṇīya Janera*, Pradip Kumar Majumdar (1995).
8. *The Sūrya Siddhānta*, A.K. Chakraborty (2001).

Āyurveda, Miscellaneous Works

1. *Flora and Fauna in Sanskrit Literature*, S.C. Banerji (1979).
2. *History of Indian Medicine* (3 vols.), G. Mukhopadhyay (1974).
3. *Caraka Saṁhitā: A Scientific Analysis* Priyadaranjan Ray and Hirendranath Gupta (1980).
4. *Suśruta Saṁhitā : A Scientific Literature*, P. Ray, et al. (1980).
5. *Rasārṇava*, ed. Prafulla Chandra Ray, Harish Chandra Kaviratna and revised by Banani Prashad (reprint) (1985).
6. *Sanskrit and Modern Medical Vocabulary*, Asoke Bagchi (2002).
7. *Carakasaṁhitār Dārśanika Bhāvanā-Samīkṣā*, Dalia Bandury (2006).

Other Sciences

1. *Art of Warfare*, P.C. Chakraborti (1980).
2. *Military Wisdom in the Purāṇas*, P.C. Sarma (1979).
3. *Kurukṣetra War: A Military Study*, P.C. Sarma (1975).
4. *Technical Terms (Glossary with Explanations) in A Companion to Sanskrit Literature*, S. C. Banerji (1989).

5. *Geographical Terms* (Glossary with Explanations) *in A Companion to Sanskrit Literature,* S.C. Banerji (1989).
6. *Kṛṣi-Parāsar, ed.* Girija Prasanna Mozumdar, Sures Chandra Banerji (reprint), (2001).
7. *Vimāna in Ancient India,* Dileep Kumar Kanjilal.

Art, Architectue, Music, Painting

1. *Fine Art in Ancient India,* A.B. Ganguli (1979).
2. *Fundamentals of Ancient Indian Music and Dance,* S.C. Banerji (1970).
3. *Story of Indian Music:* Its *Growth and Synthesis,* O. Goswami (1957).
4. *Historical Development of Indian Music,* Swami Prajnananda (1960).
5. *Aspects of Indian Culture-selected Bibliographies:* I, the Arts, R.N. Sen and H.S. Palit (1966).
6. *Concept of Iconography of the Goddess of Abundance and Fortune in Three Religions of India,* Niranjan Ghosh (1979).
7. *Saṅgītadāmodara,* ed. Sures Chandra Banerji.
8. *Saṅgīta Paricaya,* Uma De.
9. *Saṅgītacandrikā,* Gopeswar Bandyopadhyay.
10. *Bhāratīya Uchhaṅga Saṅgiter Rītiparivartana,* Binata Maitra.
11. *Saṅgītadāmodar,* (tr.) Mahua Mukherjee (2009).
12. *Aspects of Sanskrit Architectural Texts,* Manabendu Banerjee.
13. *Indian Sculpture and Painting and ideas of Indian Art,* ed. Manabendu Banerjee.
14. *Śilparatna of Śrīkumāra,* ed. Manabendu Banerjee.
15. *Devatāmūrtiprakaraṇam and Rūpamaṇḍanam (Manual of*

Indian Iconography and Iconometry), Upendra Mohan Sankhyatirtha and Manabendu Banerjee with an introduction by Haridas Mitra.

16. *Rock Art Studies in India: A Historical Perspective*, Somnath Chakraborty (2003).
17. *Mudrānuśīlana: Articles of the Seminar on Coins of Bengal and North East India*, ed. Samaresh Bandyopadhyay (2006).
18. *Late Medieval Temples of Bengal: Origin and Classification.*
19. *Vaiṣṇava Iconology in Nepal: A Study in Art and Religion*, Pratapaditya Pal (reprint), (1985).

Modern Sanskrit writings of Bengal of our period represent the confluence of the style, pattern and technicalities of the East and the West. The development of satire, short stories and changes in the concept of the character of the Nāṭaka, etc. all talk in an orchestrated manner about the influence of the West. Usage of foreign words and application of Western and Far-Eastern *chanda*s are also noticed. Some of such literary creations are as follows:

Modern Sanskrit Writings

1. *Twentieth Century Sanskrit Literature (A Glimpse into Tradition and Innovation)*, Rita Chattopadhyay.
2. *Technical Sanskrit Literature*, Dileep Kumar Kanjilal.
3. *Some Problem of Sanskrit Historiography*, Ajoy Kumar Dey.
4. *Modern Sanskrit Drama of Bengal (20th century CE)*, Rita Chattopadhyay.
5. *Select Papers mainly Indological:*, Harinatha De compiled by and ed. by Sunil Bandopadhyay.

Poetics

1. *Ānandavardhana-o-Mahimabhaṭṭa*, Bimalakanta Mulhopadhyay (1375 Baṅgābda).
2. *Kāvyatattva*, Jibendra Singha Ray (1986).
3. *Kāvyatattvavicāra*, Durgachankar Mukhopadhyay (1988).
4. *Kāvyaparimīti*, Jotindranath Sebngupta (1370 Baṅgābda).
5. *Kāvyamīmāṁsā*, Vishnupada Bhattacharya (1982).
6. *Kāvyamīmāṁsā* (Rajshekhar Viracita), Byākhyākār: Gangasagar Ray (3rd edn.) (1982).
7. *Kāvyāloka* (vol. 1), Sudhirkumar Dashgupta (5th edn.), (1386 Baṅgābda).
8. *Kālidāsa-o-Rabindranātha*, Vishnupada Bhattacharya (2nd edn.), (1386 Baṅgābda).
9. *Gadyarīti–Padyarīti*, Pabitra Sarkar (1985).
10. *Darpaṇe Pratibimba*, Bimal Kumar Mukhopadhyay (1988).
11. *Dhvanyāloka-o-Locana*, tr. Shri Subodh Chandra Sengupta, Kalipada Bhattacharya (2nd edn.), (1986).
12. *Dhvanyāloka*: (*Prathama udyota*), Satyanarayan Chakraborty, 1998.
17. Yuktivāda, Ādhunikatā-o-Ānandamīmāṁsā, Soumyendranath Thakur (1378 Baṅgābda).
18. *Rasasamīkṣā*, Ramaranjan Mukhopadhayaya, enlarged and new edn. (1384 Baṅgābda).
19. *Rājānaka Kuntakācāryer Vakroktijīvita*, ed. Rabishankar Bandyopadhyay (1st edn.), (1393 Baṅgābda).
20. *Sāhityapather Bhūmikā*, Subodh Sengupta (1957).
21. *Sāhityajijñāsā: Vastuvādī Vicāra*, Ajay Kumar Ghosh (1994).

22. *Sāhityadarpaṇa*, Haridassidhantabagish (reprint from 5th edn. with Ṭīkā) (1981).
23. *Sāhityadarpaṇa* (1-2), ed. Satyanarayan Chakraborty (1998).
24. *Sāhityamīmāṁsā*, Bishnupada Bhattacharya, (1975).
25. *Sāhityer Matra-Dvandviksūtra*, Vimal Kumar Mukhopadhyay (1981).

Traditional System of Sanskrit Learning

At this juncture it becomes pertinent to acknowledge the efforts made by Bangiyo Sanskrit Shiksha Parishat and various voluntary Sanskrit institutions running on traditional lines. Bangiyo Sanskrit Shiksha Parishat, as we know, was established by the Government of West Bengal as a department under the directorate of education. The role assigned to Bangiyo Sanskrit Shiksha Parishat was to supervise the activities of the *ṭol*s also called *catuṣpāṭhi*s, to conduct examination in traditional Sanskrit and award degrees of Adya, Madhya and Upadhi also called Tirtha.

There are more than 600 *catuṣpāṭhi*s or the centres of traditional Sanskrit-learning in the state. Amongst them there are certain *catuṣpāṭhi*s which have grown in terms of activities. The activities of some of the *catuṣpāṭhi*s are divergent enough like publications, holding international seminars, taking up and completing the academic projects of the Ministry of Human Resource Development (HRD), Govrnment of India. Example could be given of the Sanskrit Sahitya Prishad, an organisation which is more than 100 years old and can boast of a very rich library and large number of manuscripts. It publishes books, journals and also undertakes the tasks of free traditional Sanskrit teaching. It holds seminars and sanskrit dramas. Sri Sitaramdas Omkarnath Sanskrita Siksha Samsad and Sri Sitaram Vaidic Adarsh Sanskrit Mahavidyalaya, Bharati Chatuspathi (Nawadwip), Sankari Chatuspathi (Suri),

Nawadwip Sanskrit College, Sanskrit Sahitya Parisad, Bangiyo Puran Parisad and many others are equally involved in promotion of Sanskrit.

It is to be taken note of that Sri Sitaram Vaidic Adarsha Sanskrit Mahavidyalaya developed from Sri Sitaramdas Omkarnath Sanskrita Siksha Samsad and Sri Sitaram Vaidic Mahavidyalaya. Under the scheme of the Ministry of HRD, the Government of India, a section of the aforesaid organisation was developed into Adarsha Sanskrit Mahavidyalaya which receives financial assistance from the Ministry of HRD.

In the period of our consideration, two more Adarsha Sanskrit Mahavidyalayas were created by Rashtriya Sanskrit Sansthan and the Ministry of HRD, Government of India, viz. Bikram Kishore Adarsha Sanskrit Mahavidyalaya (Kaliachak) and Thakur Gadadhar Adarsha Sanskrit Mahavidyalaya (Arambag).

When we talk of traditional Sanskrit learning and the *catuṣpathis* system we cannot afford to forget the contribution of scholars, like Pandit Nityananda Smrititirtha (1923-2008), M.M. Vidhushekhar Shastri (d. 1958), Kalipada Tarkacharya (d. 1972), Siddheswar Chattopadhyay (1918-93), Pandit Dinanath Tripathi and so many others.

Pandit Nityananda Smrititirtha was a teacher in the *ṭol* section of Government Sanskrit College, Calcutta University. He was a prolific writer. He is credited to have written seven Sanskrit *mahākāvyas*, 24 Sanskrit *khaṇḍakāvyas* and more than 110 Sanskrit dramas. For recognition of this literary creation, he became the recipient of the Presidential Award in 1994.

Pandit Siddheswar Chattopadhyay will ever remain in the hearts of lovers of Sanskrit literature for his creation of (i) Athakim (a satire), (ii) Swargiya Prahasanam, (iii) and Nanavitadanam, etc.

Pandit Dinanath Tripathi is considered as a stalwart amongst the Sanskrit intelligentsia in Bengal. He is equally respected by the leading scholars of Veda, Nyāya and Vyākaraṇa. They consider him to be an authority. He has contributed richly to the three streams and produced volumes of literary creations in the aforesaid three streams. Some of his publications are:

1 *Tattvacintāmaṇi*
2 *Vedāntasāra*
3 *Vedāntasārasya ṭikā* (3 vols.)
4 *Īśāvāsyopaniṣad*
5 *Kaṭhopaniṣad*
6 *Muṇḍakopaniṣad*
7 *Vyākaraṇasya Paspaṣāhnikam*
8 *Tantrāloka*
9 *Muṇḍakopaniṣad*
10 *Praṣastpādabhāṣya* (2 vols.)
11 *Vivekacūḍāmaṇi*
12 *Vedānte Mahāvākya*
13 *Haṭhayoga-Pradīpikā*
14 *Pratiṣṭhānavidhi*
15 *Pratiṣṭhānasārasaṁgraha*
16 *Sanātankriyāvidhi*
17 *Brahmacarya, Jīvaśrāddha, Saṁnyāspaddhati*
18 *Jātibhedavarṇāśrama*
19 *Rāmakṛṣṇapūjāpaddhati*
20 *Pāṇini Aṣṭādhyāyī* (Artha)

Conclusion

When we think of the universal concomitance of smoke and fire we get reminded of another concomitance which may not enjoy the status of being called universal, is the concomitance of Bengal and Sanskrit studies. The imperishable treasures of Sanskrit literature, which form the foundation of Indian cultural heritage, has kept drenched the heart and mind of the people of Bengal which is testified by their dress pattern, the courtesies of social interaction, the folklore, and in fact, all the walks of life.

The Contributors

Bhagyalata, Pataskar, <vsm_asss@yahoo.com>.

Devanathan, K.E. <ked0410@gmail.com>.

Jha, Shankarji, Professor of Sanskrit, Deptt of Sanskrit, Panjab University, Chandigarh-160 014, <shankarjijha@hotmail.com>.

Kumar, Shashiprabha, Special Centre for Sanskrit Studies, Jawaharlal Nehru University, JNU Campus, New Delhi - 110 067 <shashiprabhakumar@yahoo.co.in>.

Mishra, Prafulla Kumar, Professor of Sanskrit, P. G. Dept. of Sanskrit, Utkal University, Vanivihar, Bhubaneswar - 751 004 (Odisha), <mprafullak@yahoo.com>.

Mishra, Somesh Kumar, Sri Sita Ram Vedic Adarsh Sankrit Mahavidyalaya, 7/2A, PWD Road, Kolkata - 35.

Muraleemadhavan, P.C., Sreekrishna Nagar, Kothakulangara, Angamaly P.O. Ernakulam Dist. 683 574, <muraleemadhavan@yahoo.com>.

Nagsampige, Dr. A.V., Director, Poornaprajna Vidyapeetha, Katriguppa Main Road, Bangalore - 560 028 <ppsmb1@gmail.com>.

Patel, Gautam Bhai, L-111, "Valam", Swatantra Senani Nagar, Nawa Vadaj, Ahmedabad - 380 013 <vedgautam@yahoo.com>.

Radhakrishnan, C.S., Department of Sanskrit, Science &Humanities block, R.V. nagar, Kalapet, Puddcherry - 605 014, <radhakri@vsnl.com>.

Sharma, Dipak Kumar, (Vice-chancellor, Kumar Bhaskar Varma Sanskrit and Ancient Studies University, Nalbari - 781335, Assam), 79 University Campus, Gauhati University, Guwahati-781014, Assam <dipaksharma2@rediffmail.com>.

Sharma, Hari Dutt, Head of Department of Sanskrit, University of Allahabad, Allahabad - 211 002, <hari_sanskrit@rediffmail.com>.

Sharma, Kedar Nath, University of Jammu, Jammu, J&K, <knaryaal@gmail. com>

Sharma, Uma Shankar 'Rishi', V-33, Vidyapuri, Kankarbagh, Patna - 800 020.

Shastry, Devarshi Kananath, C/8, Prithvi Raj Road, Jaipur - 302 001 (Raj.), <dhirendradevarshi@gmail.com>.

Siddartha, Sundari, Flat A 2 Fort Indraprastha 45, Kalakshetra Road, Chennai 600 041 (Tamil Nadu), <mahagouri@yahoo.com>.

Surendrakumar, Brahmachari, 375, Patliputra Colony, PATNA - 13, <bskumar1933@gmail.com>, <bskumar1933@rediffmail.com>.

Tripathi, Radhavallabh, Vice Chancellor, Rashtriya Sanskrit Sansthan, 56-57, Institutional Area, Janakpuri, New Delhi - 110 058, <radhavallabh2002@gmail.com>.

Varakhedi, Shrinivasa, Director, Sanskrit Academy, Adarsh Shodh Sansthan, Osmania University, Hyderabad - 07, <shrivara@gmail.com>.